CHARLIE'S CHARTS CRUISING GUIDES:

CHARLIE'S CHARTS of the Western Coast of MEXICO by Charles E. Wood
CHARLIE'S CHARTS of POLYNESIA by Charles E. Wood
CHARLIE'S CHARTS NORTH to ALASKA by Charles E. Wood
CHARLIE'S CHARTS of the HAWAIIAN ISLANDS by Charles E. Wood
CHARLIE'S CHARTS of the U.S. PACIFIC COAST by Charles and Margo Wood
CHARLIE'S CHARTS of COSTA RICA by Margo Wood

Also written by Charles E. Wood:
BUILDING YOUR DREAM BOAT, published by Cornell Maritime Press

Canadian Cataloguing in Publication Data

Wood, Charles E. (Charles Edward), 1928 - 1987
  Charlie's charts north to Alaska
  Includes index.
  ISBN 0-9697265-9-7

1. Pilot guides - Pacific Coast (B.C.) 2. Pilot guides - Pacific Coast
(Alaska) 3. Boats and boating - Pacific Coast (B.C.) 4. Boats and
boating - Pacific Coast (Alaska) 5. Pacific Coast (B.C.) - Description
and travel. 6. Pacific Coast (Alaska) - Description and travel. I. Title.
G1171.P55W66   623.89'28711   C95-910392-9

Copyright © 1986, 1995, 2001   Charles E. Wood
First published 1986, reprinted 1989, revised 1995, 2001

Revised by Margo Wood   Illustrated by Charles Wood and Richard Miller
Edited by Helen McFadden   Photographs by Charles and Margo Wood

ISBN 0-9697265-9-7

Portage Bay reflections

The Nova Scotia cutter *Ern* before Riggs Glacier

CONTENTS

ACKNOWLEDGMENTS

May I remind people that although my late husband, Charles, passed away in 1987 and I continue to revise and update *Charlie's Charts* as needed, he is the true author and creator of these guides. It was his artistry and descriptions that make the guides valuable aids when cruising. I as the caretaker and agent simply continue to update and revise material as I cruise the coast to visit new areas.

There are several people who have been generous with their knowledge and time in the preparation of this updated and enlarged edition and I wish to acknowledge their contributions:

Jerry Peters, Canadian Coast Guard Supervisor at the Vancouver office was most helpful in researching and providing current information.

Fellow sailors have shared their knowledge of this coast with me and have been most helpful during some of my (mis)adventures while sailing single-handed as well as with crew. Among them are the following who deserve special recognition:

Mike and Janet Skulsky of S/V *Amantea* who not only rafted up alongside *Ern* in the middle to Chancellor Channel to repair an engine problem but also invited me aboard for a wonderful dinner following a tiring struggle through infamous Race and Current Passage,

Bob and Ginger Bertilson of M/V *Aquila* who tried to solve a starter problem, and after agreeing with several other cruisers that the engine won that round, generously towed *Ern* through Dent Rapids some time after the optimum time for passage, and

Tom and Marg Kughler of S/V *Kadeca* who teamed up with *Ern* on a cruise to the Queen Charlotte Islands and with whom I shared many joyous times along with engine problem-solving (perhaps it's time to invest in a new engine?)

And a sincere "thank you" goes to many cruisers I've met, while cruising and at boat shows, who have volunteered information they thought would be helpful to other sailors.

Finally, I wish to express my appreciation to Helen McFadden, my meticulous, patient editor who has brought polish and clarity to this publication.

Thank you all, very much.

Margo Wood

DISCLAIMER

The word, "CHARTS," in the title of this publication is not intended to imply that these hand-drawn sketches are sufficiently accurate to be used for navigation. They and the accompanying text are meant to act solely as a handy cruising guide to harbors and anchorages in the area discussed.

The use of official Canadian Hydrographic Charts and U.S. National Ocean Service (NOS) Charts are mandatory for safe boating. The list in Appendix I is presented to assist boaters in choosing charts which cover the areas in which they are interested. Since chart numbers are constantly revised, some data may be outdated soon after publication of this guide.

Do not use any of the drawings in this book for navigation. *Charlie's Charts* and *Polymath Energy Consultants Ltd.* are in no way responsible for loss or damages resulting from the use of this book.

ADDENDA - January, 2002

P. 131a: **Port Edward**: Chinese and American food is served at Brad's Restaurant, just a short walk from the floats.

P. 220: **Marine Weather One-on-One** – Add: To speak with the weather office call 1-900-565-5555; the cost is $3. per minute.
      Marine Weather Phone – Delete Commix – 250-339-5044, insert: Comox – 250-339-0748

P. 222: **Appendix IV: Marine Weather Reporting Stations** - Add: A reporting station has been established on Fanny Island on the east side of Johnstone Strait between Chatham Point and Helmcken Island. It is reported to be more accurate in measuring westerly wind velocity than nearby stations.

September, 2002

P. 18: **Entry Procedures** – The system of entering Canada known as CANPASS was discontinued for several months following September 11/01. It resumed with the following modifications:

All CANPASS members are required to call 1-888-CANPASS up to four hours before arriving in Canada. Visitors must report to a designated Customs reporting site or an approved CANPASS Permit site. Membership in the CANPASS program saves time at security check points. The list of reporting stations should be amended as follows:
Delete: Anglers Anchorage in Sidney and the Government dock in Powell River
Add: Metro Vancouver: White Rock Government Dock, Coal Harbour in Burrard Inlet
    Approved CANPASS Permit sites available only to CANPASS members:
        Victoria ¬ Canadian Forces Sailing Association
        Nanaimo – Townsite Marina

November, 2002

P. 138: **Ketchikan** – Para 2, end of line 5: delete "while….to end of sentence and insert: "the Customs Office is in the Federal Building, beyond the Cruise Ship Docks.
Para 3, line 2: insert after "Ch 16" near the end of the line ", VHF 73 or"

P. 174: **Hoonah** – There is only one fuel dock before entering the harbor and it is marked by a sign reading "ACE." The fuel pier sits on pilings and has no camel at the base making it necessary to have horizontal fenders ready to tie to pilings. When docking for fuel tie near the ladder for it must be climbed in order to pay for the fuel. Use a pair of old gloves when climbing the ladder as it is quite dirty. The Union Oil dock shown on the sketch is now privately owned by a cannery.

P. 144: **Vixen Harbor** – Add: After departing for Wrangell an early morning visit to Anan Bay Wildlife Observatory off Bradfield Canal (SE of Wrangell Island) is highly recommended. Watch for the sandy shelf where a shoal from the stream comes quite a distance from shore before dropping off sharply into deep water. Temporary anchorage can be taken toward the east. It is wise to leave someone aboard while the rest of the crew take the 20-minute hike up the trail. At a well constructed deck and blind six people are allowed 30 minutes to watch bears eating salmon from the Anan River. For many people, this is one of the highlights of the cruise. About 10 miles to the south, just behind Deer Island is **Frosty Bay**, calm and deep with spectacular sunsets.

For updating info
visit our Website:
charliescharts.com

INTRODUCTION

Blessed with an abundance of harbors, magnificent scenery, fascinating cultures, and colorful history this region vies for the title of the greatest cruising area in the world. It is so indented with coves, fiords and inlets, and sprinkled with islands that 1,000 miles of linear distance contain over 25,000 miles of coastline. The Southeast Alaska portion alone accounts for 250 linear miles and 11,000 coastline miles. There are few other places where inland passages can be followed for hundreds of miles and where the sea's bounty can be harvested so readily in all its variety. No other cruising area has so many glaciers which discharge their bergs directly into the sea.

The area lies within the migratory low pressure system belt around the world, thus lacking a settled, continuously sunny cruising season. The annual movement of summer's North Pacific High and the winter's Aleutian Low cause variations in the pattern of the weather, but do not completely deter the passage of the low pressure systems in summer, resulting in frequently cloudy skies often laced with rain. Although more sunshine may be desirable, it must be remembered that it is precipitation that keeps these areas so heavily forested and its glaciers and rivers continuously fed.

When traversing this coast, travelers move through several different zones. The south is more populated and has islands that are generally low and provided with shallow, well protected harbors. As you move further north the inlets become fiord-like and longer, their walls and shorelines are steeper, and the harbors are correspondingly deeper and fewer in number. At the northernmost section of this guide, the snow line creeps down the steep mountains, and the heavy snow cover gives birth to glaciated mountains close to the sea.

These different zones are separated by some crucial open water passages that must be treated with care and caution. These are not of great length, and the majority of the traveling is done within the "Inside Passage" with protection from the open sea. Vessels of all types and sizes make the passage safely, and commercial fishermen move up and down the coast regularly as different areas open for fishing.

Recent years have seen an unprecedented growth in the number of visitors to the area trveling the coast in everything from small boats to luxurious cruise ships. Beauty alone can commend a visit, but its clean air and waters, and the friendly people in the small towns and villages are equally inviting. In addition, it has all the elements of "cruising foreign:" length, diversity of interest and culture, demands on vessel and crew, and even stormy conditions to be encountered in the open water sections.

DESTINATIONS and the AREA COVERED by THIS GUIDE

This guide covers the Inside Passage to Glacier Bay National Park and returns by way of Sitka. Beyond lie other portions of Alaska: Prince William Sound, the Kenai Peninsula, Cook Inlet and the arc of the remote Aleutian Islands which can be reached from this area, but are outside the scope of this guide. Also not included are the offshore Queen Charlotte Islands of British Columbia and the rugged west coast of Vancouver Island.

This volume covers the route from Victoria, B.C. through the waters between Vancouver Island and the mainland and then behind the skein of islands that make the Inside Passage up to Southeast Alaska. First-time cruisers on this coast may not have the inclination or time to make the entire voyage, and so a number of beautiful and rewarding side-trips are described. These include Princess Louisa Inlet, Fiordland Recreational Area, Kitimat and the Kitlope. In addition there are a sufficient number of suggested anchorages and alternate nearby routes that one could easily follow the basic route suggested for the Inside Passage and visit quite different anchorages on the return trip. It would be impossible in an illustrated guide such as this to include all of the possible anchorages available on the entire coast, but the best and most convenient anchorages are given in a format that has proven to be most helpful for cruising sailors for many years.

The focal destination of this guide is Glacier Bay, Alaska. The route described traverses the main beauties of an area which is growing in reputation and popularity. The criteria used in selecting anchorages and harbors are based on a nominal day's run of 50 nautical miles for a slow-moving vessel such as an auxiliary sail boat. Sources of fuel and water are other factors. However, this is no hard and fast rule, and in several sections the anchorages are more closely spaced when they are of special interest. They also allow for a wider selection of stops for fast vessels making long daily runs. At several places it is possible to make additional routes off the main circuit; to go up around Behm Canal to Misty Fiords National Monument for example, or to go into bays and anchorages not described. On the other hand, in a few cases, longer legs may be necessary due to lack of a suitable intermediate stop. This is usually true of the open water crossings i.e. across the Strait of Georgia, the run across Queen Charlotte Sound past Cape Caution, and for the crossing of Dixon Entrance. These are given special attention in the general notes that follow.

The anchorages described in this guide have been personally visited and evaluated. The sketches are all hand-drawn and it is emphasized that they are NOT TO BE USED FOR NAVIGATION. Proper charts and sailing directions should be used for actual navigation or as a back-up for plotters or other electronic navigational systems. This guide does not relieve a skipper of the responsibility of navigating his/her own vessel safely, for a good sailor is always prudent.

THE TYPE OF VESSEL

Though fuel, water and provisions are easily obtained, any vessel chosen should be sound and able to carry the requirements of those aboard for extended periods of time. The ship must be capable of being lived aboard and of facing weather and sea conditions that may worsen rapidly. The vessel should be arranged so that the dinghy can be stowed on board especially when making passages in open water such as passing Cape Caution or during any trip when rough seas prevail. An inflatable life-raft equipped with emergency supplies gives an additional element of safety.

When cruising this area the weather can be damp and cold or quite balmy, depending on the time of year and weather systems moving along the coast. However in the vicinity of the glaciers air and water temperatures are commonly very cold, an important fact that the skipper should keep in mind when outfitting the vessel.

As a long-time sailor, it is painful for me to admit that perhaps the best type of boat for this trip is a trawler-type vessel capable of at least 8 knots and with an inside steering station. This is not to say that a sailing vessel cannot be used. All areas described in this guide were visited in a 30-year-old 34-foot wooden cutter. But the prevailing winds over most of this area are such that one should expect to motor for most of the trip when heading north, and for at least some of the time on the return to the south. Moreover, the negotiation of passes (if they are traversed at slack water) requires a vessel that can make a minimum of 4 knots. Lastly, a dodger or cabin where one can be out of the cold wind is essential, as is a heater to take the chill out of a boat during the cold, rainy days that can be experienced.

Power boats (excluding high speed planing hulls) usually have these advantages along with the benefit of higher cruising speeds as compared with most sailboats. They are particularly suitable on the north-bound trip when head winds and seas of moderate level are usually encountered. However, they are less comfortable with following winds and seas and cannot handle heavy weather on the open water crossings as easily as sailboats. Power boats are constrained to wait for suitable conditions—if comfort is desired—and thus the overall times for the full passage for all types of boats does not differ by more than a few days unless exceptional conditions are experienced.

FUEL, MAINTENANCE, WATER and PROVISIONS

Both diesel oil and gasoline are available fuel stations. Prices vary but are higher in the remote areas while larger centers (where there is commercial fishing traffic) tend to have fairly similar prices. The high taxes on fuel in Canada lead to more expensive fuel when in Canadian waters as compared to U.S. prices. Propane may be obtained from dealers in towns along the route and kerosene can be purchased at most hardware stores.

It is advisable to carry a complete set of spares such as oil and fuel oil filters and water pump impellers as well as sufficient engine and gearbox oil for the entire trip. At least one spare fan belt should be aboard in addition to a supply of duct and electrical tape, miscellaneous electrical connections and a well-stocked tool box. Spare batteries for everything from flashlights to cameras should be labeled and stowed in air-tight containers.

Minor repairs to hull and engine can be undertaken in most towns where haul-out facilities and mechanics are usually to be found. Major repairs can only be done at the large towns having shipbuilding facilities—with parts probably having to be shipped from Vancouver or Seattle. A well serviced and maintained engine(s) is highly recommended for a trip in these waters.

Water available at public docks is usually good, fresh, soft water. Fresh water is also available at waterfalls and streams, but one should ascertain that the sources are from unpopulated areas, and the water should be treated. Water-makers are not an essential item of equipment when cruising this coast but they have the advantages of convenience and consistency in quality and taste.

Initial provisioning is best accomplished in Vancouver or Victoria, British Columbia or in any U.S. city in the Puget Sound area. However, there are stores at almost all stops with docks along the route and many small towns have supermarkets. Prices vary with the degree of isolation of the store and tend to be approximately 20% higher in Prince Rupert and Alaskan stores compared to southern outlets. Fresh produce in Alaska is shipped from Washington and the selection may be limited.

ANCHORING and MOORING FACILITIES

The guide describes the most convenient and protected anchorages along the route. Many more can be found if the scope of travel is wider. If desired, one can anchor during the entire cruise. However, there is moorage at all towns along the passage, and one usually uses these facilities for their convenience.

Moorage

At many places in both B.C. and Alaska, there are government installed wharves and floats that can be used on a first-come, first-served basis by either commercial or pleasure craft. These tend to be heavily used during the fishing season and rafting is a common courtesy. In the larger towns there are also public and private marinas. A section allocated to transient vessels is common in most government marinas and they are indicated on the charts. But crowding of these transient floats is so common that there is seldom space available. The harbormasters will often direct you to a berth that is temporarily vacant (hot-berthing) in order to accommodate transient traffic. This is one reason why you should report to the harbormaster as soon as possible on arrival.

Fees are usually moderate at government docks though facilities are sometimes limited for such items as washrooms and showers. Charges at private marinas may be several times those charged at public facilities and services available range from basic to luxurious. As a result of high operating costs and a very short season fees charged are higher than those in more populated, warmer areas of B.C. and U.S. which have competition and a longer business season. Inquire about charges prior to tying up for a stop-over at any marina to avoid costly surprises.

Anchoring

Good, strong tackle and experience in setting your anchor for varying bottom conditions and the type of anchorage is essential for safety and peace of mind. A feature of this area is that valuable experience is gained in the less demanding southern portion before reaching the deeper, sometimes restricted anchorages of the mid and northern sections of the guide..

At least two sets of anchors and rodes are essential, while experienced cruisers normally carry three sets (one of which may be a small "lunch hook"). Rope rodes should always include a section of good-sized chain at the anchor, and an all chain rode has some advantage in deep water anchoring. The larger the gear the more essential is an anchor winch which is a necessity with an all-chain rode. A 45 to 60 m (150- to 200-foot) length of 10 or 12 mm (3/8" or 1/2") buoyant line is useful as a shore line when swinging is to be restricted. Arrangements for its ready access and systematic stowage avoids time-consuming confusion.

The Danforth, CQR, and Bruce anchors are commonly seen and are satisfactory in most anchorages. The Bruce anchor has gained support in northern waters where its ability to hold with minimum scope helps in the deeper anchorages. The Northill is also used, and is favored by fishermen.

The minimum rode for the main anchor should be 90m (300'). Several of the anchorages in northern areas have depths of 90 feet or more, thus bringing the ratio of scope to depth close to the minimum 3 to 1. In considering the depth of an anchorage, remember that this entire area has a high tidal range. Basic anchoring etiquette involves giving ample clearance to vessels already in an anchorage.

WHEN TO TRAVEL

Glacier Bay records show that the bulk of visitors arrive from mid-May to mid-September. Although temperatures are not high in May or September they are good months for traveling in both B.C. and Alaska, as the weather is clear and fog is least likely. The winter snow gives scenic views and melts to feed innumerable waterfalls. In July and August, the weather can be warm, but fog can become a problem; notably in the area from Dixon Entrance to the northern end of Vancouver Island. By October the winter rains commence, marking the beginning of the stormy part of the year, usually lasting until March.

For a trip to be done in one season it is best to start as early as possible, perhaps by mid-May or early June, certainly no later than early July. This gives one a summer in the north, which can be adjusted or expanded to suit the vessel's capabilities, weather conditions and one's interests.

Some consider spending an extended period cruising this unique area, staying for a winter or two in Alaska. It should be noted, though, that the harsh climate and crowded docks are hard on a vessel in winter, and living aboard to care for your boat is essential.

Another possibility for some sizes and types of boats is to trailer your vessel to a launching destination, use it for as long as possible, and return the same way at the end of the season. Some quite large power boats from inland prairie provinces and western states are transported to Comox, Campbell River or Lund, B.C. to enjoy a spring and summer cruising in these waters. The B.C. and Alaska Ferry system do the same for small pleasure craft, taking care of the long journey up and down the coast in a short time and leaving the best part of the year for exploring your chosen area. Kayakers in increasing numbers are seen paddling along the coast and camping on the beaches in the countless coves dotting the shoreline.

THE CRUCIAL PASSAGES

There are four major passages along the route, though any part can be made very easy or very difficult according to weather and sea conditions.

The Strait of Georgia

You may wish to avoid crossing of Strait of Georgia by staying on the eastern side of the Strait. However, this will not eliminate the discomforts of rough conditions in the Strait, for there remain several long passages which must be made sailing against the winds and seas of the prevailing northwesterlies. Moreover, this eastern route takes a newcomer away from the scenic and attractive Gulf Islands area and numerous attractive anchorages would be missed.

As a rule, sailing vessels and large powered craft may cross the Strait almost any time, though in stormy weather the trip can be very uncomfortable. Small craft are well advised to wait for suitable conditions for an easier and safer crossing.

The weather holds the key to the conditions that will be met on the crossing the Strait. Forecasting the weather is a chancy business but in these waters there are some general conditions that can be expected. Good summer weather has settled northwesterly winds. They tend to be light in the early morning, rise during the day, and die down after about 1700 hours. A heavy dew on the decks at night is a good indicator of such a period. Thus, the early morning or the evening hours are the most suitable for traveling.

If the northwesterlies do not diminish in the evening this is because a high pressure area has stayed in position for two or three days. Crossings can be uncomfortable at this time due to the build up of seas, so it is best to wait out the weather and enjoy the Gulf Islands.

Southeasterly winds presage rain and storms. They vary in intensity and while each storm seldom lasts more than 24 hours, several successive fronts may extend this period over several days. Weather reports can usually give one an estimate of the strength of the disturbance. The lighter winds can allow travel, albeit in rain or overcast conditions, while the heavier storms should be treated with caution. In summer there are generally more good traveling days than bad, and most waiting periods are usually of short duration.

In crossing the Strait of Georgia between Nanaimo or Silva Bay and Welcome Passage a special note should be made regarding the area labeled as "Whiskey-Golf" on the charts. This area is set aside for Canadian and U.S. Navy torpedo test purposes. Its full extent is marked on current charts but may not be indicated on older ones. The direct route across the Strait passes through this zone. If you stray into the area without clearing with Winchelsea Control on VHF Ch. 16, you will be speedily apprised of the error. If permission is granted to cross the area when tests are not scheduled, you may be requested to call again when clear of the zone. Tests are not carried out over much of the summer and are usually limited to between 0700 to 1730, but the zone is reserved and must be cleared for passage. Announcements of the times when torpedo tests are to be carried out in the following 24-hour period are given at the end of weather forecasts.

The route from Silva Bay to Welcome Pass can easily be arranged to avoid this area. You should allow for a slight southerly dog-leg, or proceed about 13 miles north of Nanaimo to south of Ballenas Islands and cross via Lasqueti Island. Another route proceeds north to Comox where one can either visit Campbell River before entering Discovery Passage or cross over to Lund and proceed northward to Desolation Sound and beyond. These routes are the safest way to avoid unnecessary encounters with officialdom, and in fact provide suitable slants for the crossing.

Mid-Section Passes

The most direct route into Johnstone Strait from the Strait of Georgia is via Campbell River and Discovery Passage. Timing is crucial, for the tidal stream can run to 15 knots at springs through Seymour Narrows. Further north, Race and Current Passage (where tidal currents may reach 7 knots) must also be passed before Johnstone Strait is entered.

Before entering Seymour Narrows, the influence of the strong tidal currents can be noticeable. With the flood (south-flowing) opposed by southeasterly winds, a heavy race occurs off of Cape Mudge and Willow Point. In fact, with any strong wind opposing either stream, the various races and eddies can become quite dangerous.

Furthermore, local travel between harbors near Discovery Passage (even outside the narrows) can be greatly affected by the strong tidal currents unless the passage is made at or near slack water. The current sweeps past the entrances to Quathiaski Cove and Gowland Harbor at a fast rate; if you have been fishing and not watching the tide tables it can be a chore working back to anchor. This is the voice of experience! The Quadra Island Ferry also gives a reading of these currents, indicated by its attitude as it crosses.

The foregoing aside, the passage can be made without difficulty if done at or near slack water or going in the direction of the turning tide. The 25 miles of Discovery Passage can be done in one run, and a favorable tide often carries right to Alert Bay or Port McNeill.

The favored route for pleasure craft is following a series of passes beginning with Yuculta Rapids, Gillard Passage and Dent Rapids, then proceeding through Greene Point Rapids and Wellbore Channel and entering the final portion of Johnstone Strait through Chancellor Channel. This route is a more interesting one, and avoids both the heavy commercial traffic of cruise ships and log booms in Discovery Passage and the northwest winds which oftern build in the afternoon, and make northbound travel slow and uncomfortable. Though the various rapids can attain impressive velocities, if the first rapids are entered just before the turn of the tide it is often possible to carry an ebbing tide through the entire series. If this cannot be done there are many anchorages indicated in this guide in which to wait until the regular change of the tide when the rapids are again passable.

Queen Charlotte Sound

The passage between the north end of Vancouver Island past Cape Caution to the entrance of Fitz Hugh Sound is perhaps the most crucial of the open water passages. Though often crossed in benign conditions with just an easy NW'ly swell, Queen Charlotte Sound can develop steep and dangerous seas. This is caused by the effects of ebb currents flowing northward, a shallow basin (as little as 20 fathoms), and exposure to NW'ly winds with a long fetch. If possible, time your passage so that you have an ebb tide until reaching Cape Caution so the flood tide gives you a lift for the rest of the crossing. During winter storms this body of water is at its worst while in the late spring and summer gales are less frequent. Good anchorages are indicated for waiting out inclement weather conditions on either side of the Sound.

Most powered craft find that the crossing from Port McNeill or Port Hardy past Egg Island and Cape Caution to anchorages in Fitz Hugh Sound angles comfortably over the prevailing swell. An alternative route with less exposure to the Sound can be made by crossing Queen Charlotte Strait and keeping on the north side of it, then beginning the passage from Allison Harbor or Miles Inlet. Though this route involves shorter distances, it runs directly into the swell and prevailing northwesterly winds. In addition, this is a lee shore; thus caution is advised.

Weather reports are broadcast from Alert Bay, including observations at Egg Island lighthouse which lies along the route. The observations from lighthouses ahead give an indication of wind and sea conditions at the time the observations are made. They are of great assistance in deciding on the time to travel, but it must be remembered that as lighthouses become automated there will be a 6-hour gap between the reports and changes may occur in that time. The schedule of Canadian Coast Guard weather broadcasts is on the weather map in the Appendices.

Strong currents are found in many of the passages, and allowance should be made for them in setting courses and estimating traveling time. Preparations for the trip across should include marking in and noting the bearings of the important lights and islands. The Canadian lighthouse system is good for providing key route markers—not just for assisting night passages. GPS readings should be verified by visual means, as islands and landmarks scattered along the route are good navigational aids. Poor visibility as a result of haze or fog makes it difficult to identify landmarks against the mass of similar terrain. Without plotters at such times dead reckoning can be assisted with radar and a depth sounder.

There are two radio beacons suitable for use during this crossing. These are, from south to north:

Cape Scott	353 kHz (range 75 miles)	▬ ▬·· ·· ·· ·· ·
McInnes Island	388 kKHz (range 100 miles)	▬· ▬· · ·· ·

In addition the Canadian Coast Guard broadcasts DGPS from the following locations:

Alert Bay   309 kHz   Reference Station - 300, 301   Radiobeacon ID - 909

Because of the relative placement of these beacons a bearing crossing Cape Scott with one of the others (depending on your position) is the only choice for the route across the Sound.

Dixon Entrance

The passage of Dixon Entrance takes one across the border between Canada and the United States. This section is exposed to the full effect of the open Pacific, but with a judicious choice of route and weather, the crossing can be made without difficulty.

The hazards of Dixon Entrance include complex currents as well as fog which is a nuisance from July to September and can be a problem of several days' duration. Swells move into the area from the west and southwest, even on calm days.

Exposure to the swell and weather is reduced by crossing from Prince Rupert into the lee of Dundas Island. Thus, open seas are faced only in the 10-mile passage between Green Island (near the north end of Dundas Island) and Tree Point Light (past Cape Fox). Powered vessels may find sea conditions more of a problem on the return because following seas will be experienced on the section between Dundas Island and the entrance to Prince Rupert. The swell itself is not a problem, but with any wind the sea state is affected considerably. If the wind or swell is running contrary to the current, races of disturbed water occur at several places, and the crossing of these areas can be uncomfortable. As in other crossings, anchorages are noted where you may wait for the best time for a crossing. In addition, harbors are indicated that provide a refuge if conditions deteriorate during a passage.

Radio beacons for the crossing include:

Prince Rupert - 218 kHz (range 100 miles)

McInnes Island-388 kHz (range 100 miles)

Sandspit   -368 kHz (range 75 miles)

Open Water Passages of Lesser Extent

There are short periods of exposure when entering or crossing some of the sounds and passages which are open to the ocean, such as Milbanke Sound. Some routes pass a cape open to the sea, such as Cape Chacon or Cape Decision where weather and sea conditions are usually disturbed. In addition, some of the inner waters such as Chatham Sound and Stephens Passage are sufficiently broad and long as to offer a fetch capable of producing conditions similar to open water crossings. Usually the open water exposure in these smaller crossings is limited and not a problem. This does not mean that they should be treated casually, but the discomfort of any exposure is relatively short. Caution in choosing the time to cross and careful navigation should eliminate or reduce problems related to this open water exposure, or alternate routes may be chosen offering more protection at the expense of longer distances.

WEATHER FORECASTS

North American sailors are fortunate in being provided with weather forecasting services that relate specifically to small craft, both pleasure and commercial. In the area of this guide the remoteness of small communities does affect the overall coverage available. Since the area is also very mountainous, radio reception can be variable and though relay stations are used, there are many areas with spotty or inadequate reception. However, considering the costs and problems involved, the system is admirable, and provides a much needed service.

Because the region covered by a weather forecast is broad, the conditions experienced in a particular area can sometimes vary from the overall prediction. The information provided should be strongly considered allowing for modified conditions in your own immediate area.

Canadian Coast Guard forecasts are conceded by most sailors to be slightly more informative and to provide more data over recognizable zones than do the U.S. forecasts. Conditions reported by the manned lighthouses that lie within the area covered are of the greatest use. This data is regularly updated every few hours. The most useful information is that given by a reporting station nearest the vessel's location and planned route. A list of radio weather broadcasts and reporting stations is given in Appendix II.

The ship's barometer and the skipper's weather sense are also useful to interpret the signs and data received. Some old and useful observations that are widely applicable are:

–   The weather pattern in effect today will usually be in effect tomorrow unless definite signs of change are evident.

–   Winds usually pick up in the forenoon and increase in the afternoon, then tend to die down in the evening.

TIDES AND CURRENTS

These are of great significance to anyone traveling the waters within this guide. Tide and current tables are essential items of navigational information, particularly for the times of slack water at narrow passes. The basic tidal pattern is semi-diurnal i.e. two high tides and two low tides per day. However, the moon's declination can result in changes in this pattern so that tides can be almost diurnal. The heights of the two high waters and the two low waters vary greatly for the same reason. The tidal range is high throughout this area, varying from 3 m (10 feet) or more in the southern part to 4 m (15 feet) or more in the northern part.

The most complex tidal stream patterns occur between Vancouver Island and the mainland. The flood enters from both ends—Juan de Fuca in the south, and Queen Charlotte Strait in the north. After passing through the various channels the streams meet below Cape Mudge, in the vicinity of Middlenatch Island. Through these areas the narrowness of certain passages combined with the high sills and deep basins cause the tidal streams to pass through at high velocities. Flood and ebb streams can reach speeds of 8 knots at Gillard Islands, 9 knots at Dent Rapids, and 15 knots at Seymour Narrows in Discovery Passage. Similar speeds are reached in other passes. In the larger channels of the Inside Passage, the tidal streams follow the general direction of the passages, with the flood streams setting in from each end, meeting about the middle. The ebb streams run outwards in both directions from this central point. Examples of these flows occur in Grenville channel, Graham Reach and other similar passages.

For the long fiord-like inlets with unobstructed entrances, high and low water occur about the same time throughout the inlet. But if the entrances are obstructed and narrow, then strong tidal currents result which will affect the times and conditions of entry and exit. Examples of these are Baker Inlet off Grenville Channel and Fords Terror off Endicott Arm.

Clearly, it is important to consider the tidal currents, since the major passes can be safely traversed only at or near slack water. Also an adverse current running against a vessel for long passages extends the traveling time considerably.

A study of the tide books, and attempts to fit the day's plans in step with the currents will be as beneficial to the voyage as thinking of the wind and weather generally. For B.C. waters, the official Canadian Tide and Current Tables are:

- Volume 5: Juan de Fuca and Georgia Straits

- Volume 6: Discovery Passage to West Coast of Vancouver Island

   Volume 7: Queen Charlotte Sound to Dixon Entrance

They can be obtained from any Canadian chart dealer or by writing to:

Canadian Hydrographic Service, Dept. of Fisheries and Oceans

Institute of Ocean Sciences, Patricia Bay

9860 West Saanich Road, P.O. Box 6000

Sidney, BC V8L

The following combined volumes covering the entire coast are carried by some chart dealers:
   Ports and Passes, published by Chyna Seas and
   Pacific Northwest Tide and Current Guide, published by Shipmaster

For Alaskan waters, the official tables are:

- Tide Tables, West Coast North and South America

- Tidal Current Tables, Pacific Coast of North American and Asia –

These may be obtained from any U.S. Chart dealer, or by writing to:

Distribution Branch (N/CG 33)

National Ocean Service

Riverdale, MD 20737

Alternatively, to help determine reasonable times of passage you may also pick up the small, annually published tide tables (Dots Fishing Guides) often given away at marine stores in Ketchikan, Sitka and Juneau. These are strictly tide tables, with corrections for various local points. There is no information regarding current direction or velocity, which is included in nautical charts of the key passes.

NAVIGATIONAL AIDS

Generally speaking, the United States and the Canadian systems of lights and buoys are sufficiently alike that most sailors pass from one country to the other without much difficulty. The waters of the United States are marked by the lateral system of buoyage. In 1983 Canada adopted a buoyage which includes both lateral and cardinal buoys as recommended for use worldwide by the International Association of Lighthouse Authorities. In both cases, the main channels are marked by lateral buoys which we remember by the old stand-by, "RED RIGHT RETURNING", i.e. on proceeding upstream the starboard (right) side of the channel has red buoys. Match your green light to the red lit buoys. Fairway and bifurcation or channel buoys are similar for both countries.

Canada, however, now uses cardinal buoys to indicate the deeper water and the safe side to pass a danger, i.e. one keeps to the safe side of a cardinal buoy. The markings for cardinal buoys are now standardized, and a booklet describing them can be picked up at most chart agents, Coast Guard Stations, or from Hydrographic Departments.

In Southeast Alaska all lighthouses have been converted to automatic stations with the exception of Five Fingers light near Cape Fanshawe in Stephens Passage. Similar plans are in the works for conversion of Canadian lighthouses but fishermen, recreational boaters, and commercial seafarers are attempting to convince the Coast Guard that the safety of those on the water would be compromised by such a decision. In addition to emergency aid from lighthouse keepers, the immediate reporting of radical weather changes, so prevalent along the coast is a vital service which would no longer be available. Lighthouses that continue to be manned as at the date of printing are underlined on the weather map in the appendices.

CHARTS

Canada and the U.S. have first-class charts and navigational systems, well maintained and constantly updated. Those listed in Appendix I have been found to be essential for safe travel. The number of charts given here can be costly to obtain but this is an expense no rational skipper should neglect. Prudent navigators will keep a set of charts aboard as a back-up in the event of a break-down of electronic plotters.

All charts carried should be the newest edition available, and corrected to include the most recent changes as published in "Notices to Mariners."

TIME

The area covered by this guide is in the time zone of Greenwich or Universal Standard Time + 8 hours. Furthermore, the entire area uses Daylight Savings Time, which affects the navigator when reading the times in tide and current tables. Add one hour to the Pacific Standard Time given in the tide tables in order to convert the time to Daylight Savings Time. This is usually in effect from the first Sunday in April to the last Sunday in October.

DANGERS

Aside from the obvious and standard danger of rocks, shoals, and heavy weather, there are some additional dangers peculiar to these waters.

Kelp

There are many shoals in the vast area of this coast. Kelp often grows on rocky bottoms, its tendrils streaming out in line with surface currents. Visible kelp beds usually signify depths of less than 10 fathoms and should be avoided. Detached kelp floating on the surface is dead and does not have the same significance.

Deadheads and Log Debris

This is one of the major logging zones of the world with much of the timber transported by log booms. Thus it is no surprise to find that floating logs, deadheads, and sinkers are present in the inland passages and inlets.

Floating logs can be encountered anywhere but are most prevalent near tide lines or at the entrances to inlets during and after high tides or storms. Though they occur in Alaska as well, they seem to be more in evidence in B.C.

Deadheads are logs stuck at one end into the bottom, the other end hanging at or near the surface. They can be very dangerous to quickly moving vessels because they are not seen until one is almost upon them, and when hit at high speed they can cause serious damage.

Sinkers are the most dangerous of all, being large logs that have become waterlogged and rest vertically in the water, rising and falling with the swell. Since they float just under the surface of the water most of the time, they usually are not seen but if one rises when a vessel passes over it very serious damage can result. Report large logs, deadheads or sinkers to the nearest Coast Guard (Canadian or U.S.) who broadcast their location in the "Notice to Mariners", and take steps to remove them.

Debris includes small logs, wood chunks, branches, etc., which, though it can be a nuisance, is not usually a dangerous problem. It is as well to avoid debris in case the branches seen may be attached to partially submerged trees. Occasionally a small piece of wood may become lodged in or near the propeller causing it to vibrate or the vessel's speed to be reduced. Sometimes the obstacle may be removed by simply putting the engine in reverse for a brief period.

These dangers are not continuous, nor found everywhere. A good lookout when traveling and common sense in avoiding travel at times of low visibility or at night, will allow for a safe voyage in these waters.

Plastic Debris

Plastic bags should be retrieved and burned or deposited in trash bins whenever they are seen to prevent blockage of water intake openings on vessels.

Fishing Nets

Fishing was once as important as lumber production along this coast. Although their numbers have declined you will still share the waterways, harbors, and anchorages with fishing craft of various types since their working season falls in the summer and early autumn. Fishing periods are strictly regulated by the governments of Canada and the U.S. since the early years of uncontrolled over-fishing almost ruined this resource. There are four main types of fishing vessels seen in these waters.

Trollers may be seen working the shores, bays, and banks. They are recognizable by their long pole outriggers extended out from the boat when fishing, troll lines streaming out behind. When passing astern of them one should give them at least a 60 to 90 m (200- to 300-foot) berth in order to pass over their lines without fouling them. Troll caught salmon are the highest quality fish seen in markets.

Gillnetters are identified by the large spool and rollers—either on the stern or the bow — from which the net is let out while being supported by floats. A buoy (red or orange) marks the net's free end. DO NOT PASS BETWEEN THE ORANGE BUOY AND THE GILLNETTER as the net will foul your prop or rudder. The white floats which keep one side of the net at sea level can usually be seen between the gillnetter and the orange float. Net size and depth are regulated. Gill nets are usually strung at right angles to the current flow, with the vessel maintaining a pull on the line; but variable currents may cause the nets to curve or wind about. Openings during the fishing season for gillnetters to fish are tightly controlled by Fisheries Departments. Such openings move up or down the coast with timings determined by the salmon runs arriving at river entrances. Since the gillnetters congregate in the high yield areas of a channel, their overlapping and crowded nets can be a major problem if one is traveling on an open fishing day. They are supposed to leave a clear passage but this is seldom done and pleasure craft must weave a route around and past the ends of their nets. When a gillnetter is fishing, check to see if the net drum is on the stern or on the bow and look beyond for the buoy that marks the end of the net.

Purse Seiners are the largest fishing vessels and are clearly identified by their size, the large boom, and power winch. They are not likely to be a problem for small craft; except that when there is an opening, hordes of them can be met rushing to the site of the opening.

Long-liners fish for halibut. They set long-lines (skates) with baited hooks laid down near the bottom with the ends marked by floats. They do not operate during the summer and early fall. In any case, their lines are not a problem as they are set well underwater.

Magnetic Disturbances

There are several places within the area of this guide where local magnetic disturbances occur near land masses. These areas are marked on navigational charts and are noted in the sketches. The magnetic compass should not be relied on in these areas, for not only is there a variation in the disturbance over any zone, but the change may be unnoticed at the onset and navigational errors may occur. During fair weather and good visibility passage across these zones should be done using visual checks. If visual checks are not possible it is advisable to avoid these magnetically disturbed areas or await clearing.

Tsunamis

This danger would seem a little far-fetched except that earthquakes periodically occur in or near the Southeast. Tsunamis are not a problem to a ship at sea, as they pass harmlessly by. The major danger occurs if the vessel is at or near the epicenter of the quake, where very large waves can be generated; or if the tsunami proves dangerous as it moves into a narrowing inlet. A warning system is in operation, and is broadcast through the Canadian Coast Guard Weather reports, NOAA Weather Radio as well as local radio stations. The probability of this danger is extremely low.

Ice

Ice is a problem only in those areas fed by glaciers such as Glacier Bay, Hobart Bay, Tracy and Endicott Arms, and care and prudence will suffice to take you through safely.

Glacial ice is almost always present in the northern arms of Glacier Bay. In the summer season, the amount of ice varies considerably and some glaciers may be more active than others. However, except for the occasional berg or bergy bits in the main bay, ice will be encountered in quantities mainly as one approaches Muir, Tarr and John Hopkins Inlets. The amount of ice usually lessens as the season advances. The tides and winds move the ice up and down the inlets, tending to pack it together or disperse it. However, the circulation of water near the glacial snouts themselves is erratic, since fresh water is always being discharged and the ice movements are correspondingly unpredictable. DO NOT APPROACH A GLACIAL FACE CLOSER THAN .5 MILE. Treat large icebergs with respect and pass well clear of them, keeping in mind that only 20% is visible. Anyone who has seen an iceberg roll over will easily appreciate the reason for caution.

Glacial ice forms as snow crystals accumulate and are buried by successive falls. The pressure slowly changes the crystals resulting in changes in density and structure (a volume decrease of as much as 9 times occurs). The denser the ice, the bluer it looks, since air has been eliminated and the greater proportion of water molecules present absorb all colors except blue, which is transmitted. The bergy bits that are clear and jewel-like are from the older part of the glacier, whereas those that appear whitish are from the newer, top part. Greenish-black bergs come from near the bottom of the glacier and striped brown bergs show layers of moraine sediments from the side of the glacier.

Ice presents a different and much greater problem in winter, when in addition to glacier ice, certain bays are subject to sea ice, and vessels can be dangerously hampered by the accretion of superstructure icing. The majority of vessels using this guide should be snug in harbor during such times.

Mirages

Mirages are not in themselves dangerous. Glacier Bay provides examples of <u>towering</u>—the vertical elongation of distant objects—and of <u>superior mirage</u>—the appearance of an inverted image above an object. Mirages are a fascinating phenomena, but do not need to cause any concern.

Wind Chill, Clothing, and Hypothermia

When traveling in this area, maintaining body temperature is an important consideration even in summer, and particularly in the vicinity of snowy peaks and glaciers. The summer climate in the northern areas of this guide is temperate and tolerable, with daily mean temperatures in the mid 50's (F), and maximums that can be as high as the 80's and 90's. But when cool winds blow with the temperatures in the 50's and 60's, the wind chill factor renders conditions equivalent to much colder temperatures.

Cool winds can cause a considerable amount of body heat loss and strong cold winds can lower body temperature by causing a loss greater than the replacement rate. As this condition is affected by any barrier to the wind's effect, the value of a good dodger behind which to shelter, and windproof clothing, combined with several layers of under clothing is obvious. Except when the sun's rays beat directly down on calm days, it is worthwhile to wear heavy weather gear as an outer windproof covering with several layers consisting of sweaters, flannel shirts, and long johns underneath. Gloves are necessary at times—wool being the best in cold, and rubber fisherman's working gloves best in wet conditions. Neck scarves, wool toques and/or balaclavas help to reduce major heat loss through the head, and woolen socks in sea boots are also recommended. It is important to put rain on before getting wet for wet clothing loses much of its insulating value. Similarly, when planned trips ashore may last an hour or so, take a windproof jacket or extra sweater in case weather conditions deteriorate for even a brief rain squall accompanied by wind can cause mild hypothermia.

The mean surface water temperature in these areas in summer is about 60°F (13°C). Glacier meltwater-fed inlets have lower temperatures which become colder with increasing depth. If a person is in the water for even fairly short periods of time, the loss of deep body heat can be crucial to survival. Every effort should be made to stay aboard. Safety harness should be used before it is warranted. If a crew member does go into the water, minutes count in the recovery.

Predicted survival time without a PFD is as little as 1.5 to 2 hours when drownproofing or treading water up to 4 hours with a PFD when assuming the fetal position, or huddling if two or more people are in the water. It is especially important to realize that a person in cold water goes into shock quickly, and as hypothermia advances, the victim can become disoriented and unable to assist oneself.

When rescued, hypothermia victims should be checked for vital signs: an open airway, respiration and pulse. If there is no pulse or respiration, CPR must be started immediately. Move the victim to warmth, replace all wet clothing with dry clothing and wrap him in blankets or a sleeping bag. A warm water bottle or warm, moist towels placed on the victim's neck, groin or chest can be helpful. If the victim is conscious offer sips of warm, sweet non-alcoholic liquids. In cases of severe hypothermia, skin to skin contact in the areas of the chest and neck is most effective. Try to keep the victim awake, and exhale warm air near the victim's mouth and nose. Keep a continuous watch over the victim and get medical attention as soon as possible.

Fog

From the northern end of Vancouver Island to Alaska the highest occurrence of fog is during the summer period (June to September) when there is an average of 4 to 7 days of fog per month. Visibility is reduced below 2 miles for about 15% of the time, and below .5 mile for about 5% of the time. At any other time of the year fog can occur whenever the air is moist and much warmer than the water, but the average number of days of fog drops well below that of the summer period.

Advection fog plagues the major open water crossings of this section, and sometimes works in along nearby coastal parts of the Inside Passage. Fog is often cyclical over a period of several days if the wind patterns stay in the same quadrant. Considering the rocky coasts and danger of the various approaches, care and caution should be exercised when traveling at these times.

In the southern section of this guide, the regime for fog is slightly different, tending to occur from September to January, though fog is occasionally found in the Strait of Juan de Fuca during the summer. From May to August, the inner waters of the southern area are usually free of fog.

Radar is a valuable aid during passages in fog _if_ a member of the crew has had training to interpret the screen correctly. As long as the power supply remains constant, electronic plotters and GPS positions are reassuring. Remember when traveling toward a waypoint, a vessel may be shown to be "on the highway" but if cross-currents affect the boat's path it may drift into danger unless the bearing remains constant.

Tugs, Tows, and Log Booms

Often seen plying these waters, these are essential economic lifelines for coastal communities. Tugs and their tows are not easily maneuvered so it is the responsibility of the yacht skipper to take avoiding action when meeting them. Unless constrained by space, give them ample room. Though obvious, remember the tow-line is submerged between the tug and its tow. Most tows trail a safety line of about 60 m (200') so do not pass close astern. It is important to remember the light configuration of a tug with a tow is three vertical lights shown from the mast. At night, log booms have red hurricane lanterns lit to mark the outer limits of their tow. Since these are fairly close to sea level and are not very bright, they are often difficult to spot.

FISHING LICENSES

Licenses required for fishing in British Columbia and Alaska may be obtained from most marine service outlets, fuel docks, hardware, and sporting goods stores. An Alaska Fish and Game License is required for fishing in National Parks such as Misty Fiords and Glacier Bay. Daily and annual catch limits are described in the regulations for each area.

Sportsfishermen and cruisers have a responsibility to limit their catch to what may be consumed during the cruise. Fisheries Officers strictly enforce regulations regarding the number and size of fish of various species that a person/boat may have possession of at any time. Similarly, the size of crabs that may be kept are clearly listed in the booklet given along with fishing licenses, and Fisheries Officers monitor pleasure boats regularly. Female crabs of any size must be released. Some cruisers feel they are being hounded by the authorities, but without limits being regulated the fish and shellfish would be decimated by both commercial fishers and sportsfishers alike.

The entire coastal area was once a Mecca for salmon and other seafood which could be found in abundance. Unfortunately, destruction of spawning streams by logging, over-fishing and poaching has resulted in a serious degradation of the salmon population. The escape of east coast salmon from fish farms happens frequently and the unknown long-term consequences are of concern. Other factors which may have had an effect on fish habitat are El Nino and the gradual warming of the earth's temperatures.

> To make connections to any Port of Entry call 1-888-226-7277 at any time up to four hours before your arrival.

ENTRY PROCEDURES

The majority of pleasure boaters cruising waters covered by this guide will be citizens of Canada or United States and there are only a few rules and formalities with which to comply. These are primarily aimed at stopping illegal drug traffic and preventing abuse of the customs and immigration laws of both countries, which pride themselves on their long standing open border. The major requirements are to check in and clear with Customs and Immigration, and to obtain a Cruising Permit allowing freedom to travel in the waters of the country with a minimum of red tape. Entry requirements are listed on the following page.

Vessels and crew who are not Canadian or American may have to follow more detailed entry procedures. Cruising Permits can be obtained easily if the country of origin has reciprocal arrangements with Canada and the U.S.A. Visas may be needed for the skipper and crew, depending on the nationalities involved.

In order to streamline entry into Canadian waters pre-approved Canadian and U.S. citizens may enter Canada by calling Canada customs provided their application has been approved by the Citizenship and Immigration Department and a Permit has been issued. Application forms for a permit may be obtained from marinas in BC, offices of Revenue Canada or Citizenship and Immigration or by writing to: CANPASS Processing Centre, #28 - 176 Street, Surrey, BC V4P 1M7 CANADA. Following approval of the application a Permit is issued along with a letter of authorization, a decal and a small triangular identification flag. When permit holders are admitted to Canada by a Customs Official they ~~are given a Clearance Number or they~~ will be told to report to one of the following designated reporting stations for an inspection.~~which is done on a random basis:~~

Metro Vancouver: Crescent Beach, False Creek or Steveston
Victoria; Oak Bay Marina, Customs Dock, RVYC (Cadboro Bay or Tseum Harbor
Sidney: Anglers Anchorage, Canoe Cove, Port of Sidney, Vancouver Isle Mar)
South Pender: Bedwell Harbour (only from May 1 to September 1)
North Coast: Nanaimo: Brechin Pt. Marina, Nanaimo Hbr. Commission Yacht Basin
  Campbell River: Discovery Chevron Dock, Discovery Marina Dock
  Powell River Government Dock
  Prince Rupert: Fairview Government Dock, PRYC, Prince Rupert
  Government Dock, Rushbrook Government Dock

Vessels without permits are required to proceed to one of the above Ports of Entry where only the skipper (or his representative) may go ashore to report to the Customs Office. In some southern centers it is possible to make first contact with the Customs Officer by telephone, whereupon he will meet the vessel at the Customs dock to check it in. The person reporting must return aboard immediately after reporting and remain aboard unless clearance is given by telephone. Note that the vessel may not land, anchor or meet with another boat until Customs clearance has been given. Though there are some small variations, the customs and immigration laws of both Canada and the United States require the following:

1. The yacht's registration, documentation or license papers.
2. A letter or statement from the owner allowing the skipper to move the boat if the owner is not aboard.
3. Passports, birth certificates, or acceptable identification of the crew.
4. Visas for crew members, when necessary.
5. Limits to the amount of alcohol, beer, and cigarettes for each person. Certain fruits, vegetables or other agricultural products may be prohibited entry.
6. Pets should have a valid certificate for rabies vaccination within the last three years.
7. Prescription drugs for personal use should have labels and have copies of the physician's prescription or a letter stating the necessity for their use.
8. Canada prohibits hand guns, automatic firearms, and mace and applies a criminal charge to anyone in violation of this rule. In the United States hand gun regulations are a state responsibility. To determine current regulations for Alaska write to: Alaska Dept. of Fish and Game, P.O. Box 3–2000, Juneau, AK 99802.

Failure to conform to the requirements for declaration and check-in procedures make the vessel subject to seizure and/or fines. Recent cases include a $100 fine for not declaring liquor on board in excess of the allowed amount; $100 fine for being 24 or more hours late in reporting in; and $300 fine, for persistent disregard of entry procedures by local boaters near border points.

FLAG ETIQUETTE

"There is a certain accepted procedure to which pleasure boats should properly adhere when they cross international boundaries into the waters of another nation," is a quotation worth repeating from Charles F. Chapman's *Piloting, Seamanship and Small Boat Handling (PP 470-472)*. Though the position of the foreign flag varies depending on the type of vessel, the general practice is for it to be flown from the foremost starboard spreader on sailing vessels and from the starboard yardarm on powerboats. If the motor vessel is mastless then the courtesy flag is flown alone from the bow staff (thus replacing the club burgee).

GARBAGE DISPOSAL

The increasing number of vessels cruising this coast has placed severe strains on small communities to deal with garbage. Boaters can lessen this impact several ways:

1. Beer, liquor, juice and pop containers purchased in B.C. should be returned to outlets selling similar products, where a refund will be made for the deposit charged.

2. Other glass and tins can be cleaned and returned to recycling depots in your home port. There was sufficient space to stow the full containers on board prior to the start of the cruise, so the same space can accommodate empty containers, plus additions since tins can be flattened.

3. Any garbage left over should be sorted into that which can be burned and 'other,' so that shore facilities can deal with the trash as efficiently as possible.

If boaters make an effort to reduce the amount of garbage left in communities along this coast and refrain from discarding trash in an irresponsible manner we can help to preserve the pristine beauty of this coast for future generations.

WHALE WATCHING

This is a highlight of any cruise in these waters. A small cruising vessel provides many excellent opportunities to observe whales closely. The whales found in these coastal waters include four baleen whales: Gray, Humpback, Minke and Finback and three toothed whales: Orca or Killer Whale, the Dalls and Harbor Porpoises.

Whales will often maintain their course and pass near a small vessel. The chances of collision are unlikely, since not only do whales have good eyesight, but they have a built-in sonar facility. However, it is important to maintain a good lookout and take action to avoid a collision as needed. Never chase whales, steer directly toward them, or corner them in bays or narrow inlets where they might feel threatened.

To assist in identification at a distance, sketch silhouettes of the whale's blow characteristics and surface attitudes are given.

Gray Whale

A stocky whale having no distinct dorsal fin, the Gray whale may grow to 12m (40 feet) and reach 40 tons. It is slate or gray in color with whitish patches of barnacles and whale lice. A few grooves may be seen on the throat. It is a slow swimmer, its normal speed being 5 to 8 knots. It may be seen in the Gulf of Georgia and adjacent bays, or traveling along the outer coasts as it migrates from the Baja Peninsula in Mexico to the Bering Sea each year.

Surfacing & Blowing   Beginning a Dive   Sounding (Diving)

Debris Harms Our Marine Life

Rex Herron

Endangered species also suffer. Sea turtles mistake plastic bags for jelly fish (a major source of food) and choke to death.

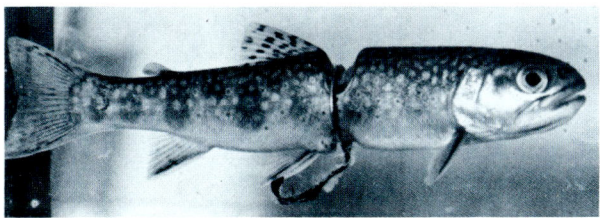

Michigan Dept. of Natural Resources

Fishermen and boater safety is jeopardized when debris fouls propellers or causes engines to overheat. Heavy losses of time and money are reported from debris damage to vessels and equipment.

George Antonelis

Brian Lawhead

Some 30,000 Northern Fur seals die yearly from entanglement in netting, a 50% decline in population in 30 years has been noted.

Common items like six-pack rings, fishing line, and strapping bands entangle and kill sea birds, fish and mammals. Plastics can last many hundreds of years, harming even large mammals like the gray whale.

Pierce Harris

This page and the one following marked ⚡ have been reprinted (with permission) from a brochure published by the National Marine Fisheries Service, Maine Refuse Disposal Project, Newport, Oregon.

Plastics can last for hundreds of years. A careless moment lasts generations. The best method of disposal is at a recycling depot.

Dale Snow

Frans Lanting

Birds, fish and mammals mistake plastic for food. Some birds even feed it to their young! With plastic-filled stomachs, animals die of starvation or poisoning.

Bill Keay

Six-pack rings can result in starvation and death to seabirds such as this Great Blue Heron and other marine life.

⚡ DON'T TEACH YOUR TRASH TO SWIM!
WGM

Western Canada Wilderness Committee

Oil spills such as the disasters caused by the Exxon Valdez in 1989 (which ran aground in Prince William Sound) and the leaking oil barge (which was deliberately hauled out to sea from near Grays Harbor, Wash. in 1988) caused the deaths of thousands of seabirds and damage to marine habitats along the coasts of Washington, British Columbia, and Alaska.

Public pressure is needed to have a moratorium on offshore drilling, require the transport of oil in double-hulled vessels and establish a Law of the Sea making the owners of oil shipments liable for all clean-up costs and damages anywhere in the world. This would encourage oil companies to act responsibly toward the fragile marine environment.

Jim Boeder

⚡ You can help!
* Make boat policy that no trash is discarded, washed, or blown overboard.
* Minimize the amount of non-degradable products on board. Provision your vessel using bulk-refillable containers.
* Stow trash for disposal in port. Encourage your port to provide convenient refuse disposal facilities.
* Where possible retrieve trash found on the ocean.
* Share your concern with friends, fellow mariners and politicians.
* Participate in beach clean-ups, and leave the beach clean after visits.

Orca or Killer Whale

This striking whale is black, with white patches along the flanks and bottom. It may grow to 9 m (30 feet) and reach 10 tons. Its high, triangular dorsal fin may reach 1.8 m (6 ft.) in mature males but only .9m (3 feet) in females and immature males. Orcas are rarely seen alone as they travel in groups, reaching speeds of 20 knots or faster. Their range includes all areas of the guide but they are most common in waters south of Prince Rupert.

| Surfacing and Blowing | Beginning a Dive | Sounding (Diving) |

Humpback Whale

Known both for its acrobatics and its haunting songs, this whale is distinguished by its 15-foot slender flippers and the knobs (stove bolts) on its head. It may grow to 15 m (50 feet) in length and reach 45 tons. When sounding, it raises its tail flukes high. Traveling individually or in groups, it usually cruises at 5 knots, but is capable of 10 knots. It can be seen in much of the Southeast Alaskan waters, but is most likely in Lynn Canal, Chatham Strait, and along the outer coast. In Glacier Bay the number of boats is restricted, to reduce disturbances to the Humpback's habitat.

Finback Whale

The second largest of the whale species, these can reach over 21 m (70 feet) and up to 60 or 70 tons. They are fast travelers, swimming at up to 20 knots, and when feeding they can be even speedier. They have a curved dorsal fin and a short ridge about two-thirds of the way along the back. When diving, the back arches deeply but the tail does not break the surface. At close range they can be identified by the asymmetrical color pattern of the head—blue-gray on the left, and white on the right lower jaw.

Minke Whale

Pronounced Min - ke, this small whale reaches only 9 m (30 feet) and about 7 tons in weight. It has a short curved dorsal fin two-thirds of the way along the back with white patches across the flippers. Its blow is low, hardly visible. On the rise, the pointed nose breaks the water first. It may be seen in inlets and bays, and sometimes approaches boats closely. Frederick Sound is a place to look for this whale. It is occasionally seen in northern British Columbian waters.

Surfacing and Blowing   Beginning a Dive   Sounding (Diving)

Dalls Porpoise

Friendly and playful, they will come to cavort in the boat's bow wave. Black with white patches on the belly, throat, and flippers, they could be mistaken for killer whales except that they are small (2 m/7 feet long) and have a small dorsal fin. Porpoises lack the dolphin's beak. They are fast, and traveling in groups, may be found anywhere in South East Alaska waters.

Rising   Blowing   Diving

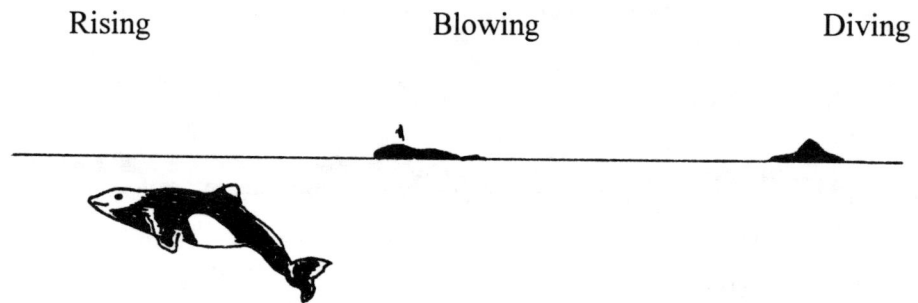

Harbor Porpoise

The smallest of the whales, averaging 1.5m (5.5 feet), they are usually all black or brown. They are more aloof than the Dalls and rarely approach boats closely. A small curved dorsal fin is in the center of the back. Sometimes alone, sometimes in large groups, they can be seen hunting inside small anchorages or passing near their entrances throughout Southeast Alaska.

THE NATIVE CULTURES

Travel along this coast and visits to any its towns develops a growing interest in the art and culture of the First Nations people. Totem poles are the first and most impressive of the symbols one sees, but almost every object in native life, even the most utilitarian, was decorated with design—as, for example, berry baskets and beautifully carved wooden halibut hooks. This guide can do no more than introduce the tribal areas and point out other sources of information.

From Victoria to about Campbell River, Coast Salish dominate followed by Kwakiutl until north of Bella Bella and the Tsimshian to the Alaska border with an intrusion around Metlakatla. The sea-going Haida inhabit the Queen Charlotte Islands and the southern end of Prince of Wales Island. The Tlinglit tribe are found in the long remaining stretch of the South East. There are similarities as well as marked differences in tribal cultures, and the local museums are a good way of finding out about them; the University of British Columbia Museum of Anthropology is a major source, as are the museums in Campbell River, Alert Bay, Prince Rupert, Juneau and the Sheldon Jackson in Sitka.

BOOKS AND REFERENCES

Duart Snow, Editor. *BC Marine Parks Guide*. Vancouver, BC: Pacific Yachting Magazine (This is an excellent accompaniment to *Charlie's Charts*.)

Blanchet, M. Wylie. *Curve of Time*. Sidney, B.C.: Gray's Publishing.

Chappell, John. *Cruising Beyond Desolation Sound*. Vancouver, B.C.: Naikoon Marine.

Cummings, Al and Bailey-Cummings, Jo. *Gunkholing in Desolation Sound and Princess Louisa*. Edmonds, WA: Nor'Westing Inc.

Douglass, Don and Reanne Hemingway-Douglass. A series of books *Exploring* selected sections of BC and Alaskan waters. Anacortes, WA Fine Edge Productions, LLC

Flaherty, Chuck. *Whales of the Northwest*. Seatttle, WA: Cherry Lane Press.

Eppenbach, Sarah. *Alaska's Southeast, Touring the Inside Passage*. Seattle, WA: Pacific Search Press.

Flaherty, Chuck. *Whales of the Northwest*. Seattle, Cherry Lane Press.

Hale, Robert. *The Waggoneer*. Seattle, Robert Hale Publishing

Halpin, Marjorie J. *Totem Poles - an Illustrated Guide*

Lange, Owen. *The Wind Came All Ways*. Ottawa, ON Environment Canada

State of Alaska, Dept. of Transportation *Southeastern Alaska Harbor and Boating Facility Directory*. Juneau, AK: Southeast Graphics Media.

Wolferstan, Bill. *Cruising Guide to British Columbia: Volume I, II and III*. Vancouver, B.C.: Pacific Yachting.

Woodward, Walt. *How to Cruise to Alaska Without Shaking the Boat Too Much*. Edmonds, WA Nor'Westing Inc.

SECTION I - Victoria to Campbell River

Additional B.C. Marine Parks and marinas where moorage is available:

Cabbage Island off the northeast coast of Tumbo Island, east of Saturna Island. Local knowledge and is needed to approach the mooring area for many unmarked reefs and shoals are in the vicinity. Mooring buoys are available in Reef Harbour where anchorage may be taken.

Sidney Spit at the northern tip of Sidney Island between Miners Channel and Sidney Channel. Enter from Sidney Channel. Fees are charged for the use of mooring buoys and a landing dock is available for easy access to the shore.

Wallace Island provides limited moorage at a float in Conover Cove where snug anchorage may be taken with a stern line ashore recommended. Avoid nearby reefs and shoals.

Winter Cove at the northern tip of Saturna Island. Enter from Plumper Sound and Navy Channel giving Minx Reef a safe berth. At low tide the anchorage has about 2 m (7 feet) of water. Boat Passage joins the cove to the Strait of Georgia and has strong tidal currents; reefs and shoals in the area discourage use of this passage without local knowledge.

Princess Margaret - on Portland Island, between Satellite Channel and Prevost Passage, SE of Saltspring Island. Caution must be exercised for reefs and shoals surround the island. Passable anchorage may be taken in North Bay, with Chads Island providing protection.

Copeland Islands (Ragged Islands). Enter from Thulin Passage giving a clear berth to reefs extending off the small islands where the Marine Park sign is posted

Sandy Island (Tree Island) off the northern tip of Denman Island. Anchorage during good, settled weather may be taken off the south side of the island. The spit connecting Sandy Island and nearby Seal Islets dries at low tide.

Squitty Bay near the southeast tip of Lasqueti Island north of Young Point. Enter from Sabine Channel staying close to the south shore to avoid rocks near the entrance.

Mitlenatch Island is a nature reserve near the north end of Georgia Strait and is home to a multitude of various seabirds. Temporary good weather anchorage may be taken in Northwest Bay on the west side of the island and in Camp Bay on southeast side.

Jedediah Island between Lasqueti Island and the southern end of Texada Island. Excellent anchorage may be taken in Deep Bay on the northwest shore, east of Paul Island. and in a cove on the southeast side of the island behind a number of small islands.

Rebecca Spit is on the east side of Quadra Island off Drew Harbour. Anchorage may be taken off the northwestern end of the spit on hard sand bottom. The anchor must be well set to avoid dragging.

Teakerne Arm on the west side of West Redonda Island. Enter from Lewis Channel. Anchorage may be taken on a steeply sloping shelf in the vicinity of the falls or further into the bay.

Walsh Cove on the east side of West Redonda Island is entered from the south via Waddington Channel. A stern line ashore is needed in this popular spot.

Schooner Cove Resort Hotel and Marina is a major marine center just to the north of Nanoose Harbour. This luxurious facility offers both permanent and transient moorage (look for orange cleats). Guests have complimentary use of showers, pool, spa, sauna, tennis, shuttle to grocery stores and shuttle to Fairwinds Golf Course. The office monitors VHF 73 or call 1-800-663-7060.

Looking toward the entrance from within Prideaux Haven

Entering Gorge Harbour on Cortes Island

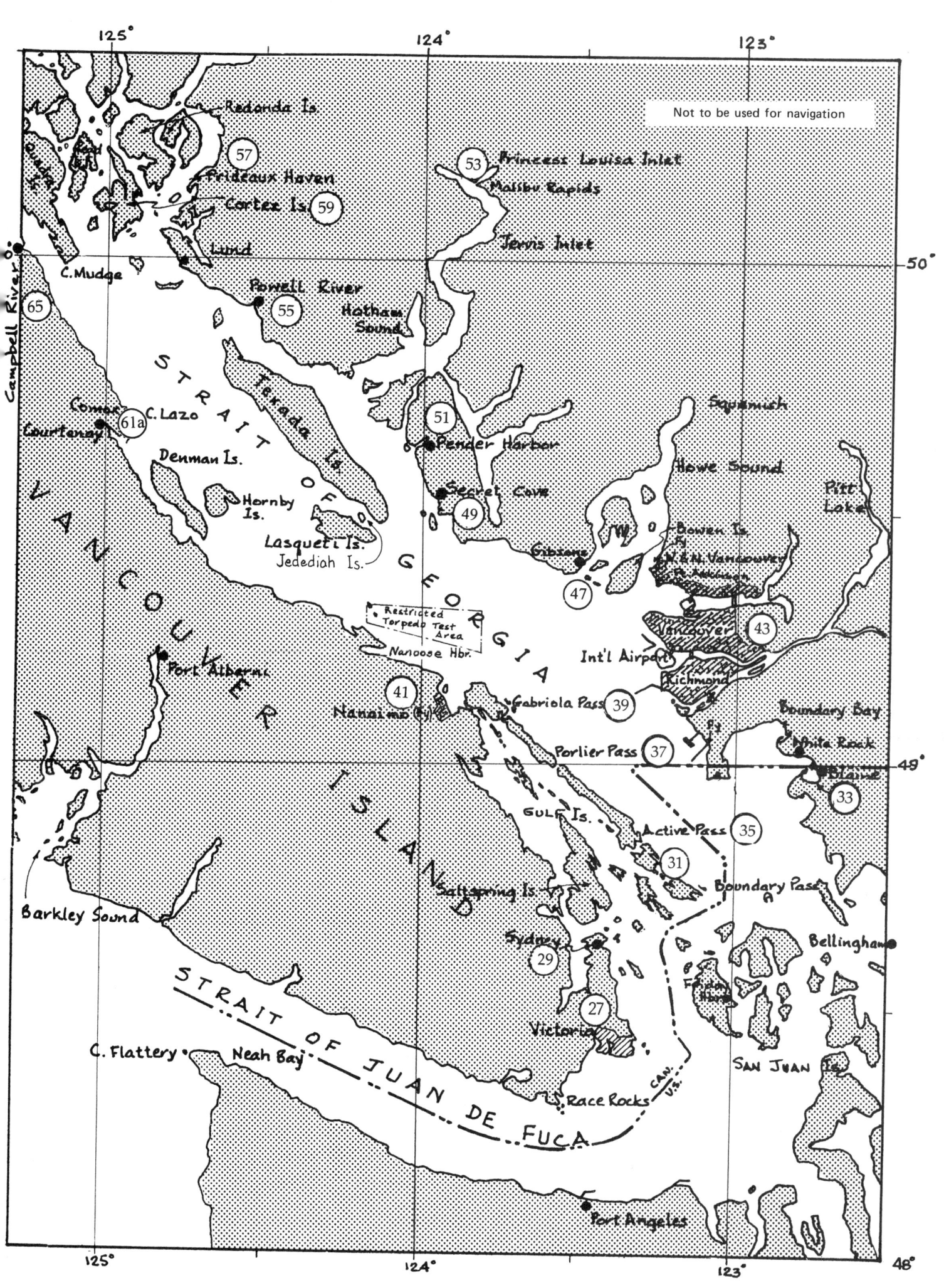

Not to be used for navigation

125°   124°   123°

Redonda Is.
⑤⑦
Prideaux Haven
Cortex Is. ⑤⑨   Princess Louisa Inlet ⑤③
Lund   Malibu Rapids
C. Mudge
⑥⑤   Jervis Inlet   50°

Campbell River
Powell River ⑤⑤   Hotham Sound
S   Squamish
T   Howe Sound
R   Pender Harbor ⑤①
Comox C. Lazo ⑥①ₐ   A   Pitt
Courtenay   I   Secret Cove   Lake
Denman Is.   T   ⑤①④⑨
Hornby   O   Gibsons   Bowen Is.
Is.   F   ⑤①④⑦   N. & N. Vancouver
Lasqueti Is.   G   Anmore
Jedediah Is.   E   Vancouver ⑤①④③
Restricted   O
Torpedo Test   R   Int'l Airport
Area   G   Richmond
Nanoose Hbr.   I   Boundary Bay
Port Alberni   A   Gabriola Pass ⑤①③⑨
⑤①④①   White Rock
Nanaimo (y)   I   Porlier Pass ⑤①③⑦   Blaine
S   ⑤①③③   49°
L
A   Gulf Is.   Active Pass ⑤①③⑤
N   ⑤①③① Boundary Pass
Saltspring Is.   Bellingham
Barkley Sound   Sydney ⑤①②⑨
⑤①②⑦   San Juan Is.
S T R A I T   Victoria
C. Flattery Neah Bay O F   J U A N   D E   F U C A
Race Rocks

Port Angeles

125°   124°   123°   48°

VICTORIA

Victoria is the capital of the province of British Columbia and is a **Port of Entry**. Promoted for many years as a "bit of Merry Old England," this beautiful city is a unique and attractive blend of turn-of-the-century architecture and modern development.

Entry to the harbor is clear and simple as is passage to the inner harbor in the heart of the city. A feature of this location is the magnificent view of the Provincial Parliament Buildings and ivy-clad Empress Hotel overlooking the waterfront.

Upon arrival vessels must tie to the Customs dock to complete entry requirements unless a CANPASS clearance number has been obtained and the Customs called for telephone clearance. Until clearance has been obtained no one may leave the vessel except the skipper whether or not Customs Officers inspect the vessel. Several telephones with direct lines to the Customs Office are on the dock and the skipper should phone in to report if a Customs Officer is not present on the dock. The telephone number of the Customs Office is 363-3339. Flag etiquette requires foreign vessels to fly the Canadian flag while in Canadian waters.

Moorage in Victoria harbor is on a first-come, first-served basis. Docks have power and water; shower and bathroom facilities are nearby. The traditional visitors' floats, enjoying the best location in the harbor, are at the head of the Inner Basin. Operated by the city of Victoria, they are the most expensive moorage in the harbor. The Wharf St. floats are also conveniently close to the downtown area though space is limited. Inquiries can be made by calling 363-3273 or by calling the wharfinger on VHF Ch. 73. During July and August when the fishing fleet is off to the fishing grounds Fisherman's Wharf has reasonably-priced transient moorage. Occasionally this facility becomes so congested on holiday weekends that rafting becomes necessary. Vessels over 15 m (50 feet) are advised to call the dockmaster at Fishermen's Wharf on VHF Ch. 73 when they are about a half hour from entering the harbor.

Victoria has many interesting shops, points of interest, and ongoing cultural activities. Good restaurants are available which feature international and North American cuisine; many are within walking distance of the inner harbor. Afternoon tea at the Empress Hotel though extremely expensive, is considered a "must" provided you are dressed appropriately. A visit to the Provincial Museum (next to the Parliament Buildings) introduces visitors to the heritage and resources of B.C. Many shops feature beautiful arts and crafts of the various Indian tribes found in the province.

For many visitors, to see Victoria is to see **Butchart Gardens**. These world-famous gardens are easily reached by bus or taxi from all of the moorages described on pages 26 - 29. In addition, cruisers staying at **Angler's Anchorage Marina** in Brentwood Bay may walk to the main entrance or take their boats or dinghies to the water-side entrance where day moorage may be available at a float or overnight at a mooring buoy. See next page for more details.

When proceeding north from Victoria the first harbor is at **Oak Bay** which can be approached using CHS Chart #3424. Tide rips, rocks and shoals in the vicinity of Discovery Island demand careful navigation. The entrance to Oak Bay is between the breakwater at Turkey Head and the breakwater projecting south from Mary Tod Island. Buoy "V26" marks the outer end of a reef extending west from Mary Tod Island. Additional cautionary buoys and private buoys lie to the west of the island. The fully modern facility of **Oak Bay Marina** welcomes transient sailors and offers convenient access to both downtown Victoria and Butchart Gardens.

VICTORIA

Approx. Scale. n.m. (and feet)

Not to be used for navigation

1000' 0 ¼ ½ n.m.

Pandora St.

Johnson St.

Yates St.

Fort St.

Wharf St.

Showers
Washrooms
Laundry

Empress
Hotel

Parliament
Buildings

City
Floats

Undersea
Gardens

Ship
Point

Black
Ball Ferry

Customs

Air West

JAMES BAY

5f

Discovery
Rk.

Bn.

West Coast
Air

Wharf
St. Floats

Booms

5f

Ok Fl.G

Tuzo Rk.

Songees Pt.

Ok Fl.R

Laurel Pt.

Shell Oil

Shipyards

Fuel

FG

5f

N

5f

Pelly Is.
Fl.G

Booms

Colville Is.

Sleeper Rk
Bn.

5f

Fuel

FR FG FR

Crane

Marine
Store

Harbour
master

Fisherman's
Docks

Shoal Pt.
Heliport

Fl.R.

SIDNEY

Sidney is a **Port of Entry** located near the northern end of the Saanich Peninsula. It has two locations from which Customs clearance may be obtained. When approaching the Port of Sidney keep the red buoy to starboard and the black one to port. A breakwater protects the northern floats where pleasure craft may moor while clearing Customs. At the outer end of the public wharf is a telephone with a direct line to Customs. Note: Tidal streams are strong near the wharf making it advisable to berth at slack water, especially during southeasterly weather.

Customs clearance may also be obtained at the Customs float in All Bay in Tsehum Harbor by phoning the Customs House in Sidney at 356-6645 to request clearance. No one may leave the vessel except the skipper until clearance has been obtained. Flag etiquette requires foreign vessels to fly the Canadian flag while in Canadian waters. See page 19 for the proper placement of the courtesy ensign.

Tsehum Harbor has the greatest concentration of boating services and pleasure craft facilities to be found on Vancouver Island. Entry to this beautiful area is between Armstrong Point and Curteis Point; the channel into the harbor is marked by numerous daybeacons. Shoals line the shoreline and patches of kelp are scattered about. Beacons and buoys clearly mark the route to be followed when entering All Bay, Blue Heron Basin, the Royal Victoria Yacht Club facilities and other facilities. This intricate series of bays and coves is lined with docks, yacht clubs, shipyards and repair shops of every kind. Fuel, water, and supplies can be obtained from marinas operating here and hull, engine, and equipment repairs are available in the boatyards and shops clustered about. Haul-out facilities can handle vessels up to 24 m (80').

Brentwood Bay is reached by a short trip around the north end of Saanich Peninsula. Several marinas, fuel docks, and restaurants are in the southeastern part of the bay which is dominated by the huge Port Royal Condos sprawling over the slopes at the southern end. This first-class marina can accommodate vessels up to 45 m (150') and features a marine store, restaurant, and transient moorage. A local ferry runs between Brentwood Bay and Mill Bay which is located on the western shore of Saanich Inlet. Customs clearance can be obtained by calling the Sidney Customs House at 356-6645 from the Customs float at Anglers Anchorage Marina.

Caution: A drying rock located southwest of the ferry landing is marked by buoy U22. Do not approach the marina close south of the ferry wharf between U22 and the day beacon, for drying rocks lie between the buoy and the shore.

Although this is a pretty spot to visit, the main reason for coming here is its close proximity to the world famous **Butchart Gardens**. During July and August out-door stage shows are performed in the amphitheater on week nights and Saturday night fireworks at the Gardens can even be seen (and heard) as they add a festive note to a stop-over in the bay.

VICTORIA & SIDNEY
Ports of Entry

Approx. Scale n.m.

Not to be used for navigation

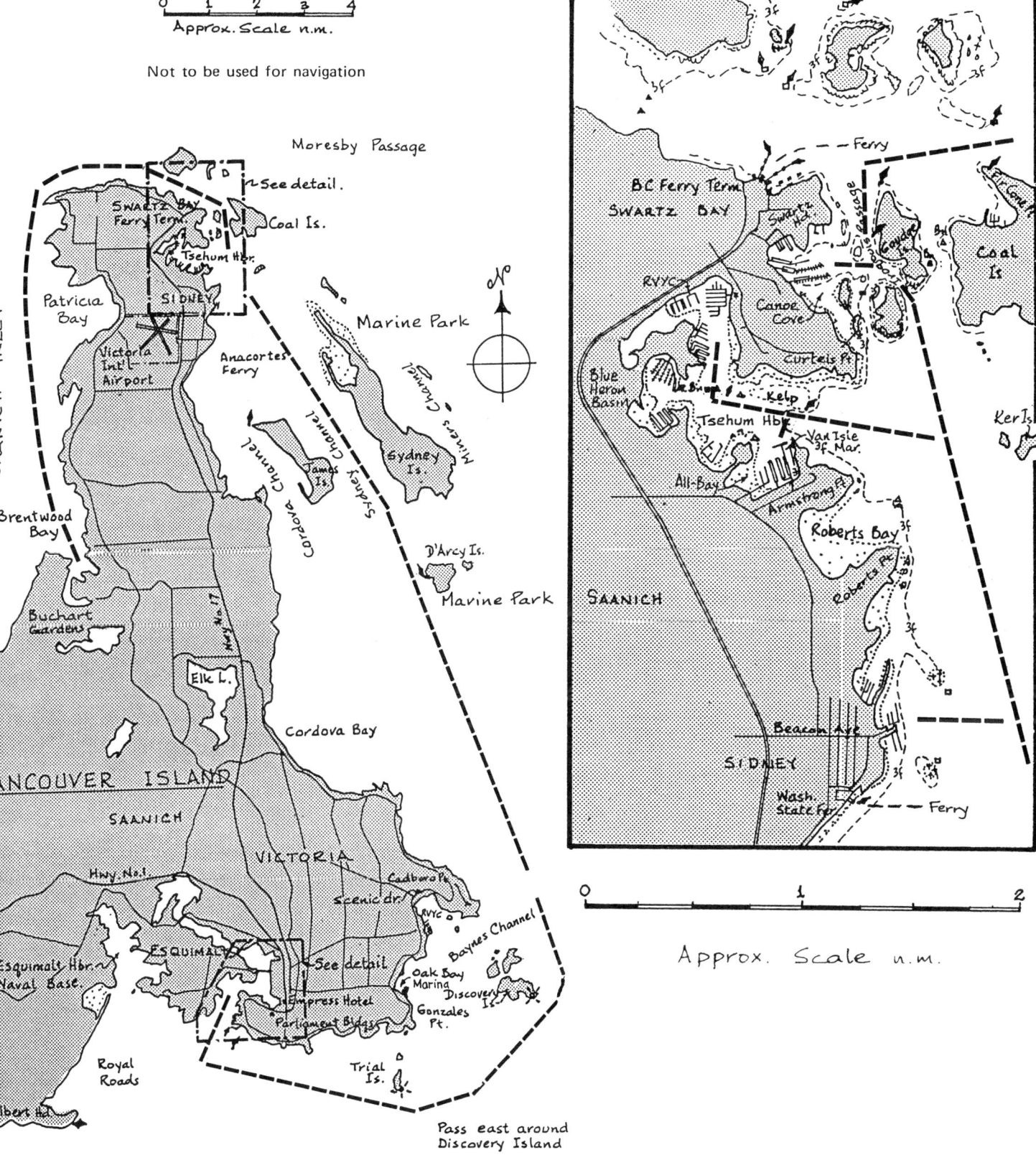

Moresby Passage

See detail.

Coal Is.

Swartz Bay Ferry Term.

Tsehum Hbr.

SIDNEY

Patricia Bay

SAANICH INLET

Victoria Int'l Airport

Anacortes Ferry

Marine Park

Minrso Channel

Sydney Is.

Brentwood Bay

Cordova Channel

Sidney Channel

James Is.

D'Arcy Is.

Marine Park

Buchart Gardens

Hwy. No. 17

Elk L.

Cordova Bay

VANCOUVER ISLAND

SAANICH

VICTORIA

Hwy. No. 1

Cadboro Pt.

scenic dr.

RVYC

Baynes Channel

Oak Bay Marina

Discovery Is.

Esquimalt

See detail

Esquimalt Hbr. Naval Base

Empress Hotel

Parliament Bldgs.

Gonzales Pt.

Royal Roads

Trial Is.

Albert Hd.

Pass east around Discovery Island

STRAIT OF JUAN DE FUCA

BC Ferry Term.
SWARTZ BAY

Ferry

Swartz Hd.

Passage

Coal Is.

RVYC

Canoe Cove

Curteis Pt.

Blue Heron Basin

Kelp

Tsehum Hbr.

Ker Is.

Van Isle 3f Mar.

All-Bay

Armstrong Pt.

Roberts Bay

Roberts Pt.

SAANICH

Beacon Ave.

SIDNEY

Wash. State Fer.

Ferry

Approx. Scale n.m.

BEDWELL HARBOUR*

This **Port of Entry** is tucked in a bay in the northern part of South Pender Island. Two bodies of water, Port Browning and Bedwell Harbour separate North Pender Island from South Pender Island where they meet at Pender Canal. This shallow waterway has a least depth of 2.2m (7'). A bridge with a vertical clearance of 8.5m (28') crosses the canal near its north end. Tidal streams reach a maximum of 4 knots during springs.

Egeria Bay is about midway along the southwestern shore of South Pender Island. A breakwater built out from Richardson Bluff on the northern shore of the bay gives harbor facilities protection from northerly winds. Approach and entry to the harbor pose no difficulties. Connected to the public float located at the head of the bay are the Customs docks where Customs officers clear vessels from May 1 to September 1 from 8 am to 10 pm daily. Vessels entering Canada that have not received a Clearance Number under CANPASS regulations are required to clear Customs at the dock before proceeding elsewhere.

Bedwell Harbour Marina is just to the north of the Customs docks. The moorage office monitors VHF 68 and sells fuel, ice and pop. Shore facilities for the use of cruisers and hotel guests include a restaurant, heated pool, washrooms, showers, movies, dog walk, tennis courts, bike rentals, snack bar, playground and grocery store. Moorage may be reserved by telephone at (250) 629-3212 or (800) 663-2899. Moorage rates vary from $.50 per foot to $1.10 per foot depending on the month, with the high season being July and August. A 4 km. walk along a road leads to an ocean lookout, while another trail leads to the top of Mount Norman where the view is well worth the effort.

Since water is scarce here boaters are asked to conserve it and dispense with washing the boat or leaving taps running. The island does not have a landfill site, so trash is not collected and boaters must take their garbage to a community that has collection facilities.

Beaumont Marine Park is a strip of land less than .2 miles wide and about 5 miles long, bordering part of the coast. The steep shores are covered with arbutus, fir and the rare and beautiful Garry oak. About 15 mooring buoys are east of Skull Islet and excellent anchorage can be taken to the south of the buoyed area. Fees for use of the mooring buoys are collected on the honor system at the self-registration stations in the information shelters.

******

Both Pender Island and Bedwell Harbour were named by Captain Richards, commander of the survey ship *Plumper*, after second masters Daniel Pender and Edward Bedwell who surveyed the B.C. coast from 1857 to 1860. Egeria Bay was named after a steam screw sloop *Egeria*, built in 1874 that was used exclusively for survey of the coast until 1902. Port Browning was also named by Captain Richards after George Browning, second master of the survey ship *Hecate,* a paddle wheel sloop..

Though violent altercations between Indians and settlers were rare in Canada a settler named Brady was killed by Cowichan Indians in Bedwell Harbour in April, 1863.

*The Canadian spelling, harbour, is used in Canadian place names and the U.S. spelling, harbor, is used elsewhere in the guide

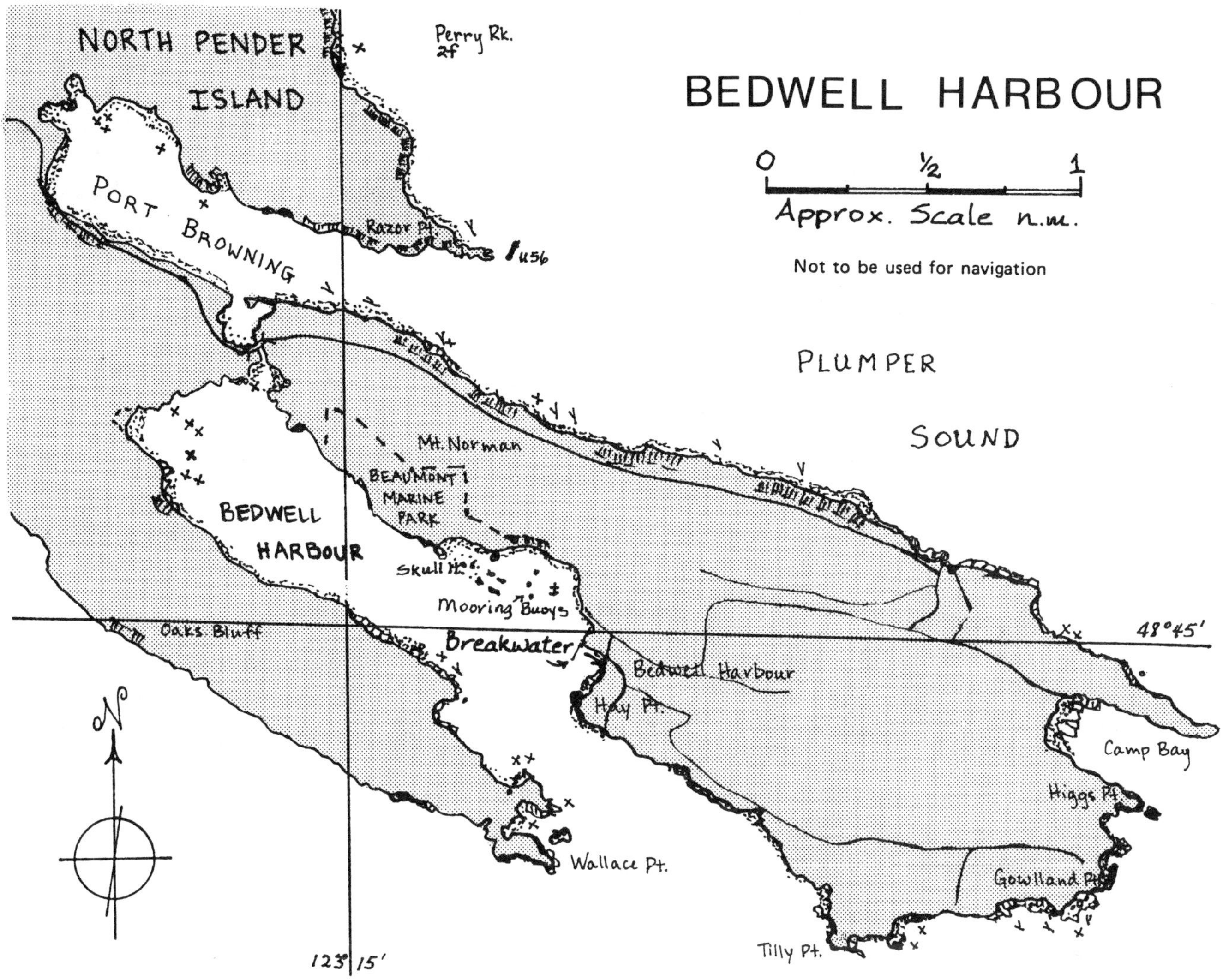

BEDWELL HARBOUR

NORTH PENDER ISLAND

Perry Rk.
2f

PORT BROWNING

Razor Pt.
Y
fu56

0 ½ 1
Approx. Scale n.m.

Not to be used for navigation

PLUMPER

SOUND

Mt. Norman
BEAUMONT MARINE PARK
BEDWELL HARBOUR
Skull Is.
Mooring Buoys

Oaks Bluff
Breakwater
Bedwell Harbour
Hay Pt.

48°45'

N

Camp Bay

Higgs Pt.

Wallace Pt.

Gowlland Pt.

123° 15'

Tilly Pt.

Detail –

Bedwell Harbour Marina

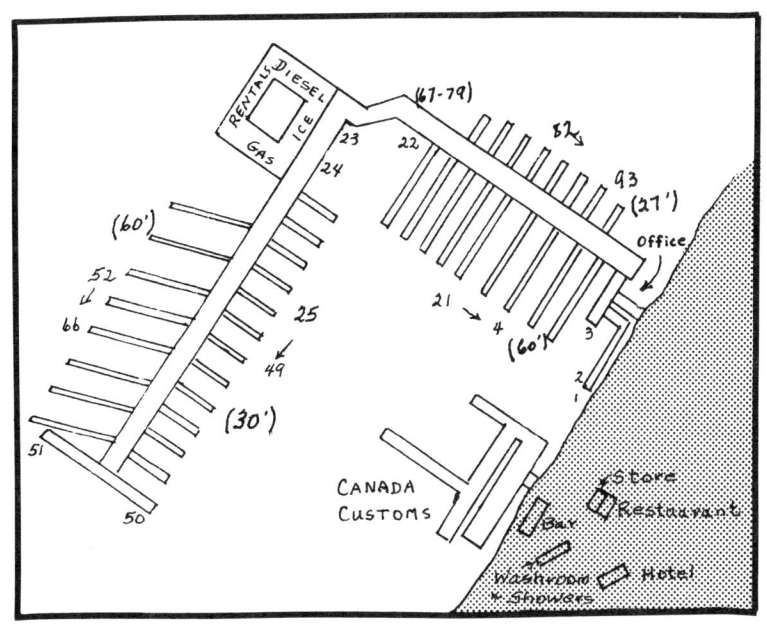

RENTALS DIESEL
GAS ICE
(67-79)
23 22
24
82
93 (27')
Office
(60')
52
66
25
21 4
(60')
3
49
2
1
(30')
51
50
CANADA CUSTOMS
Store
Restaurant
Bar
Washroom + Showers
Hotel

BLAINE, WASHINGTON

Semiahmoo Spit helps to enclose the protected area known as Drayton Harbor. On the eastern side of the harbor lies Blaine, a **U.S. Port of Entry.** A protective dike and breakwater encloses the port of Blaine, which is entered through an opening opposite the end of Semiahmoo Spit.

The eastern end of Blaine harbor (a subsidiary of the Port of Bellingham, which is operated by Whatcom County) has a series of long docks forming a boat haven. The western portion of these floats is for commercial fishing vessels; the eastern floats are for yachts in Blaine Harbor, and here transients can usually find moorage. The harbormaster monitors VHF Ch. 16; working channels are 9 and 68. The Harbor Office is in the one-story building at the head of the gangway.

The western end of Blaine harbor is commercial and includes a repair yard with haul-out facilities, and fish unloading docks. A fuel dock is opposite the main entrance to the harbor. The main part of the town is about .25 mile to the east.

Semiahmoo Yacht Basin is an alternative which can be entered through an opening in the floating breakwater behind Semiahmoo Spit. Immediately to starboard on the inside of the breakwater is a fuel station, where temporary moorage can be taken while the harbormaster is being contacted. His office is in the large building beyond the head of the wharf. Moorage is usually available for transient vessels. Facilities are very clean and include a laundromat, shower, and a store handling marine supplies, groceries, and sundry items. Any major shopping will have to be done in Blaine, which though less than .25 mile away by water, is about 7 miles by road.

Anchorage can be taken in **Drayton Harbor** west of Semiahmoo Yacht Basin. The sketch shows the extensive shoal area. Southerly or southeasterly winds can kick up a nasty chop in the harbor.

Entry into the U.S. can be easily made from either marina. Call U.S. Customs at 332-6318 from telephone booths ashore; clearance may be obtained either by phone or an inspector will come out to check the vessel and crew. After 5 p.m. or on Sundays and holidays, call 1-800-562-5943.

Blaine is a small border town, so if any major refitting is needed better prices may be obtained in Bellingham or Seattle (a short trip by bus) or across the border in Vancouver.

WHITE ROCK, BRITISH COLUMBIA

Across the bay is White Rock, a **Canadian Port of Entry**. A long pier protrudes from the shore with a short breakwater at right angles to the end. Proceed around the breakwater to the dock on the eastern side. A call can be made from the telephone booth at the shore end of the pier to Canadian Customs at 1-888-226-7277.

BLAINE, WASH.; WHITE ROCK, B.C.
Ports of Entry

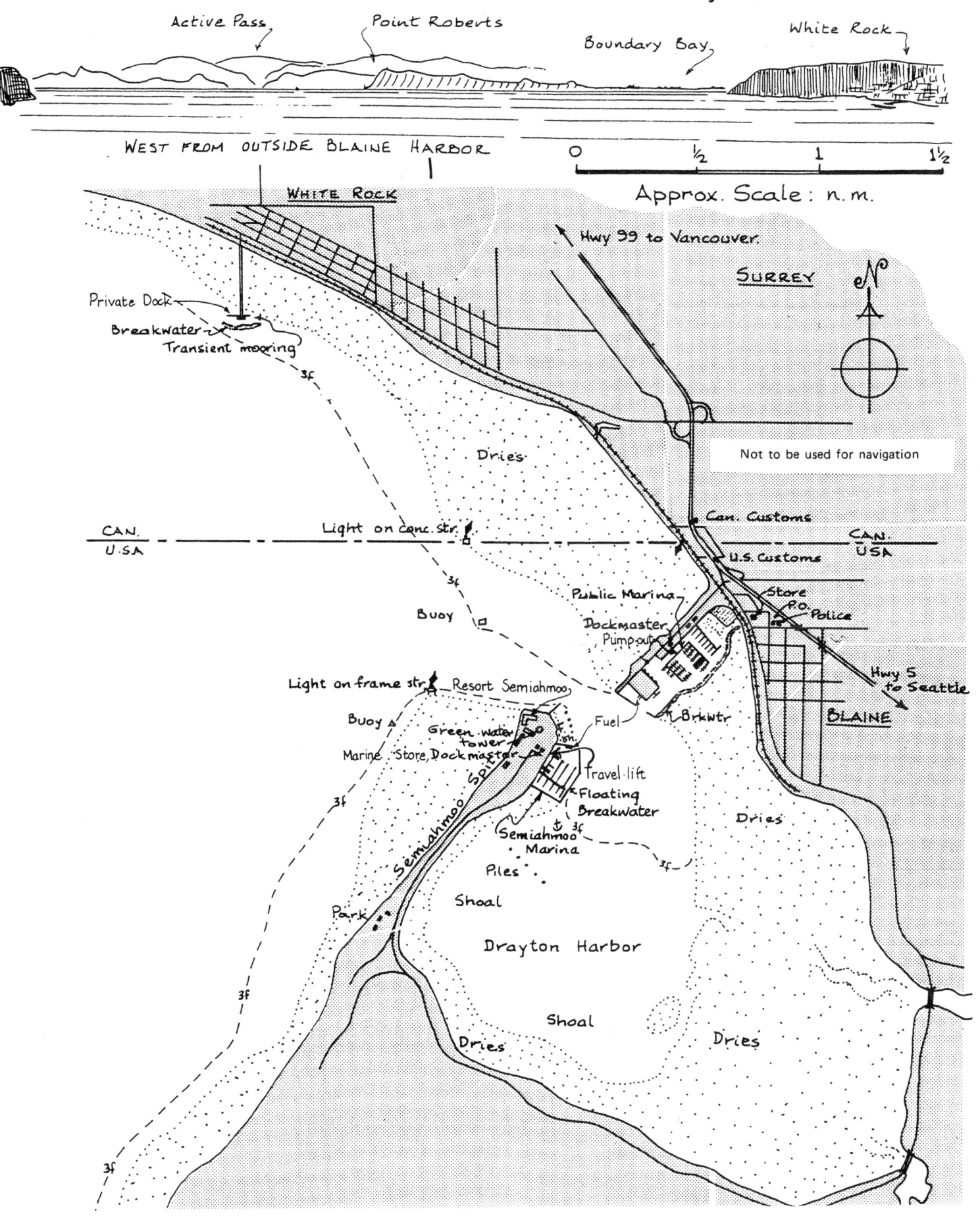

Active Pass

Point Roberts

Boundary Bay

White Rock

WEST FROM OUTSIDE BLAINE HARBOR

0   ½   1   1½

Approx. Scale : n.m.

WHITE ROCK

Hwy 99 to Vancouver

SURREY

N

Private Dock

Breakwater

Transient mooring

3f

Not to be used for navigation

CAN.
U.S.A

Light on conc. str.

Can. Customs

CAN.
USA

3f

U.S. Customs

Buoy

Public Marina

Store
P.O.
Police

Dockmaster
Pump-out

Light on frame str.   Resort Semiahmoo

Hwy 5
to Seattle

Buoy

Green water
tower

Fuel

Brkwtr

BLAINE

Marine Store, Dockmaster

Travel lift

Floating
Breakwater

Semiahmoo   SPIT

Semiahmoo
Marina

3f

Dries

Piles

3f

3f

Shoal

Park

Drayton Harbor

Shoal

3f

Dries

Dries

3f

ACTIVE PASS

Of the four passes of the Gulf Islands, this is the longest and the busiest. Not only is it used by many yachts, but swarms of small sports-fishermen frequent each end and the B.C. Ferries vessels meet each other every hour within the pass on their routes to Swartz Bay or Tsawwassen. Even tugs towing log booms occasionally use the pass.

During the springs, the tides set through the pass at 7 to 8 knots. Even during normal days, the current is considerable. Small vessels, particularly deep draft power and sail boats should use the pass at or near slack water. It is generally possible to use the pass for an hour on either side of slack water, though it is better to do so going with the tide. But during these periods of use near slack water the concentration of vessels, requires careful and alert seamanship. The pass is crooked and after dark, well lit, and can be used by skippers familiar with it at any time. First-time visitors should use the pass only during daylight hours. One of the greatest advantages of Active Pass is that it has anchorages available on either side, as well as within the pass.

The pass is deep and clear except for a well marked and lighted area at Gossip Shoal near the eastern entrance and a drying patch with a light near Collinson Point at the western end. These are more of a hindrance for large vessels than for small ones, for the pass is quite wide. On any passage, favor the starboard side and allow for lots of room if a ferry is being passed or met. They kick up a considerable wash which, when combined with current boils and swells, can be most unsettling for small craft. Provided care is taken and the pass is used near slack water, the passage through Active Pass is relatively easy.

On the eastern side of the Pass, anchorages are available in **Whalers Bay** or **Sturdies Bay**. The former has the larger area, with drying shoals at its ends and several rocky reefs along its perimeter. Enter in mid-channel. Sturdies Bay has a terminal for the inter-islands ferry, and there is a small resort alongside where moorage is available. Beware of the reef that projects slightly across the direct passage to the wharf.

Within the pass itself, you can find anchorage in **Miners Bay** to the east of the wharf at the village of Mayne. A back current can be felt here, but the anchorage is otherwise comfortable.

Montague Harbour is at the western end of Active Pass and its relation to the pass is shown on the sketch. This B.C. Marine Park is one of the most popular anchorages in the Gulf Islands. In addition to cruising families who arrive by pleasure craft there are many who come by ferry to stay at the public campground nestled among the trees. Pleasant walks through the trees give you a chance to stretch your legs; one trail goes past an abandoned orchard and then to a beach on the other side of the peninsula.

Near the government wharf is a ferry dock which is used intermittently. At the head of the wharf is a small store which stocks a few groceries and sundry items. Mooring buoys in the northern part of the bay are usually claimed early in the day. Anchorage may be taken anywhere in the bay; the southern part has deeper water. Anchorages which can be found within a relatively short distance are at **Fulford Harbour** and **Long Harbour** on Saltspring Island and at **Prevost Island**.

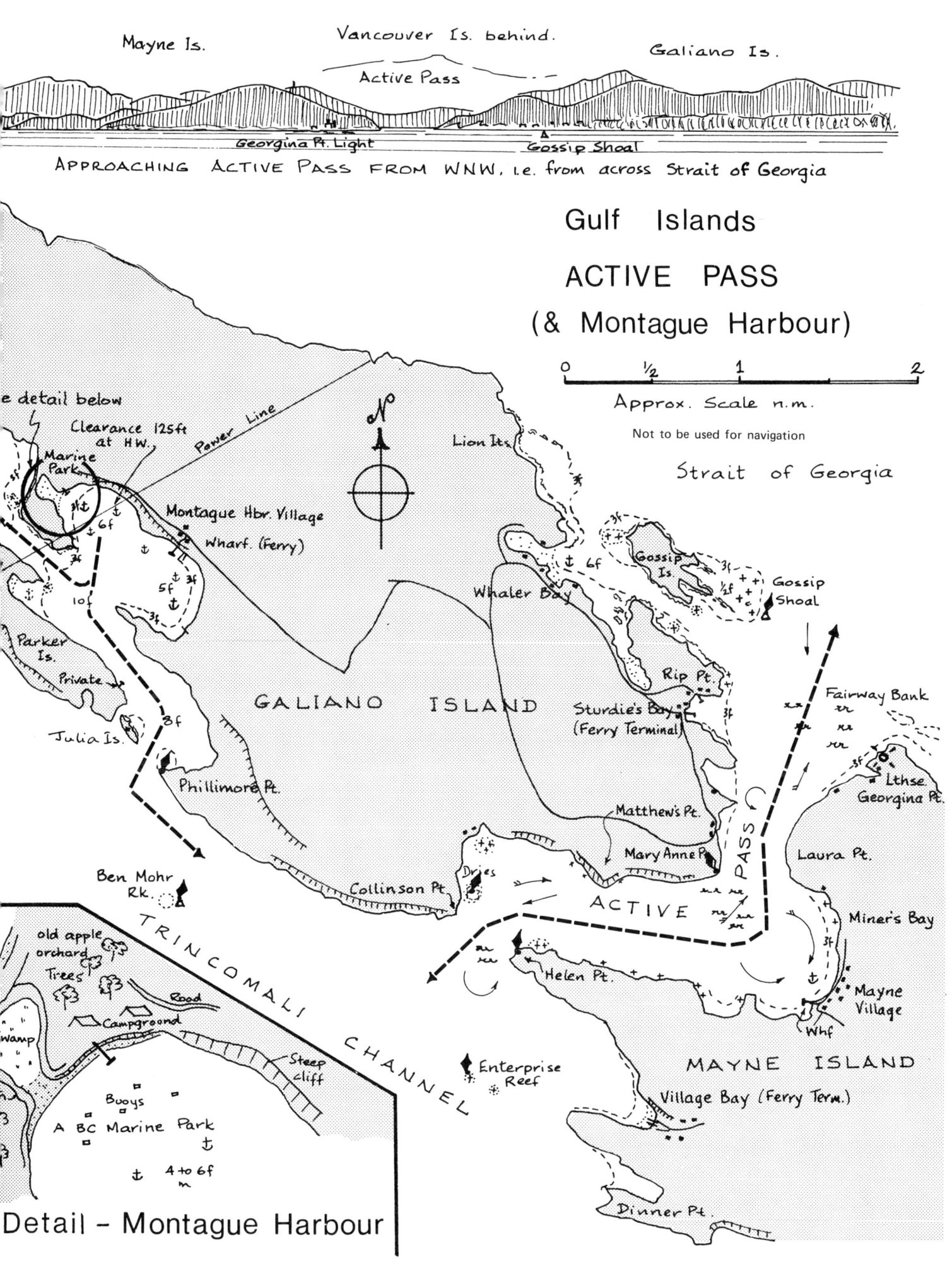

Mayne Is.   Vancouver Is. behind.   Galiano Is.

Active Pass

Georgina Pt. Light   Gossip Shoal

APPROACHING ACTIVE PASS FROM WNW, I.E. from across Strait of Georgia

Gulf Islands
ACTIVE PASS
(& Montague Harbour)

0   ½   1   2

Approx. Scale n.m.

Not to be used for navigation

Strait of Georgia

e detail below

Clearance 125ft at H.W.

Power Line

Marine Park

Montague Hbr. Village
Wharf. (Ferry)

Lion Its.

Gossip Is.

Gossip Shoal

Whaler Bay

6f

Parker Is.

Private

Rip Pt.

Julia Is.

8f

GALIANO ISLAND

Sturdie's Bay (Ferry Terminal)

Fairway Bank

Lthse Georgina Pt.

Phillimore Pt.

Matthew's Pt.

Laura Pt.

Ben Mohr Rk.

Collinson Pt.

Dries

Mary Anne Pt.

Miner's Bay

ACTIVE   PASS

old apple orchard
Trees

Road

Campground

wamp

Steep cliff

TRINCOMALI   CHANNEL

Helen Pt.

Mayne Village

Whf

Buoys

A BC Marine Park

4 to 6f
m

Enterprise Reef

MAYNE ISLAND

Village Bay (Ferry Term.)

Detail – Montague Harbour

Dinner Pt.

PORLIER PASS

Located between Galiano and Valdes Islands, this is the next pass north of Active Pass. It is much used by cruising vessels bound for the Gulf Islands and by fishermen. No deep sea vessels use this pass as Romulus Rock at its western end limits the apparent opening.

This is the shortest and straightest of the three Gulf Island passes. As such, it would normally be the favored route, except that the underwater dangers of the western side make it less attractive for large vessels, and the lack of immediate anchorages on either side reduce its appeal for small craft awaiting slack water. As a result, there is less traffic here than in Active Pass.

Though short, this pass should be traveled at or near slack water. The current can reach 8 or 9 knots at springs and boils, and small whirlpools can make passage hazardous for an under powered small craft. But taken within an hour of each side of slack water, the pass is relatively straightforward.

Although Romulus Rock, on the western side is more of a hazard for large vessels, for small craft the best route through Porlier Pass is to hold about 225 m (700 feet) off the light at Race Point, and set a course to pass a similar amount off of Alcala Point on Galiano Island. This should take small vessels clear of any effects of Romulus Rock. There are more shoals and rocky patches on the northern side of Porlier, including a drying patch called Black Rock, so it is recommended that vessels favor the southern side in passing either way.

A small niche just to the west of the lighthouse can give shelter, but most vessels passing through Porlier proceed to one of the many anchorages available in the Gulf Islands. A particularly nice little one is **Retreat Cove,** about 6 miles south, on the west coast of Galiano Island. Enter only the southern portion, where the government wharf is built, for the northern section of the cove and behind Retreat Island is shallow and is suitable only for very small boats. Though the cove is small, it has good holding in mud, and there is space at the wharf as well. The road ashore offers a scenic, rural walk with many fine views of the area.

Other anchorages within reasonable reach of Porlier Pass are: **North Cove** and **Telegraph Harbour** on Thetis Island, and **Tent Island Marine Park** which is south of Thetis and Kuper Islands.

Fishing is productive at most passes and Porlier Pass is no exception. The salmon congregate at the downstream ends of passes, changing ends as the tide changes. This results in some congestion of small fishing craft which follow the movement of the tides and the fish. When fishing the passes, mooching with bait and lures seems to be the most successful, followed by trolling.

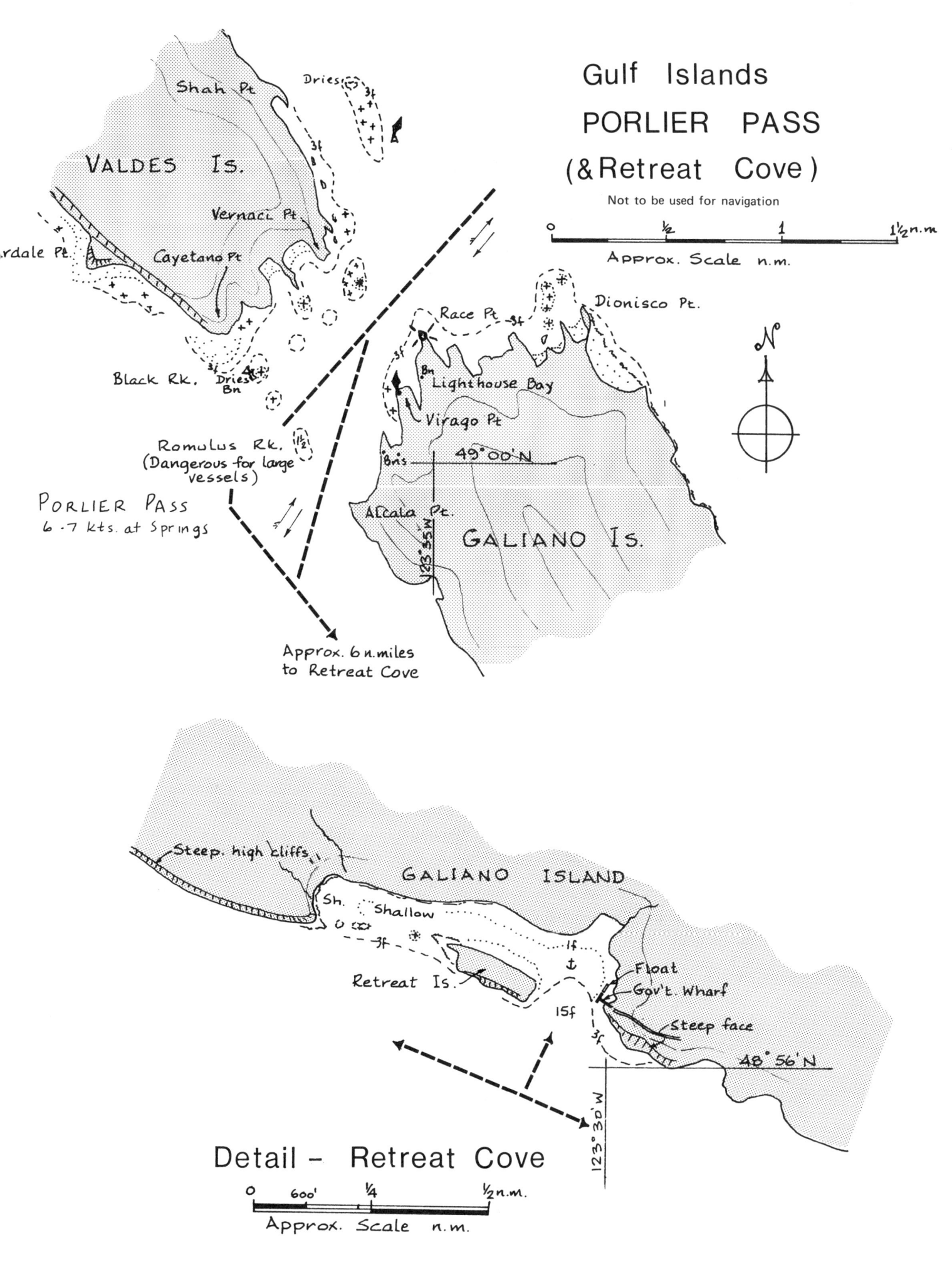

Gulf Islands
PORLIER PASS
(& Retreat Cove)

Not to be used for navigation

Approx. Scale n.m.

0   ½   1   1½ n.m.

N

Shah Pt.

Dries

VALDES Is.

Vernaci Pt.

rdale Pt.

Cayetano Pt.

Black Rk. Dries Bn

Race Pt.

Dionisco Pt.

Bn Lighthouse Bay

Virago Pt

Bns 49°00'N

Alcala Pt.

GALIANO Is.

123°55'W

Romulus Rk.
(Dangerous for large vessels)

PORLIER PASS
6·7 kts. at Springs

Approx. 6 n.miles to Retreat Cove

Steep. high cliffs

GALIANO ISLAND

Sh. Shallow

Retreat Is.

1f

Float

Gov't. Wharf

15f

Steep face

48° 56'N

123° 30'W

Detail - Retreat Cove

Approx. Scale n.m.

0   600'   ¼   ½ n.m.

GABRIOLA PASS

This is the most scenic of the three passes. It has good anchorages on each side of the pass and another one half way through. It is a good location from which to commence crossing the Georgia Strait either to Vancouver or to Welcome Pass.

The eastern end of the pass is fronted by Breakwater Island, which divides the current. The dangers are marked, and a mid-channel course is clear of all problems. The constriction between Josef Point on Gabriola Island, and Cordero Point on Valdes Island, is where the currents are strongest. Boils, swells and occasional whirlpools occur downstream of this area when the current is running. Passage should be made at or near slack water—no more than an hour on either side. Large power boats have been known to fail to make headway against the full current and have had to turn back.

At the proper time, however, the passage is simple and straightforward. Once past Josef Point, the opening to the north is **Degnen Bay** where good anchorage can be taken in its northern end near a public wharf. As you continue through the Pass, effects of the current are less noticeable and once through the next section, you are free to roam the Gulf Islands.

On the Gulf Islands side, a very good anchorage is at **Pirates Cove** Marine Park in the southern part of De Courcy Island. When entering the enclosed harbor, favor the De Courcy Island shore, heading toward the private house, for a reef, marked by a concrete marker, projects underwater from the spit. At low water, there may be less than a fathom over the rocky sill of the entrance, so pass between the marker and a buoy marking a rock. This cove is crowded in summer. The holding is in mud on rock, and with strong winds it will be wise to let out additional scope if space permits.

Silva Bay is one of the nicest anchorages on the Strait of Georgia side of the Gulf Islands. The harbor is formed by the protection of the many Flat Top Islands around a cove of Gabriola Island. Shelter is available from all winds and seas, and there is room for many vessels. Beware of the plastic water pipes laid across the bay from the village to Tugboat Island — vessels anchoring in the northern part of the bay can often foul their anchors on these pipes. The harbor is very crowded in summer, since it is a popular place. There is an RVYC outstation on Tugboat Island.

The entrance to Silva Bay is from the east, through Commodore Passage. Note the jog that must be made around the reef which is marked with a concrete pedestal and light. Stay at least 18 m (60 feet) off, for the reef extends beyond the marker. Do not pass between the marker and the south shore.

Those familiar with the bay also use the passage between Sear Island and Gabriola Island. At low water, the maximum draft that can be carried through this passage is 2 m (6 feet)—rocks and other dangers show clearly. This passage leads to the entrance of Gabriola Pass behind Breakwater Island.

Thrasher Rock and Gabriola Reefs lie about 1.5 miles northwest of Breakwater Island. Pass north around Thrasher Rock, which is a good departure or destination point to or from the mainland. Good fishing can be had around the reefs and around Breakwater Island.

Commodore Passage

Reef

ENTERING SILVA BAY

0   600'   1800'   ½   1   1½

Approx. Scale n.m.

Not to be used for navigation

N

Gaviola Is

3f

Lily Is

Vance Is

Acorn Is

Gaviola Is

3f

FLAT TOP IS.

Approx. 19 n.m. to
Pt. Grey buoy, Vancouver.

Note: Water pipes are
laid across the harbor
under-water.

Silva Bay
Dock
Floats

Fuel

Tugboat
Is.
RVYC

Commodore
Passage

Dries Thrasher Rock
Light

GABRIOLA Is.

Only vessels drawing
less than 6ft. can use this passage

Seal
Is.

Dries

3f   3f

Bath Is.

Saturnina Is.

Local knowledge
needed for passage.

Dries

Gabriola Reefs

Good trolling

Wharf

2f

Degnen Bay

4f   3f

Josef Pt.

cliffs

Breakwater
Is.

3f

Cordero Pt.

3f   3f

Steep Cliffs

VALDES IS.

Gabriola Pass.
Currents 6-8 kt at Springs
Travel at slack.

Vancouver Is.

Valdes Is.

Beacon

Silva Bay

Breakwater Is. behind.

Bath Is

To Gabriola Pass

Commodore
Passage

Acorn Is.

APPROACHING THE FLAT TOP IS. FROM NNE, distant about 2 miles.

NANAIMO

As the second largest city on Vancouver Island, Nanaimo acts as a hub for much of the activity in the central part of the island. It is the second major terminal of the B.C. Ferry Corporation which links the island and Vancouver. It is also the home of the zany annual Bathtub Race held in July, when hundreds of dedicated entrants take of in their souped-up special tubs to race to Vancouver.

Nanaimo lies north of the Gulf Islands area and can be approached from the Strait of Georgia or from the inside waters via Dodd Narrows, which is north of Gabriola Passage, and between Mudge Island and Vancouver Island. As with other passes in the Gulf Islands, Dodd Narrows should be traversed only at or near slack water. The harbor of Nanaimo lies ahead up Northumberland Channel.

False Narrows, to the east of Dodd Narrows, leads from Pylades Channel. Though narrower and a little more complex, it can also be traversed at or near slack water. A large scale chart is useful, though there are ranges in the channel. Kelp is prevalent in summer.

Newcastle and Protection Islands lie in front of the main small craft facilities in Nanaimo harbor. Approach from the north around Newcastle, or from the south around Protection Island. Do not attempt the channel between these islands, as it is shoal and encumbered by kelp. Mooring buoys and anchorage can be taken in Mark Bay, which is part of the **Newcastle Island Marine Park**. A passenger ferry connects the island to Nanaimo.

Several small craft facilities are located along the Newcastle Passage shore of Nanaimo. Favor the Newcastle Island side of the passage to avoid the marked rocks, particularly Rowans Rock which has bent many a propeller. The harbor has a 5-knot speed limit.

The yacht club station and the Nanaimo harbor basin are near the southern part of the harbor, opposite the end of Protection Island. The old octagonal harbor bastion is a good marker, though it now has a large hotel rising behind it. There are many berths in the basin, controlled by the harbormaster. As fishing vessels moor here in winter and are out during the summer, space may be available. Showers and restrooms are provided, while across the street is the Harbour Park Mall, with supermarkets, restaurants, laundromats and other facilities. Fuel floats are moored along the harbor front and repair yards are available.

A B.C. Ferry Terminal is Departure Bay, in the northern part of the harbor. The large ferries run every hour (sometimes more frequently in the summer) to Horseshoe Bay in West Vancouver. A second B.C. Ferry Terminal is south of Nanaimo at Duke Point and it runs to Tsawwassen Ferry Terminal in Delta. As the ferries have a big wash, care should be taken when encountering them.

When leaving Departure Bay the grassy hump of Snake Island and (when bound for Vancouver) the barren sandstone Entrance Island are both passed on their north side. A lighthouse and fog signal are located on Entrance Island. If crossing to Welcome Pass, note the comment on page 6 of the Introduction regarding the restricted area designated as "Whiskey-Golf."

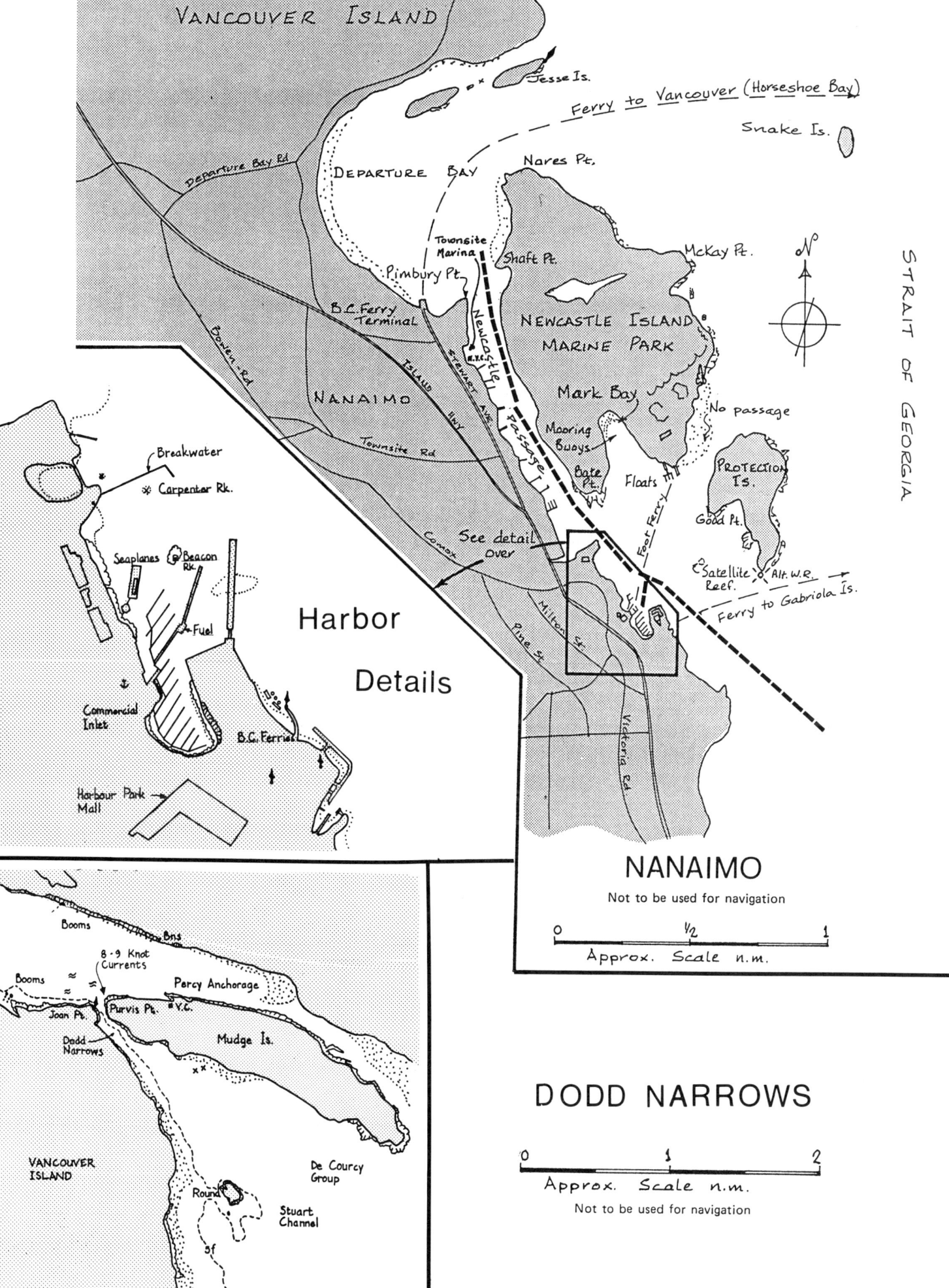

VANCOUVER ISLAND

Jesse Is.

Ferry to Vancouver (Horseshoe Bay)

Snake Is.

Departure Bay Rd

DEPARTURE BAY

Nares Pt.

Townsite Marina

Pimbury Pt.

Shaft Pt.

McKay Pt.

STRAIT OF GEORGIA

B.C. Ferry Terminal

NEWCASTLE ISLAND MARINE PARK

Bowen Rd

Nanaimo R.

Stewart Ave.

Newcastle

N.Y.C.

Mark Bay

No passage

NANAIMO

Townsite Rd

Mooring Buoys

Floats

PROTECTION Is.

Passage

Bate Pt.

Foot Ferry

Good Pt.

See detail Over

Comox

Milton St.

Satellite Reef.

Alt. W.R.

Ferry to Gabriola Is.

Pine St.

Victoria Rd

Harbor

Details

Breakwater

* Carpenter Rk.

Seaplanes

Beacon Rk.

Fuel

Commercial Inlet

B.C. Ferries

Harbour Park Mall

NANAIMO

Not to be used for navigation

|0| | |1/2| | |1|

Approx. Scale n.m.

Booms

Bns

8·9 Knot Currents

Percy Anchorage

Booms

Joan Pt.

Purvis Pk.

Y.C.

Dodd Narrows

Mudge Is.

VANCOUVER ISLAND

De Courcy Group

Round

Stuart Channel

3f

DODD NARROWS

|0| |1| |2|

Approx. Scale n.m.

Not to be used for navigation

VANCOUVER

Vancouver is the principal city of British Columbia and is a **Port of Entry**. Including the surrounding municipalities, Greater Vancouver has over 2 million people, almost half that of the entire province of British Columbia and this is the largest city in the area covered by this guide. It has its own special attractions as well as the disadvantages of big cities anywhere. When Sir Francis Drake explored the coast in 1579 followed by Captain Vancouver who sailed past First Narrows into Burrard Inlet in 1792, who could have imagined that a city such as this would grow from these densely wooded shores.

This city enjoys one of the most beautiful natural harbors in the world. The surrounding mountains offer a scenic backdrop, as well as good skiing in season. The mild Pacific coast climate allows year-round sailing (though winter's cooler weather needs to be taken into consideration with layers of clothes and a source of heat aboard).

Beginning from the south and proceeding northward the centers of population—Delta, Richmond, Vancouver, North Vancouver, and West Vancouver—will be described.

Deriving its name from being part of the delta of the Fraser River, Delta is a sprawling district on the south side of the Fraser River. Significant landmarks seen as one sails northward are the B.C. Ferries Terminal at Tsawwassen and a container terminal adjacent to the huge Roberts Bank Coal Port facility. The silt of the Fraser River has laid two large shallow banks— Roberts Bank off of Delta and Sturgeon Bank off of Richmond. Both banks are well buoyed and courses past them should pass clear of the extensive areas of shoal water.

The South Arm of the Fraser River exits through a buoyed channel protected by a breakwater which ends at Sand Heads Light at the edge of the bank. This route is navigable by deep sea vessels as far as the Port of New Westminster, about 20 miles upstream. Cruising yachts can enter the small town of Steveston for fuel, moorage and provisions, though this is mainly a commercial fishing vessel center. **Captain's Cove Marina** is 9.5 miles up the river from Sand Heads; transient moorage is available and facilities include a travel-lift, restaurant, showers and laundromat. From April till July the melting snows that feed the Fraser cause freshet currents that can run to 5 knots. Upstream travel is affected by these currents and the state of the tide.

Richmond extends between the North and South Arms of the Fraser River. It is one of the largest residential suburbs of Vancouver, and includes the expanse of Sea Island on which Vancouver International Airport is located. Depending on the prevailing winds the jets land from either inland or over the Strait of Georgia. Entrance to Richmond marinas is through the North Arm which exits just south of Point Grey. There are several marinas at the southeastern end of Sea Island. The Arthur Lang bridge has clearance of 19 m (65 feet) and the airport swing bridge beyond it has only 5.5 m (18 feet). Many of the marinas are southwest of this bridge.

The high bluff of Point Grey marks the tip of the peninsula on which Vancouver proper is located. Immediately behind it are the extensive lands and buildings of the University of British Columbia. High-rise towers of the city center can be seen from some distance before Lion's Gate Bridge comes into view.

E. Side, Str. of Georgia

VANCOUVER AREA

MARINAS — DOCKS, FUEL, ETC.

- C Fisherman's Cove — WYYC, EHYC, Thunderbird Marina, fuel
- I Coal Harbour — RVYC, VRC, Commercial docks, fuel, see next map
- M Burrard Bridge — Civic Marina, fuel, boat launch
- N Jericho — Royal Vancouver Yacht Club docks
- R False Creek — Marinas, fuel, and marine services of every kind
- V Richmond — Marinas, fuel, and marine services
- X Steveston — Fishboat docks, fuel and marine services
- Y Fraser River — Captain's Cove Marina, fuel, boat launching

PARKS & ATTRACTIONS

- A Horseshoe Bay — BC Ferry Terminal, docks, fuel, great view
- B Whytecliff Park — Walks, diving, views
- D Lighthouse Park — Pt. Atkinson Light, walks, large trees, views
- E Grouse Mountain — Skyride, view, restaurant, skiing
- F Cleveland Dam — Canyon Park, walks, views, tourist attractions
- H Ambleside Park — Beach, view
- I Stanley Park — 1,000 acre (404 Ha) park, walks and aquarium
- J Gastown — Shops, curios, restaurants, tourist attraction
- K Chinatown — North America's 2nd largest Chinatown, shops
- L False Creek North Shore — B.C. Place Stadium
- M Kitsilano — Maritime Museum, Planetarium, Museum, beach
- O Spanish Banks — Beaches, views
- P University of B.C. — Museum of Anthropology, Nitobe Japanese Garden
- Q Granville Island — Public Market, restaurants, marine equipment
- S VanDusen Bot. Gardens — Acres of manicured gardens, restaurant
- T Queen Elizabeth Park — Gardens and conservatory for tropical plants
- Z Tsawwassen — BC Ferry terminal, nearby town with services

SHOPPING CENTRES

(The four major centres easily accessible by bus, car or walking are shown.)

- G Park Royal Centre — Marine Drive in West Vancouver
- J Downtown Vancouver — Several malls and large stores
- U Oakridge Centre — 41st and Oak St.
- W Richmond, Lansdowne Ctr. — No. 3 Rd., Richmond

For Tourist Information about Greater Vancouver - phone 682-2222

Not to be used for navigation

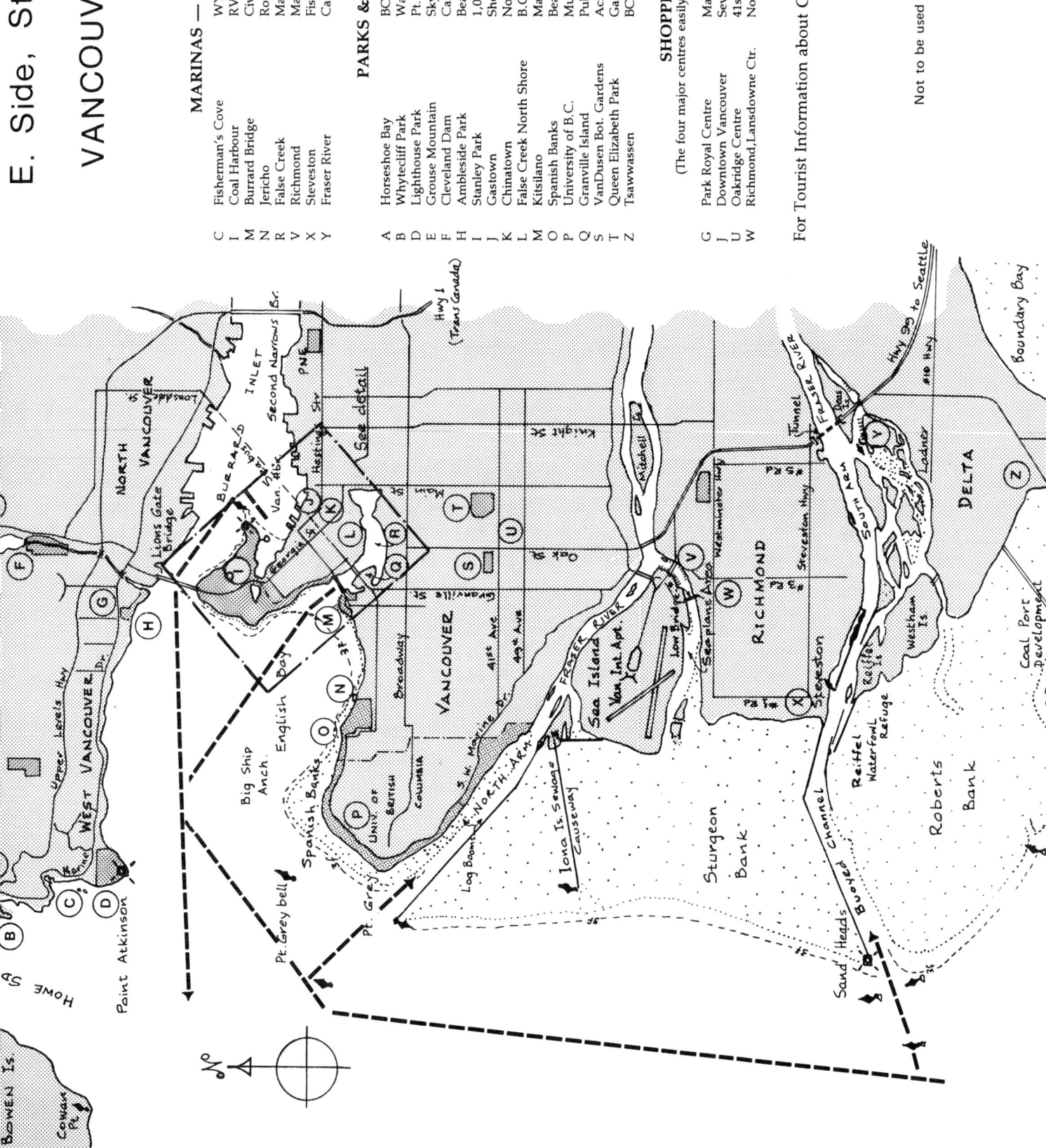

Point Grey, and Point Atkinson, to the north mark the 3.5 mile wide entrance to Vancouver Harbour. Spanish Banks extend out for .5 mile; a light and bell mark the northwestern edge of this bank which is covered at high water. The outer harbor includes English Bay which is used as an anchorage for freighters as well as by myriads of pleasure boaters from the city for recreational use. The Royal Vancouver Yacht Club Station, protected by breakwaters, lies midway along English Bay.

Most Vancouver marinas are in False Creek (between the downtown city center and the residential area of Kitsilano) and Coal Harbour (east of First Narrows, tucked behind Stanley Park). There are other marinas in Burrard Inlet and Indian Arm, but they are less convenient for the transient boater.

The Burrard Street bridge marks the boundary between False Creek and English Bay. The distinctive buildings of the Maritime Museum (large A-frame) and the McMillan-Bloedel Planetarium and Museum complex (onion-shaped) are easily identified on the south shore west of the bridge. Both the Burrard and Granville Street Bridges (to the east) have a clearance of 27 m (90 feet). The north bank of False Creek was the site of EXPO 86, a world's fair with a transportation and communication theme held in 1986.

The Burrard Civic Marina, a Coast Guard Station and a fuel barge are to starboard just before passing under the Burrard Street bridge (westernmost of the two bridges). Strong tidal currents flow through this passage. Transient moorage is not available at this marina.

Fisherman's Wharf lies between the two bridges. In winter it is filled with fishing vessels, but in summer space is rented to pleasure craft—transient vessels can try for space here. A harbormaster's office is located near the gate at the south side of the complex. Several other marinas lie within False Creek but space is usually taken by local boats.

The entrance to Vancouver Harbor proper is through First Narrows and under Lions Gate Bridge which has a clearance of 60 m (200 feet). Tidal currents of up to 6 knots run through the Narrows. Large vessels have the right of way through First Narrows because of their limited maneuverability in confined passages.

The magnificent green expanse of Stanley Park with its 1,000 acres of woodland and park facilities, is well worth visiting. The lighthouse at Brockton Point marks the eastern tip of the Park. After rounding the buoy which marks Burnaby Shoal turn southwest to enter Coal Harbour, where mooring is available. Fuel barges are anchored on the eastern side of Stanley Park. On the Stanley Park side are the Royal Vancouver Yacht Club Station and the Vancouver Rowing Club facilities, both private clubs where reciprocal club arrangements may allow guest moorage for transient boats. On the Vancouver waterfront there are moorings at the Westin Bayshore Inn (the home of many charter vessels) or at the marinas towards the west (relatively less expensive moorage).

The sketch map indicates the location of the various attractions in Vancouver. Tourist information offices, hotels and most businesses will be glad to give assistance and advice for visiting centers of interest or generally finding one's way around this beautiful city.

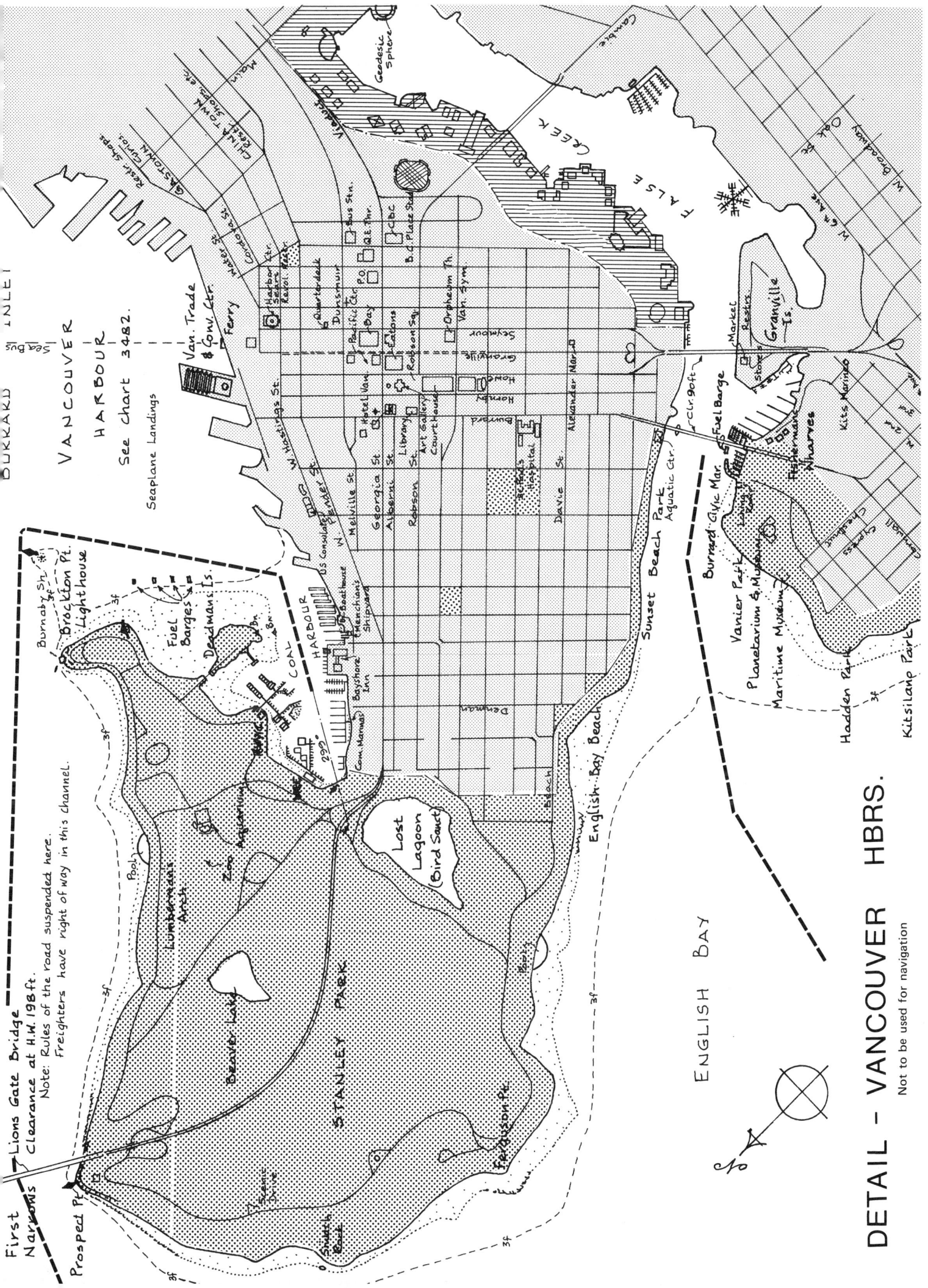

DETAIL – VANCOUVER HBRS.

Not to be used for navigation

ENGLISH BAY

First Narrows

Lions Gate Bridge
Clearance at H.W. 198 ft.
Note: Rules of the road suspended here.
Freighters have right of way in this channel.

Prospect Pt.

BURRARD INLET

VANCOUVER HARBOUR
See chart 3482.

Seaplane Landings

Burnaby Sh.
Brockton Pt. Lighthouse

Fuel Barges
Deadmans Is.

STANLEY PARK

Beaver Lake

Lumberman's Arch

Zoo & Aquarium

Pool

Ferguson Pt.

Siwash Rock

Lost Lagoon (Bird Sanct.)

COAL HARBOUR

Bayshore Inn

Menchions Shipyard

Gov. Marina

Van. Trade & Conv. Ctr.

Ferry

SeaBus

CHINA TOWN
GASTOWN
Recstr. Shops
Cypress
Water St.
China Shop Etc.
Cordova St.

Harbour Ctr. Sears
Royal Bank

Quarterdeck
P.O.

Pacific Ctr.
Bay
Eatons
Robson Sq.

Bus. Stn.
Q.E. Thr.
CBC
B.C. Place Stad.

Dunsmuir

W. Hastings St.
W. Pender St.

US Consulate

Melville St.

Hotel Van.

Georgia St.
Alberni St.

Robson St.

Library
Art Gallery
Court House

Orpheum Th.
Van. Sym.

Seymour
Granville
Howe
Hornby
Burrard

St. Paul's Hospital

Davie St.

Denman

Beach

English Bay Beach

Sunset Beach Park
Aquatic Ctr.

Alexander Man.D

Burrard Civic Mar.

Cr. 90 ft.

Fuel Barge

Vanier Park
Planetarium & Museum
Maritime Museum

Hadden Park

Kitsilano Park

False Creek

Geodesic Sphere

Market
Restr.
Granville Is.

Stores
False Creek Mar.
Fishermans Wharves

Kits Marina

ENGLISH BAY

N

KEATS ISLAND and GIBSONS

Howe Sound is a popular sailing area, not only because of its protected waters but also because of its proximity to Vancouver. Across from West Vancouver on Bowen Island are two marinas and a public dock in Snug Cove. As you enter the cove, **Bowen Island Marina** is the first marina seen on the north side. It consists of a 100m (340')dock with a least depth of 2.3 fathoms on the outer side. Further into the cove, beyond the prominent government dock is **Union Steamship Marina** which monitors VHF Ch 68. Both marinas have slips for transient cruisers. Stores and a post office are found nearby and a local ferry links the island to Horseshoe Bay in West Vancouver.

Located at the southwestern entrance to Howe Sound, Shoal Channel lies between Gibsons and Keats Island. The bar that gives the channel its name has only 3m (10 feet) of water at low tide. Opposing wind and currents cause short steep seas in this channel which is often filled with small sportsfishing boats "mooching" for salmon. Depending on the draft of the vessel the channel is normally passable on rising tides—a mid-channel course is best.

Plumper Cove Marine Park is on the western shore of Keats Island, with Shelter Islands to the southwest providing a lee. The islands are joined by a drying ledge. The Park Warden collects a nominal fee for the use of mooring buoys in the cove, or anchorage can be taken nearby. There is a small dock which a few small vessels can use. Beyond the gravel beach is a campground.

Gibsons is a small town on the Sechelt shore of Howe Sound. Steep Bluff is an easily recognizable point at the southern end of Gibsons. Some drying rocks extend roughly northeast from the foot of the bluff into Shoal Channel. A breakwater protects the harbor where a government dock and **Gibsons Marina** are located.

Transient vessels can usually find moorage at the marina on a hot-berth basis. Fuel, water, charts, and provisions are available in the marina store or you can walk to supermarkets and other stores in this quickly growing town. The highway which commences at the Ferry Terminal at Langdale (about 2 miles north along the shore) passes by Gibsons on its way up the Sechelt Peninsula to Powell River. A local ferry connects Langdale to Vancouver from this terminal.

Other anchorages in Howe Sound include:

Center Bay is a small cove in the western side of Gambier Island midway into the long bay. Good anchorage can be taken here.

Halkett Bay is the small, easternmost bay on Gambier Island. It offers a good anchorage although care must be taken to avoid a rock near the center of the bay at its head.

Fishermans Cove located in West Vancouver has no anchorage as it is filled with floats of the West Vancouver Yacht Club and Thunderbird Marina. Transient space is seldom available at these docks. Enter as shown on the sketch, to the north of Eagle Island.

Point Atkinson Lighthouse is a prominent landmark south of Fishermans Cove. It is the datum for many tidal calculations along this coast, and marks the northwestern boundary of Vancouver Harbour.

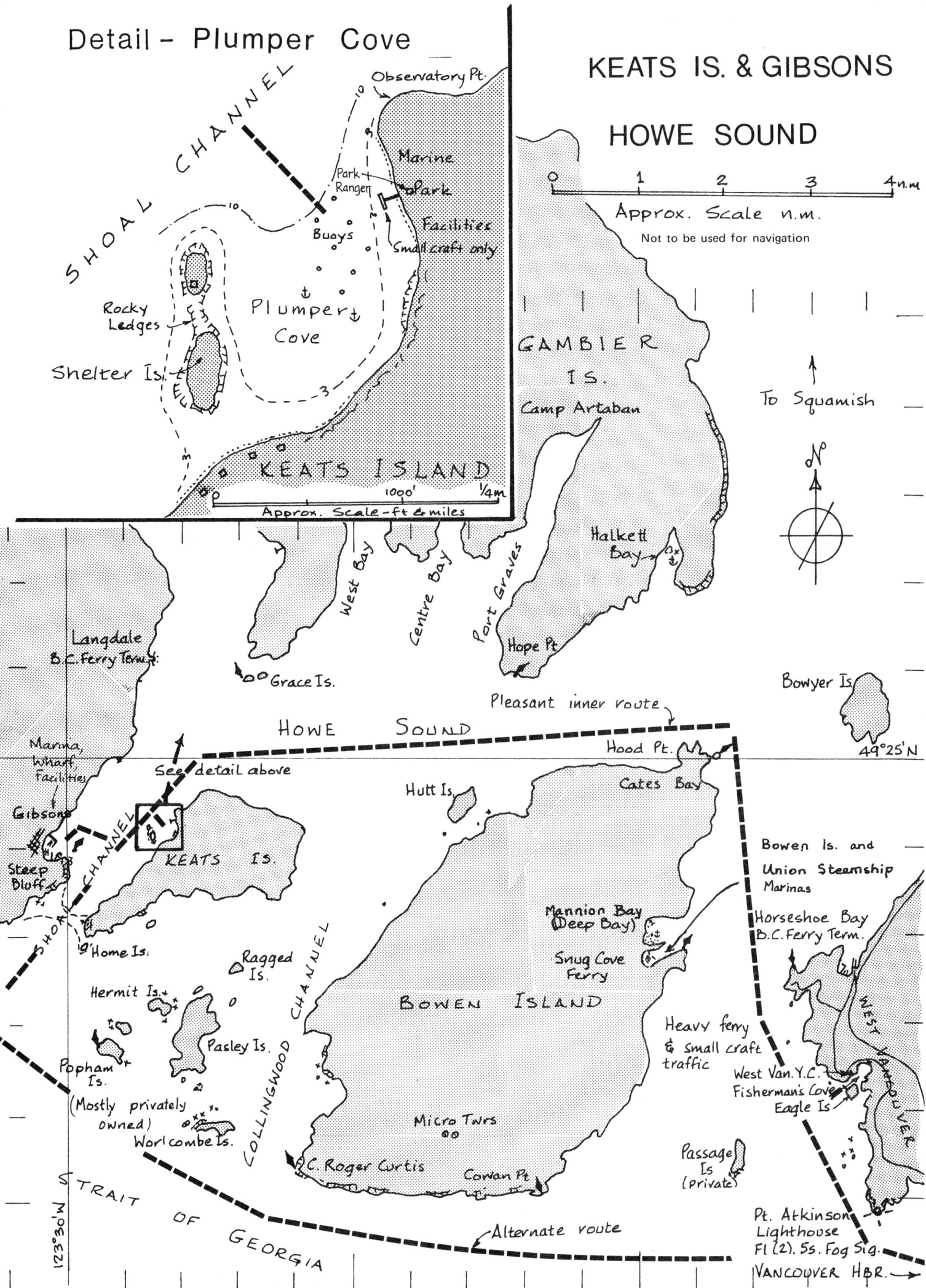

Detail - Plumper Cove

SHOAL CHANNEL

Observatory Pt.

KEATS IS. & GIBSONS

HOWE SOUND

Approx. Scale n.m.

Not to be used for navigation

Park Ranger

Marine Park Facilities

Small craft only

Buoys

Rocky Ledges

Plumper Cove

Shelter Is.

GAMBIER IS.

Camp Artaban

To Squamish

N

KEATS ISLAND

1000'   1/4m

Approx. Scale - ft & miles

West Bay

Centre Bay

Port Graves

Halkett Bay

Langdale B.C. Ferry Term.

Grace Is.

Hope Pt.

Bowyer Is.

Pleasant inner route

49°25'N

Hood Pt.

Cates Bay

HOWE   SOUND

See detail above

Hutt Is.

Marina, Wharf Facilities

Gibbons

SHOAL CHANNEL

KEATS IS.

Bowen Is. and Union Steamship Marinas

Steep Bluff

Mannion Bay (Deep Bay)

Horseshoe Bay B.C. Ferry Term.

Home Is.

Ragged Is.

Snug Cove Ferry

Hermit Is.

COLLINGWOOD CHANNEL

BOWEN   ISLAND

Heavy ferry & small craft traffic

Popham Is.

Pasley Is.

West Van. Y.C. Fisherman's Cove Eagle Is.

(Mostly privately owned)

Worlcombe Is.

Micro Twrs

Passage Is (private)

123°30'W

STRAIT

C. Roger Curtis

Cowan Pt.

OF   GEORGIA

Alternate route

Pt. Atkinson Lighthouse Fl (2). 5s. Fog Sig.

VANCOUVER HBR.

SMUGGLER and SECRET COVES

Though passage up the Strait of Georgia can be accomplished on either side, the more popular route is along the mainland coast. For this route, cross from Nanaimo or Silva Bay to either Howe Sound or the Sechelt Peninsula (known as the Sunshine Coast). Merry Island makes a good reference point as it is marked by a light and is close to Smuggler and Secret Coves. Beyond Merry Island is Welcome Passage is straightforward and clear of dangers except for occasional log debris.

Smuggler Cove Marine Park, on the mainland, comes very shortly after exiting from the northern end of Welcome Passage. The opening is about 21 m (70 feet) wide and is marked by a Marine Park sign on the northern side of the passage. Favor the north or port side when entering, staying fairly close to the rocky cliffs where the water is deeper. While popular, this anchorage has no facilities.

Once you are through this passage the cove opens up. Protected anchorage is available in the outer basin. Ahead lies a small island with a home built on it. By continuing on between this island and the north shore (still favoring the north side) make a fairly sharp turn to starboard leads to an inner basin. The sharp bend may seem to limit the size of vessel that can enter the inner anchorage but 12 m (40-foot) vessels can enter without difficulty. Here, safe and protected by the hills and islands, quiet anchorage on good holding is available no matter what the weather is in the Strait. The space is not large, but as the depths are about 1.5 fathoms, several vessels can be accommodated. Do not anchor in the small cove opening to the north as it is quite shallow, and only small sportsfishing vessels and multi-hulls can anchor here. In order to accommodate the many vessels which congregate in both anchorages it is common practice for boats to drop a bow anchor and tie a stern line to the trees or rocks ashore.

Just 2.5 miles further up the coast is the popular Sechelt harbor of **Secret Cove**. When entering leave the entrance light (located on a drying ledge) to starboard. The cove is congested, with little space for anchoring. Secret Cove Marina offers transient moorage as well as fuel, groceries, washrooms, showers, marine supplies and liquor. Buccaneer Marine has facilities to haul sailboats up to 9m (32ft.) and powerboats up to 12m (40 ft.) and provides mechanical and electrical repairs. The Jolly Roger Inn is one of the more popular places for dining on this coast. A Royal Vancouver Yacht Club outstation is located here and this is the home of the specially formed Sechelt Yacht Club which was responsible for *CANADA I* and its entry in the 1984 America's Cup Races.

In settled weather anchorage may be taken at **Buccaneer Bay Marine Park,** off the drying shoal between North and South Thormanby Islands but northerly winds make this a poor spot. A better one is in the small cove off the private dock in Water Bay. Care is needed to avoid Tattenham Ledge when approaching the area.

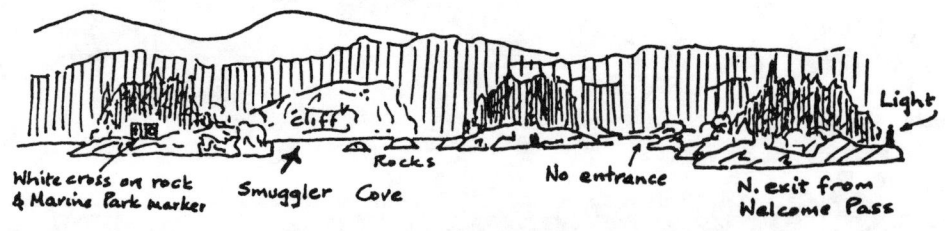

ENTRANCE TO SMUGGLER COVE MARINE PARK

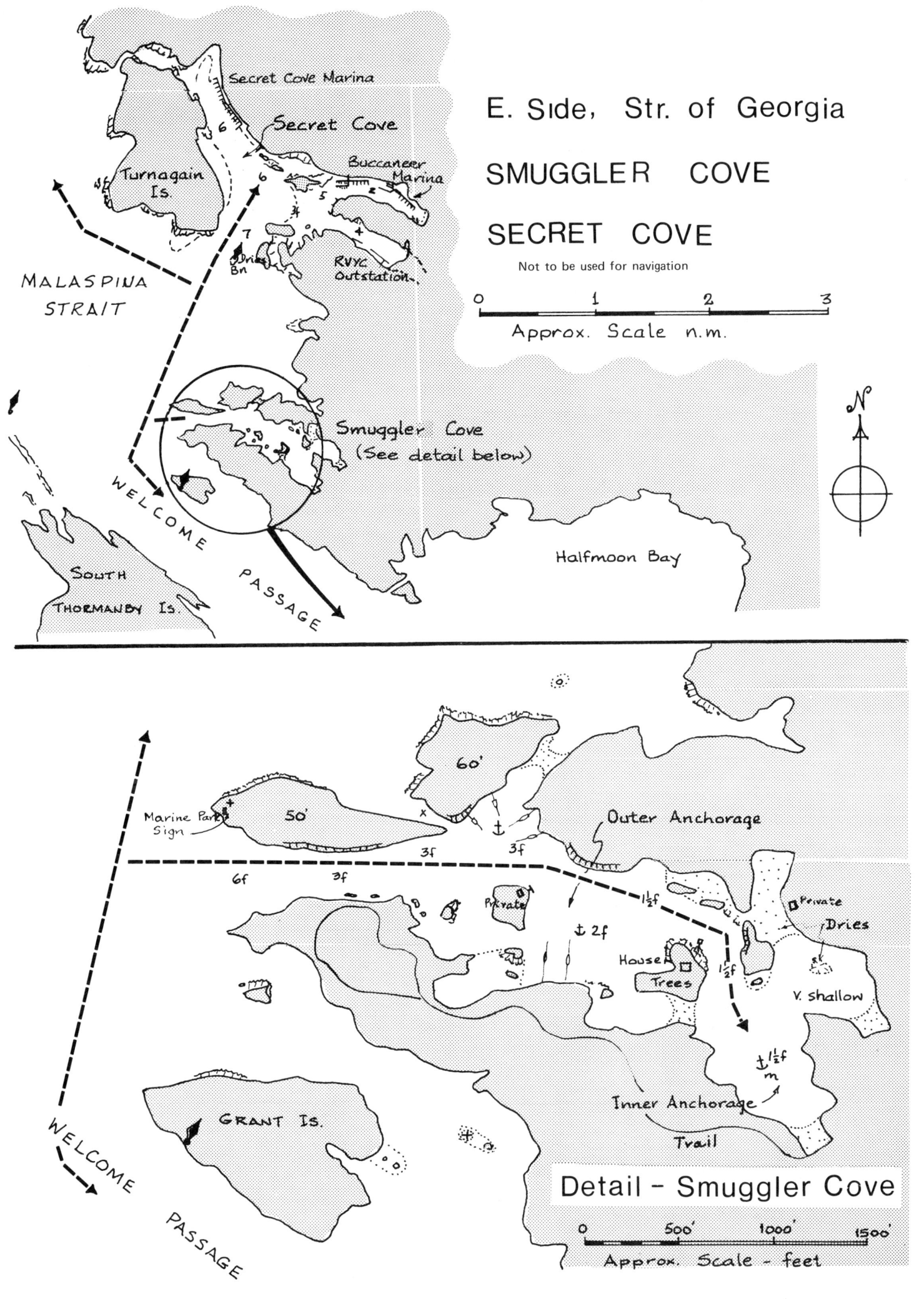

E. Side, Str. of Georgia
SMUGGLER COVE
SECRET COVE

Not to be used for navigation

0   1   2   3
Approx. Scale n.m.

Secret Cove Marina

Secret Cove

Buccaneer Marina

Turnagain Is.

Dries Bn

RVYC Outstation

MALASPINA STRAIT

WELCOME PASSAGE

SOUTH THORMANBY Is.

Smuggler Cove
(See detail below)

Halfmoon Bay

N

Detail — Smuggler Cove

60'

50'

Marine Park Sign

Outer Anchorage

3f   3f

6f   3f

1½f

Private

Private

Dries

‡ 2f

House
Trees

1½f

V. shallow

Inner Anchorage

‡ 1½f
m

Trail

WELCOME PASSAGE

GRANT Is.

0   500'   1000'   1500'
Approx. Scale - feet

PENDER HARBOUR

This popular harbor has a narrow entrance opening into an extensive basin with many fingers and small bays. It has been developed into a busy sports fishing center with several marinas and communities scattered along its shores.

The entrance to the harbor looks complicated because of the many islands, but it is not difficult if a mid-channel course is taken between them. The light at the north end of Williams Island marks the south side of the entrance, which is about 400' wide. A speed limit of 5 knots is enforced in the harbor (past the entrance) because of the numerous docks and floats.

There are several marinas offering moorage, fuel, water, showers and laundry services. The first one seen on entry is **Irvines Landing Marina** (604-883-1145) in Joe Bay. After passing four small coves the sizable bight of Hospital Bay is seen where a Government Wharf is found near its eastern end. Other Government Wharves, located in Garden Bay and Welbourne Cove, can also be identified by their distinctive red railings. Off the western tip of Garden Peninsula is **Fisherman's Resort and Marina** (604-883-2336) where transient moorage is available and facilities include showers and laundry. Next door to the east is **John Henry's Marina** (604-883-2253) where fuel groceries, liquor, propane and post office facilities are located.

East of Garden Peninsula is Garden Bay where a small area on the waterfront has been reserved as the Garden Bay Marine Park. Garden Bay is the only protected area in Pender Harbour where anchorage can be taken. When anchoring here be sure to set your anchor well, for gusty winds sometimes sweep the bay, creating havoc when anchors drag or insufficient space has been left between anchored vessels. At the western end of the bay is the Royal Vancouver Yacht Club outstation consisting of docks and a club house. Next door are the floats of the Garden Bay Hotel and Marina where a pub is located. To the east is the Seattle Yacht Club outstation.

Madeira Marina (604-883-2266) in Welbourne Cove has haul-out facilities which can accommodate vessels up to 50 ft. Engine servicing and fiberglass repairs can be done at this facility. Their marine supply store has a fairly good inventory, mainly for power boats.

From Pender Harbor a side trip via 8-mile long Agamemnon Channel leads to Jervis Inlet. This 44-mile fiord with high mountains on each side leads to beautiful Princess Louisa Inlet (6 miles from its head). For details see the following page.

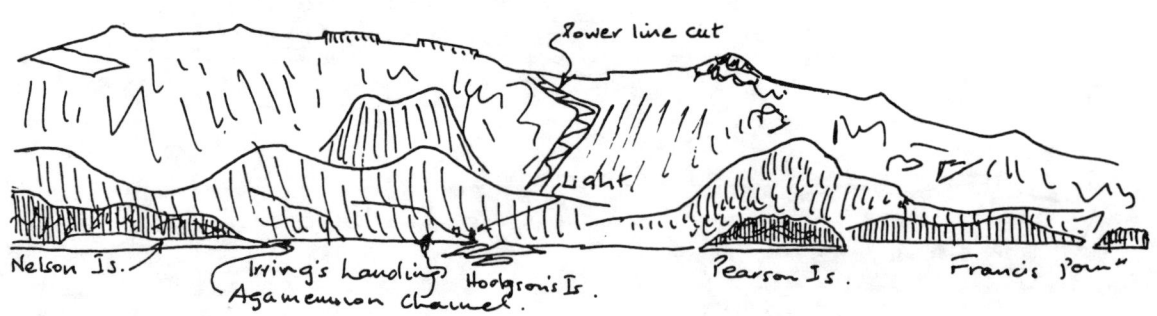

APPROACHING PENDER HARBOR FROM ENE, i.e. coming down Malaspina Str.

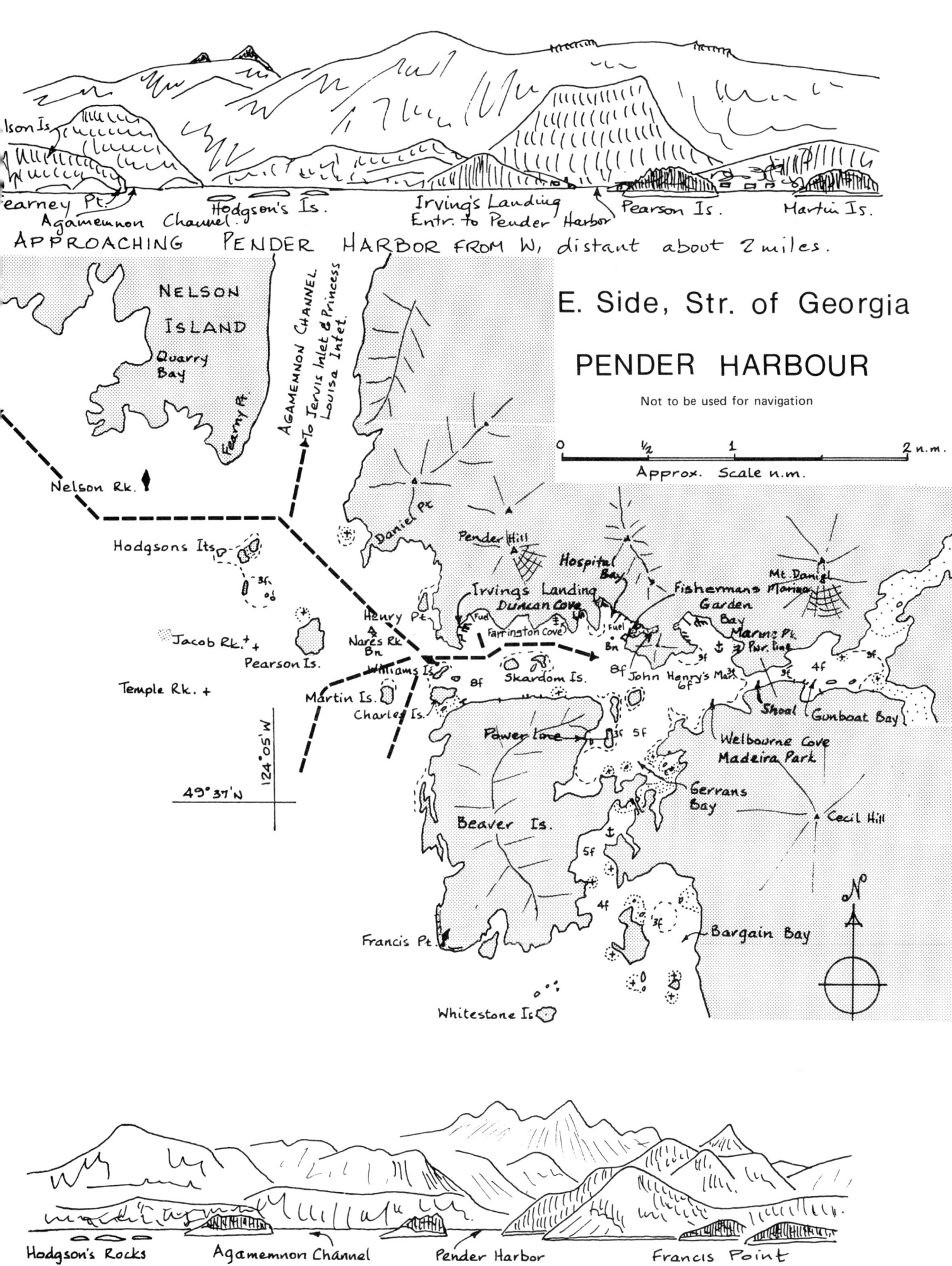

APPROACHING PENDER HARBOR FROM W, distant about 2 miles.

E. Side, Str. of Georgia

PENDER HARBOUR

Not to be used for navigation

0   ½   1   2 n.m.

Approx. Scale n.m.

NELSON ISLAND

Quarry Bay

Fearney Pt.

Agamemnon Channel

To Jervis Inlet & Princess Louisa Inlet.

Nelson Rk.

Hodgsons Its.

3f

Jacob Rk. +

Pearson Is.

Temple Rk. +

Daniel Pt.

Pender Hill

Hospital Bay

Irvings Landing

Duncan Cove

Henry Pt.

Fuel

Farrington Cove

Nares Rk. Bn

Williams Is.

8f

Skardom Is.

Martin Is.

Charles Is.

Fuel

Bn

John Henry's Mall

6f

8f

Fishermans Garden

Mt. Daniel

Marina

Garden Bay

Martins Pt.

Pwr. line

3f

4f

3f

Shoal

Gunboat Bay

Welbourne Cove

Madeira Park

Power line

3f 5f

Gerrans Bay

Cecil Hill

Beaver Is.

5f

4f

3f

Bargain Bay

N

124°05'W

49°37'N

Francis Pt.

Whitestone Is

APPROACHING PENDER HARBOR FROM S, distant about 3 miles.

Hodgson's Rocks   Agamemnon Channel   Pender Harbor   Francis Point

Ison Is.

Fearney Pt.

Agamemnon Channel

Hodgson's Is.

Irving's Landing
Entr. to Pender Harbor

Pearson Is.

Martin Is.

PRINCESS LOUISA INLET and ANCHORAGES ENROUTE

One of the most photographed sights in British Columbia is Chatterbox Falls at the head of Princess Louisa Inlet. To arrive at this site you must travel for 44 miles up deep and winding Jervis Inlet which penetrates the Coastal Range. A number of beautiful anchorages are available soon after leaving Malaspina Strait which shouldn't be missed even though your destination is Princess Louisa Inlet. During unsettled weather the winds in Jervis Inlet can be quite gusty and during rainy weather the cloud level can be so low as to obliterate the opposite shore.

On the south side of the entrance to Jervis Inlet is Hardy Island is and Fox Island is south of it. Between these two islands is **Musket Island Marine Park.** This secure anchorage can accommodate many vessels (with stern ties ashore) in the double-lobed basin. There is easy access to the shore where large rocks make safe scrambling for all ages. In addition to picnic spots, from here you can view sea conditions in Malaspina Strait.

Just around the corner to the south, on the north side of Nelson Island is a magical little cove where several vessels can anchor in **Ballet Bay.** Though the approach channel south of Nocturne and Clio Islands ends with a reef on the starboard side that seems to extend much further than the chart indicates, and signs ashore announcing private property prohibit shore trips, this is a lovely spot. A host of rocky islets outside the bay can provide hours of delightful exploration by dinghy.

When leaving the bay some excitement can be added by entering Jervis Inlet via narrow **Telescope Passage** which separates Hardy Island from the NW corner of Nelson Island. Avoid the rock in the narrowest part of the passage by favoring the Nelson Island side of the passage.

The next available anchorage is at **Harmony Islands Marine Park** on the east side of 7-mile long Hotham Sound, south of Syren Point. Avoid the rock (covered 1 m/3 ft.) at the entrance to the basin. The water here is surprisingly warm, and snorkeling and diving can be enjoyed.

Jervis Inlet can also be reached via Agamemnon Channel and near its northern end is the village of **Earl's Cove.** Regular ferry service to Saltery Bay on the north shore of Jervis Inlet carries road traffic from Powell River and Lund southward to the Sechelt Peninsula and beyond to Gibsons. A public dock is located here as well as a cafe and small grocery store. To the southeast is Skookumchuck Narrows at the north end of Sechelt Inlet. It is worth stopping over to take a hike to view Sechelt Rapids at the peak of the tidal flow. The turbulent waters can be seen from ledges along the shore and the dramatic display makes one a believer in the use of tide tables!

When proceeding up Jervis Inlet, take advantage of a rising tide and plan your arrival at **Malibu Rapids** near slack water for currents in the restricted entrance can reach 9 knots at springs and the turbulence even at half tide is impressive. Slack water occurs about 24 minutes after high water at Point Atkinson and 36 minutes after low water. The actual time is seen by the cessation of white overfalls in the channel. Malibu Lodge, overlooking the rapids, is a Young Life Summer Camp site where each year several groups of teen-agers congregate for a week or so before returning to homes in various parts of the US and Canada.

Precipitous mountains reaching 2,450 m (8,000 ft.) streaked with lacy waterfalls (especially after a rain) line the shores of **Princess Louisa Inlet**. Chatterbox Falls are at the head of the 4-mile inlet where a 120 m (400 ft.) float is located. Because of its popularity, space at the dock is at a premium especially during the summer months, and rafting is normal. When walking ashore care must be taken to stay on the trails and watch your step for the footing is extremely slippery.

PRINCESS LOUISA INLET and Approach

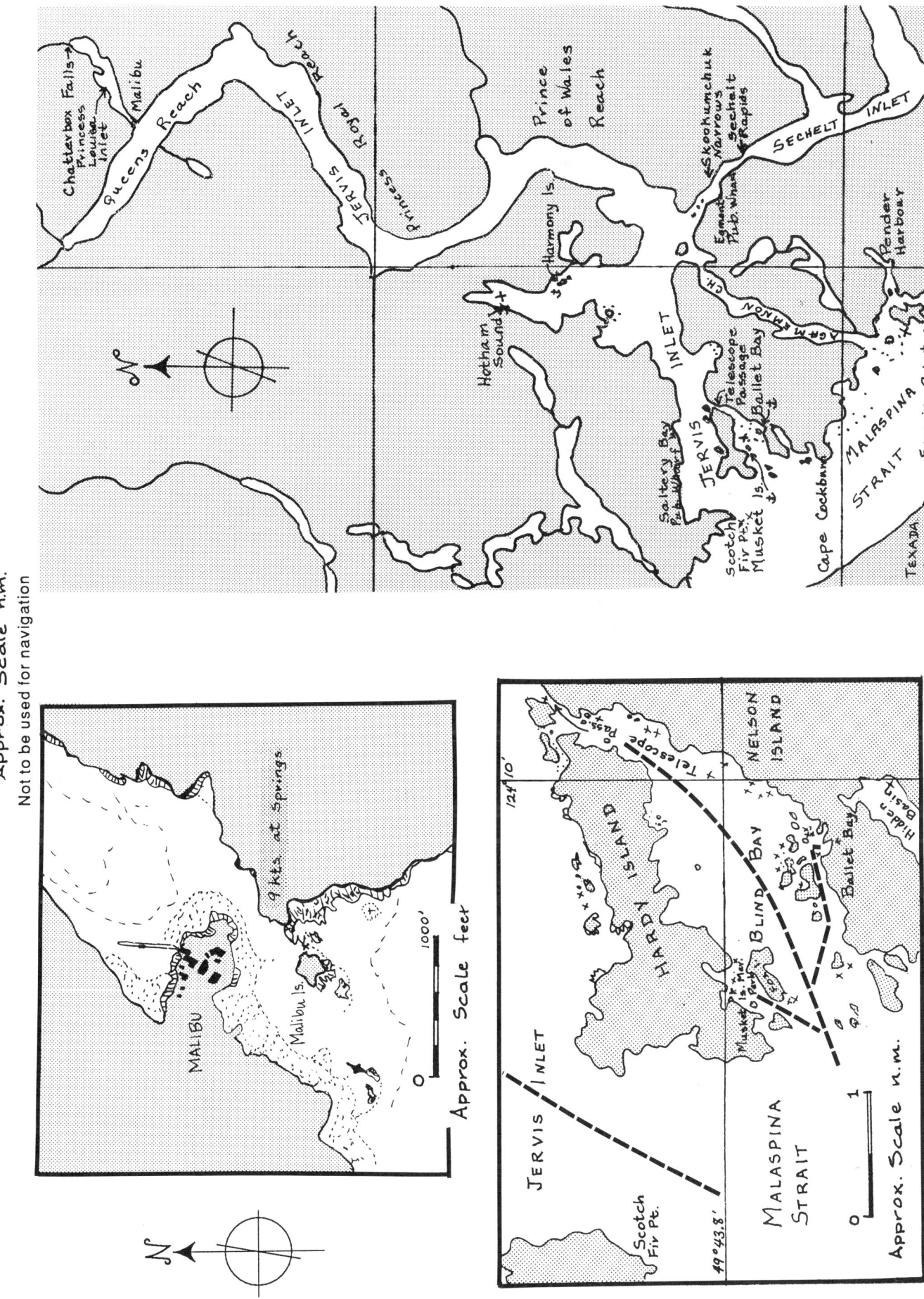

Approx. Scale n.m.

0   5   10

Not to be used for navigation

Chattavbox Falls→
Princess Louisa Inlet
←Malibu
Queens Reach
JERVIS INLET
Princess Royal Reach

Prince of Wales Reach

←Skookumchuck Narrows
Sechelt Rapids
SECHELT INLET
Egmont Pub Wharf

Harmony Is.

Hotham Sound

JERVIS INLET

AGAMEMNON CH.

Pender Harbour

Saltery Bay Pub Wharf

Telescope Passage
Bullet Bay
Scotch Fir Pt.
Musket Is.

Cape Cockburn

MALASPINA STRAIT

Francis Point

TEXADA ISLAND

N

MALIBU

9 kts at Springs

Malibu Is.

Approx. Scale feet

0   1000'

N

JERVIS INLET

Scotch Fir Pt.

49°43.8'

124°10'

×Telescope Passage×

HARDY ISLAND

NELSON ISLAND

Musket Is. Pt. Marg
Musket Is.

BLIND BAY

Hidden Basin

Bullet Bay

MALASPINA STRAIT

Approx. Scale n.m.

0   1

POWELL RIVER, WESTVIEW and LUND

The town of Powell River surrounds the mill which is conspicuous because of the tall power plant stack and its constant plume of dark smoke. The mill is the major employer in the town. The harbor near the mill, behind the breakwater and some half-sunken ships and barges, is a log booming ground.

The city harbor is at **Westview**, a residential suburb south of the mill site. A large rock breakwater extends on either side of the B.C. Ferry Dock. Tanks and long buildings on shore are visible from some distance as identifying features as you approach the harbor. The northern basin is a pleasure craft basin filled with local vessels. The southern basin is public, its wide floats shared by both fishing vessels and transient yachts. Call the harbormaster on VHF Ch. 16 when approaching the harbor to arrange for moorage. Enter at the southern end where a fuel barge is moored in a tight little spot at the end of the harbor. The harbormaster's office is in a building at the side of the main ferry pier. Next door is Harbor Marine, a well stocked marine supply store.

Stores and restaurants are just up the hill and supermarkets and larger shops are within a mile. Taxi service is available. Buses and airlines link Powell River and Westview to Vancouver.

Grief Point is the low sandy point about 2 miles south of Powell River, backed by many residential houses. The point marks the turn from Malaspina Strait (which can be quite windy) into the more open water of the Strait of Georgia. On the south side of the point is **Beach Gardens Resort and Marina** behind a rock breakwater. Moorage and accommodation are available where one can find refuge if winds in Malaspina Strait become boisterous. Turning space at the marina entrance is quite limited, so enter slowly, bearing to starboard.

Lund is a small town at the end of the coastal road from Vancouver. A steel pontoon, wooden plank and steel frame breakwater protect a small niche in the rocky coast. Entrance is around either side of the breakwater, through narrow openings. The small harbor has a fuel dock, government wharf, post office, grocery store, bar, restaurant, arts and crafts store, outdoor eatery and excellent bakery at Nancy's. Note the green buoy marking a rock between the dock and the N shore of the basin. A launching ramp allows small power boats towed from southern areas to cruise waters in the northern part of the Strait of Georgia, Desolation Sound and beyond.

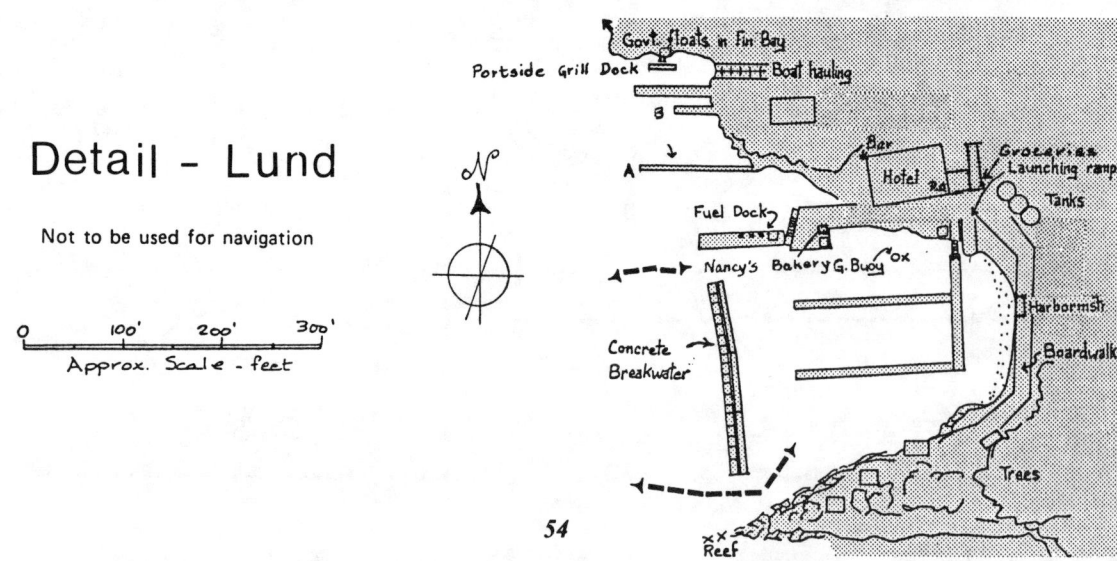

Detail - Lund

Not to be used for navigation

0   100'   200'   300'
Approx. Scale - feet

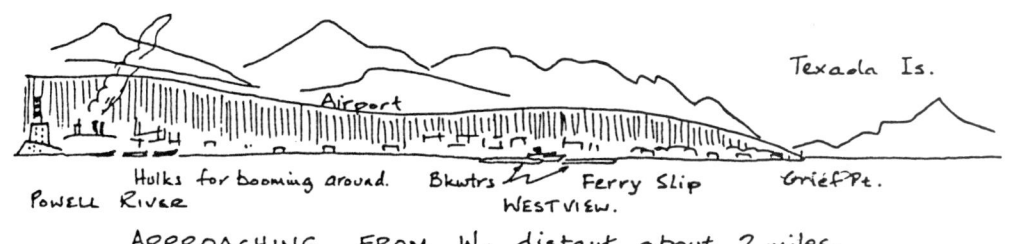

Texada Is.

Airport

Hulks for booming around.   Bkwtrs   Ferry Slip   Grief Pt.

Powell River   WESTVIEW.

APPROACHING FROM W, distant about 2 miles.

POWELL RIVER - WESTVIEW

Not to be used for navigation

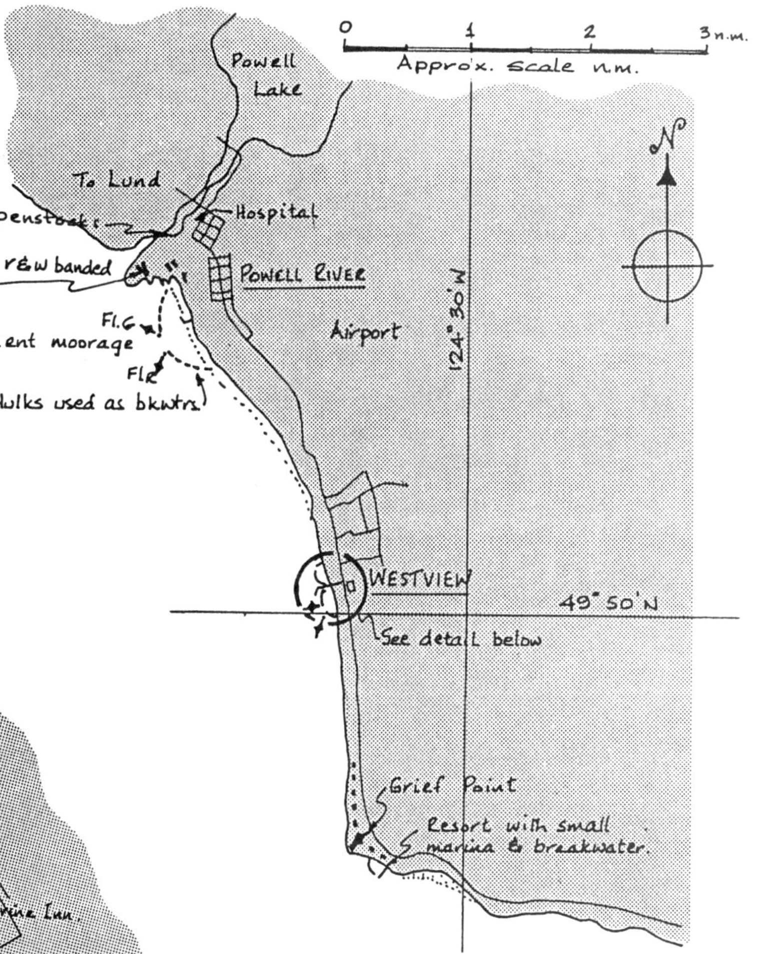

0   1   2   3 n.m.

Approx. scale n.m.

Powell Lake

To Lund

Dam & penstocks

Hospital

Mill with r&w banded stack

Powell River

Fl.G

No transient moorage

Airport

Fl.R

Hulks used as bkwtrs

124° 30'W

N

WESTVIEW

49° 50'N

See detail below

Grief Point

Resort with small marina & breakwater.

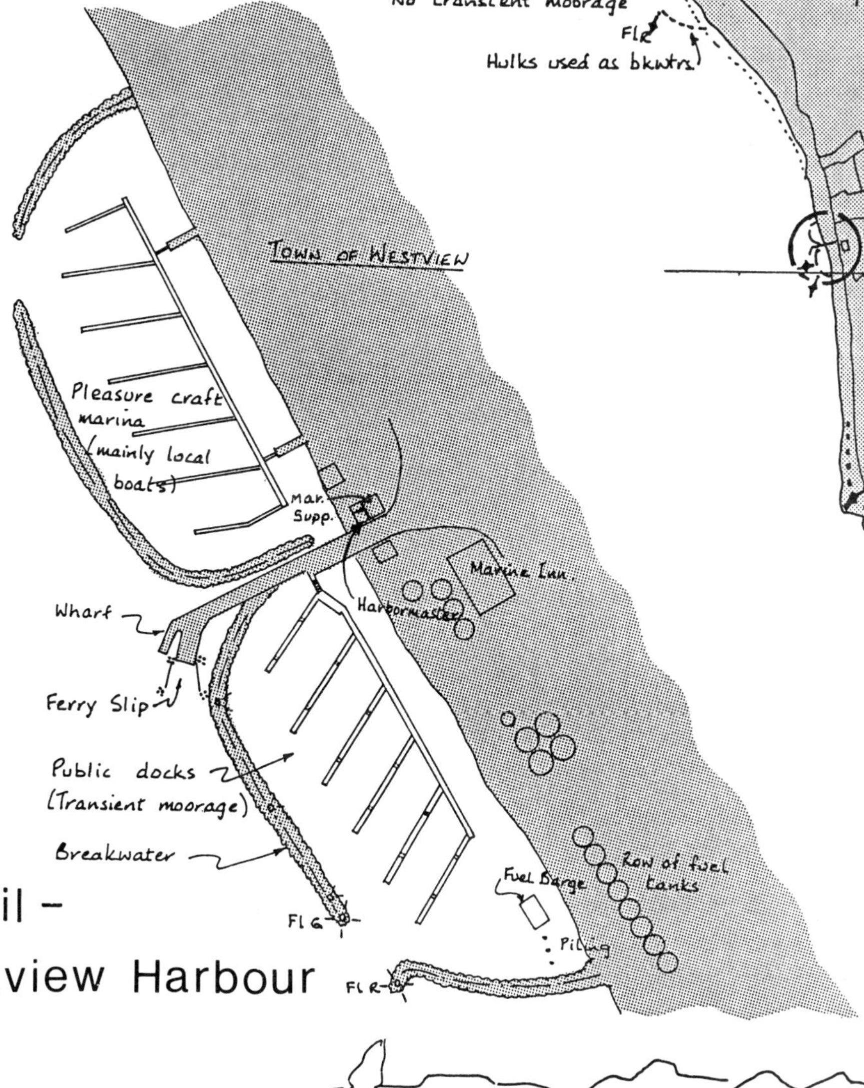

Town of Westview

Pleasure craft marina (mainly local boats)

Mar. Supp.

Marine Inn.

Harbormaster

Wharf

Ferry Slip

Public docks (Transient moorage)

Breakwater

Fl G

Row of fuel tanks

Fuel Barge

Piling

Fl R

Detail – Westview Harbour

Powell River   Westview   Grief Point

APPROACHING FROM SE, i.e. up Malaspina Strait

DESOLATION SOUND ANCHORAGES

This pretty and deservedly popular area is worth a slight digression off the direct passage to the north. The most attractive areas are largely dedicated as B.C. Marine Parks, and there is often over-crowding during the summer months when Pacific Northwest yachtsmen congregate during the summer vacation. There is little tidal action in this area, so it is designated a no-discharge zone, and cruisers must use their holding tanks.

With a spectacular back-drop of beautifully sculpted mountains, **Desolation Sound** opens to the northeast as one rounds Sarah Point at the tip of Maslaspina Peninsula. On a lovely summer's day it is difficult to reconcile the name that Captain Vancouver gave this unique area.

Separating Malaspina Peninsula from Gifford Peninsula is Malaspina Inlet. In this passage, watch for unmarked dangerous rocks. **Grace Harbour** may be tricky to find but is worth a visit, and **Okeover Inlet** has a restaurant and Public Dock.

After passing bold Zephine Head, **Galley Bay** opens up. It is open to the north but good anchorage can be taken in calm weather. **Tenedos Bay** lies ahead. Give Bold Head a wide berth as a dangerous rock lies close to it while Ray Rock and its reef lie offshore. Once into the cliff-edged, deep bay there are three choices for anchorage. On the eastern side is a cove with a beach and a stream descending from Unwin Lake; avoid the rock in the middle of the cove. Other anchorages are on the shelves on either side of the island in the northwest head of the bay. The island is connected to the shore by a drying ledge and anchorages are in the narrow coves on each side. The holding is moderate (rock and mud), stern lines ashore are helpful.

Several anchorages further along Homfray Channel are around the bulk of land forming Bold Head. These are the **Prideaux Haven** anchorages noted below:

Otter Island Anchorage lies between the island and the mainland. It is a narrow, but navigable space allows room for one or two boats. Avoid Sky Pilot Rock (dries) which lies about .25 mile north off the entrance into the channel.

Eveleigh Anchorage is the southwestern cove between Eveleigh Island and the mainland. A drying reef connects the island to the mainland and separates this anchorage from Prideaux Haven on the southwest side.

Prideaux Haven and **Melanie Cove** are entered through the narrow channel between Lucy Point (the east end of Eveleigh Island) and Oriel Rock (part of the William Islands group). The passage is clear in mid-channel. A drying rock is close to Lucy Point and a shelf extends a short distance south of the point. Prideaux Haven anchorage lies to the west where it is fairly open and deep. Beyond Melanie Point to the east, Melanie Cove is a long, narrow inlet with clear, green water and a stream emptying into the head of the bay. The shores of the cove are deeded to the University of British Columbia. Please heed signs asking that no fires be lit ashore. A garbage barge is conveniently moored just outside Melanie Cove.

Laura Cove is entered between Copplestone Point and a rock off the east end of Copplestone Island. Passage should not be taken between the rock and the island. This is an attractive, good anchorage with a narrow but easy entrance.

Roffey Island anchorage is entered from the north, off Homfray Channel and is a very snug anchorage for a maximum of two boats. Drying ridges on the sides reduce the available space.

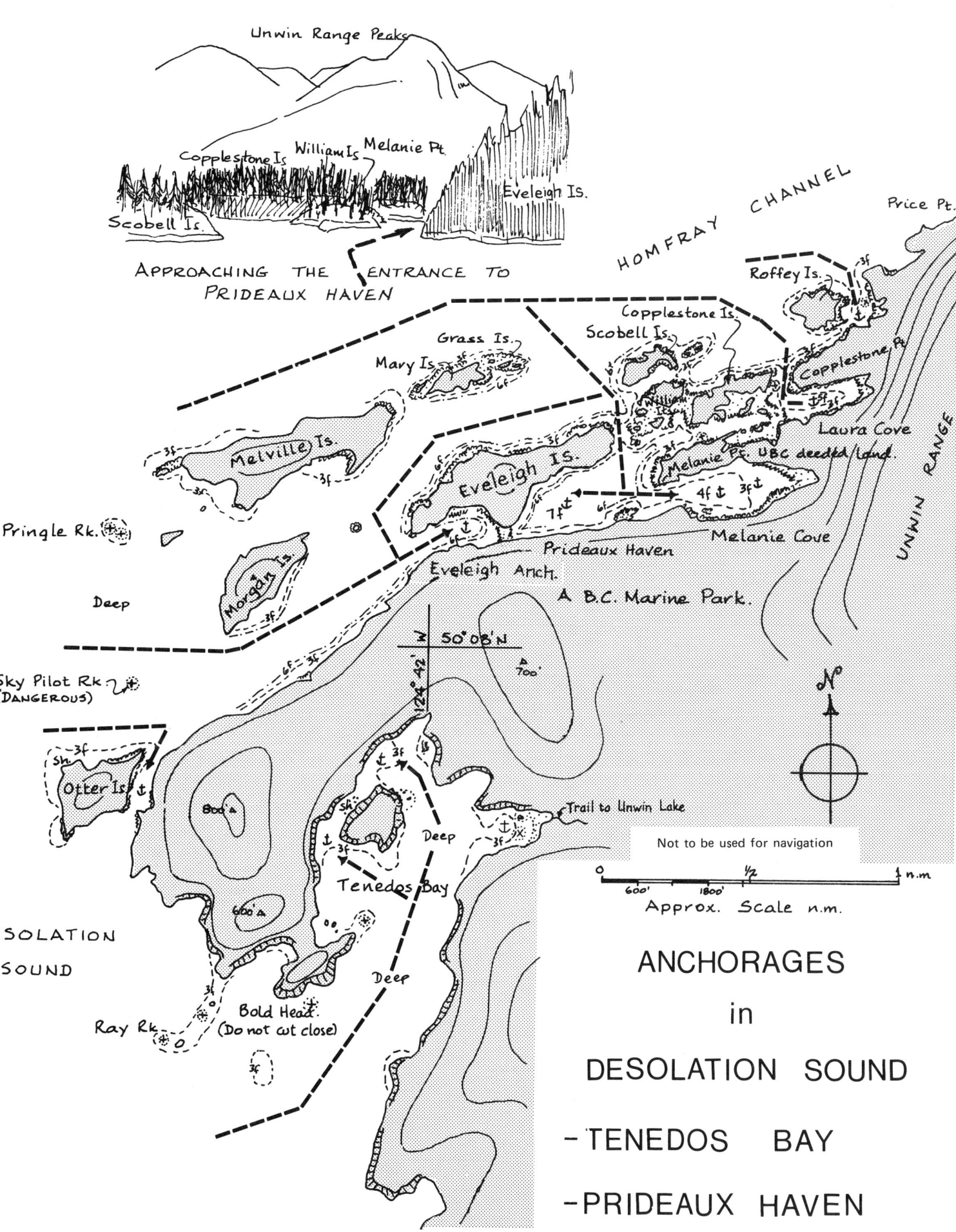

Unwin Range Peaks

Copplestone Is. William Is. Melanie Pt.

Eveleigh Is.

Scobell Is.

APPROACHING THE ENTRANCE TO
PRIDEAUX HAVEN

HOMFRAY CHANNEL

Price Pt.

Roffey Is.

Copplestone Is.
Scobell Is.

Copplestone Pt.

Grass Is.
Mary Is.

Laura Cove

William Is.

Melville Is.

Eveleigh Is.

Melanie Pt. UBC deeded land.

Pringle Rk.

Morgan Is.

Deep

Melanie Cove

Prideaux Haven

Eveleigh Anch.

A B.C. Marine Park.

50°08'N

124°42'

A
700'

Sky Pilot Rk.
(DANGEROUS)

Otter Is.

800'

Trail to Unwin Lake

Deep

Not to be used for navigation

Tenedos Bay

SOLATION
SOUND

600'

Deep

0   ½   1 n.m.
600'   1800'
Approx. Scale n.m.

Ray Rk.

Bold Head.
(Do not cut close)

ANCHORAGES

in

DESOLATION SOUND

-TENEDOS BAY

-PRIDEAUX HAVEN

CORTES ISLAND ANCHORAGES

This is an island with a wealth of good harbors that are well worth exploring. The anchorages will be described in a clockwise sequence, beginning from Mary Point on the southeast corner of the island.

Mary Point is rocky, with a few stunted trees. To the north are two islands close to shore connected by drying ledges to Cortes Island. About 1 mile east of Mary Point is the first harbor.

Cortes Bay must be approached by steering well clear of the three small, white, rocky islets and the drying rocky ledge near them. At the entrance to the harbor is a rock with a lighted beacon, which should be kept to starboard on entering. A public wharf and float is on the west side of the bay. Anchorage can be taken almost anywhere in about 4 or 5 fathoms, soft mud bottom. Allow plenty of scope for holding is moderate and sometimes winds funnel into the bay. In the SW part of the bay is an outstation of the Seattle Yacht Club with facilities for members only.

Sutil Point is the southern end of Cortes Island. Using Baker Passage pass outside the lighted red buoy to clear the shoals extending south from Sutil Point. The route turns northward towards other Cortes Island anchorages.

Manson's Landing lies behind some small islands on the shore of Manson's Bay, beyond which lies a drying lagoon. Near the public wharf is a store, fuel and other facilities. Temporary a anchorage can be taken in the bay.

Gorge Harbour though not a true gorge, has a unique entrance with a spectacular high, rocky buttress guarding its western shore where pictographs can be seen on some flat rocks. The eastern side is much lower with boulders once used as burial caverns. On an approach from the south the two small Guide Islets indicate the entrance. Pass on either side of these islets (not between) then passage through the gorge is taken. The entrance is about .5 mile long, the narrowest part (60 m /200 feet wide) being very short. While currents can be felt which sometimes reach 4 knots, passage is always possible. At the inner end pass between small, bare, rocky Tide Islet and the steep western shore. The government wharf to the south was condemned in 1995 and should not be used until repairs have been completed. Moorage, fuel, a well stocked grocery store, laundry and shower facilities and a good restaurant are available at **Gorge Harbour Marina** which monitors VHF Ch. 73. For reservations call (250) 935-6433. Garbage receptacles require sorting into glass, tins and miscellaneous. Two large anchorage areas with good holding in 5 - 10 fathoms, mud may be taken west or east of the marina.

Uganda Passage is a little pass between Shark Spit on Marina Island and Cortes Island. Although it appears tricky it is quite easy as it is well marked with buoys. Stay within the buoyed channel, keeping the black buoys to port and red buoys to starboard when westbound. Influenced by northern tides, the current floods east and ebbs to the west, with 3-knot currents at springs. Anchorage can be taken behind Shark Spit. Caution: The shallow shelf that runs around Marina Island drops off sharply into deep water.

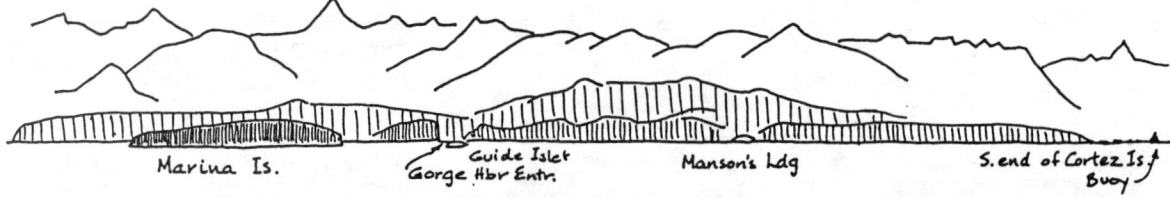

Marina Is.   Guide Islet
Gorge Hbr Entr.   Manson's Ldg   S. end of Cortez Is.
Buoy

CORTES IS. FROM SE, distant about 6 miles, WITH BACKGROUND PEAKS

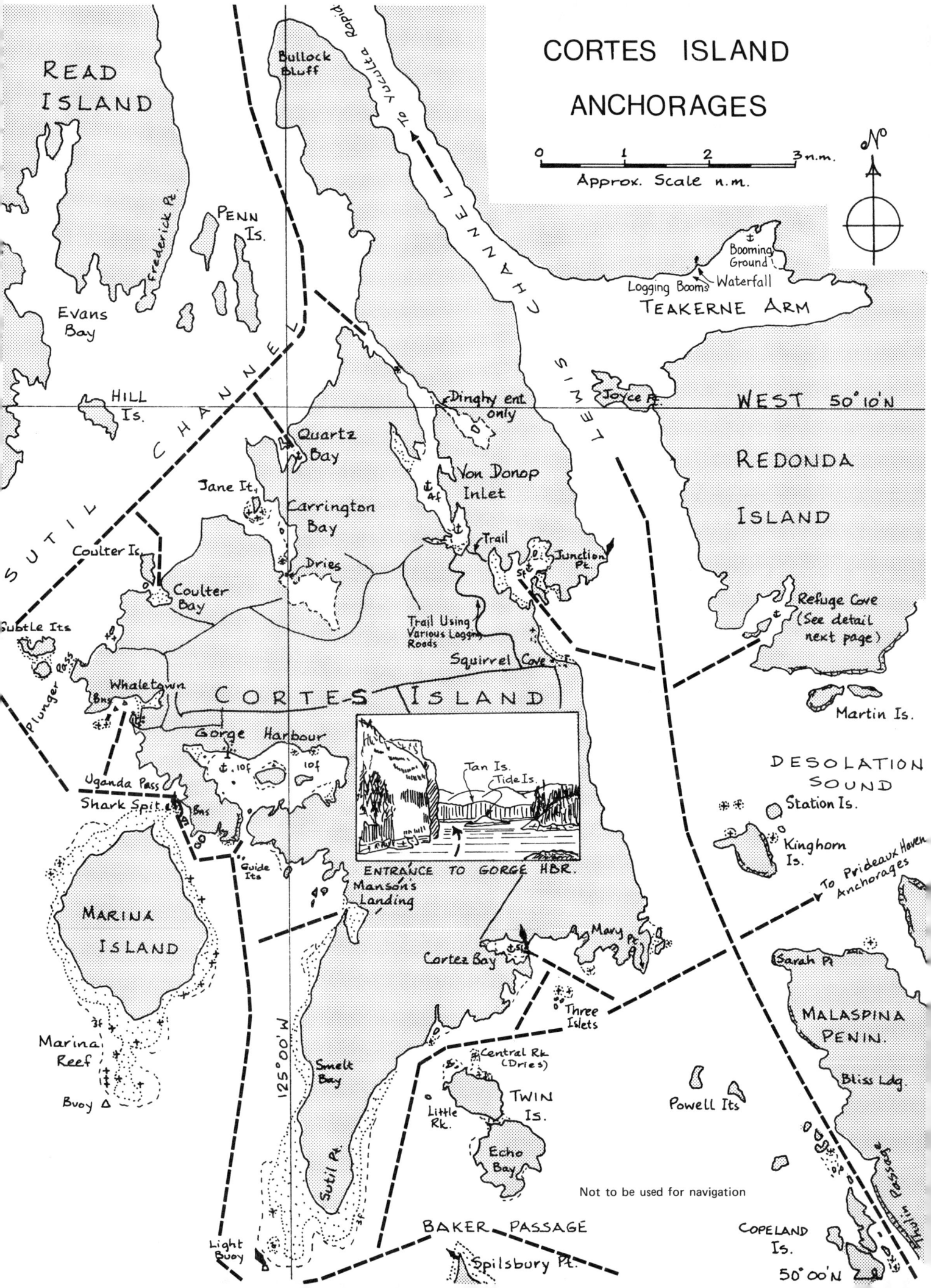

CORTES ISLAND
ANCHORAGES

Approx. Scale n.m.

0   1   2   3 n.m.

READ ISLAND

Frederick Pt.

PENN Is.

Evans Bay

HILL Is.

Bullock Bluff

To Yuculta Rapids

CHANNEL

Booming Ground

Logging Booms — Waterfall

TEAKERNE ARM

LEWIS CHANNEL

Joyce Pt.

WEST 50°10'N

REDONDA

ISLAND

SUTIL CHANNEL

Coulter Is.

Subtle Its.

Plunger Pass

Whaletown

Bns

Uganda Pass

Shark Spit.

Bns

Quartz Bay

Jane It.

Carrington Bay

Dries

Coulter Bay

Dinghy ent. only

Von Donop Inlet

4f

Trail

Junction Pt.

Spit

Trail Using Various Logging Roads

Squirrel Cove

Refuge Cove (See detail next page)

Martin Is.

DESOLATION SOUND

Station Is.

Kinghorn Is.

To Prideaux Haven Anchorages

CORTES   ISLAND

Gorge Harbour

10f

10f

Guide Its

Manson's Landing

Tan Is.   Tide Is.

ENTRANCE TO GORGE HBR.

MARINA ISLAND

Marina Reef

Buoy △

125°00'W

Smelt Bay

Sutil Pt.

Cortez Bay

Mary

Three Islets

MALASPINA PENIN.

Sarah Pt.

Bliss Ldg.

Central Rk. (Dries)

Little Rk.

TWIN Is.

Echo Bay

Powell Its

Not to be used for navigation

BAKER   PASSAGE

Light Buoy

Spilsbury Pt.

COPELAND Is.

50°00'N

Whaletown is in the small indentation of Whaletown Bay. Enter from the south, allowing for shoals and rocks which are marked by beacons. Moorage at the public wharf is often crowded during the summer and the seaplane area must be kept clear. A small grocery store with large ice cream cones makes a visit worthwhile. The tiny church in the village often merits a photograph.

Coulter Bay is the next stop, where good anchorage can be taken in the lee of Coulter Island. Enter as shown on the sketch.

Carrington Bay is a large bay with a drying lagoon. Though anchorage can be tried the rocky bottom has poor holding.

Quartz Bay is smaller than the previous bay but is more acceptable. Enter via the northeastern channel. Good anchorage can be taken in the inner southwestern part of the bay behind the islets, in about 6 fathoms.

Von Donop Inlet is the boater's entrance to (**Ha'Thayim Marine Park**) This 3-mile long narrow entrance inlet provides excellent anchorage with complete protection. The entrance has a rock (covered 1.5m/5'), about mid-channel in the passage at the narrowest part, about .75 mile from the entrance. Enter slowly and favor the south side where overhanging trees mark the rock. Anchorage can be taken almost anywhere either in the widening near the lagoon, where there is little evidence of the out-going current, or further in near the head in 4 fathoms, good holding mud. At the southeast corner of the bay is a short trail leading to the northwestern shore of Squirrel Cove; another trail beyond the islet follows a mixture of tracks and logging roads before joining the paved road linking the village of Squirrel Cove to Manson's Landing.

Squirrel Cove is a popular, pretty and well protected anchorage. Enter the cove through the opening south of Protection Island. The west and northwest arms of the bay are shoal, but anchoring can be done anywhere in the bay and when stern lines are tied ashore over 100 vessels can be accommodated. Off the settlement of Squirrel Cove is a very small government wharf with shoal water close by. A telephone is at the head of the dock. The general store has a good variety of groceries and a surprisingly well stocked hardware downstairs.

REFUGE COVE, WEST REDONDA ISLAND

Across Lewis Channel from Squirrel Cove is the busy fueling and provisioning depot of **Refuge Cove**. The cove can be entered on either side of the unnamed island at the entrance, though the south side is usually preferred. Facilities include floats, water, fuel, showers, laundry, ice, and a fast food stand. The store is well stocked with groceries, fresh produce and liquor.

ROSCOE BAY MARINE PARK, WEST REDONDA ISLAND

Roscoe Bay is north of Marylebone Point on the east side of the island. Unfortunately, this is such a popular spot from June to September that vessels lining the shore resemble a supermarket parking lot. Enter from Waddington Channel at or just before high water. A drying shoal lies within the entrance channel and care must be taken to avoid rocky outcrops on the north side of the narrow passageway. A short trail through the forest leads to Black Lake, where large smooth rocks give gentle access to a popular swimming spot. Unfortunately, planned clear-cutting of the mountains surrounding the lake will ruin the ambiance of this lovely hideaway.

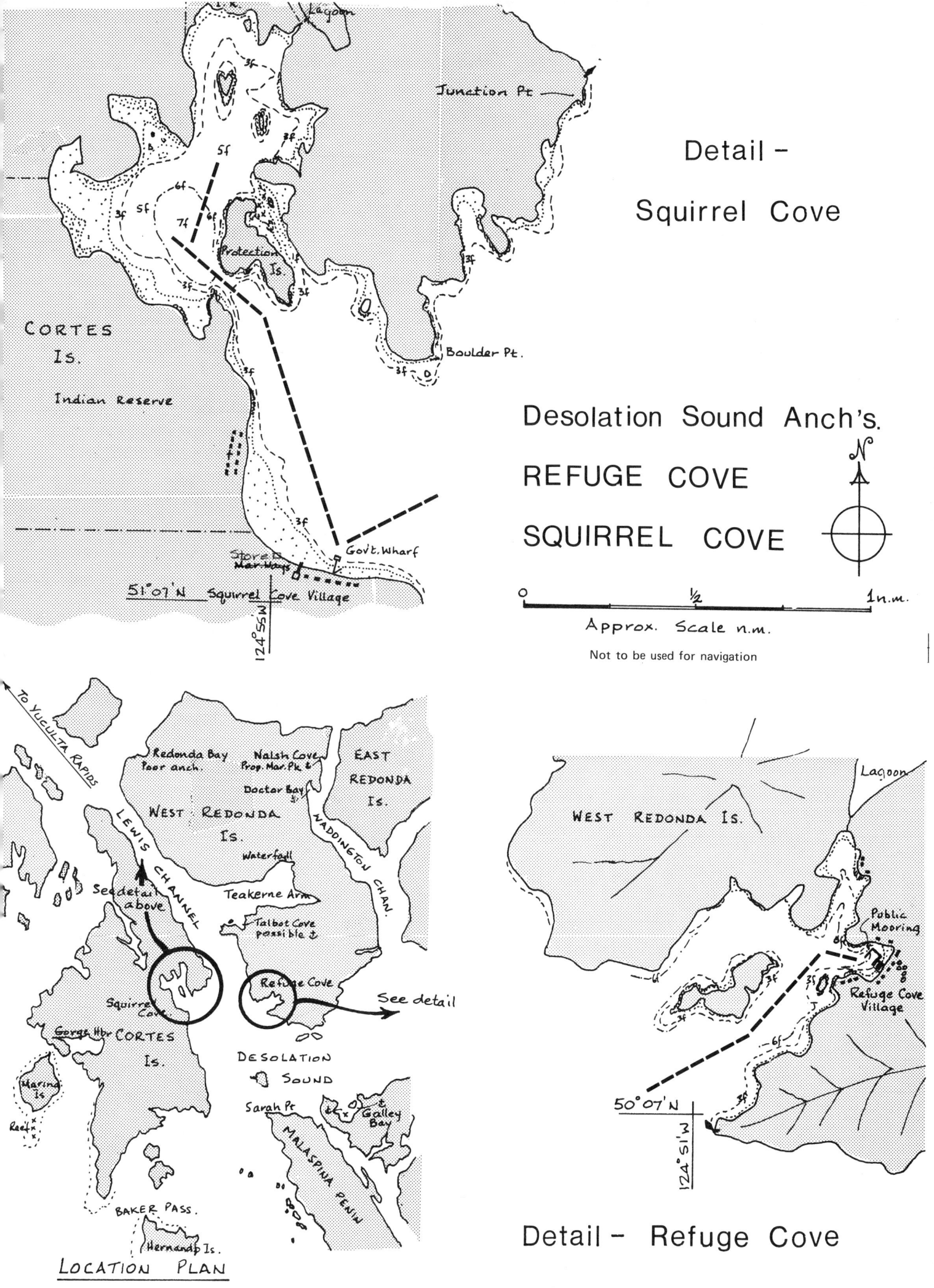

Detail -
Squirrel Cove

Lagoon

Junction Pt.

5f

6f

5f

7f   6f

Protection Is.

3f

CORTES
Is.

Boulder Pt.

3f

Indian Reserve

3f

3f

Govt. Wharf

Store
Mar. Ways

51°07'N   Squirrel Cove Village

124°56'W

Desolation Sound Anch's.

REFUGE COVE

SQUIRREL COVE

N

0   ½   1 n.m.

Approx. Scale n.m.

Not to be used for navigation

To Yuculta Rapids

Redonda Bay   Nalsh Cove   EAST
Poor anch.   Prop. Mar. Pk. ‡   REDONDA
Is.

Doctor Bay

WEST REDONDA
Is.

LEWIS CHANNEL

WADDINGTON CHAN.

Waterfall

See detail
above

Teakerne Arm

Talbot Cove
possible ‡

Squirrel
Cove

Refuge Cove   See detail

Gorge Hbr   CORTES
Is.

DESOLATION
SOUND

Marina Is.

Sarah Pt   Galley
Bay

Reef

MALASPINA PENIN.

BAKER PASS.

Hernando Is.

LOCATION PLAN

WEST   REDONDA   Is.

Lagoon

Public
Mooring

3f

Refuge Cove
Village

3f

6f

50°07'N

3f

124°51'W

Detail - Refuge Cove

COMOX

Comox makes an excellent stop-over for vessels following the Vancouver Island shore of Georgia Strait. A home base for fishing vessels and pleasure craft, Comox also can provide accommodation for many transient vessels. A scenic backdrop for the town is provided by the Beaufort Mountains and beautiful Comox Glacier. The area is a haven for recreation, with summertime water sports, hiking and camping followed by skiing and snow-boarding during the winter. Comox is a weather reporting station, the communication center for airborne search and rescue and the site of the Canadian Coast Guard radio station monitoring calls as far north as Bella Bella.

The harbor is located four miles southwest of Cape Lazo, a prominent landmark with a flat top and distinctive yellow clay bluffs. When approached from the south the cape resembles an island but seen from north of Hornby Island its connection to Vancouver Island becomes evident. When approaching from the north clear Cape Lazo by at least one mile to avoid the foul ground seaward of the Cape. When crossing Comox Bar use extreme caution and follow the route indicated by the buoys and range. The least depth of the passage is 2.4 m (8 ft.) and strong variable currents tend to push the vessel off the desired route. Use Chart No. 3513 when transiting this area.

Comox Harbour is entered between Gartley Point on the south (marked by buoy P47) and Goose Spit on the north (where the end of the spit is marked by a light). Two breakwaters protect the marine facilities, cluster of four marinas offering moorage and associated services to cruisers. Moorage, both transient and permanent, is available at all marinas except the Municipal Marina which has permanent moorage only. Facilities differ and the following summary can help you to choose the facility that best suits your needs. Daily moorage rates for transient vessels start at $.50 per foot.

1. **Black Fin Marina** monitors VHF 68 and provides Fuel, ice, water and a store. Sail Pacific Yacht Charters operates from this location.

2. **Comox Bay Marina** has showers, laundromat and garbage collection facilities. Desolation Sound Yacht Charts operates from this location and can be reached at (250) 339-7222.

3. **Harbour Authority/Government Dock** monitors VHF 68, provides garbage collection facilities and has water on the dock.

4. **Municipal Marina** has washrooms, garbage collection and oil disposal facilities and a launch ramp.

Well protected anchorage can be taken north of Goose spit. A block from the waterfront is a sizable shopping mall which includes a well stocked grocery store, a liquor store and several banks. Charts and marine supplies are available at The Crowsnest; fishing gear and charts are sold at Ted's Trolling.

COMOX

Approx. Scale, n.m.

0   1   2   3

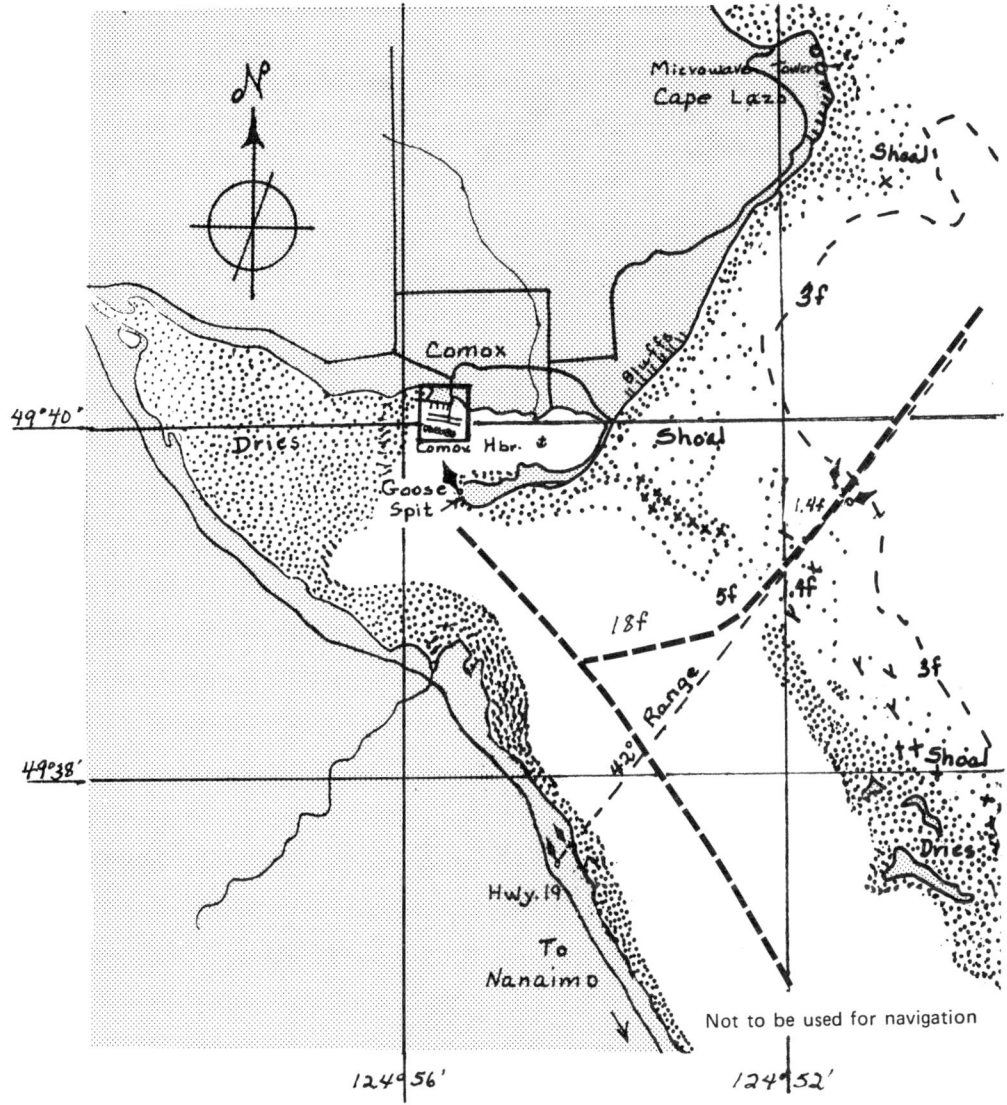

N

Microwave tower
Cape Lazo

Shoal x

3f

Comox

Bluff

49°40'

Dries

Comox Hbr.

Shoal

Goose Spit

1.4f

18f   5f   4f

Range   42°   3f

Shoal

Dries

Hwy. 19

To Nanaimo

Not to be used for navigation

124°56'   124°52'

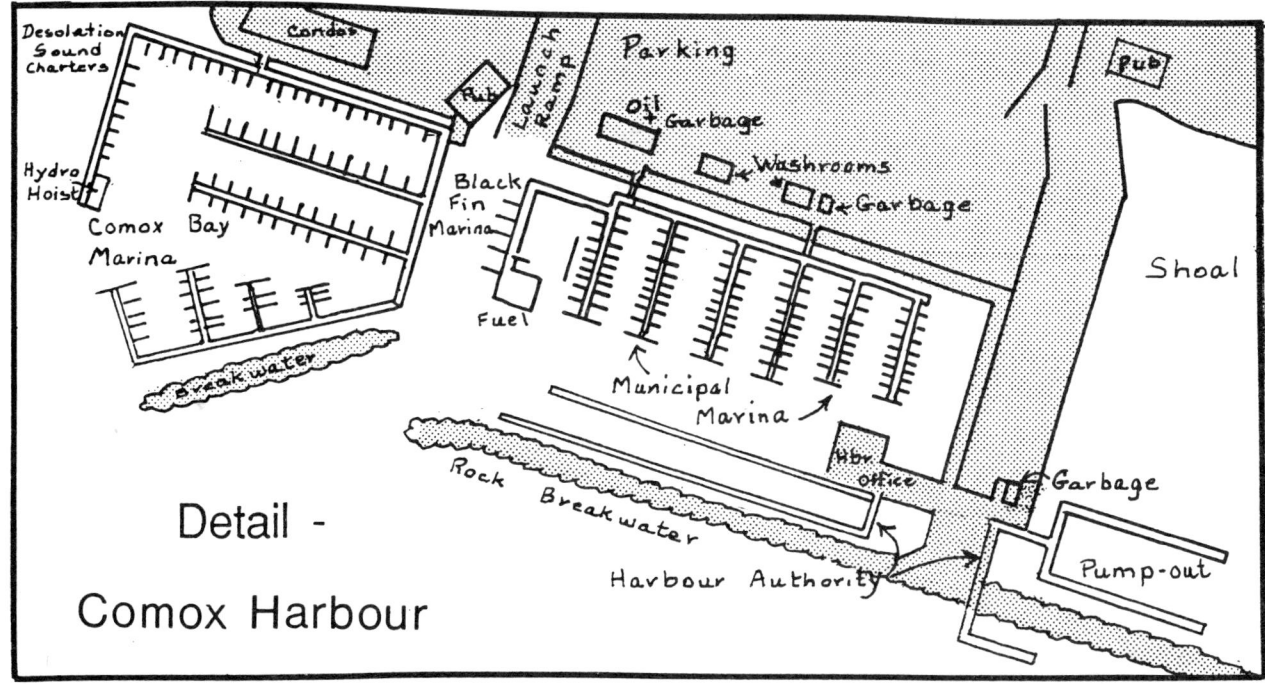

Desolation Sound Charters

Condos

Parking

Pub

Pub

Launch Ramp

Oil

Garbage

Hydro Hoist

Comox Bay Marina

Black Fin Marina

Washrooms

Garbage

Fuel

Shoal

Breakwater

Municipal Marina

Rock Breakwater

Hbr office

Garbage

Harbour Authority

Pump-out

Detail -

Comox Harbour

Broughton Archipelago is at the southern end of Queen Charlotte Strait off the west coast of Gilford Island. A multitude of islands and islets are home to seabirds and marine animals. It is a haven for kayakers and canoeists who pull ashore in countless sandy coves. Several anchorages are available for cruising vessels, the preferred ones are Joe Cove on Eden Island and Farewell Harbour on Berry Island.

Beaver Cove, a sizable bight on Vancouver Island is entered between Ellis and Lewis Points. Much of the bay is utilized by logging operations and it is of interest to cruisers only in an emergency. On its east side is **Telegraph Cove** where a small marina is located. The significance of this area is its fame as site where orca can often be sighted because they frequent these waters to enjoy conveniently located and comfortably shaped rubbing stones. Campsites dot the overlooking cliffs on the east side of the Strait and whale-watchers in kayaks and tour boats from Port McNeill are a comon sight.

Tidal overfalls at Sechelt Rapids, Skookumchuk Narrows

Approaching Dent Rapids from Gillard Passage

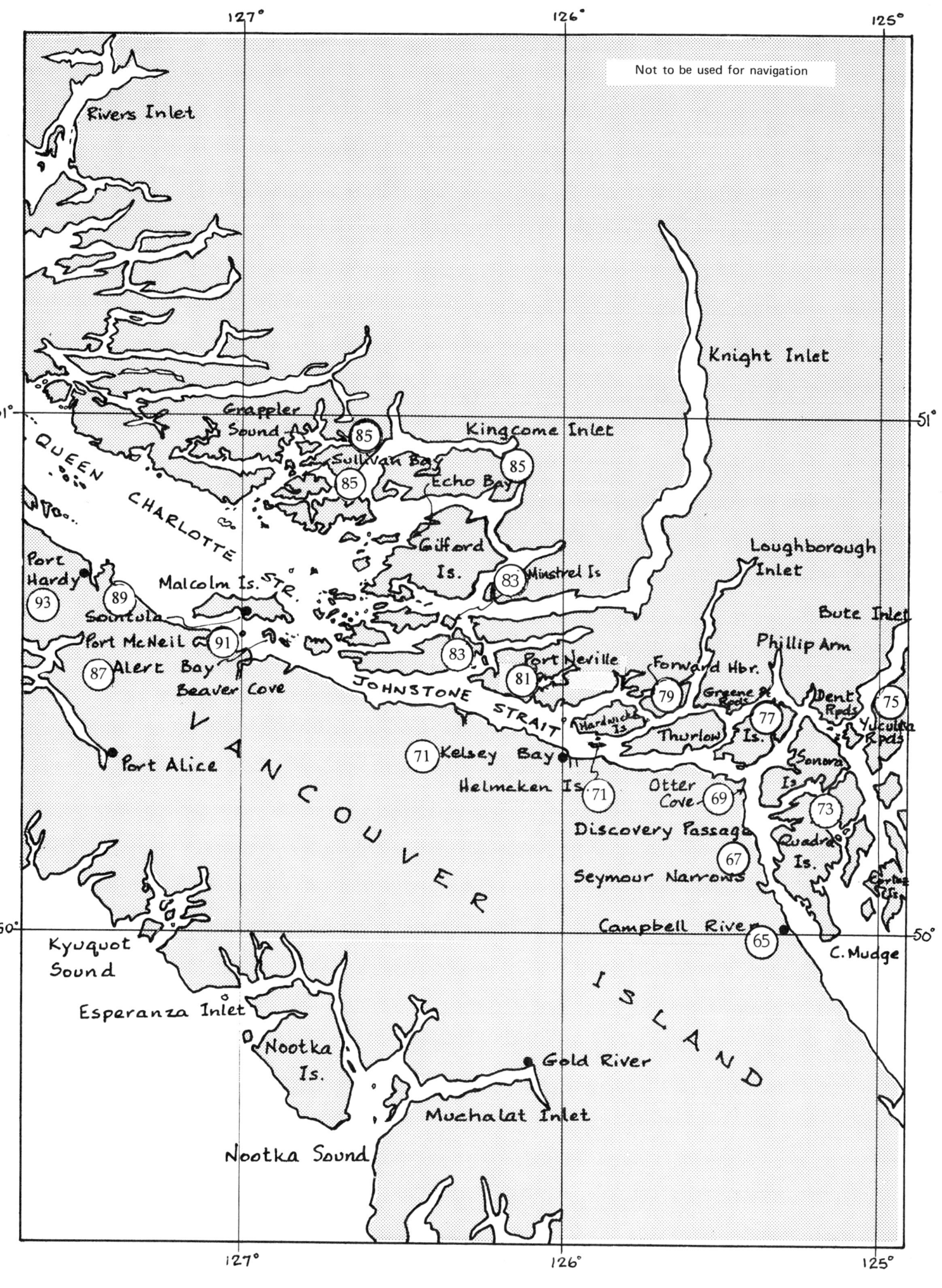

Not to be used for navigation

Rivers Inlet

127° 126° 125°

Knight Inlet

51° Grappler Kingcome Inlet 51°
Sound 85
QUEEN Sullivan Bay 85
CHARLOTTE 85
Echo Bay

Gilford Loughborough
Is. Inlet
Port Malcolm Is. STR. 83 Minstrel Is Bute Inlet
Hardy 93 89 Phillip Arm
Sointula 91 Forward Hbr. Dent
Port McNeil 83 Port Neville 79 Greene Pt Rpds
87 Alert Bay 81 Rpds 77 75
Beaver Cove JOHNSTONE Hardwicke Thurlow Is. Yuculta
STRAIT Is Sonora Rpds
71 Kelsey Bay Is
Port Alice Helmcken Is. 71 Otter 69
Discovery Passage Cove 73
Quadra
Seymour Narrows 67 Is.
50° Campbell River 50°
Kyuquot 65
Sound C. Mudge

Esperanza Inlet
ISLAND
Nootka
Is. Gold River

Muchalat Inlet

Nootka Sound

VANCOUVER

127° 126° 125°

CAMPBELL RIVER

Campbell River is situated at the south end of Discovery Passage, and lies almost exactly midway along Vancouver Island. This is the center of activity at the north end of Georgia Strait and the largest town in this area. As the importance of marine-related tourism has grown, facilities for cruising vessels of all sizes have been developed. A range of facilities are available, from the basic public wharf to all-service marinas.

Because of the proximity of Discovery Passage to Seymour Narrows the tidal currents are quite noticeable here.. They do not pose a particular problem, but one should be aware of the state of the tide when approaching Campbell River and when maneuvering in the area.

Two rock breakwaters angle out from the shore to protect the floats for moorage. The southern basin is the larger one and has **public floats** for both pleasure craft and fishing vessels. The harbormaster's office is in a small building on shore near the walkway leading from the wharves. A nominal fee is charged for moorage. The docks are often crowded and rafting may be necessary.

The next basin to the north, adjacent to the Quadra Island Ferry Terminal, is privately owned. A short distance beyond is **Discovery Harbour Marina** where moorage for over 300 vessels is protected by a large breakwater. They monitor VHF Ch 73 and can be reached at (250) 287-4911. This full-service modern marina offers transient moorage and an easily accessible fuel dock. The harbor office is on the second floor of a clearly marked building housing showers and restrooms on the ground floor. Adjacent to the parking area is a huge shopping mall. In addition, the Harbour Grill restaurant overlooks the waterfront and serves good meals, and several other cafes and pubs are nearby. Three magnificent totem poles carved by Bill Henderson stand before an excellent Native craft shop attached to a theater featuring live performances by Native dancers.

Other alternatives for a stop-over in the area include anchoring in Gowlland Harbor or tying to the dock in Quathiaski Cove. The ferry can be used for getting across to Campbell River.

At the south end of **Quathiaski Cove**, beside the ferry dock, is a government dock with floats, where rafting is almost always necessary. A fuel dock and a repair yard are in the harbor. Quathiaski Cove can be entered on either side of Grouse Island. The current stream that sweeps past the entrance and creates tidal rips does not affect the cove.

April Point, the location of a luxurious fishing resort is about 1 mile north of Quathiaski Cove. The flagpoles of the lodge are prominent at the point. The landing dock at the lodge is meant for lodge skiffs. The small marina connected with the lodge is about .5 mile southeast along the inner shore of the point. Rates at the marina are high during summer, though you do have access to the lodge and its facilities. Anchorage is good beyond the marina, but the head of the cove is shoal.

Gowlland Harbor can be entered north of Steep Island and Gowlland Island, taking care to avoid Entrance Rock. Anchorage can be found behind Crow and Doe Islands. Many private docks line the harbor. Do not attempt the pass south of Gowlland Island leading to the cove at April Point as it has many rocks.

Rebecca Spit is on the east side of Quadra Island off Drew Harbour. Anchorage may be taken off the NW end of the spit on hard sand bottom. Set the anchor securely, for brisk winds can test how well you have set your gear.

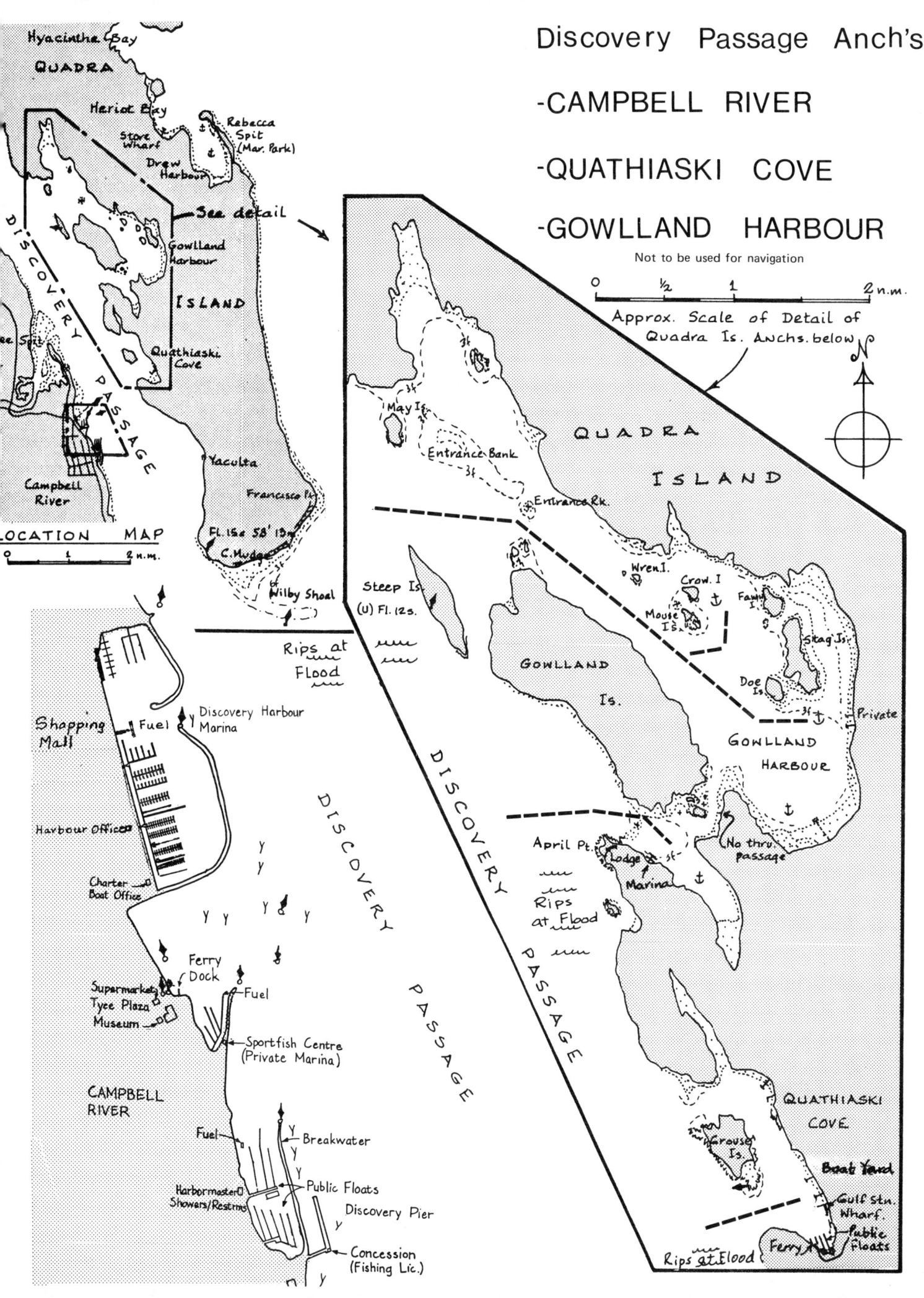

Discovery Passage Anch's.

-CAMPBELL RIVER

-QUATHIASKI COVE

-GOWLLAND HARBOUR

Not to be used for navigation

0   ½   1   2 n.m.

Approx. Scale of Detail of
Quadra Is. Anchs. below

N

Hyacinthe Bay
QUADRA
Heriot Bay
Store Wharf
Drew Harbour
Rebecca Spit
(Mar. Park)
See detail
Gowlland Harbour
ISLAND
Quathiaski Cove
Discovery Passage
e Spit
Campbell River

LOCATION MAP
0   1   2 n.m.

Yaculta
Francisco Pt.
Fl. 15s 58'15n
C. Mudge
Wilby Shoal

May Is.
Entrance Bank
Entrance Rk.
QUADRA ISLAND
Wren I.
Crow I.
Fawn I.
Mouse Is.
Stag Is.
Doe Is.
Private
GOWLLAND HARBOUR
GOWLLAND Is.
No thru passage
April Pt.
Lodge
Marina
Rips at Flood
Steep Is.
(U) Fl. 12s.
Rips at Flood

DISCOVERY PASSAGE

DISCOVERY PASSAGE

Shopping Mall
Fuel
Discovery Harbour Marina
Harbour Office
Charter Boat Office
Ferry Dock
Fuel
Supermarket
Tyee Plaza
Museum
Sportfish Centre
(Private Marina)
CAMPBELL RIVER
Fuel
Breakwater
Harbormaster
Showers/Restrms
Public Floats
Discovery Pier
Concession
(Fishing Lic.)

QUATHIASKI COVE
Grouse Is.
Boat Yard
Gulf Stn. Wharf
Public Floats
Ferry
Rips at Flood

SEYMOUR NARROWS AND DISCOVERY PASSAGE

This famous passage, with its high-velocity tidal currents, appears to be a big obstacle when approached for the first time. However, as the B.C. Coast Pilot points out, navigation through the passage is simple if done at or near slack water. For most of the passage a mid-channel course is all that is needed.

When going north leave Campbell River against the last of the flood, which sets south, planning to reach Seymour Narrows about 8 miles from Campbell River at slack water. At Race Point, on the flood, there are rips and swirls that occur well to the east of it, so give it a wide berth on passing—it is less disturbed on the ebb. If Seymour Narrows is taken at the slack there is little problem in passing through and a favorable stream can be carried all the way through Johnstone Strait. However, if anchorages are needed, several are available.

A similar pattern should be followed when going south, i.e. taking the northern part of Discovery Passage against the last of the ebb to reach Seymour Narrows at Separation Head about slack water. Again, the passage should be simple and the favoring stream will carry one to Campbell River or out past Cape Mudge.

Anchorages are available on either side of Seymour Narrows to allow passage through at slack even if the turn is to an unfavorable direction. Since the velocity of the stream can increase quite rapidly an hour or so past the change, it behooves a slow vessel to reach its anchorage before the current becomes too strong.

The hazards caused by Ripple Rock were eliminated in 1958 when it was destroyed by the largest non-nuclear explosive charge of its time. The rips, whirlpools and swirls associated with the current at full strength are still awe-inspiring. Only large vessels with speeds in excess of 17 knots can attempt the channel at times other than near slack water. Even for them this can be dangerous, and quite large vessels have been swamped when caught in the violent rips and whirlpools. If you are in the passage at other than slack water remember that a vessel going with the current has less control than one going against it. It is strongly recommended that travel through Seymour Narrows be done only at, or near, slack water.

Anchorages on the south side of Seymour Narrows are:

- **Campbell River**, **Quathiaski Cove**, and **Gowlland Harbour** as described

- **Menzies Bay**, behind Defender Shoal (if anchorage close to the Narrows is needed)

Anchorages on the north side of Seymour Narrows are:

- **Otter Cove** at the end of Discovery Passage, 2.5 miles north of Elk Bay

- **Kanish Bay** and **Small Inlet** on Quadra Island - use Chart 3539

- **Plumper Bay** towards its southeast corner, keeping clear of the shoal area

- **Brown Bay** on the west shore, opposite Plumper Bay, where there is a resort with mooring
    slips behind a floating tank-car breakwater. Fuel, water and other supplies are available.

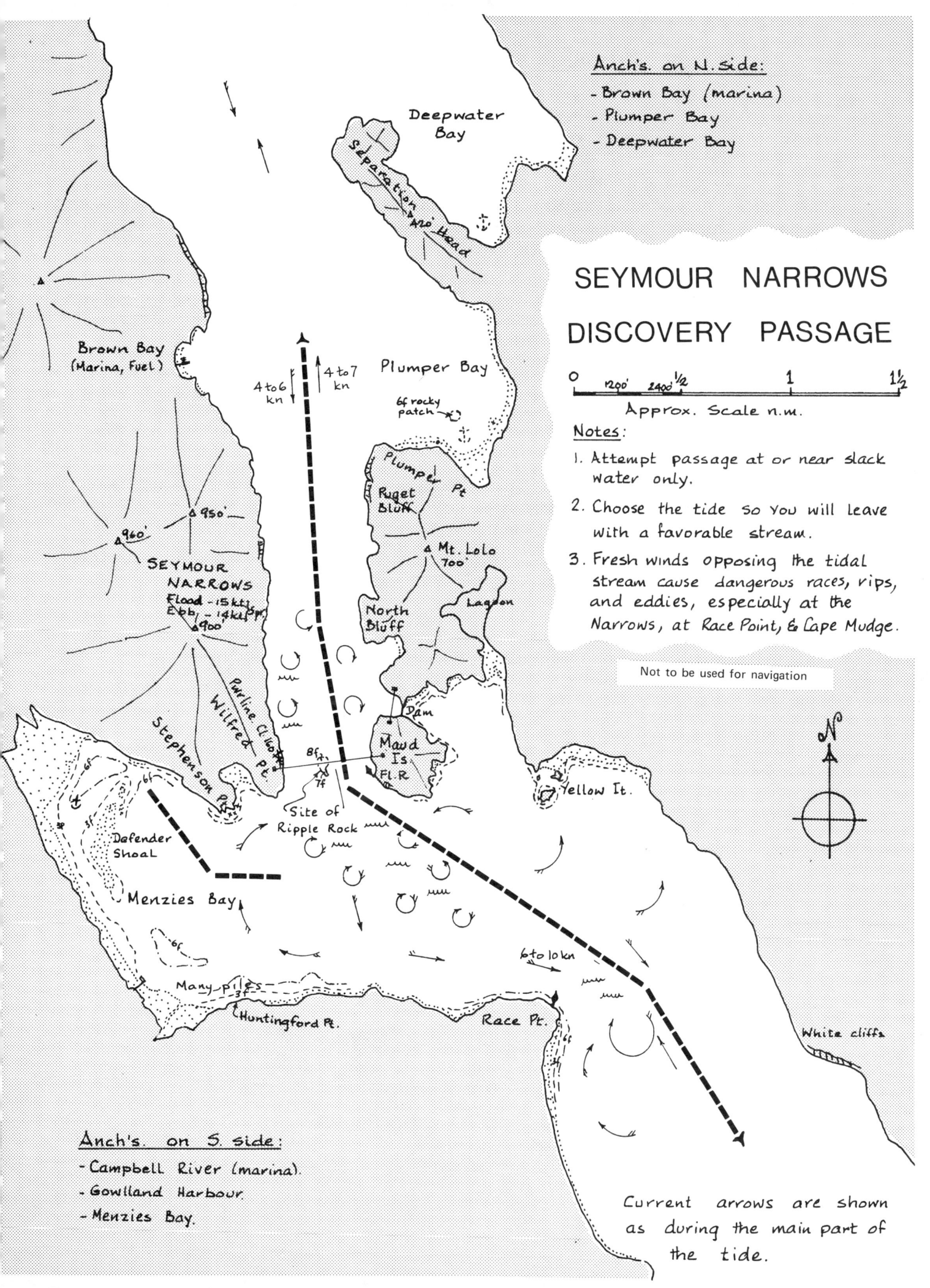

Deepwater Bay

Anch's. on N. side:
- Brown Bay (marina)
- Plumper Bay
- Deepwater Bay

Separation Head

SEYMOUR NARROWS
DISCOVERY PASSAGE

Plumper Bay

Brown Bay
(Marina, Fuel)

4 to 6 kn   4 to 7 kn

6f rocky patch

Plumper Pt.

0   1200' 2400' 1/2   1   1 1/2

Approx. Scale n.m.

Puget Bluff

Notes:

1. Attempt passage at or near slack water only.

2. Choose the tide so you will leave with a favorable stream.

3. Fresh winds opposing the tidal stream cause dangerous races, rips, and eddies, especially at the Narrows, at Race Point, & Cape Mudge.

△ 950'

△ 960'

SEYMOUR NARROWS
Flood - 15 kt.
Ebb - 14 kt.
△ 900

Mt. Lolo 700

Lagoon

Not to be used for navigation

North Bluff

Purline Cliffs

Wilfred Pt.

Dam

Stephenson Pt.

Maud Is
Fl. R.

8 ft.

7 f

Yellow It.

N

Site of Ripple Rock

Defender Shoal

Menzies Bay

6 to 10 kn

White cliffs

Many piles
3 f

Huntingford Pt.

Race Pt.

Anch's. on S. side:
- Campbell River (marina).
- Gowlland Harbour.
- Menzies Bay.

Current arrows are shown as during the main part of the tide.

OTTER COVE (ROCK BAY MARINE PARK)

This cove lies at the north end of Discovery Passage, where the channel turns almost at right angles to become Johnstone Strait. Housing for the lighthouse keeper's are at the point of the turn on Chatham Point, but the light itself is erected on Beaver Rock almost 300m (1,000 feet) to the north. The light is on a white painted steel tank on top of a white polygon-shaped concrete base. The foghorn of this station sounds every 20 seconds in fog, from a small building on the rocky point to the west of the light. This separation of light, houses, and foghorn is notable because if one is approaching Chatham Point in fog without radar, it is important to pass north and east of the light. It is dangerous to hold close to the shore in fog since rocks off the point prevent passage between it and the light where swirls and strong currents occur on the flood.

Immediately south of Chatham Point is a tiny cove with a cable strung across it to moor the keeper's boats. Two small islands, Rocky Islets, lie off the south side of Chatham Point. They are connected by a drying rocky ledge and have other ledges extending around their sides.

Otter Cove can be entered only by passing between Rocky Islets and Limestone Island. This rocky, 18m (60 foot) island has a few shrubs and trees. South of Limestone Island, between it and Slab Point (the southern point of Otter Cove entrance) there are shoal areas with kelp. Do not enter Otter Cove through this southern passage.

Anchorage can be found in the cove well in towards the head, in 5 to 8 fathoms, mud and rock; this area gives good protection from westerly winds. Though strong currents and swirls occur in Discovery Passage off Chatham Point the anchorage is relatively unaffected. This cove is a convenient base either to wait for slack water when southbound in Discovery Passage, to await quiet conditions in Johnstone Strait when northbound.

Several other anchorages in this locality are:

- **Turn Island,** across Johnstone Strait from Chatham Point has an anchorage behind it in a cove on Thurlow Island. Take care on entry from the east to avoid reefs found on both sides. There may be some sunken debris remaining for the logging camp that was located here..

- **Cameleon Harbour** and **Thurston Bay**, around the corner in Nodales Channel, offer several anchoring locations. Thurston Bay is an undeveloped Marine Park where anchorage may be taken behind Block Island.

- Rock Bay on Vancouver Island appears to be a possible anchorage but this is not the case. The government pier does not have a float and currents sweep the bay.

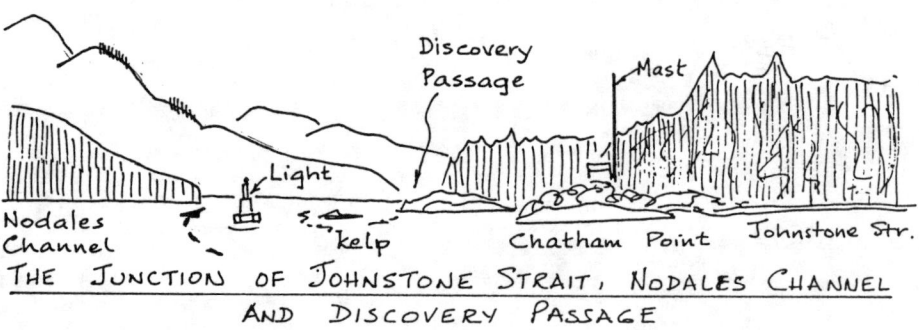

THE JUNCTION OF JOHNSTONE STRAIT, NODALES CHANNEL AND DISCOVERY PASSAGE

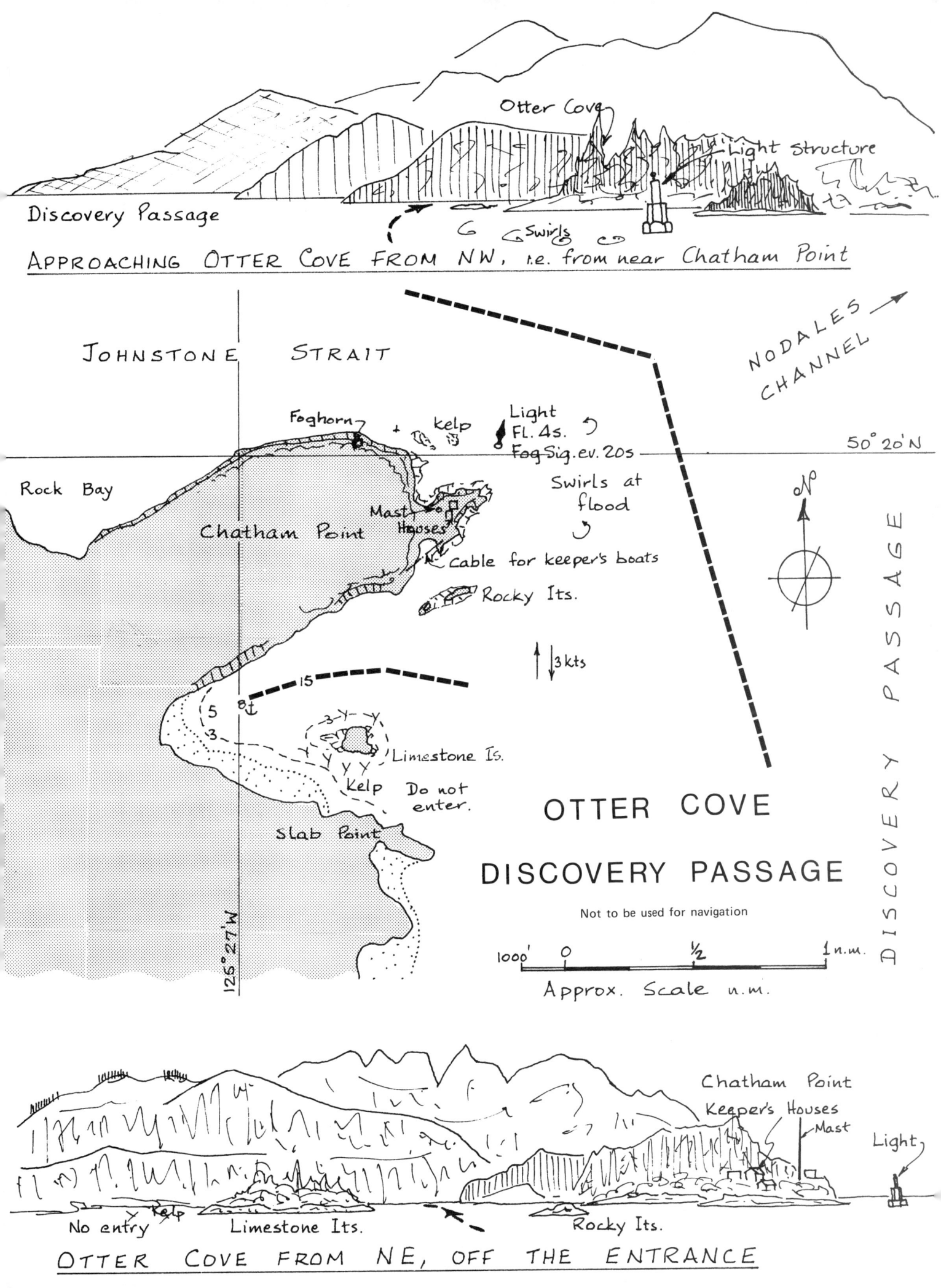

Discovery Passage

APPROACHING OTTER COVE FROM NW, i.e. from near Chatham Point

Otter Cove

Light structure

Swirls

JOHNSTONE STRAIT

NODALES CHANNEL

Foghorn

kelp

Light
Fl. 4s.
Fog Sig. ev. 20s

50° 20'N

Rock Bay

Chatham Point

Mast
Houses

Swirls at
flood

Cable for keeper's boats

Rocky Its.

3 kts

15

5

3

3

Limestone Is.

Kelp

Do not
enter.

Slab Point

DISCOVERY PASSAGE

OTTER COVE

DISCOVERY PASSAGE

Not to be used for navigation

1000'   0   ½   1 n.m.

Approx. Scale n.m.

125°27'W

Chatham Point
Keeper's Houses
Mast

Light

No entry   Limestone Its.   kelp   Rocky Its.

OTTER COVE FROM NE, OFF THE ENTRANCE

RACE and CURRENT PASSAGES and KELSEY BAY

The eastern portion of Johnstone Strait from Chatham Point to Kelsey Bay (about 21 miles) has steep mountains along the southern side, with no chance for anchorage The mountainous islands on the north side are not as high, and several large channels open into the Strait joining it to the northern passes. Though the passage has much beautiful scenery it has some drawbacks for small vessels.

This relatively narrow part of the Strait has strong currents, made more turbulent at certain areas such as Ripple Shoal and Race and Current Passages. Strong summer northwesterlies can kick up seas that make it a testing passage. Sometimes, too, summer fog hangs on in this part of the channel long after it has burned away in the other inside waters. In addition, traffic is heavy as cruise ships (often four or five in row) as well as log booms and fishing craft transit this area. Mayne Passage enters Johnstone Strait on the north side, opposite Ripple Point. A short distance west, Knox Bay is deep but can offer some respite from the westerly wind and sea.

Chancellor Channel enters the Strait about 12 miles along, leading to Helmcken Island, with Current and Race Passages on the N and S sides respectively. Favor the shore to avoid the eddies and rips near Ripple Shoal. The 1-mile long shoal lies in the red sector of the Helmcken Island light, about 1 mile east of Helmcken Island.

Large vessels observe a traffic separation pattern, with westbound craft passing north of Helmcken Island in Current Passage and eastbound using Race Passage. Small vessels do not always heed this requirement. The current can run to 6 knots in these passages, and it is always a good feeling to get by them. If an anchorage is needed, **Billy Goat Bay** on the north side of Helmcken Island can be used. Enter with care, for there are several rocks, islets and shoal areas nearby though the entrance is clear. Earl Ledge extends off Hardwicke Island for about .25 miles into the channel. Stay well clear of the light marking its end to avoid the turbulence found here.

As a result of snowmelt from the various inlets pouring into Johnstone Strait the current runs westward for long periods, and the tide and current tables will often show a continuous ebb current even while the water level is rising with the flood tide. This is a curious feature of the basins and sills of the various passages, one that confuses many transient skippers. *The tide and current tables are to be believed.* Since the prevailing westerly winds seem to develop their strongest force through this section seas can build seas against the ebb flow that make this passage lumpy and uncomfortable. Rainy weather or an early start assist in transiting this section during its quietest conditions.

Kelsey Bay is on the Vancouver Island side of the Strait, at the mouth of the Salmon River. The wide, shallow delta of the river has six sunken freighters forming a breakwater for a booming ground. This feature, together with buildings behind at Sayward and numerous tanks identify Kelsey Bay. If strong westerly winds are blowing against a high ebb tide in the Strait, heavy tidal rips will be encountered off Kelsey Bay. Alternate anchorages are justified when the rips are particularly turbulent or when tidal currents make progress in the area difficult.

The small craft floats are behind the rock breakwater west of the prominent ferry slip, where your vessel is protected from the wind and sea. The fuel dock is behind the high pier beyond the breakwater. Facilities are limited and are exposed to wash through the pilings making it unsatisfactory as an overnight stop.

RACE & CURRENT PASSAGES

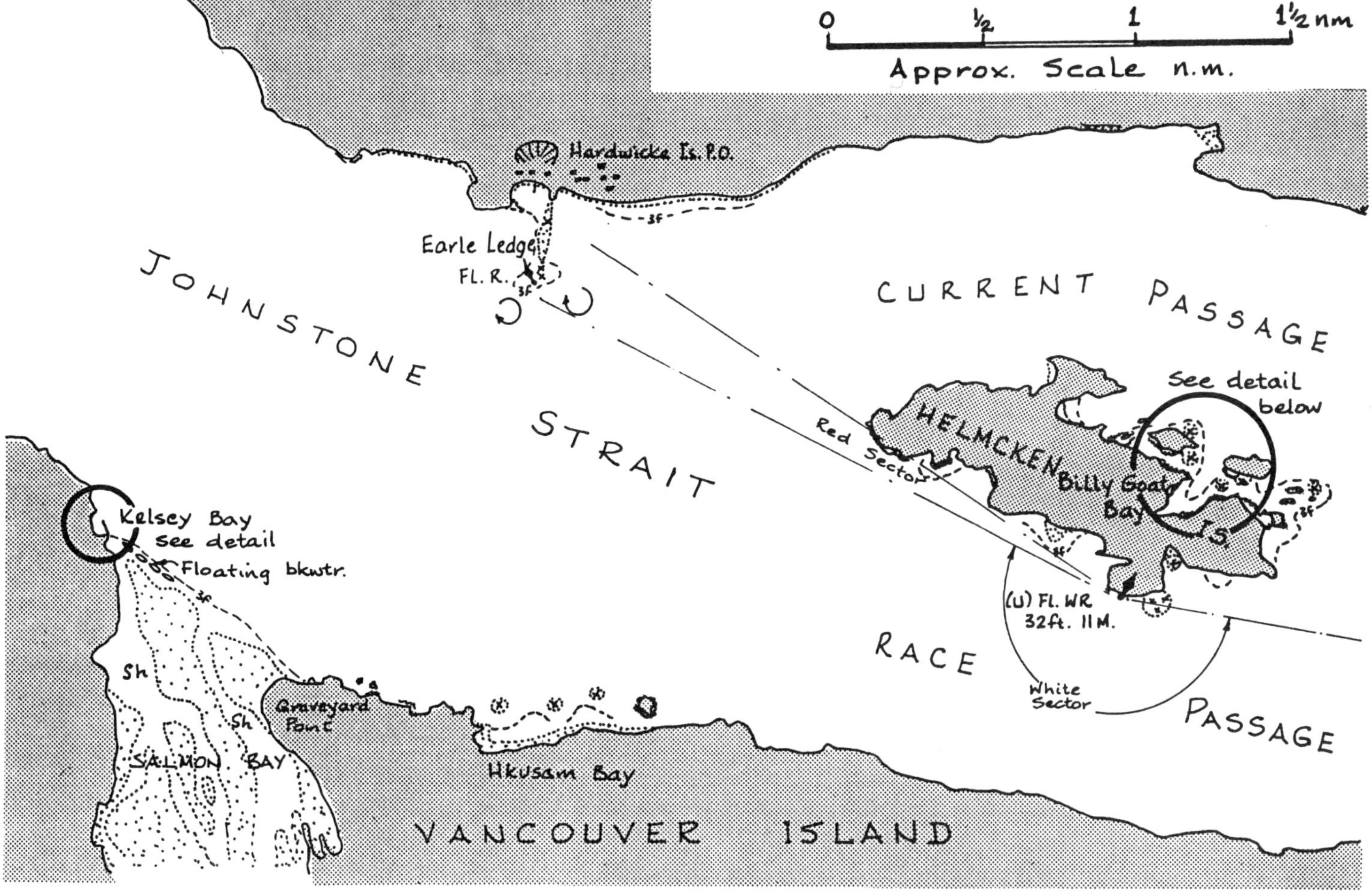

0   ½   1   1½ nm

Approx. Scale n.m.

Hardwicke Is. P.O.

Earle Ledge
Fl. R.

JOHNSTONE STRAIT

CURRENT PASSAGE

Red Sector

HELMCKEN

See detail below

Billy Goat Bay

Kelsey Bay
see detail

Floating bkwtr.

Sh

Sh

SALMON BAY

Graveyard Point

Hkusam Bay

(u) Fl. WR
32ft. 11M.

White Sector

RACE

PASSAGE

VANCOUVER ISLAND

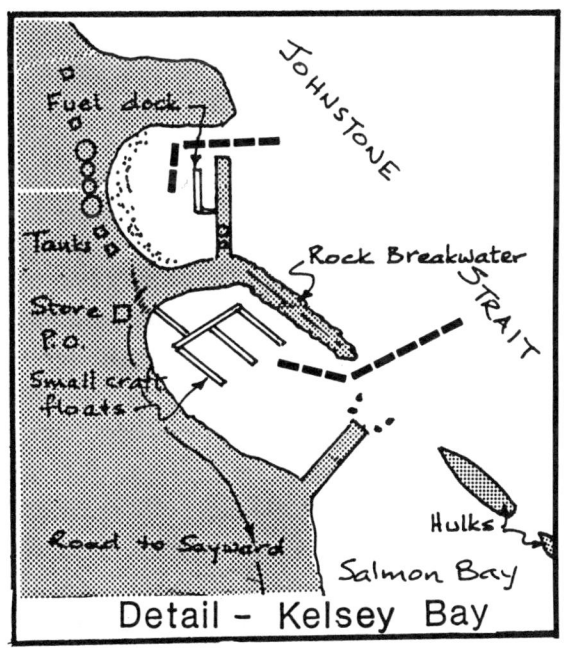

Fuel dock

JOHNSTONE

Tanks

Store
P.O.

Small craft floats

Rock Breakwater

STRAIT

Hulks

Road to Sayward

Salmon Bay

Detail - Kelsey Bay

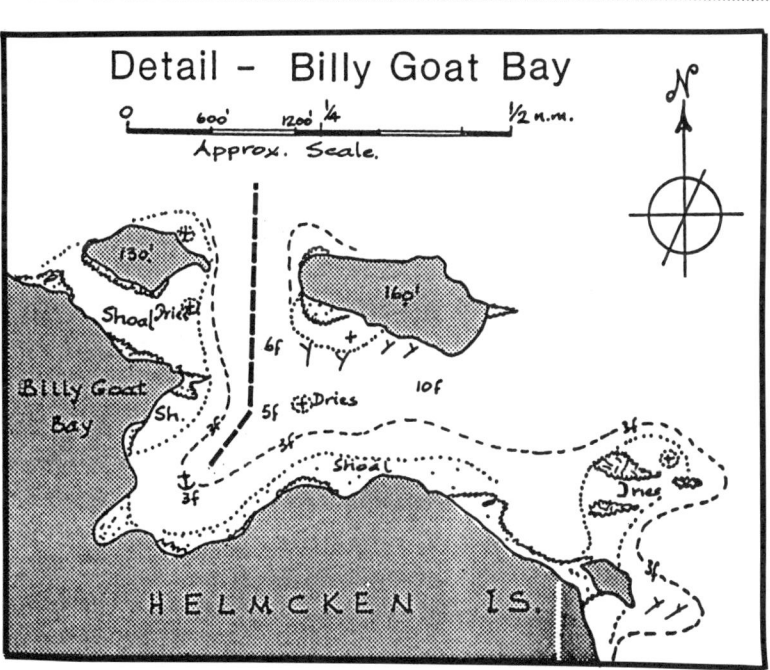

Detail - Billy Goat Bay

0   600'   1200'   ¼   ½ n.m.

Approx. Scale.

130'

Shoal

160'

6f

Billy Goat Bay

Sh.

5f Dries

10f

Dries

Shoal

3f

Ines

HELMCKEN IS.

Old hulks used as a breakwater for the booming ground

Sayward Clearing

Breakwater

High wharf with piling

APPROACHING KELSEY BAY FROM NNW, i.e. down Johnstone Strait abt. 1mile.

OCTOPUS ISLANDS MARINE PARK

This beautiful marine park is a destination for many families from the Pacific Northwest and southern B.C. who find Desolation Sound and the Gulf Islands to be overcrowded during July and August. If time permits, it is also a side-trip worth taking when cruising the coast to or from Alaska. Located near the northeast tip of Quadra Island, it can be reached by one of three routes: from Okisollo Channel (joining Discovery Passage north of Seymour Narrows), through Hole in the wall (connecting Okisollo Channel to Calm Channel just to the north of Cortes Island) or via Surge Narrows (joining Okisollo Channel to Hoskyn Channel through Beazley Passage). Regardless of the approach taken, strong tidal currents with swirls, eddies and overfalls combined with a profusion of rocks and shoals demand careful timing and precise navigation.

Approaching the park from the west via Okisollo Channel must be timed for slack water in the Upper and Lower Rapids, as tidal currents can reach 9 knots accompanied by heavy overfalls and turbulence. Several anchorages are available while waiting for slack water. **Chonat Bay** on the south shore provides anchorage in the middle of the bay, but don't go too far in as much of the bay is shoal. **Barnes Bay** offers anchorage in the eastern part on a rocky bottom. The entrance to **Owen Bay** is affected by currents and eddies from the Upper Rapids unless entry is made less than an hour before slack. Clearance must be given to the drying reef .1 mile SW of Grant Island and rocks on the SE side of Walters Point. This is a pretty anchorage.

When approaching the park from Hole in the Wall timing of slack water at the western end is essential, for tidal currents can reach 12 knots while those at the eastern end, are only 2 knots. A convenient anchorage to await slack water is on the south shore at **Florence Cove** where a private dock is located. At the western end a mid-channel course must be followed when entering Okisollo Channel to avoid the drying rocks lying close to both the north and south entrance points where a 3.5 fathom band of water reaches across the opening.

The entrance to the Marine Park is through Bodega Anchorage followed by an interesting passage through a narrow channel having depths of 3 - 4 fathoms Anchorage may be taken in the first cove to starboard, taking care to avoid a large underwater rock extending off the shore to port. Further along the channel is another bay to starboard where many vessels find good anchorage. The tidal range must be considered when anchoring in the western bay where extensive shoals line the western and northern shores.

Approaching the park from the south via Surge Narrows is not recommended for first-time visitors. The route is narrow (Beazley Passage is only 60 m/197 feet wide) and many rocks and shoals must be negotiated only at slack water as tidal currents reach 12 knots.

Many pleasant hours can be spent rowing around the islets exploring this peaceful, undeveloped park. During high tide you can row to a little stream which empties into a small niche on the western shore to have a freshwater wash. Cruisers who prefer a less crowded anchorage may proceed further to anchor in **Waiatt Bay** in 4 - 5 fathoms, mud. A trail at the head of the bay leads to Small Inlet on the other side of Quadra Island and beyond to a lovely protected area surrounding Newton Lake where a quiet approach is often rewarded by hearing the melancholy song of loons.

OCTOPUS ISLANDS

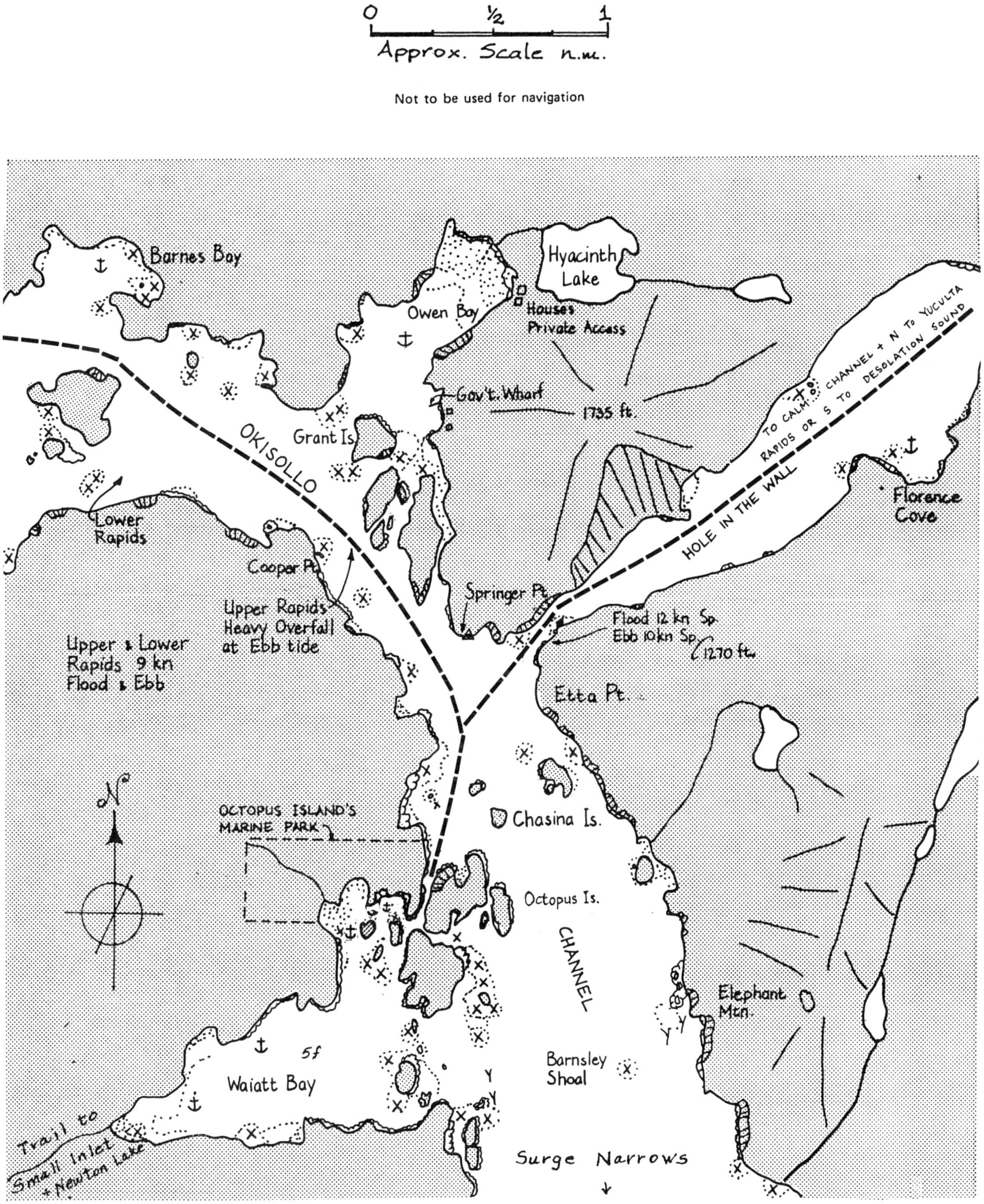

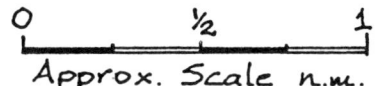

0   ½   1

Approx. Scale n.m.

Not to be used for navigation

Barnes Bay

Owen Bay

Hyacinth Lake

Houses Private Access

Gov't. Wharf

1735 ft.

TO CALM CHANNEL + N TO YUCULTA RAPIDS OR S TO DESOLATION SOUND

OKISOLLO

Grant Is.

HOLE IN THE WALL

Florence Cove

Lower Rapids

Cooper Pt.

Upper Rapids Heavy Overfall at Ebb tide

Springer Pt.

Flood 12 kn Sp Ebb 10 kn Sp

1270 ft.

Upper & Lower Rapids 9 kn Flood & Ebb

Etta Pt.

N

OCTOPUS ISLAND'S MARINE PARK

Chasina Is.

Octopus Is.

CHANNEL

Elephant Mtn.

Waiatt Bay

5f

Barnsley Shoal

Trail to Small Inlet + Newton Lake

Surge Narrows

YUCULTA RAPIDS and DENT RAPIDS

Two routes lead from the north end of Georgia Strait to Johnstone Strait and on to the waters of northern British Columbia. The Seymour Narrows- Discovery Passage route is more direct, although it is influenced throughout its length by currents. It is heavily used by commercial fishermen, tugs, etc. The more interesting, alternative route uses the northern passes where the high currents are interspersed by stretches of calm water. Yachtsmen tend to favor these northern passes.

The entrance into this northern route is through Calm Channel which is between Stuart and Sonora Islands. A tiny cove north of Harbott Point at the southern entrance to Calm Channel is the location of a private resort.

When traveling north, leave Harbott Point about one hour before the tide turns to the ebb. (Remember the flood runs south and the ebb runs north in this channel.) Hold close to the Stuart Island shore till off Kelsey Point, then cross over to take advantage of a back eddy along the Sonora Island shore. Swing clear of Sea Lion Rock. There is a light on the east tip of the largest Gillard Island and the pass is immediately north of the light. One should enter Gillard Pass no more than 20 minutes before high water slack. The current tables are essential for correct timing, for the change in current direction does not always coincide with the tidal change.

Barber Passage lies northeast of Gillard Passage. While free of dangers, it is not as convenient to use. Big Bay is east of these rapids and provides a refuge from nearby currents. A detached shoal, marked by kelp, with a least depth of 4 m (13 ft.) lies in the center of the bay. A 204 m (699 ft.) public wharf is protected by a breakwater. Nearby is **Big Bay Resort**, a well known fishing resort for the rich and famous and is also a popular stop-over for cruisers. The office monitors VHF Ch. 73 or can be called at (250) 830-7524

Dent Rapids are 2 miles northwest of Gillard Passage along Cordero Channel. The narrowest section is about .25 mile wide. The strong currents at peak flow create a standing wave off the tip of Little Dent Island with a large whirlpool "Devil's Hole," occurring down current. Favor the Sonora Island shore to avoid these turbulent waters. Do not pass close to Little Dent Island for the back eddy draws a vessel toward the whirlpool. When traveling south plan to be at Dent Rapids at low slack. Since this occurs 25 minutes prior to Gillard Passage enter it at the right time to pass through Yuculta Rapids about a half-hour into the flood. Do not attempt Tugboat Passage between Dent Islands as local knowledge is essential. Mermaid Bay is frequently used by log booms and pleasure craft find little space here to anchor.

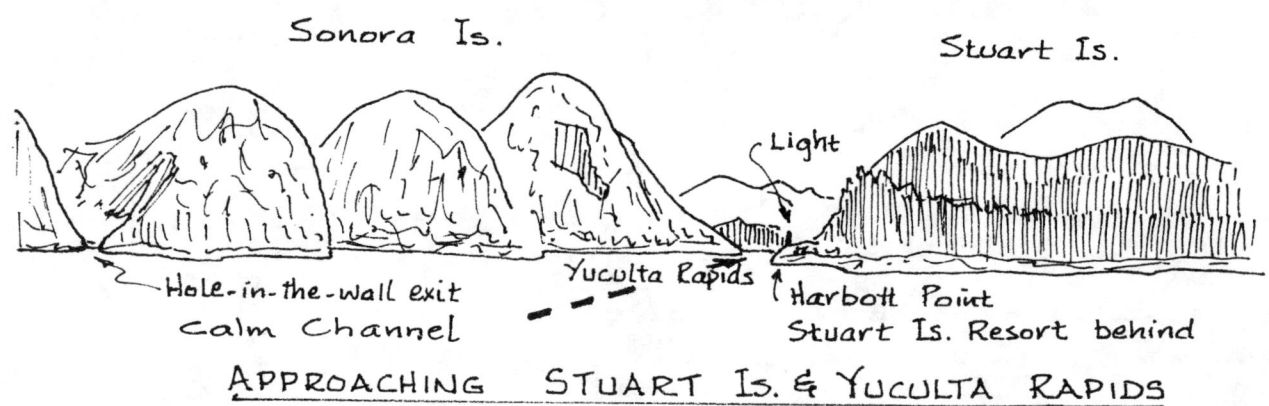

APPROACHING STUART IS. & YUCULTA RAPIDS

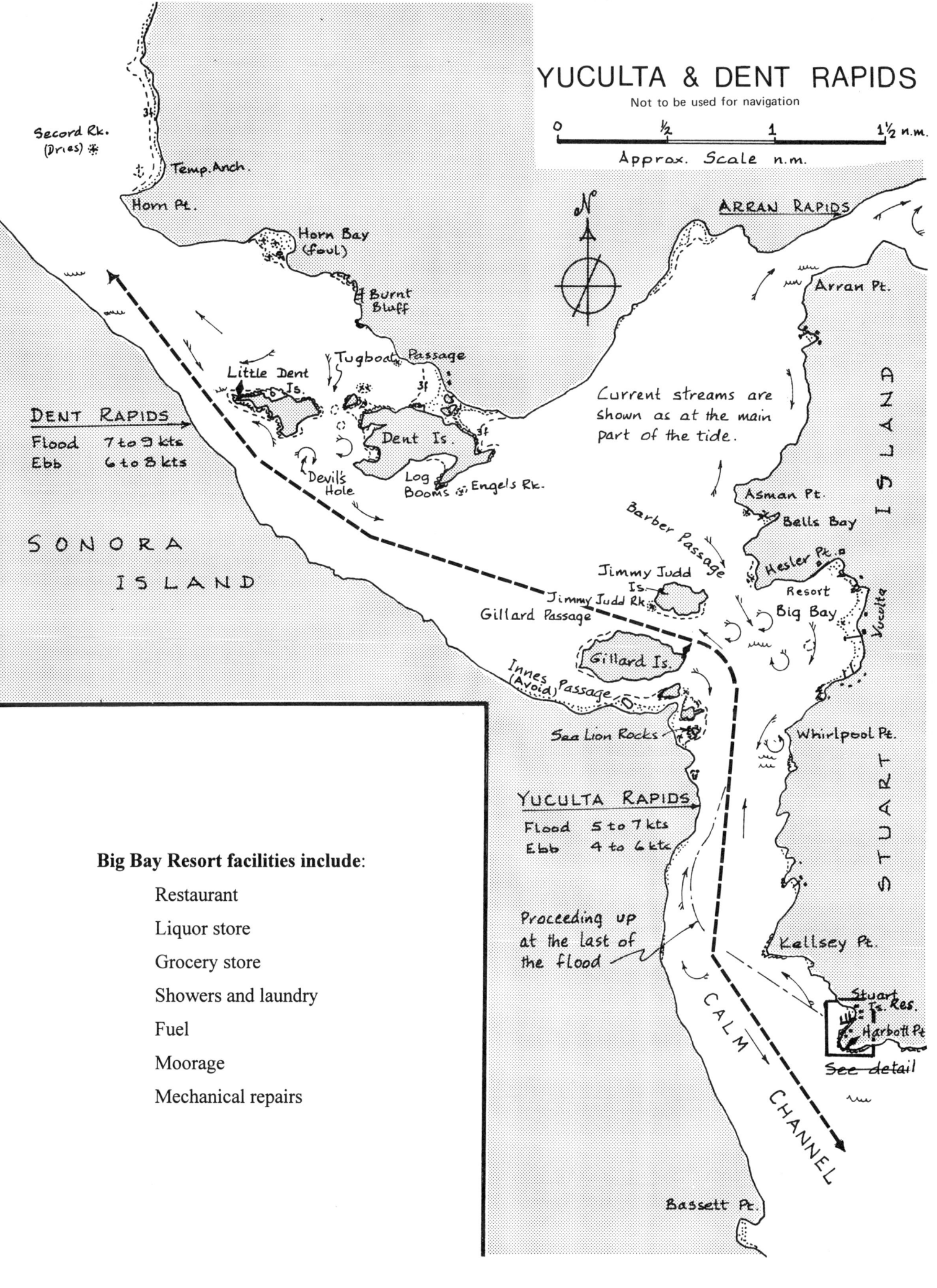

YUCULTA & DENT RAPIDS

Not to be used for navigation

Approx. Scale n.m.

Secord Rk. (Dries)

Temp. Anch.

Horn Pt.

Horn Bay (foul)

Burnt Bluff

Tugboat Passage

Little Dent Is.

DENT RAPIDS

Flood   7 to 9 kts
Ebb   6 to 8 kts

Devil's Hole

Dent Is.

Log Booms

Engels Rk.

S O N O R A
I S L A N D

ARRAN RAPIDS

Arran Pt.

Current streams are shown as at the main part of the tide.

Asman Pt.

Bells Bay

Barber Passage

Hesler Pt.

Jimmy Judd Is.

Jimmy Judd Rk.

Gillard Passage

Resort
Big Bay

Innes Passage (Avoid)

Gillard Is.

Sea Lion Rocks

Whirlpool Pt.

YUCULTA RAPIDS

Flood   5 to 7 kts
Ebb   4 to 6 kts

Proceeding up at the last of the flood

Kellsey Pt.

S T U A R T   I S L A N D

Yuculta

Stuart Is. Res.

Harbott Pt.

See detail

Big Bay Resort facilities include:

Restaurant

Liquor store

Grocery store

Showers and laundry

Fuel

Moorage

Mechanical repairs

CALM CHANNEL

Bassett Pt.

GREENE POINT RAPIDS

Cordero Channel continues in a northwesterly direction beyond Dent Rapids. At Hall Point, the northern tip of Sonora Island, Nodales Channel leads off Cordero Channel in a southwesterly direction to join Johnstone Strait near Chatham Point. The northern pass route continues along Cordero Channel.

Shoal Bay is on the south side of the channel about 2 miles from Nodales junction. A government dock with a long pier is at the southwest corner of the bay, where a boardwalk leads to an old hotel. If the small float at the dock is fully occupied you may anchor east of the dock in 3 - 4 fathoms, mud. The head of the bay shoals for a considerable distance.

Two miles further west on the south side of the channel is another large bay is. **Bickley Bay** is a convenient anchorage if it is necessary to wait for passage of Greene Point Rapids. If carrying the favoring current from entering Gillard Passage just before high slack, you can plan on transiting these rapids (if the vessel's speed is at least 6 knots). Depending on the vessel's speed they will be commencing to ebb, and though milder than Dent or Gillard they should not be treated lightly.

Greene Point Rapids are a T-shaped meeting of channels. Cordero Channel continues along the head of the T, while Mayne Passage leads southward to join Johnstone Strait. At the junction there are several groups of islands that narrow the passage and which should be passed with care. The ebb shows swirls and small overfalls from south of Cordero Islands for a considerable distance west along Cordero Channel. Slow vessels need to favor the south shore to avoid being pushed towards Griffith Islet, marked by a light. On the flood, going east, swirls and currents extend past Erasmus Island. Here too, a slow vessel should avoid being set towards the island.

About 1.5 miles east of Greene Point Rapids is Lorte Island with light and a prominent "restaurant" sign. In the cove nearby are the floats of an excellent dining room at **Camp Cordero**. Approaching the dock is easy near slack water but at other times strong currents in the cove make mooring the vessel somewhat challenging and care is needed.

Anchorage can be found in the Cordero Islands, approaching as indicated on the sketch. The islands block most of the effect of the current. Chart No. 3566 and other publications mention Crawford Anchorage behind Erasmus Island, but this anchorage appears so restricted by rocks and current flow that it is not recommended.

Tide and current effects should be kept in mind when entering or leaving Blind Channel. In the narrow section of Mayne Passage rips and eddies are encountered. A mile south in Mayne Passage, on the west side is **Blind Channel Resort.** This well run resort provides a welcome rest spot with very good facilities, including grocery, showers and a laundromat as well as an excellent dining room. The government dock is in the SW part of the bay with floats on either side. This is a busy spot in summer so rafting may be necessary. Fuel and water are available at the float. A pleasant walk along a forest trail leads to a point of interest-the ancient Thurlow Cedar which is more than 6 m (20 ft.) in diameter.

Charles Bay, roughly opposite Blind Channel, offers a beautiful anchorage in good holding mud for two or three vessels. Keep clear of shoal areas and allow for slight swinging about as some current effects are felt in the vicinity of Eclipse Island in the middle of the bay. This is a perfectly protected anchorage which also allows you to escape the hubbub of a congested marina to the serenity of the calls of eagles, gulls and sometimes loons.

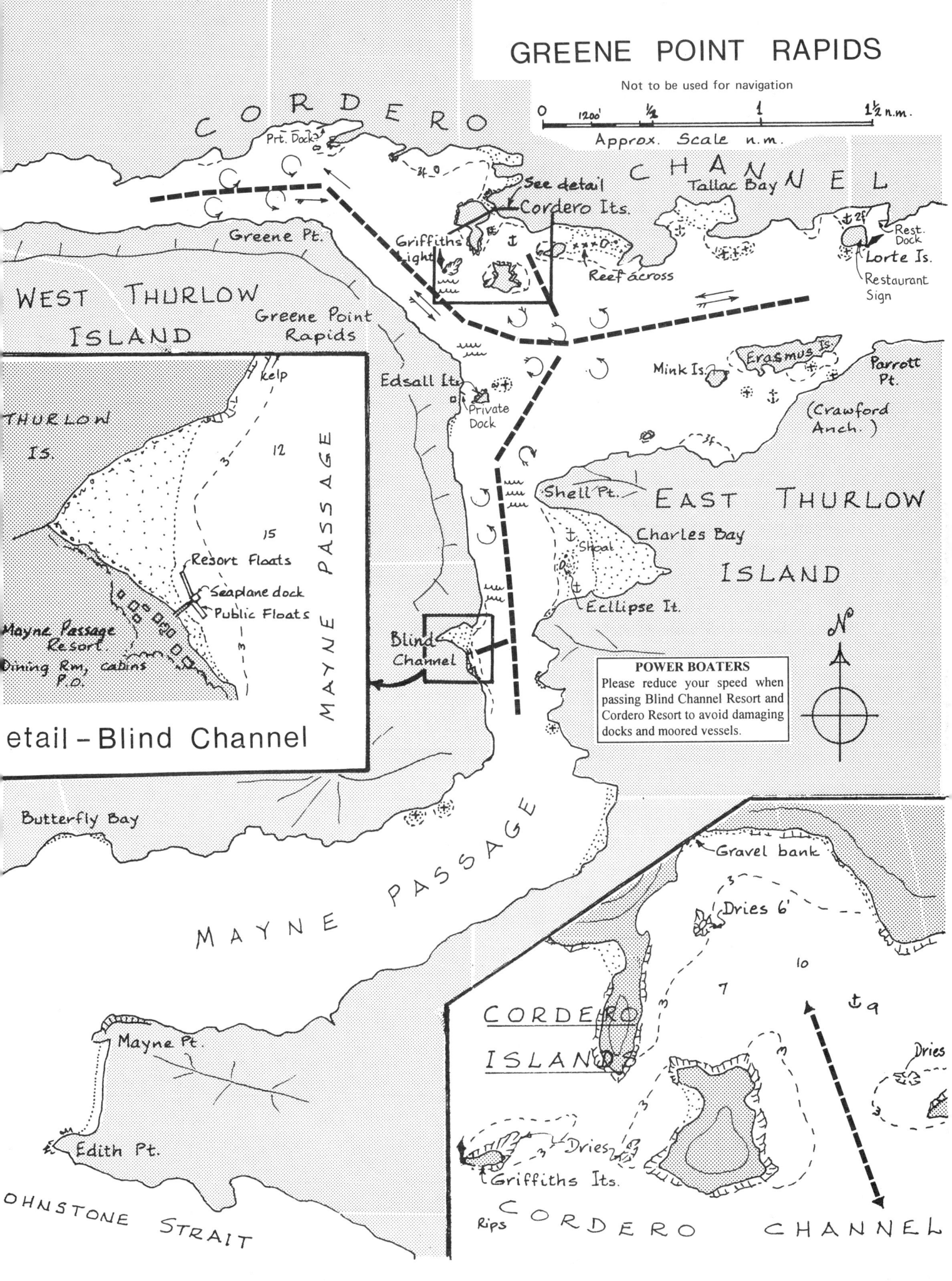

GREENE POINT RAPIDS

Not to be used for navigation

0　1200'　½　1　1½ n.m.

Approx. Scale n.m.

C O R D E R O

Prt. Dock

C H A N N E L

Tallac Bay

See detail

Cordero Its.

⚓2f

Griffiths light

Rest. Dock

Lorte Is.

Reef across

Restaurant Sign

Greene Pt.

WEST THURLOW ISLAND

Greene Point Rapids

Edsall Its

Private Dock

Mink Is.

Erasmus Is.

Parrott Pt.

(Crawford Anch.)

Shell Pt.

EAST THURLOW

Charles Bay

ISLAND

Shoal

Ecllipse It.

N

POWER BOATERS
Please reduce your speed when passing Blind Channel Resort and Cordero Resort to avoid damaging docks and moored vessels.

Blind Channel

Detail – Blind Channel

THURLOW Is.

kelp

3　12

15

Resort Floats

Seaplane dock

Public Floats

Mayne Passage Resort

Dining Rm, cabins P.O.

M A Y N E   P A S S A G E

Butterfly Bay

M A Y N E   P A S S A G E

Mayne Pt.

Edith Pt.

OHNSTONE STRAIT

Gravel bank

Dries 6'

10

7　⚓9

C O R D E R O

I S L A N D

Dries

Dries

Griffiths Its.

Rips

C O R D E R O   C H A N N E L

WELLBORE CHANNEL

Cordero Channel continues west from Greene Point Rapids for 3.5 miles to join Chancellor Channel marked by a light on Lyall Island. North of this junction, Loughborough Inlet* extends 18 miles to the north. The ebb effects of Greene Point Rapids are felt as far as this point. Chancellor Channel leads southwest for about 7 miles to join Johnstone Strait east of Helmcken Island and Race and Current Passages. If the weather is calm this exit into Johnstone Strait can be taken to shorten the distance to be traveled. However when strong westerlies are blowing they create disturbed seas in Chancellor Channel (as well as Johnstone Strait) and the side-step via Wellbore Channel can offer more miles but greater comfort.

For a slow vessel running the northern passes all together, the ebb will be well advanced by the time the entrance to Wellbore Channel is reached. The channel can be taken if the tides and currents (as given in the tables), are not large. But for bigger tides, or if the tide is too far advanced you should wait to enter Wellbore Channel nearer slack water. Small craft can find good anchorage close to shore in the little bays on either side of **Shorter Point,** depending on wind direction.

The effect of the currents are felt throughout Wellbore Channel. The main current effects are at Whirlpool Rapids off Carterer Point. The south-flowing flood effects extend south of Carterer Point, with the strongest back-eddy and whirlpools on the west side. Small floods have lesser effects and a vessel can pass through even at mid flood. Snug anchorage can be taken in a small cove west of Robson Point for one boat.

The north-flowing ebb has a narrow center section with large back-eddies and whirlpools on each side. The eastern back-eddy, together with the effects from Forward Harbour is strong. Entering Forward Harbour when the ebb is strong will require considerable power and it is best avoided. On small ebb flows the current effects are diminished, but swirls and currents sweep out past Althorp Point almost across Bessborough Bay.

Forward Harbour has a clear entrance channel leading to an attractive anchorage. It can be easily negotiated except, as noted when strong ebb currents exit the inlet. Douglas Bay provides good anchorage off the muddy beach. The depths drop off fairly quickly and stern ties to trees or rocks can be helpful. Good protection is provided during westerly winds, but if strong easterly winds are expected the log booms which are sometimes tied along the south shore may offer a more comfortable moorage. A seasonal restaurant operates near the logging camp is at the head of the bay. The operators sometimes offer a launch pick-up/drop-off service to patrons anchored in Douglas Bay or you can make the trip with your outboard in a few minutes. The food is reported to be good although, understandably, the menu is limited.

In Sunderland Channel a small anchorage can be found in the lee of Murray Islet in **Topaze Harbor.** Otherwise, some protection may be obtained behind log booms in Jackson Bay. Strong westerlies in Johnstone Strait also affect Sunderland Channel but the seas are not as heavy due to a shorter fetch. Sunderland Channel enters Johnstone Strait west of Kelsey Bay. Most vessels keep to the north shore, except when avoiding the rips off Gunner Point. If the seas are bad, respite can be found in the bay east of Gunner Point, in **MacLeod Bay, Tuna Point** or **Port Neville**

*If westerly winds pick up and make westbound progress in Cordero Channel slow or uncomfortable, moorage is available a few miles to the north in Loughborough Inlet at Heyden Bay where you can tie to log booms or anchor near the head of Jane Bay in 4 to 5 fathoms, mud.

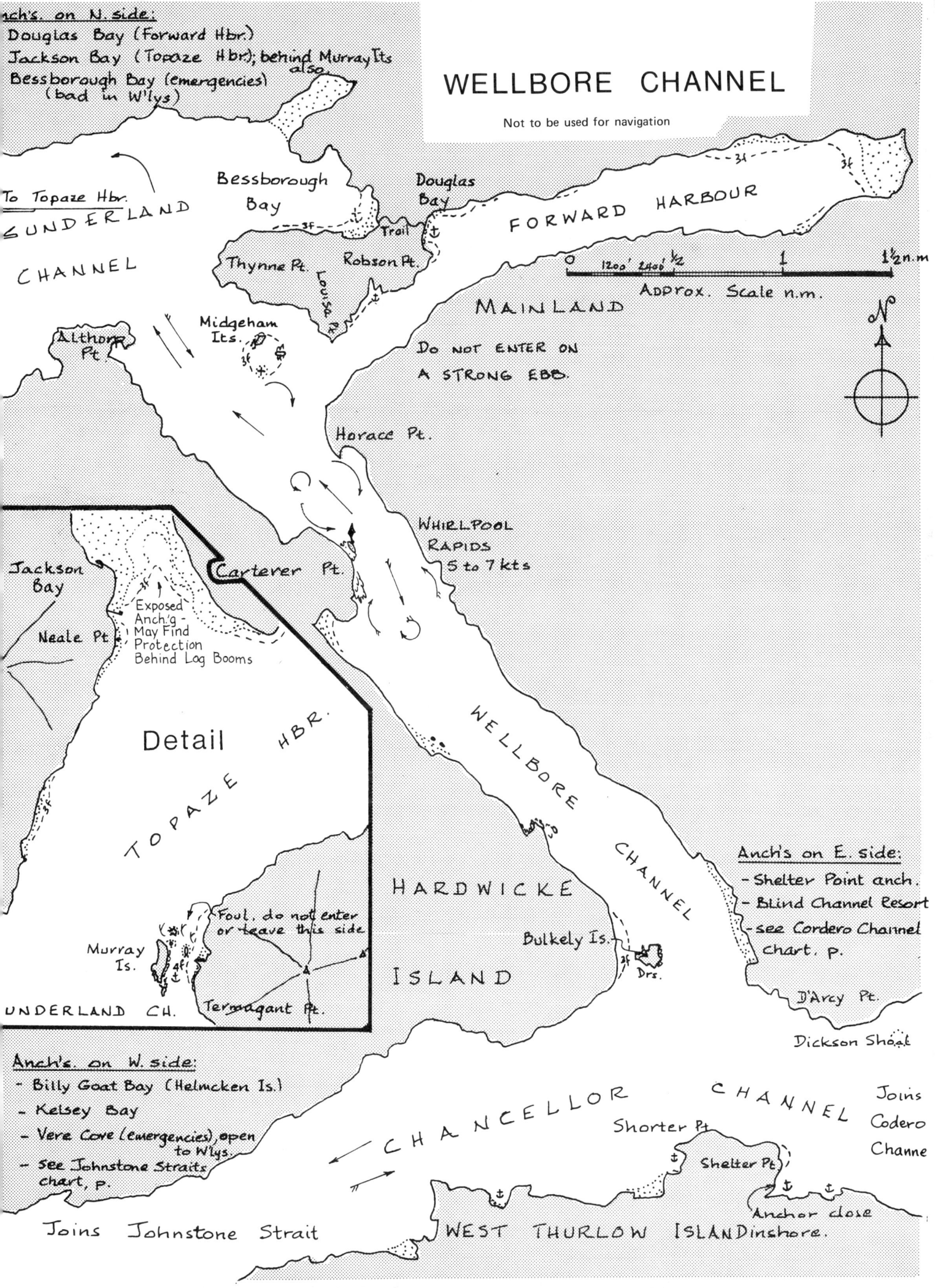

WELLBORE CHANNEL

Not to be used for navigation

Anch's on N. side:
- Douglas Bay (Forward Hbr.)
- Jackson Bay (Topaze Hbr.); behind Murray Its. also.
- Bessborough Bay (emergencies) (bad in W'lys)

To Topaze Hbr.

SUNDERLAND CHANNEL

Bessborough Bay

Thynne Pt.

Louise Pt.

Robson Pt.

Trail

Midgeham Its.

$

3f

Althorp Pt.

Douglas Bay

FORWARD HARBOUR

3½

3f

MAINLAND

DO NOT ENTER ON A STRONG EBB.

0   1200' 2400   ½   1   1½ n.m
Approx. Scale n.m.

N

Horace Pt.

WHIRLPOOL RAPIDS 5 to 7 kts

Jackson Bay

Carterer Pt.

Exposed Anch'g — May Find Protection Behind Log Booms

Neale Pt.

Detail

TOPAZE HBR.

WELLBORE CHANNEL

Foul, do not enter or leave this side

Murray Is.

4f

HARDWICKE

ISLAND

Bulkely Is.

3f

Drs.

SUNDERLAND CH.

Termagant Pt.

Anch's on E. side:
- Shelter Point anch.
- Blind Channel Resort
- see Cordero Channel chart, P.

D'Arcy Pt.

Dickson Shoal

Anch's on W. side:
- Billy Goat Bay (Helmcken Is.)
- Kelsey Bay
- Vere Cove (emergencies), open to W'lys.
- see Johnstone Straits chart, P.

CHANCELLOR CHANNEL

Shorter Pt

Shelter Pt.

Joins Cordero Channe

Joins Johnstone Strait

WEST THURLOW ISLAND

Anchor close inshore.

PORT NEVILLE

The central portion of Johnstone Strait is where vessels transiting Seymour Narrows meet those traveling the northern route through the Yuculta, Dent and Greene Point Rapids. Some join Johnstone Strait at the junction of Chancellor Channel, others connect at the western end of Sunderland Channel (probably following a stop-over at Forward Harbour). Because prevailing northwesterlies funnel down Johnston Strait it is often uncomfortable to pass through this section when proceeding up the coast, yet all vessels must pass this way.

Sunderland Channel enters Johnstone Strait west of Kelsey Bay. On its north side the large opening of Blenkinsop Bay looks attractive, and can be used as an anchorage in calm weather, but westerlies tend to blow into the Bay.

Tuna Point anchorage, behind the little point and Mary Island gives relief from turbulent seas and apart from some effect of strong northwesterlies, the waters are calm. The cove has limited space and the middle and east part of the anchorage have some kelp and grass so care is needed to set the anchor securely. McLeod Bay is very small, offering protection to a single boat.

Port Neville, about four miles northwest of Tuna Point, is a popular stop-over for anchorage can be taken if the public wharf is filled. The wide, easily recognized entrance is between Ransom Point and Neville Point. The most noticeable feature marking the point is the nearby steep and rocky Milly Island where a prominent house overlooks the Strait. Kelp beds line much of the entrance channel to the bay but a mid-channel course presents no problems. Because of the large volume of water passing through the entrance, tidal currents can reach three knots. The direction and speed of these currents must be considered when mooring or anchoring in the bay.

Anchorage may be along the western shore of the outer part of the inlet taking care to set the anchor securely and have extra scope to prevent dragging as a result of strong currents or changes in depth with a rising tide. When proceeding further into the inlet you pass over an area with least depths of about 1.5 fathoms where it is easy to thread a way through lengthy tendrils of kelp waving at the surface. Within the inlet, anchorage in 4 to 5 fathoms, mud, may be taken in a wide area during settled weather. However, during easterly winds a considerable chop can develop making this exposed anchorage unsatisfactory and a spot in the lee of Robbers Nob off the shoal can give better protection.

A peaceful walk can be taken along the shore and grounds of Port Neville. The log buildings beyond the public dock have such an interesting history that there has been considerable pressure from cruisers and local inhabitants to have the area declared a Provincial Park. The log buildings date from 1916 when the Hansen family first settled here. For many years when logging and fishing were the economic life-blood of many small operators working the coast this was a center of activity. The small log store which operated from 1924 to 1960 is still standing and the daughter of the original settlers lives here and acts as a postmistress but there are no facilities ashore. Deer are often seen browsing in the open green spaces.

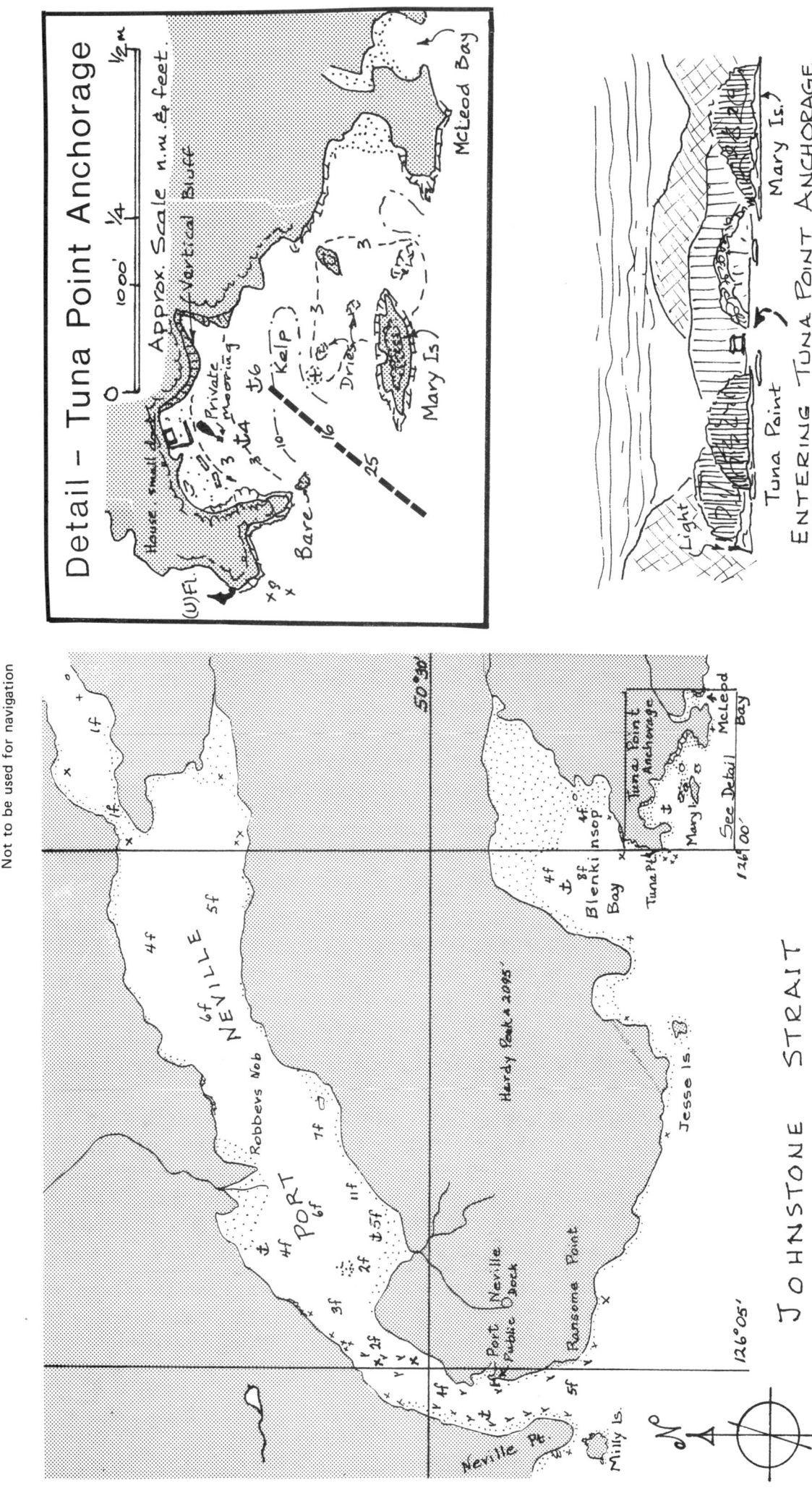

PORT NEVILLE

Not to be used for navigation

Detail – Tuna Point Anchorage

Approx. Scale n.m. & feet.

Vertical Bluff

McLeod Bay

Private mooring

House (small float)

Kelp

Dries

Mary Is.

Bare

(W)Fl.

ENTERING TUNA POINT ANCHORAGE

Tuna Point

Mary Is. →

Light

PORT NEVILLE

Robbers Nob

Hardy Peak 2095

Jesse Is.

Milly Is.

Neville Pt.

Ransome Point

Port Neville Dock

Port Public Dock

Blenkinsop Bay

Tuna Point Anchorage

Mary Is.

See Detail

McLeod Bay

50°30'

126°00'

126°05'

JOHNSTONE STRAIT

PORT HARVEY, LAGOON COVE and other anchorages

This inlet indents the coast for 3 miles off Johnstone Strait, between East and West Cracroft Islands.* The entrance is wide, but there are several dangers that require attention when turning off the Strait. Broken Islands, a group consisting of two large islands, some islets and many rocks, lies to the east of the point where Havannah Channel joins Johnstone Strait. Escape Reef is about .5 miles off the south shore of West Cracroft Is. and 2 miles west of Broken Is. Hull Rock is a detached rock off the southeast shore of West Cracroft Is. and about .75 miles west of Domville Point. Slightly favor the southeast side of the passage to clear all dangers in the area.

A number of pretty anchorages with good holding are available. **Open Cove** is a small cove on the east side of Port Harvey between Transit and Harvey Points. It can be used as an anchorage during easterly winds, but is open to westerlies and the swell they create in Johnstone Strait.

A few sparsely scattered houses and private docks dot the shoreline of the upper end of **Port Harvey**. Though anchorage may be taken NNW of Mist Island, it is fairly restricted by rocks. A large area where anchorage may be taken is off the large private floats and dolphins, north of Range Island. Northeast winds can affect the anchorage so set your anchor well. Do not anchor northeast of Range Island as the bottom shoals until becoming a marshy area.

Cruisers who wish to top up their fuel or visit a lovely area often take a side trip via Havannah and Chatham Channels to Minstrel Island. From this spot a route can be chosen which reaches Greenway Sound and Sullivan Bay and proceeds to Queen Charlotte Strait. Havannah Channel leads to two attractive anchorages before approaching Chatham Channel. **Boughey Bay** is a spacious anchorage with good holding in 4 - 6 fathoms, mud. It can be affected by southerly winds and you must not anchor too far into the bay as the head is shoal. A few miles to the north is **Burial Cove** where excellent protection can be obtained in similar depths.

Chatham Channel is best traversed near slack water as 4- to 6-knot currents are found in the narrow, shallow channel where kelp shows at mid-tide. Range markers must be watched carefully and speeds should be kept down so that your wake does not disturb the safe course of other vessels in this restricted channel.

Cutter Cove is a long, narrow bay opening off the northeast end of Chatham Channel. The anchorage can become lumpy when winds pick up; anchor on the north shore during westerlies and on the south shore during easterlies. There is excellent crabbing here.

Minstrel Island was once a popular resort but now has limited facilities. Passage through the Blow Hole, a narrow channel separating Minstrel Island from East Cracroft Island, must be made at high water via a mid-channel course, by vessels drawing no more than 1.8 m (6 feet). Beyond the Blow Hole is the entrance to **Lagoon Cove** where good anchorage can be taken by many vessels. Lagoon Cove Marina is a popular stop-over for fuel, water, moorage and supplies. The nightly BBQs are becoming a legend! A walk through the creatively decorated grounds (to receptacles where sorted garbage may be left) is sure to bring chuckles to all ages. About 6 miles to the southwest in Clio Channel is a beautiful refuge in **Potts Lagoon**. There are no facilities but the outer coves and inner lagoon provide fascinating exploration by dinghy.

*When proceeding west in Johnstone Strait the next anchorages are at Boat Bay, .5 mile east of Swaine Point (entering along the shore of W. Cracroft) to gain protection from west winds or 1.5 miles further west to a bight opposite Sophia Islands (avoid offlying rocks) when winds are easterly.

PORT HARVEY & VICINITY

```
0        1        2        3
```
Approx. Scale n.m.

Not to be used for navigation

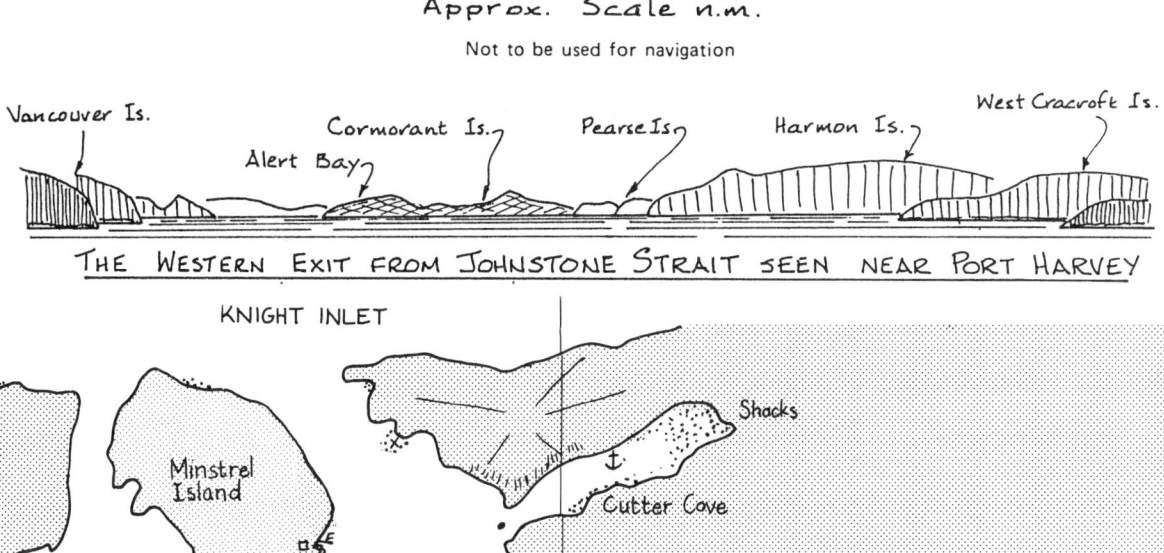

Vancouver Is.   Alert Bay   Cormorant Is.   Pearse Is.   Harmon Is.   West Cracroft Is.

THE WESTERN EXIT FROM JOHNSTONE STRAIT SEEN NEAR PORT HARVEY

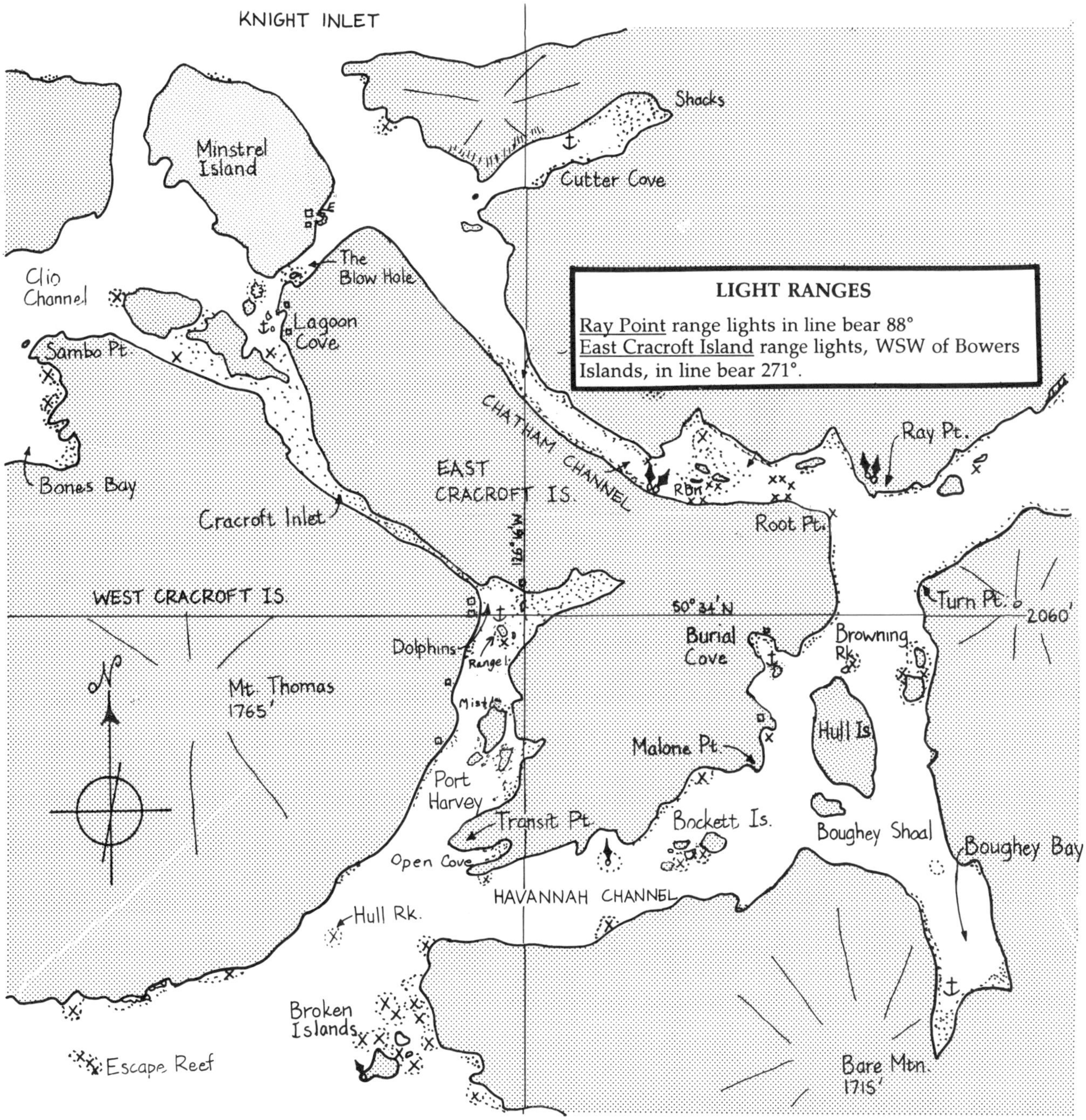

KNIGHT INLET

Minstrel Island

Shacks

Cutter Cove

Clio Channel

The Blow Hole

Lagoon Cove

Sambo Pt

Bones Bay

CHATHAM CHANNEL

LIGHT RANGES

Ray Point range lights in line bear 88°
East Cracroft Island range lights, WSW of Bowers Islands, in line bear 271°.

Ray Pt.

EAST CRACROFT IS.

Rbn

Root Pt.

Cracroft Inlet

WEST CRACROFT IS.

50° 34' N

Turn Pt.   2060'

Dolphins

Range

Burial Cove

Browning Rk.

Mt. Thomas 1765'

Mistle

Malone Pt.

Hull Is.

Port Harvey

Transit Pt.

Bockett Is.

Boughey Shoal

Boughey Bay

Open Cove

HAVANNAH CHANNEL

Hull Rk.

Broken Islands

Bare Mtn. 1715'

✗✗ Escape Reef

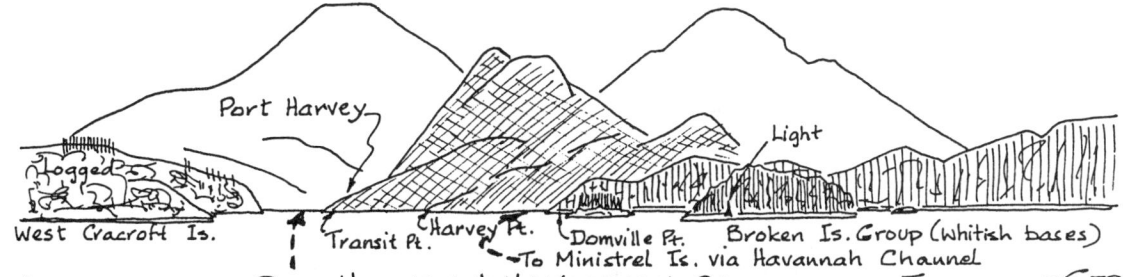

Port Harvey   Light

Logged

West Cracroft Is.   Transit Pt.   Harvey Pt.   Domville Pt.   Broken Is. Group (whitish bases)
To Ministrel Is. via Havannah Channel

APPROACH TO PORT HARVEY & HAVANNAH CHANNEL FROM JOHNSTONE STRAIT

GREENWAY SOUND, BLUNDEN and ALLISON HARBORS

Queen Charlotte Strait may be reached either by proceeding west through Johnstone Strait or by following a protected but very indirect course from Port Harvey to Minstrel Island and crossing Knight Inlet to follow Tribune and Sutlej Channels to Wells Passage which joins the Strait. This is a popular cruising area in itself as there are many spots where anchorage may be taken in addition to marina facilities which can satisfy cruising needs. If prolonged exploration of this area is planned you should have a copy of John Chappell's excellent guide, *Cruising Beyond Desolation Sound.* If your destination is Alaska, a visit to this delightful area might be best postponed until the return trip.

Several marina facilities in the area provide fuel, groceries, laundry, liquor, ice and moorage; all marinas monitor VHF Ch. 73. Services and facilities range from basic to luxurious and they are constantly being improved and enlarged. Since the cruising/business season is very short for these establishments, higher fees for services are charged than those in more populated areas with a longer business season. In addition to cruisers in their own boats, many visitors arrive by float plane to enjoy fishing, clean air, and a relaxed atmosphere.

On the NW coast of Gilford Island, opposite the E end of Baker Island is **Echo Bay Marine Park** which is undeveloped. Nearby are **Echo Bay Resort** and **Windsong Sea Village Resort of Echo Bay**. Further to the W, on the N shore of Broughton Island is a sizable bay off Greenway Sound where deluxe **Greenway Sound Marine Resort** and restaurant are located. Just 5 miles W of the junction of Greenway Sound and Sutlej Channel on the N shore of North Broughton Island is **Sullivan Bay Marine Resort**. This location is the site of logging operations which began in the area almost 100 years ago and is now a popular reprovisioning and fuel stop for northbound vessels. Clearence must be given to rocks near Atkinson Island and shoals off the E entrance point of the bay.

Dickson Island (50°50.50'N 126°56.00'W) at the south end of Wells Passage provides anchorage near Queen Charlotte Strait which gives protection in all but southerly weather. Approach from the south between Vincent and Percy Islands, then pass between Broughton and Dickson Islands. On at the NE end of the island is a small cove where anchorage can be taken on the eastern side. Avoid the mud shoals in the western part of the bay which dry at low water.

Blunden Harbour is about 22 miles from Sullivan Bay and is the next spot where anchorage may be taken by cruisers proceeding up the coast. Careful use of CHS Chart #3548 is necessary to thread a route through numerous rocks and dangers near the entrance. Anchorage may be found off the beach in 7 fathoms, mud. The abandoned Indian burial site on Byrnes Island and the shell middens ashore must not be disturbed as they are protected by law.

The turn to **Allison Harbour**, the next jumping off point for vessels heading up past Cape Caution, is about 13 miles NW of Blunden Harbour. There are many outlying rocks off the coast on the north side of Queen Charlotte Strait and caution is needed when traveling in this area. Entry to Allison Harbour is between Ray Island and City Point. Depending on the direction of the wind, anchorage may be taken north of the old settlement (8 fathoms), 1 mile north of the 2.4 m (8 foot) drying rock, or near the head of the harbor in 4 fathoms. All locations have good holding, mud bottom. Formerly an active logging center, the settlement is now abandoned and there are no facilities ashore. Aptly named **Murray Labyrinth** is in the middle of the group of islands northwest of City Point. The intricate entrance to this magical hideaway demands vigilance and calm nerves, but as an extra reward, you may be welcomed by the resident grey whale. It is essential to use CHS Chart #3921, details of Allison Harbour and its approach.

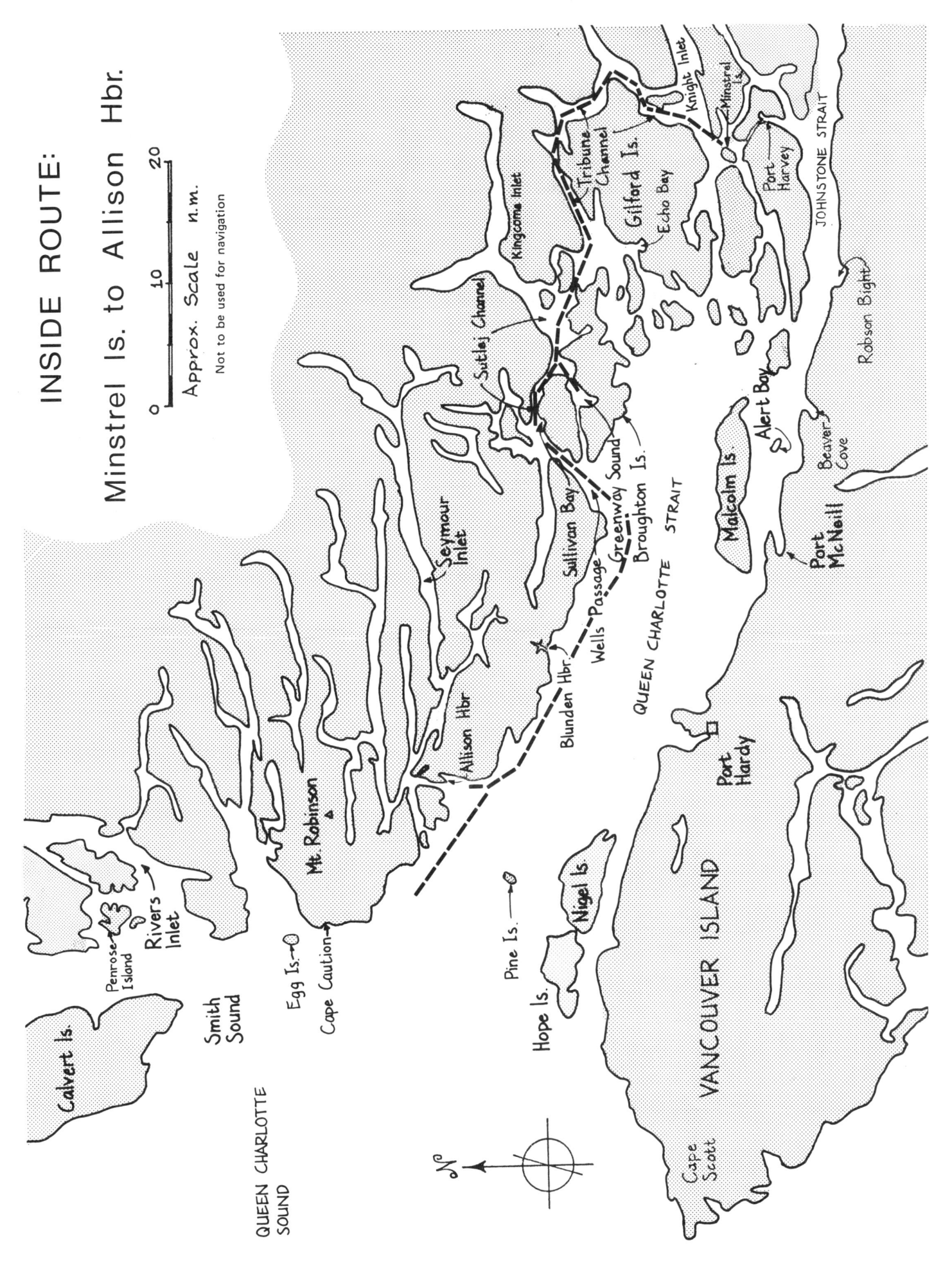

INSIDE ROUTE:

Minstrel Is. to Allison Hbr.

Approx. Scale   n.m.

0   10   20

Not to be used for navigation

Calvert Is.

Penrose Island

Rivers Inlet

Smith Sound

QUEEN CHARLOTTE SOUND

Egg Is.

Cape Caution

Mt. Robinson

Seymour Inlet

Sutlej Channel

Kingcome Inlet

Tribune Channel

Knight Inlet

Minstrel Is.

Gilford Is.

Echo Bay

Port Harvey

JOHNSTONE STRAIT

Allison Hbr.

Sullivan Bay

Greenway Sound

Broughton Is.

Wells Passage

Blunden Hbr.

QUEEN CHARLOTTE STRAIT

Robson Bight

Malcolm Is.

Alert Bay

Beaver Cove

Port McNeill

Pine Is.

Nigel Is.

Hope Is.

Port Hardy

VANCOUVER ISLAND

Cape Scott

N

ALERT BAY, CORMORANT ISLAND

This town is the center of much of the activity in northern Vancouver waters. The town and a major Nimpkish Indian village are almost inseparable, and lie along the southern inner curve of Cormorant Island. The comma-shaped island lies where Johnstone Strait ends and Broughton Strait begins.

Southwest of Alert Bay the Nimpkish River flows out of Vancouver Island. A large bank, which dries in some places and is shoal elsewhere, extends a considerable distance out from the Vancouver Island shore. Two beacons mark the edge of these shoals. Vessels should stay well over to the Alert Bay side from these beacons, and as the currents can be strong the course should be checked often. There are many wharves and docks along the waterfront. Perhaps the simplest way to orient oneself is by referring to the totem poles.

Near the southern end of the town the totem poles in the clear space of the Nimpkish Burial Grounds stand out. A walk along the road will give you a closer look at these impressive poles. Please heed the posted signs asking visitors to stay off the sacred grounds.

A few hundred yards or so to the north is a government wharf and a float. There is seldom much space here as it is in the center of town. A short distance beyond is a fuel dock.

About 1 mile northwest of the Burial Grounds is a tall totem pole on the hill behind the old three-story Indian School. At one time this was the tallest totem pole in the world. About midway between this totem pole and the burial grounds (north of the ferry dock) is a long, angled rock breakwater. The entrance to the small craft floats is around the northern end of the breakwater. When the fishing fleet is out there is plenty of room at the floats. But when the fleet is in port there may not even be sufficient space for rafting.

A strong current runs along the shore which must be taken into account when maneuvering in this harbor. The many facilities include: a supermarket, laundromat, hospital, drug store, post office, hotels, and restaurants. Several craft shops are on the main street. Near the tall totem pole is a Long House where Indian dancers perform in costume when arrangements have been made by 15 or more people. The U'Mista Cultural Center and Museum have an exceptional collection of Native Indian masks and other artifacts and are well worth visiting.

On the hill above the town the antenna of Alert Bay Coast Guard VHF Radio is conspicuous. The weather broadcasts on VHF Ch. 21, 26, and 2054 KHz are given several times daily. They are a welcome source of information along this coast.

Some significant distances related to Alert Bay are as follows:

Campbell River to Alert Bay	83 miles
Kelsey Bay to Alert Bay	41 miles
Port Harvey to Alert Bay	29 miles
Alert Bay to Sointula	6 miles
Alert Bay to Port Hardy	26 miles
Alert Bay to Blunden Harbor	24 miles

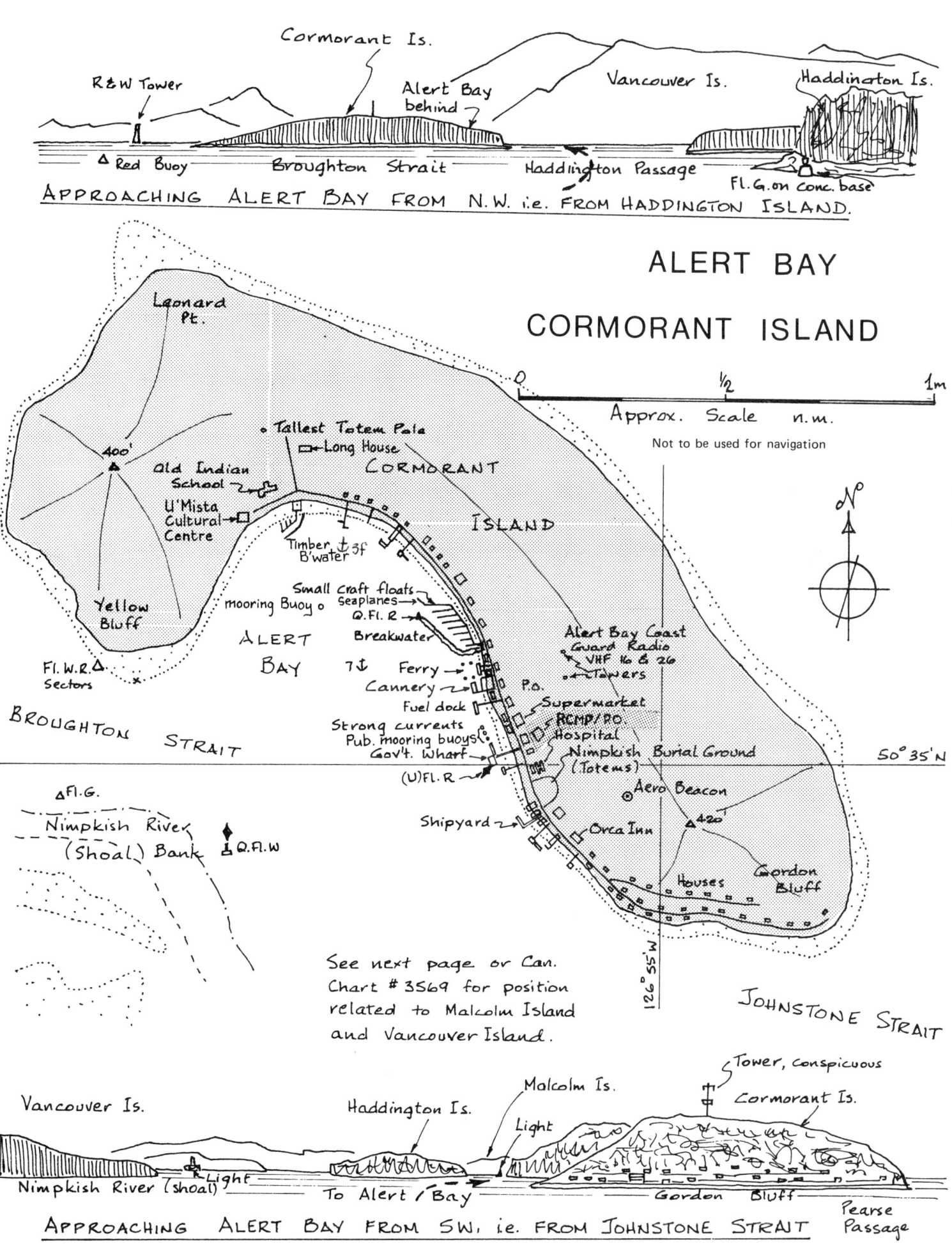

APPROACHING ALERT BAY FROM N.W. i.e. FROM HADDINGTON ISLAND.

Cormorant Is.
R&W Tower
Alert Bay behind
Vancouver Is.
Haddington Is.
△ Red Buoy
Broughton Strait
Haddington Passage
Fl.G. on conc. base

ALERT BAY
CORMORANT ISLAND

Leonard Pt.

0 .... ½ 1m
Approx. Scale n.m.
Not to be used for navigation

Tallest Totem Pole
Long House
CORMORANT
400'
Old Indian School
ISLAND
U'Mista Cultural Centre
Timber B'water ⚓ 3f
Small Craft floats
Seaplanes →
Q.Fl. R
Breakwater
mooring Buoy o
ALERT
BAY
Yellow Bluff
Alert Bay Coast Guard Radio
VHF 16 & 26
Towers
Fl. W.R. △
Sectors
7⚓ Ferry →
Cannery
P.O.
Supermarket
RCMP/PO
Hospital
BROUGHTON STRAIT
Fuel dock
Strong currents
Pub. mooring buoys
Gov't. Wharf
Nimpkish Burial Ground (Totems)
50°35'N
(U)Fl. R →
△Fl.G.
Nimpkish River (Shoal) Bank
⚓ Q.Fl.W
Aero Beacon
420'
Shipyard →
Orca Inn
Gordon Bluff
Houses

See next page or Can. Chart #3569 for position related to Malcolm Island and Vancouver Island.

JOHNSTONE STRAIT

APPROACHING ALERT BAY FROM SW. i.e. FROM JOHNSTONE STRAIT

Vancouver Is.
Haddington Is.
Malcolm Is.
Light
Tower, conspicuous
Cormorant Is.
Nimpkish River (shoal)
Light
To Alert Bay
Gordon Bluff
Pearse Passage

SOINTULA, MALCOLM ISLAND

Malcolm Island was settled by Finnish immigrants of the Kalevan Kansa Colonization Company in 1900 in one of the first attempts at a socialist cooperative commune. The hard working settlers made their living from fishing, farming and logging. Sointula, which means "Place of Harmony," was the site of their main village. Personality conflicts, particularly with the irascible leader, caused a break-up in 1905. Many of the original residents remained and the community survived in a slightly different form. A walk through the cemetery gives proof of the strong family ties of the Finnish forebears.

The calm simplicity of Sointula, the neat cottages with their carefully tended flower gardens and the industrious residents gave this place a feeling of peace, in contrast to the raw, rough land around it. Much of the success was due to the fact that there was no liquor, no religious intolerance and no police force on the island, until the 1960's when the island became popular with hippies.

Malcolm Island and Sointula are connected to the B.C. road system by a three-town ferry that calls at Port McNeill and Alert Bay. The ferry dock is northwest of Dickenson Point. The small craft harbor is about 1 mile further into Rough Bay, behind an L-shaped breakwater.

This is a busy place during the fishing season as many vessels from southern B.C. use Sointula as a base in summer. In addition to the old wharf and four finger floats, a newer wharf and three finger floats have been added to the north. Both sets of floats are approached around the end of the breakwater.

A harbormaster, based in the small hut on the old wharf, controls all berthing in the small craft harbor and collects government fees. Check with the harbormaster on arrival, or if after hours find any berth and check in the next morning.

At the head of the wharf and across the road is the marine hardware branch of the Cooperative Store. The main store, post office, hotel, restaurant, and a museum are at the center of town, a pleasant walk from the wharf.

Just across Broughton Strait from Sointula, on Vancouver Island is Port McNeill, a modern town, with many facilities described on the following page. The approach from Alert Bay to Sointula or Port McNeill passes Haddington Island. A traffic separation scheme (for cruise ships and large freighters) is established for each side of the island. Lights mark the reefs, ledges, and shoals. The passages are wide enough to cause small vessels few problems if the lights and marks are carefully identified.

Continuing west from Sointula through Broughton Strait, the route enters Queen Charlotte Strait after passing Pulteney Point Lighthouse. This lighthouse on the southwest tip of Malcolm Island is an important weather reporting station whose deep fog horn can be very welcome in poor visibility.

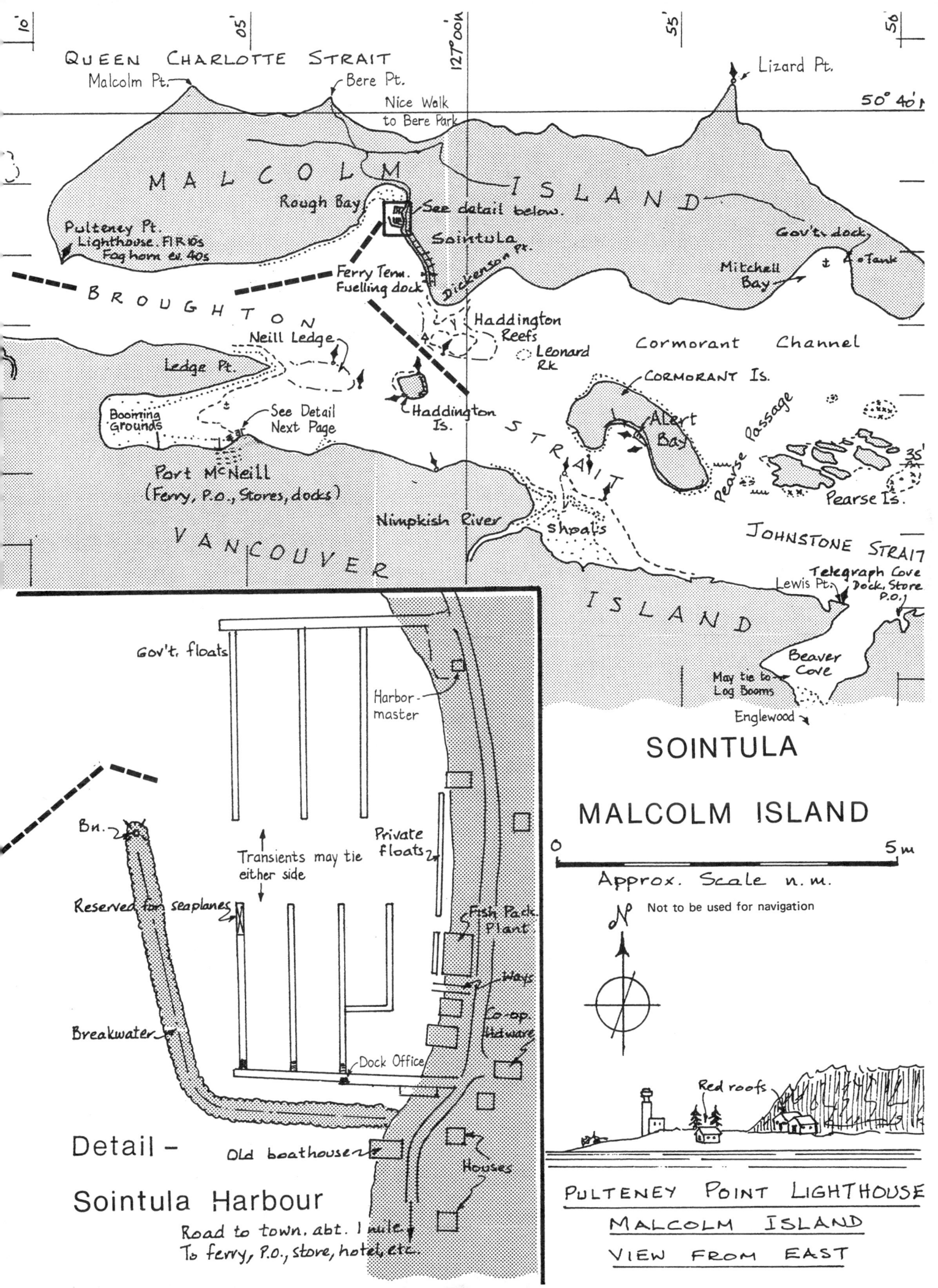

QUEEN CHARLOTTE STRAIT

Malcolm Pt.

Bere Pt.

Nice Walk to Bere Park

127°00N

55'

Lizard Pt.

50° 40'N

M A L C O L M   I S L A N D

Rough Bay

See detail below.

Sointula

Gov't. dock

Pulteney Pt.
Lighthouse. Fl R 10s
Fog horn ev. 40s

Ferry Term.
Fuelling dock

Dickenson Pt.

Mitchell Bay

Tank

B R O U G H T O N

Neill Ledge

Haddington Reefs

Leonard Rk

Cormorant   Channel

CORMORANT IS.

Ledge Pt.

Booming Grounds

See Detail Next Page

Haddington Is.

Alert Bay

Pearse Passage

35'

Port McNeill
(Ferry, P.O., Stores, docks)

S T R A I T

Pearse Is.

V A N C O U V E R

Nimpkish River

Shoals

JOHNSTONE STRAIT

I S L A N D

Lewis Pt.

Telegraph Cove
Dock, Store
P.O.,

Beaver Cove

May tie to
Log Booms

Englewood

SOINTULA

MALCOLM ISLAND

0   5 m

Approx. Scale n.m.

Not to be used for navigation

N

Gov't. floats

Harbor-master

Transients may tie
either side

Private floats

Reserved for seaplanes

Fish Pack. Plant

Breakwater

Ways

Bn.

Co-op Hdware

Dock Office

Detail –

Sointula Harbour

Old boathouses

Houses

Road to town. abt. 1 mile.
To ferry, P.O., store, hotel, etc.

Red roofs

PULTENEY   POINT   LIGHTHOUSE

MALCOLM   ISLAND

VIEW   FROM   EAST

PORT McNEILL

At this bustling logging and tourist town on the south side of Broughton Strait, the municipal floats and floatplane dock are sandwiched between two sets of breakwaters. The high structure of the ferry dock extending northeast from the end of the causeway is prominent from a distance. For a mile or two the coast is lined with neat homes, and a cement block seawall protects the foreshore against winter storm action. The breakwater along the northwestern side of the basin backs on to a large dump site where logging trucks unload. The inner part of the bay is a booming ground.

This busy town has become such a popular provisioning and fueling stop for vessels cruising the coast that sometimes during July and August it is quite overcrowded. Federal Docks, intended for use by commercial fishermen lead off the causeway. Here overflow pleasure craft from the Municipal Floats are often rafted alongside workboats as space permits. Rafting (sometimes as much as three abreast) is often the norm. The alternative is laying at anchor on the north side of the channel.

Moorage is under the control of the harbormaster who should be contacted prior to entering the harbor by phoning (250) 956-3881 or calling VHF Ch. 73 which is monitored from 8 a.m. to 7 p.m. Moorage is on a first-come, first-serve basis; reservations are not accepted. Water and 15 and 30 amp power are on most docks. A short walk from the basin leads to the town center where there is a laundromat, telephone, post office, liquor store, marine repair and supply store and several supermarkets (which will deliver groceries to you boat). The friendly shopkeepers and accessible, well stocked stores make this an excellent location for provisioning. Showers with towels supplied are available at the Delwood Hotel for $5. Arrangements for the purchase of propane can be made at the fuel dock.

The tri-Island ferry route links Port McNeill to Alert Bay on Cormorant Island and Sointula on Malcolm Island. The town is linked by Highway 19 to Port Hardy to the north and southern Vancouver Island and bus and air services operate daily. Airplane and boat charters for fishing nearby waters and inland lakes as well as whale watching trips to nearby Robson Bight and Telegraph Cove (famous for its whale rubbing stone beach) have added much tourist activity.

Named after Captain William McNeill who explored this part of the coast in 1825, Port McNeill's first permanent white settlement was established in 1937 by a lumber company. The economy continues to be based on logging as the old steam donkey featured on the shore and a logging museum demonstrate. A Logger Sports Day, held annually in June attracts competitors from far afield to compete in such events as log scaling, log birling and log splitting. Incidentally, the world's largest burl weighing more than 22 tons measures 14 m (45 feet) in circumference can be seen about 2 miles north of the town on Hwy. 19.

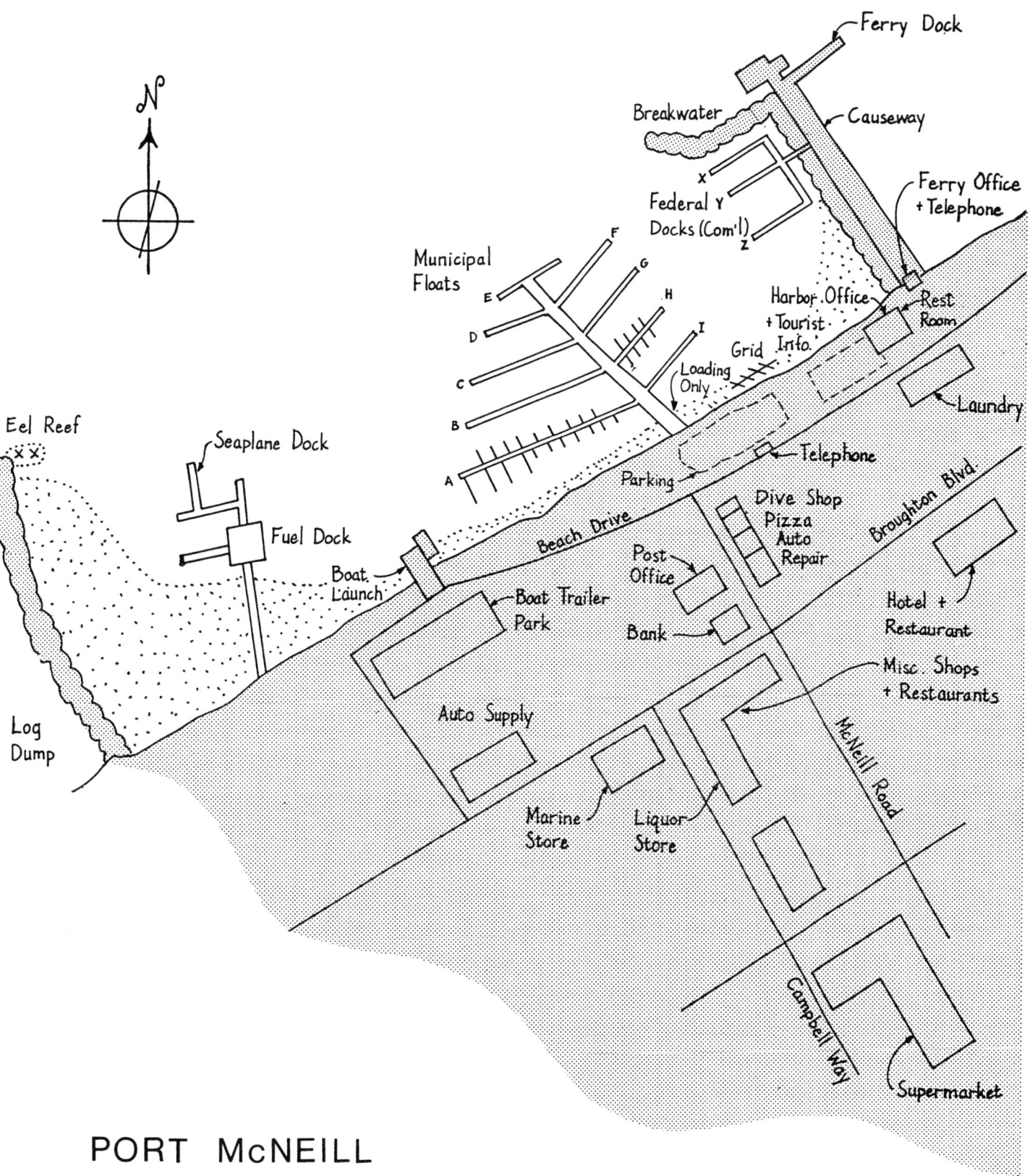

N

Ferry Dock
Breakwater — Causeway
Ferry Office + Telephone
Federal Docks (Com'l)
X Y Z
Municipal Floats
F
G
E
H
D
I
Harbor Office + Tourist Info.
Rest Room
Grid
C
Loading Only
B
Laundry
A
Eel Reef
X X
Seaplane Dock
Parking
Telephone
Dive Shop
Pizza
Auto Repair
Broughton Blvd
Beach Drive
Fuel Dock
Boat Launch
Post Office
Bank
Hotel + Restaurant
Boat Trailer Park
Misc. Shops + Restaurants
Log Dump
Auto Supply
McNeill Road
Marine Store
Liquor Store
Campbell Way
Supermarket

PORT McNEILL

Not to be used for navigation

PORT HARDY

A pleasant, small town situated near the northern end of Vancouver Island, this is the last fuel and provisioning center before sailing to the north. It marks the end of the island highway from the south and is the terminus for the B.C. Ferry, *Queen of the North,* which sails to Prince Rupert. Although many vessels depart from Port McNeill for the Queen Charlotte Sound crossing, some choose to leave from Port Hardy.

Hardy Bay is large, and marked at its eastern end by a light on Masterman Islands about .5 mile off Dillon Point. **Port Hardy** lies at the southern end of the bay, beyond the two shoal bars marked by lighted buoys at their seaward ends. A government wharf lies between the buoys, but the small craft harbor lies beyond the southern shoal buoy. Pass on the east side of the buoy before entering between the two breakwaters. The harbor offers two small craft facilities.

The government wharf is popular with commercial fishing vessels but can be used by cruisers when space is available. Locally called "Fisherman's Wharf, during the fishing season it is extremely busy and rafting may be necessary.

Quarterdeck Marina, in the southern part of the harbor, offers transient moorage. Reservations are recommended during July and August when space is at a premium; call ahead on VHF Ch. 73. A marine supply store, showers, laundry, and other facilities are at the head of the dock and a restaurant is nearby. Fuel may be obtained at a Chevron station at Quarterdeck Marina or just outside the breakwaters to the north at an Esso Marine Station. Both stations are very busy in summer, and short waits may be necessary.

Goletas (Schooner) Channel leads WNW from Hardy Bay to the northern end of Vancouver Island at Cape Sutil. Vessels heading for the west coast of Vancouver Island or north to Rose Harbour in the Queen Charlotte Islands use this channel to reach **Bull Harbour** on Hope Island, as the departure point for these destinations.

The route for transiting Queen Charlotte Strait follows Goletas Channel to Noble Islets where a light is located. Here, Christie Passage separates Hurst and Balaklava Islands. Hurst, Bell and adjacent small islets are included in **God's Pocket Marine Park**. Harlequin Bay on the north side of Hurst Island provides sheltered anchorage from S and W winds. God's Pocket Resort is in the indentation on the west side of Hurst Island off Christie Passage. This small bay even though it is hardly noticeable on regular charts provides adequate shelter close to Queen Charlotte Sound. **God's Pocket Resort** welcomes cruisers, with a small dock where moorage may be arranged and shower facilities are available. The two white tire floats in the bay are often used by rafted fishing vessels, leaving little space for anchoring.

Scarlett Point Lighthouse on the northeast tip of Balaklava Island is 2 miles northwest of God's Pocket. This is a good departure or destination point for the crossing of Queen Charlotte Sound. The favored northbound route proceeds northwesterly in Gordon Channel passing west of Pine Island. The course is then changed more to the north to pass Cape Caution and Egg Island across South Passage to Fitz Hugh Sound.

If the weather deteriorates after leaving God's Pocket, refuge may be found in the Walker Group, between Kent and Staples Is. Avoid Nye Rock and Sussex Reefs southeast of Redfern Island.

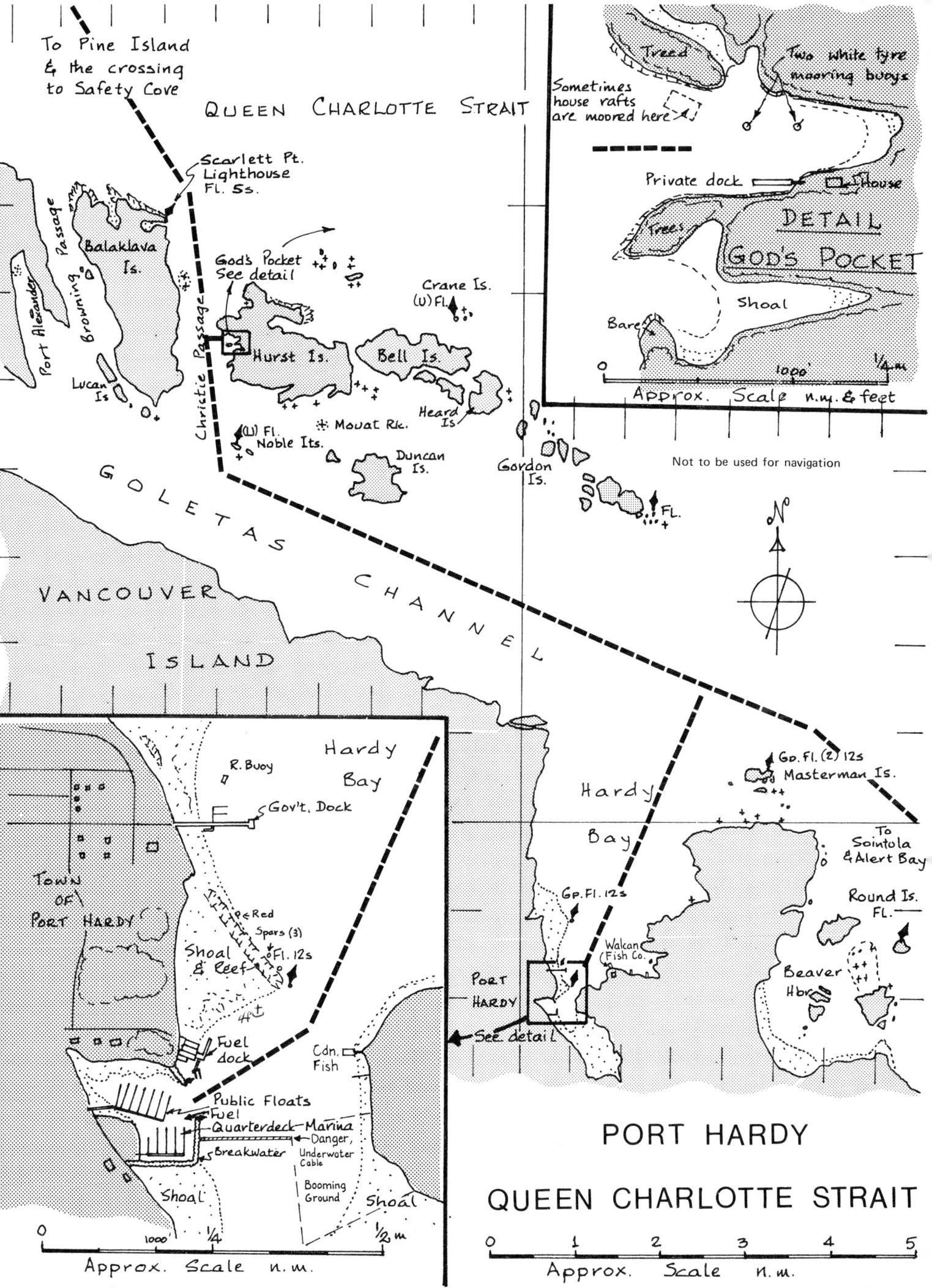

To Pine Island
& the crossing
to Safety Cove

QUEEN CHARLOTTE STRAIT

Scarlett Pt.
Lighthouse
Fl. 5s.

Balaklava
Is.

Browning Passage

Port Alexander

Lucan
Is.

Christie Passage

God's Pocket
See detail

Crane Is.
(U) Fl.

Hurst Is.

Bell Is.

Heard
Is.

Mouat Rk.

(U) Fl.
Noble Its.

Duncan
Is.

Gordon
Is.

Fl.

GOLETAS

CHANNEL

VANCOUVER

ISLAND

Treed

Two white tyre
mooring buoys

Sometimes
house rafts
are moored here

Private dock

House

DETAIL

GOD'S POCKET

Trees

Shoal

Bare

0   1000'   1/4 n.m.
Approx. Scale n.m. & feet

Not to be used for navigation

N

Hardy
Bay

R. Buoy

Gov't. Dock

Red
Spars (3)

Fl. 12s.

Shoal
& Reef

4'

TOWN
OF
PORT HARDY

Fuel
dock

Cdn.
Fish

Public Floats
Fuel
Quarterdeck Marina
Danger,
Underwater
Cable

Breakwater

Shoal

Booming
Ground

Shoal

0   1000'   1/4   1/2 m
Approx. Scale n.m.

Hardy

Bay

Gp. Fl. (2) 12s
Masterman Is.

To
Sointula
& Alert Bay

Gp.Fl. 12s

Round Is.
Fl.

Walcan
Fish Co.

Beaver
Hbr.

PORT
HARDY

See detail

PORT HARDY

QUEEN CHARLOTTE STRAIT

0   1   2   3   4   5
Approx.   Scale   n.m.

Kwakiutl Totem
(Eagle and Grizzly Bear)

Peaceful Oliver Cove Marine Park off Reid Passage

Boat Bluff Lighthouse on Sarah Passage

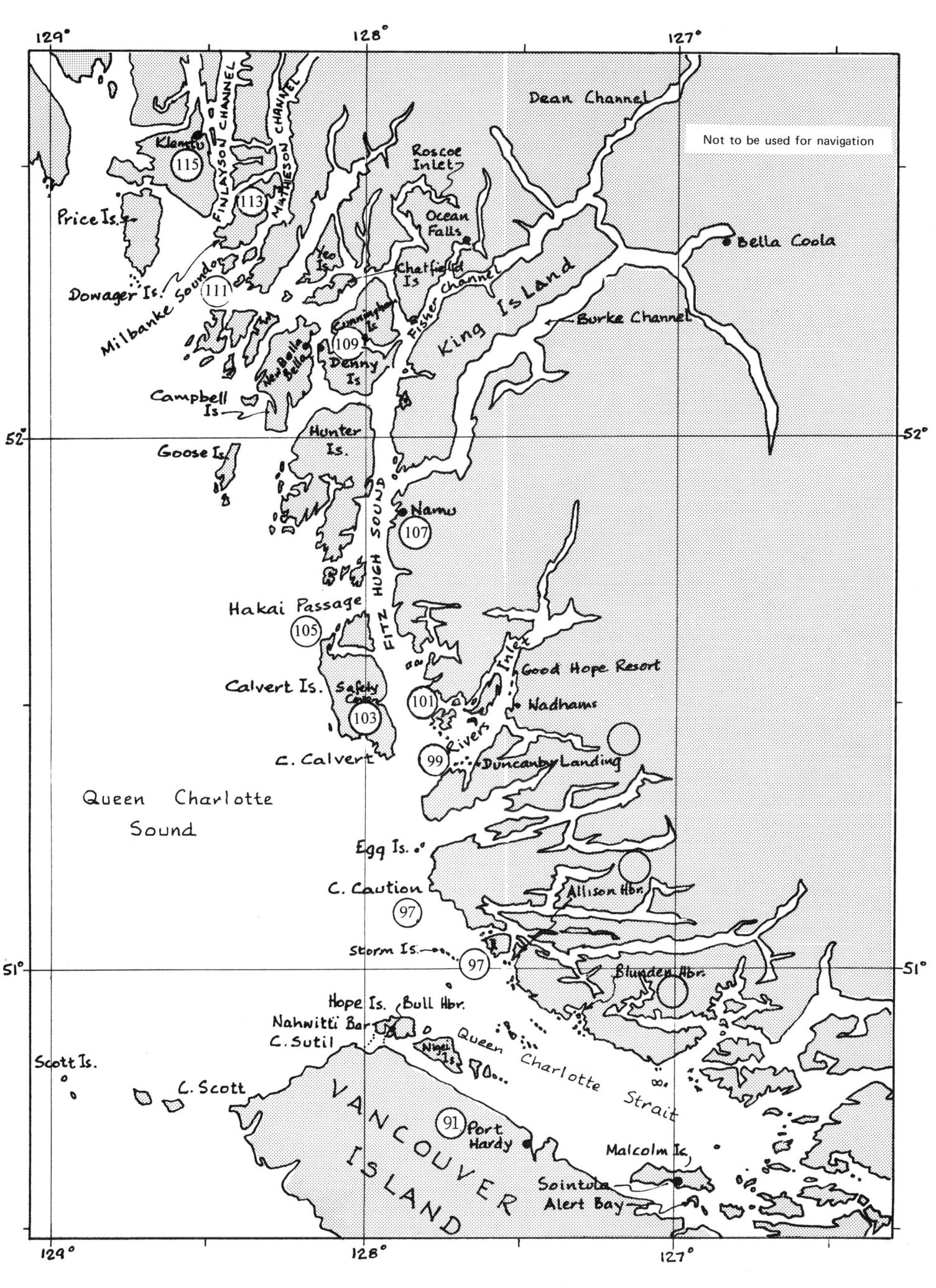

Not to be used for navigation

129°   128°   127°

Dean Channel

Roscoe Inlet?

Ocean Falls

Bella Coola

Klemtu (115)

(113)

Price Is.

Yeo Is.

Chatfield Is.

Dowager Is.

(111)

Milbanke Sound

King Island

Burke Channel

Cunningham Is.

(109)

New Bella Bella

Denny Is.

Campbell Is.

52°

Hunter Is.

Goose Is.

Namu (107)

Hakai Passage

(105)

Calvert Is.

Safety Cove

Good Hope Resort

(101)

Wadhams

(103)

C. Calvert

Rivers Inlet

(99)

Duncanby Landing

Queen Charlotte Sound

Egg Is.

C. Caution

(97)

Allison Hbr.

Storm Is.

(97)

Blunden Hbr.

51°

Hope Is.

Bull Hbr.

Nahwitti Bar

C. Sutil

Nigei Is.

Queen Charlotte Strait

Scott Is.

C. Scott

VANCOUVER

Malcolm Is.

(91)

Port Hardy

Sointula

ISLAND

Alert Bay

129°   128°   127°

ROUTES PAST CAPE CAUTION

The crossing of Queen Charlotte Sound past Cape Caution is one of the key passages of the trip. Departure can be made from either Port McNeill or Port Hardy. If you are departing from Greenway Sound in a low-powered vessel you will probably be making the crossing in two days with a stop-over along the way. The route from Port Hardy is detailed on page 92.

The most direct route from Port McNeill uses Pulteney Point as a departure and a course is laid to Echo Island in the Deserters Group. This takes you about .25 miles west of Ewen Rock, where if the weather is deteriorating you can seek refuge in Miles Inlet, shown on the following page, or in the Walker Group where a protected anchorage is found between Kent and Staples Islands approaching from the west. A course change in the vicinity of Ewen Rock to clear Cape Caution by about a mile will be followed by a further change to clear Egg Island and northward to the desired anchorage.

In clear weather these routes have interest but offer no problems other than those that nature provides in the wind and sea. The entire coast is well marked with lights and lighthouses that provide assurance and useful bearings. Summer fog can be disconcerting but with the help of a professionally swung compass, a depth sounder and fog signals at key lighthouses, navigation of the crossing can be safely made. Of course radar, GPS and electronic plotters assist greatly in reducing navigational concerns. Pine and Egg Island Lighthouses are manned but the light at Cape Caution is unmanned.

Two elements affect the sea conditions on a passage through Queen Charlotte Strait: weather and the state of the tide when reaching Cape Caution. Unfortunately you can't always adjust your departure to take advantage of the optimum time for both of these considerations. By leaving early in the morning from either Port McNeill or Port Hardy you can complete a good part of the voyage before the afternoon northwesterlies pick up resulting in headwinds and seas that slow progress and make the boat's motion uncomfortable. On the other hand, by departing with an ebb tide and timing your arrival off Cape Caution at low water, the vessel will also get a lift from the a flood tide as you pass through South Passage and enter Fitz Hugh Sound.

Most cruisers usually like to get an early start regardless of tidal considerations, especially if they have a low-powered vessel. If weather conditions dictate a stop-over then you can look for the most convenient refuge that can be reached depending on the direction of the wind and seas. Several anchorages are available it may be prudent to make the passage in two or more steps as long as the new course is carefully plotted to avoid intervening dangers. For details on anchorages south of Miles Inlet (Blunden Harbor and Allison Harbour) see page 84.

Miles Inlet is a wonderful anchorage on the north side of the Strait, a convenient refuge regardless of your departure point or whether you are north- or southbound. The light on McEwen Rock makes a prominent landmark both for avoiding coastal dangers and as an important marker of the approach to the Inlet one mile to the east. For details see the following page.

Gods Pocket — Scarlett Pt. Lighthouse

Hurst Is.

APPROACHING SCARLETT POINT LIGHTHOUSE FROM WNW, about 3 miles

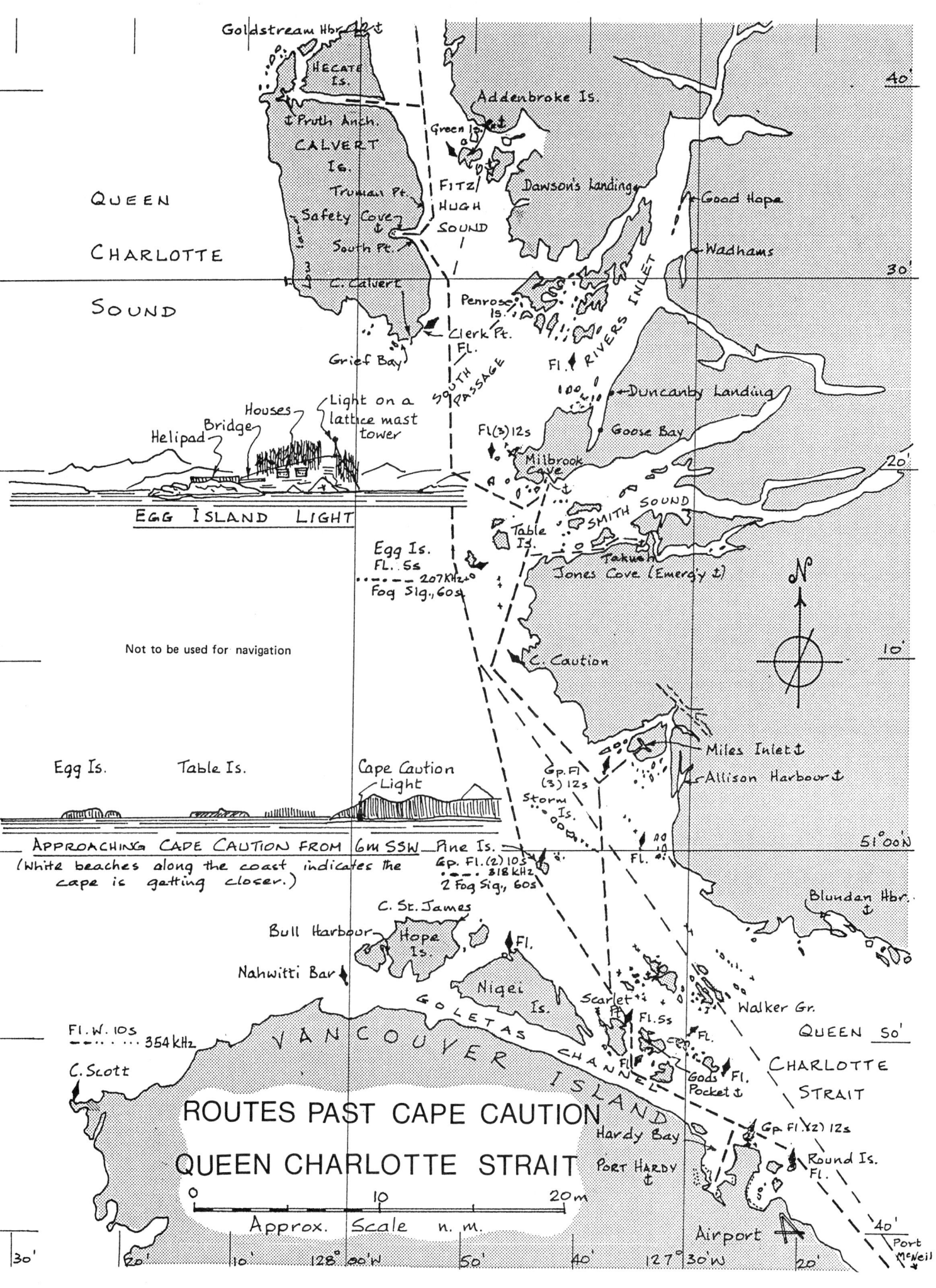

Goldstream Hbr ⚓

HECATE Is.

⚓ Pruth Anch.

CALVERT Is.

Truman Pt.

Safety Cove ⚓

South Pt.

C. Calvert

Clerk Pt. Fl.

Grief Bay

QUEEN

CHARLOTTE

SOUND

Addenbroke Is.

Green Is. ⚓

FITZ/HUGH SOUND

Dawson's Landing

Good Hope

Wadhams

Penrose Is.

RIVERS INLET

Fl.

Duncanby Landing

Goose Bay

Fl(3)12s

Milbrook Cove

SMITH SOUND

Table Is.

Takush

Jones Cove (Emergy ⚓)

SOUTH PASSAGE

EGG ISLAND LIGHT

Helipad
Bridge
Houses
Light on a lattice mast tower

Egg Is. Fl. 5s
207 kHz
Fog Sig., 60s

Not to be used for navigation

C. Caution

N

Miles Inlet ⚓
Allison Harbour ⚓

Egg Is.   Table Is.   Cape Caution Light

APPROACHING CAPE CAUTION FROM 6m SSW
(White beaches along the coast indicates the cape is getting closer.)

Gp. Fl (3) 12s
Storm Is.

Pine Is.
Gp. Fl. (2) 10s
318 kHz
2 Fog Sig, 60s

Fl.

51°00'N

Bluudan Hbr. ⚓

C. St. James

Bull Harbour
Hope Is.

Nahwitti Bar ↓

Nigei Is.

GOLETAS CHANNEL

Fl.

Scarlet Pt.
Fl. 5s
Fl.

Walker Gr.

QUEEN

CHARLOTTE

STRAIT

50'

Fl. W. 10s
354 kHz

C. Scott

VANCOUVER ISLAND

Gods Pocket ⚓
Fl.

ROUTES PAST CAPE CAUTION
QUEEN CHARLOTTE STRAIT

Hardy Bay
PORT HARDY ⚓

Gp. Fl (2) 12s

Round Is. Fl.

0   10   20m

Approx. Scale   n. m.

30'
20'
10'
128° 00'W
50'
40'
127° 30'W
20'

Airport

40'
Port McNeil

MILES INLET and ANCHORAGES NORTH of CAPE CAUTION

The amphitheater-like entrance to **Miles Inlet,** a narrow cut in Bramham Island, lies between McEwen Point on the north and Bramham Point on the south. Many small islets and detached rocks are clustered along the northern shore, and after about .5 mile the opening narrows to only 22 m (75 feet). Its dramatic entrance is a narrow rock-walled corridor that branches to the northwest and southeast in the form of a T at its inner end.

Depths in the entrance vary between 3 to 4 fathoms. Good anchorage in 2 to 3 fathoms, mud, can be taken in both channels. The northwestern end is a lagoon sealed off by shallows that dry 4 m (13 feet) at low water. The bottom shoals quickly in the southeast arm past a rocky mid-channel islet, beyond which is an interesting area to explore by dinghy. Westerly winds blow through the entrance, but are more of a nuisance for causing sloppy seas outside the entrance than for their effect within the anchorage.

After passing Cape Caution the nearest anchorage is small and can be difficult to identify the first time it is entered. **Jones Cove** lies on the northeast side of Macnicol Point. When entering steer clear of a reef that extends 180 m (600 ft.) southwest of Turner Islands, and round the east point of Jones Cove entrance by at least 90 m (300 feet). The cove is small but offers some shelter in an emergency. However, when heavy seas are breaking in the area the entrance is difficult to identify and anchorage should be taken elsewhere if you are unsure of the proper approach.

Takush Harbour is about 7 miles east of Table Island. It provides excellent protection from all winds and is worth visiting for its beauty as well as for a refuge from stormy weather. The most popular spot is in Anchor Bight, the west arm of the Harbour entered between Gnarled Islets and Anchor Islets. Bull Cove, on the east side of the entrance, south of Bull Point offers snug, secure protection for 2 or 3 vessels in 4 - 5 fathoms, mud.

Smith Sound can be entered from the south through Alexandra Passage between Egg Island and Macnicol Point (about 5 miles north of Cape Caution) or through Radar Passage north of Egg. The Sound can be entered from the north through Irving Passage south of False Egg Island. There are several dangers in both entrances and a large scale chart should be used in determining safe courses. The main dangers are drying rocks that are usually visible or are indicated by breakers.

Milbrook Cove is on the north shore of Smith Sound close to the east of Shield Island. A buoy marks Milbrook Rocks midway in the entrance which should be passed on the west. Once in the cove stay in mid-channel and pass between the two islands in the north end of the cove to anchor behind them in 4 to 5 fathoms, sand. This is a snug and pleasant anchorage.

Duncanby Landing is on the south side of Rivers Inlet. Approach by passing SSE of Bull Island until clear of the southern extremity of Cow Island when the marina facilities are seen ashore. Facilities here include: moorage, fuel, water, showers, laundry, liquor and provisions. Anchorage may be taken on the west side of the island .8 mile west of the facilities.

Penrose Island is located between the entrance to Rivers Inlet and Darby Channel adjoining Fitz Hugh Sound. The anchorages are described on the next page.

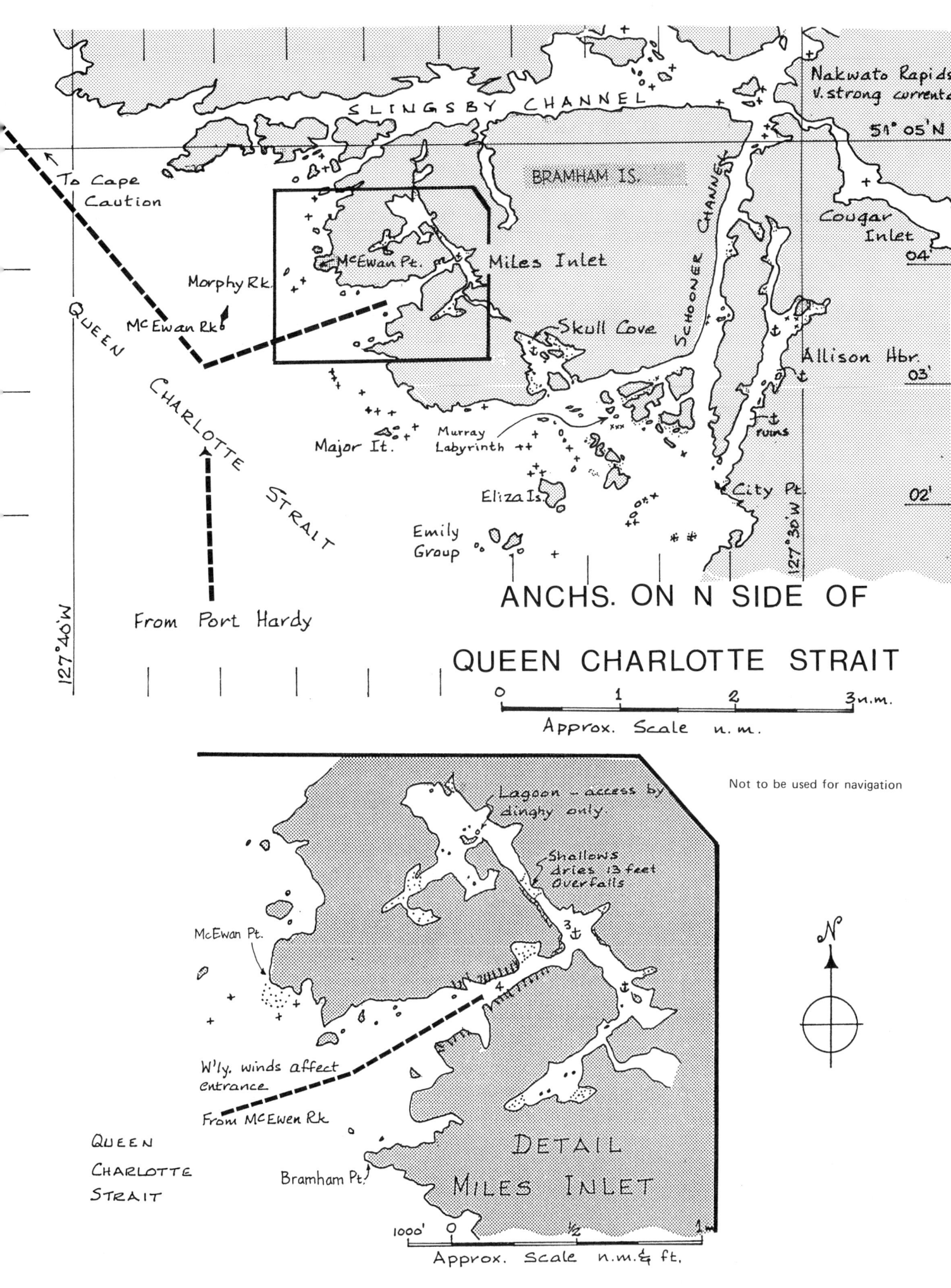

SLINGSBY CHANNEL

Nakwato Rapids
V. strong currents

51° 05'N

BRAMHAM IS.

To Cape
Caution

Cougar
Inlet

04'

McEwan Pt.

Miles Inlet

Morphy Rk.

Schooner Channel

Queen

McEwan Rk

Skull Cove

Allison Hbr.

03'

127°30'w

ruins

Major It.

Murray
Labyrinth

Charlotte

City Pt.

02'

Eliza Is.

Strait

Emily
Group

ANCHS. ON N SIDE OF

QUEEN CHARLOTTE STRAIT

From Port Hardy

0   1   2   3 n.m.

Approx. Scale n. m.

127°46'w

Not to be used for navigation

Lagoon – access by
dinghy only

Shallows
dries 13 feet
Overfalls

N

McEwan Pt.

3

4

W'ly. winds affect
entrance

From McEwen Rk

QUEEN
CHARLOTTE
STRAIT

DETAIL

MILES INLET

Bramham Pt.

1000'   0   ½   1 m.

Approx. Scale n.m. & ft.

PENROSE ISLAND MARINE PARK and DAWSONS LANDING

At the southern end of Fitz Hugh Sound is Calvert Island on the west and numerous islands, islets, rocks and reefs on the east, the largest being Penrose Island. It provides several anchorages, the most useful one for cruisers being **Fury Cove** on the west coast. This is an ideal departure point to use when southbound for it is easy to exit and conveniently close Queen Charlotte sound. It is best to make your first entry to the cove during settled weather, for the intricate entry can be quite intimidating when seas are breaking on the many offlying rocks and reefs lining the western edge of the archipelago. The identification of Rouse Reef is of prime importance, for .75 mile to the southeast of it the opening through Schooner Retreat to Exposed Anchorage becomes evident. The many treed islets merging one with the other seem to be confusing, but the entrance is clear and once within Exposed Anchorage a turn to the only narrow opening to the northwest leads into the sanctuary of Fury Cove. Anchorage for many vessels can be taken in the bay in 3 to 5 fathoms, mud. In addition to being a protected anchorage the view to the west provides a sneak preview of sea conditions in Fitz Hugh Sound.

There are a multitude of dangerous rocks and shoals in Klaquaek Channel which separates Penrose Island from Walbran and Ripon Islands to the east. It is essential that the most recent edition of Chart 3934 is used. If the chart you are using has been published prior to August 12, 1998 you should make a note of two rocks reported in the immediate area by the Prince Rupert Notice to Mariners for that date at the following locations: 51°29.49'N and 127°42.1'W and at 51°29.51'N, 127°41.9'W

Anchorage may be taken in **Frypan Bay** tucked into the center of the inner part of a cove in the south part of the bay. Another spot is in the center of the wider cove to the east, allowing for the shoals that restrict the useable space. The southern coves of **Big Frypan Bay** provide secure anchorage in 4 - 5 fathoms, mud.

East of Klaquaek Channel is a very popular anchorage in **Sunshine Bay**. Follow a mid-channel route in the narrow entrance, but favor the port side just before the channel turns eastward. Anchor in the center of the bay in 5 fathoms, mud. The next channel to the north leads to an unnamed basin with an islet in the middle. Pass to the east of the islet giving sufficient clearance to avoid a rock off its southeastern tip and another near the northeast end where a shoal extends in a northeasterly direction. Anchor northeast of the islet in 4 fathoms, sand. It is important to move slowly within these restricted areas in order to identify the location of rocks and shoals.

Moorage can be found on the floats in **Finn Bay** where divers congregate to explore the clear waters of the bay. A rock with a least depth of 2 m (6.5 ft.) is on the north side of the bay approximately .2 mile within the entrance. In southeasterly weather Finn Bay provides very good protection.

Dawsons Landing is about 12 miles up Rivers Inlet near the north end of Walbran Island. The store has a good selection of groceries and is a liquor outlet. Fuel, water and moorage are available. In days gone by this was once a very busy spot during the fishing season but reduction of the fishing fleet due to a lack of salmon has resulted in much less activity during the summer months.

PENROSE ISLAND

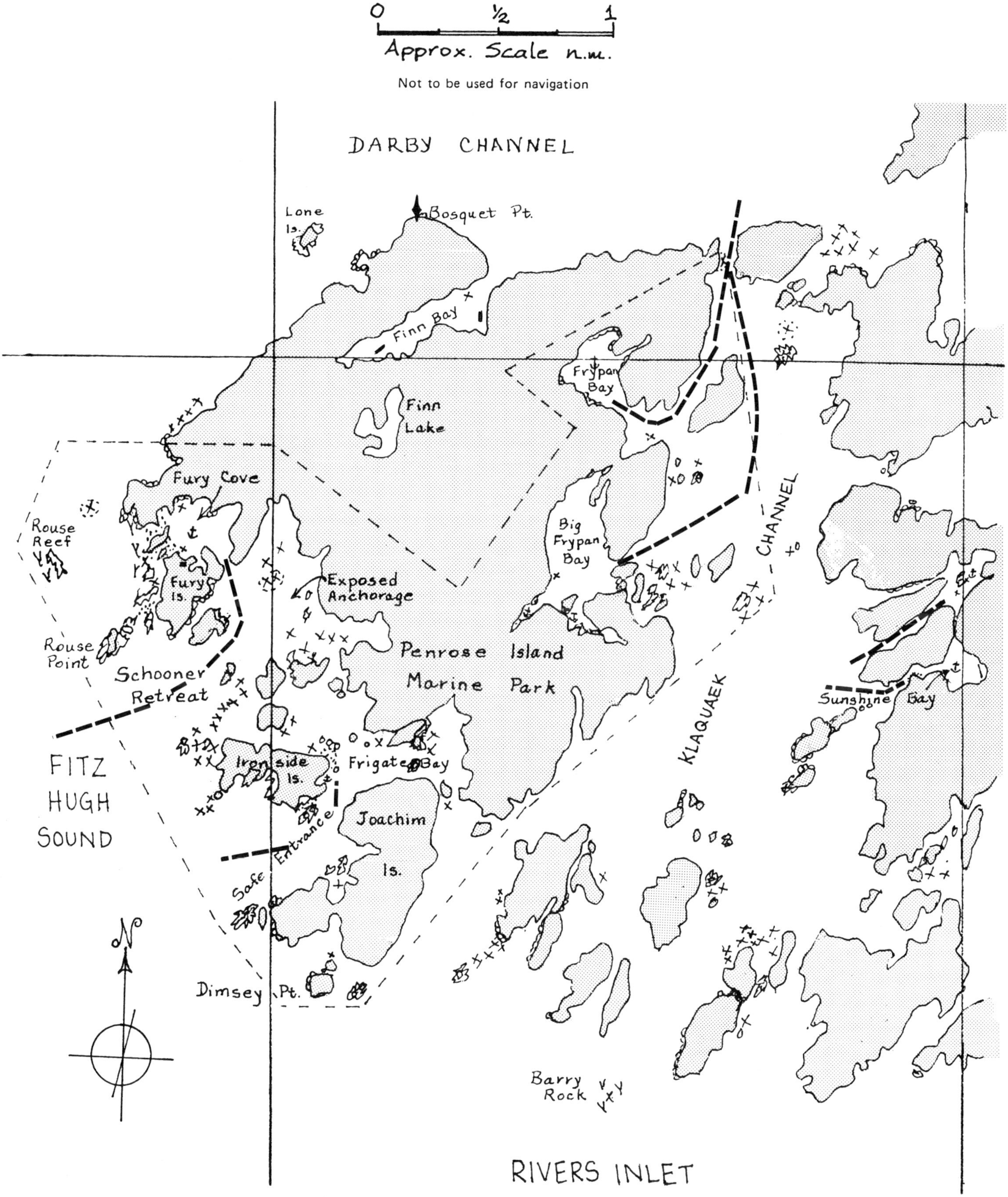

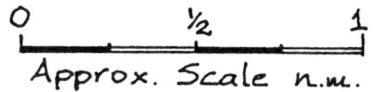

0 ½ 1

Approx. Scale n.m.

Not to be used for navigation

DARBY CHANNEL

Lone Is.

Bosquet Pt.

Finn Bay

Finn Lake

Frypan Bay

Fury Cove

Rouse Reef

Fury Is.

Exposed Anchorage

Big Frypan Bay

Rouse Point

Schooner Retreat

KLAQUAEK CHANNEL

Sunshine Bay

Penrose Island Marine Park

FITZ HUGH SOUND

Ironside Is.

Frigate Bay

Safe Entrance

Joachim Is.

Dimsey Pt.

N

Barry Rock

RIVERS INLET

SAFETY COVE, FIFER BAY and GREEN ISLAND ANCHORAGE

THE HEAD OF SAFETY COVE

Calvert Island shelters the entrance of Fitz Hugh Sound off Queen Charlotte Sound. The triangular profile of highest mountains of the Cape Range (602 m/1,975 ft.) can be seen from a considerable distance. Cape Calvert is the SE extremity of Calvert Island, but it is not an obvious landmark. Clark Point, slightly northeast has a light and is more noticeable. The shore, with the bulk of Entry Cone above the point, is steep and hides any indication of the indentation of the cove, which lies about 6 miles to the north. Calvert Island is a welcome sight after passing Cape Caution and there are several anchorages where you can recuperate after a long day's run. Details for Penrose Island anchorages are on the previous page.

Safety Cove penetrates almost a mile into Calvert Island and is about .3 miles wide. Two islets lie off the northern point, but are not particularly noticeable on an approach from the south. The cove's wide entrance makes it easy to identify. It is deep throughout, but shoals quickly at the head where an extensive mud and sand bank dries for almost 300 m (1,000 feet) from shore. Anchorage can be taken anywhere in the middle of the cove in 10 to 12 fathoms, mud. There is usually a breeze in the cove which can become gusty if a gale is blowing on the ocean side, but the anchorage is secure. This anchorage is popular with large craft and fishing vessels. The coast adjacent to the entrance points are productive areas to troll for salmon.

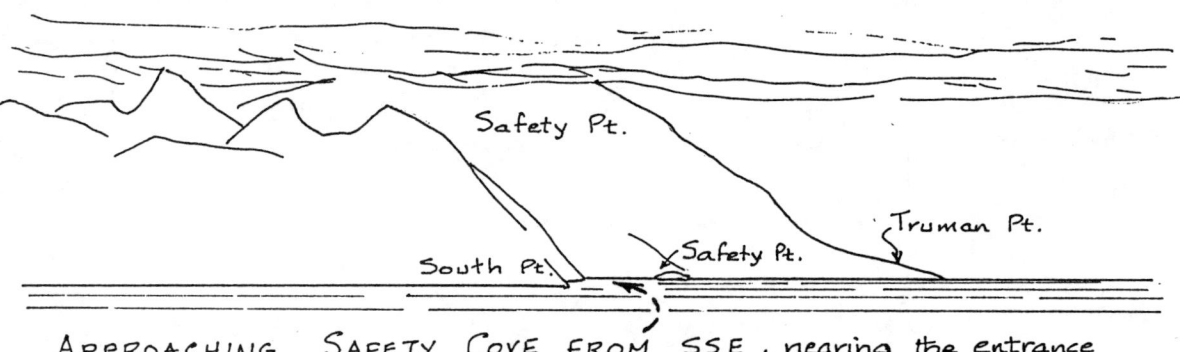

APPROACHING SAFETY COVE FROM SSE, nearing the entrance

About four miles to the north the forested islands of Blair and Addenbroke jut into Fitz Hugh Sound. There are two beautiful anchorages in the vicinity and a night spent at either one is very pleasant. **Fifer Bay** is a large irregularly shaped indentation in the middle of the western shore of Blair Island. It provides excellent protection from all winds for a limited number of vessels. When entering, care is needed to avoid the reef extending off the north end of the entrance islet and the rock slightly to the northeast. The passage to south end of the bay appears narrow but anchorage within is beautiful and secure.

A mile north of Fifer Bay is the more spacious well protected anchorage at **Green Island**. Entry can be made from the south by proceeding north of Fifer Bay through a narrow channel separating Blair Island from an unnamed island east of Sweeper Island. Fishing is usually productive in this passage. Many vessels can anchor with good protection in the outer and inner bays in 4 to 6 fathoms, good holding mud. Interesting trips can be taken in the dinghy exploring the varied coastline of the island's shores. The mound of clam shell fragments mark a midden.

FIFER BAY & GREEN IS. ANCH.

Approx. Scale n.m.

0   1200'   ½   1   1½ n.m.

Green Island Anchorage

51°38'

SOUVENIR PASSAGE

SALVAGE ISLAND

FAIRMILE PASSAGE

CORVETTE ISLANDS

PATROL PASSAGE

ADDENBROKE ISLAND

FIFER BAY

BLACK ISLAND

51°36'

127°50'

Not to be used for navigation

CALVERT ISLAND

Safety Mtn.

Safety Pt.

Entry Cove

South Pt.

Clerk Pt. behind

Bay Pt.

South Passage

APPROACHING SAFETY COVE FROM N. distant about 1 mile.

127°56'W

51°32'N

North Pt.

Safety Pt.

Good fishing

FITZ HUGH SOUND

0

17

15

12½ soft

10

House with a galvanized roof visible behind trees.

Forested hillside

Stony Beach

Shoal

Low col and hill behind

Rough road cutting into the bank

Forested hillside

South Pt.

Good Fishing

SAFETY COVE
CALVERT ISLAND

Approx. Scale n.m. & feet

100'   0   ¼   ½ n.m.

Not to be used for navigation

Low out towards open ocean

Safety Mtn 2550'

Grief Bay

Cape Calvert

CALVERT ISLAND

Entry Cove 185'

Clerk Pt. (Light)

Fitz Hugh Sound

To Safety Cove

APPROACHING CALVERT ISLAND FROM S. distance about 4 miles.

PRUTH BAY and GOLDSTREAM HARBOUR

These anchorages are within Hakai Recreation Area and are a short day's travel from anchorages just described. Each has its own attraction and is well worth visiting. Kwakshua Channel lies between Calvert Island and Hecate Island to the north. The entrance off Fitz Hugh Sound is about 7 miles north of Safety Cove. The channel is about 5 miles long with remarkably parallel, steep-to sides. At the eastern end it divides into several fingers, while the main Kwakshua Channel turns sharply northward in a right-angled turn.

Keith Anchorage lies on the south side, opposite Whittaker Point at the turn of the channel. Telus (the province-wide telephone company) microwave towers stand atop the low summit, and a small house and dock lie at the head of the bay. Anchorage can be taken here although winds may blow down the channel through the low passes.

Pruth Bay lies at the western end of Kwakshua Channel where it divides into three fingers. Anchorage in about 6 to 7 fathoms is best towards the head of the center finger, off the long pier and walkway of the Hakai Beach Resort. The unobtrusive buildings of the resort are tucked behind a screen of trees. A trail leads from the beach across the neck of land to a lovely sandy beach on the Pacific side of the island. A fantastic mask is carved into a cedar tree just off the trail.

Anchorage can also be taken .5 mile north of Whittaker Point. The south part of the cove is deep and shoals rapidly at the eastern side. Two small islands (separated by a drying rock) mark the northern part of the cove. Pass on either side of the rock to enter the northern section for anchorage. There is sufficient space for two or three boats, sand bottom.

Proceeding north in Kwakshua Channel, Meay Islets and the surrounding reef and shoals constrict the channel, which is otherwise clear. At the northern end you may choose to go to the west to use **Adams Harbour**, a snug spot though not recommended during strong westerlies, or turn northeast to pass through the narrow channel between Rattenbury Island and Hecate Island. In both cases, use the chart as a guide, generally favoring the Rattenbury Island side. Eagles nest alongside the channel on Rattenbury Island. Upon leaving Kwakshua Channel you enter Hakai Passage where the effect of the open sea is felt.

Goldstream Harbour, at the northern tip of Hecate Island, is on the south side of Hakai Passage as it joins Fitz Hugh Sound. An unnamed island lies off the tip to form the harbor, which is entered from the east. Midway into the harbor the channel is narrowed by Evening Rock (a drying reef) in mid-channel, and Hat Island which lies off the Hecate Island shore. Pass between to enter the basin where good anchorage can be taken in 7 to 12 fathoms, sand and mud.

The best nearby anchorage on the east shore of Fitz Hugh Sound is **Kwakume Inlet,** ESE of Goldstream Harbour. Give clearance to a rock awash about .1 mile west of the entrance. The narrow entrance is between a heavily treed islet on the north side of the north opening and two smaller islets topped with 4 or 5 trees to the south. The S opening is foul and should not be used. The actual entrance is easily lost in the background trees but when one is directly in front of it, it becomes obvious. Anchor in the south part of the bay in 3 - 4 fathoms, mud. Fishermen often raft together in the northern part where a rock awash at 1.6 m (5.5ft.) is half way between the southeast tip of the islet and the shore. **Koeye River Anchorage**, 5 miles to the north is strongly affected by west winds funneling down Hakai Passage and can be quite a rolly and uncomfortable spot.

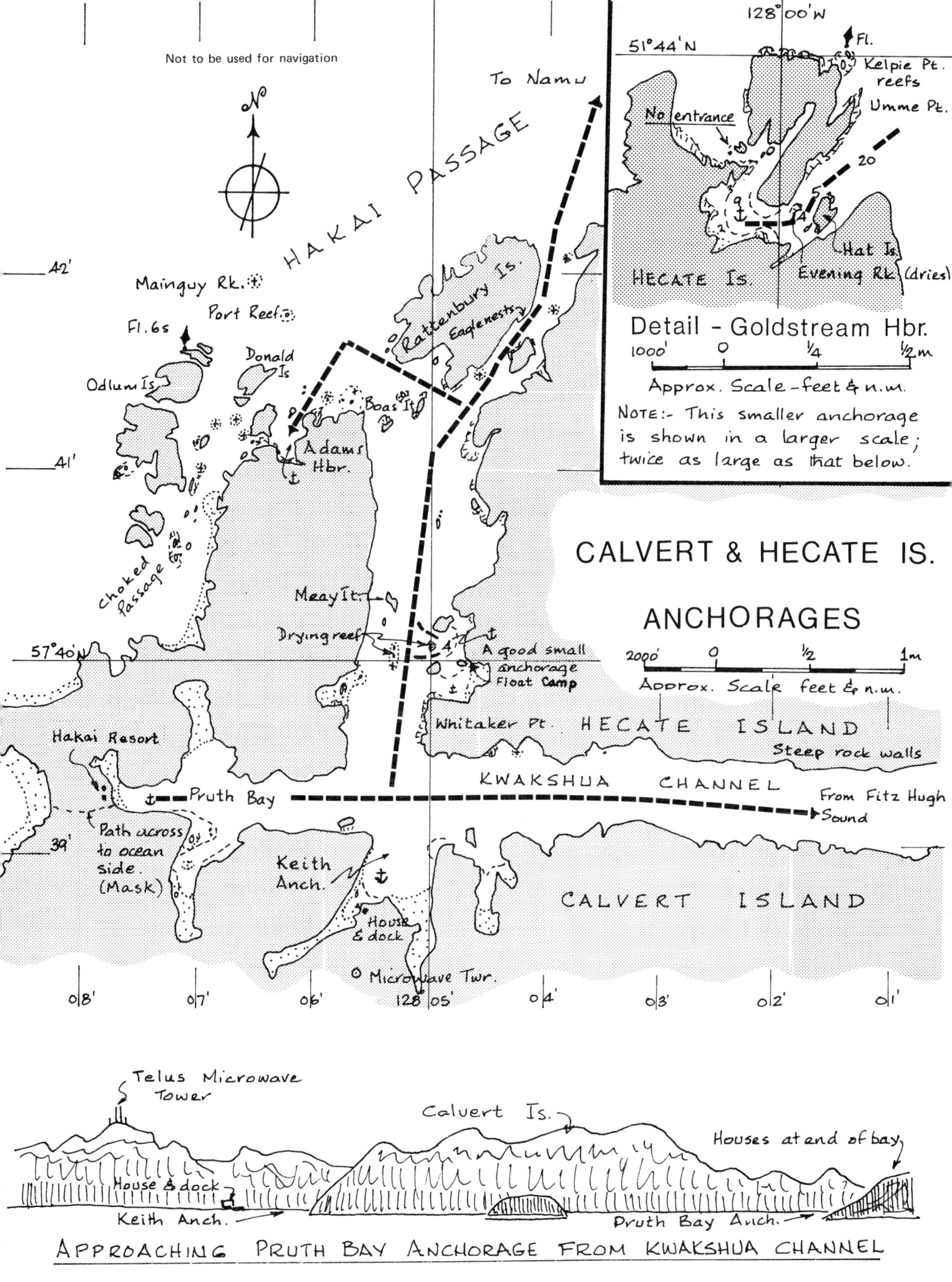

Not to be used for navigation

HAKAI PASSAGE

To Namu

128° 00'W

51° 44'N

Fl.
Kelpie Pt.
reefs
Umme Pt.

No entrance

20

HECATE Is.
Evening Rk. (dries)
Hat Is.

Detail - Goldstream Hbr.

1000' 0 ¼ ½ m

Approx. Scale - feet & n.m.

NOTE:- This smaller anchorage is shown in a larger scale; twice as large as that below.

42'

Mainguy Rk.
Port Reef.

Fl. 6s

Odlum Is.

Donald Is.

Rattenbury Is.
Eaglenest

Boas Is.

Adams Hbr.

41'

Choked Passage

Meay It
Drying reef

A good small anchorage
Float Camp

CALVERT & HECATE IS.

ANCHORAGES

2000' 0 ½ 1m

Approx. Scale feet & n.m.

57° 40'N

Whitaker Pt. HECATE ISLAND
Steep rock walls

KWAKSHUA CHANNEL

Hakai Resort

Pruth Bay

From Fitz Hugh Sound

Path across to ocean side. (Mask)

39'

Keith Anch.

House & dock

CALVERT ISLAND

O Microwave Twr.

128° 05'

08' 07' 06' 04' 03' 02' 01'

Telus Microwave Tower

Calvert Is.

Houses at end of bay

House & dock

Keith Anch.

Pruth Bay Anch.

APPROACHING PRUTH BAY ANCHORAGE FROM KWAKSHUA CHANNEL

NAMU

Namu is in Whirlwind Bay on the east shore of Fitz Hugh Sound. For many years, when fishing was a major economic resource in B.C. waters, this small community was very active. Now, the ruins are a stark reminder of a vibrant natural resource that was mismanaged and abused.

The rotting remains of cannery buildings and various workshops are visible when entering the bay through either Morehouse or Cloverleaf Passes on either side of Kiwash Island. Several owners have had proposals to rejuvenate the facilities but their plans have not materialized.

When approaching the facilities the vessel passes south of a small red buoy marking Loo Rock, about 90 m (300 feet) NNW of an open cove where a small float is located. At the present time limited moorage is provided and fuel is sometimes available at a floating dock around the corner. Many buildings in reasonable condition are scattered about and a caretaker lives in one of the houses on the hill. A trail beyond the houses provides a pleasant, but sometimes muddy walk.

Whirlwind Bay is not a good anchorage, for it suffers from willi-waws and is too deep. Neither Rock Inlet nor Harlequin Basin nearby offer anchorage.   Anchorage can be taken in **Fougner Bay** in Burke Channel, just 3 miles north.   There are many islets and rocks but the chart can be used to guide an entry to find protected anchorage.

Burke Channel leads northeasterly to the coastal town of Bella Coola, about 50 miles distant. If the weather is good this can be a very attractive trip, as the channel lies between high peaks which increase in height towards the head of the channel. **Eucott Bay**, three miles northeast of Fougner Point, provides good anchorage in 2.4 to 3.7m (8 to 12 ft.). Nearby is Eucott Hot Springs, and a float on the east shore marks the location of a fresh water pipe.

In Dean Channel **Sir Alexander MacKenzie Park** is northeast of Elcho Point. A monument commemorates MacKenzie's historic trip overland as the first European to reach the Pacific Ocean in July, 1793. Nearby is the rock in which he made a lasting inscription, "Alex MacKenzie from Canada by land 22nd July 1793." This epic journey was completed twelve years before the American expedition led by Lewis and Clark, who reached the mouth of the Columbia River in November, 1805.

* * * * *

The Inside Passage proceeds north through Fitz Hugh Sound into Fisher Channel, past Fog Rocks, across to Pointer Island and into Lama Passage. An excellent all-weather anchorage at **Codville Lagoon** can be entered off the east coast of Fitz Hugh Sound opposite the entrance to Lama Passage. Enter from Fisher Channel taking care to avoid reefs to starboard in the inner part of Lagoon Bay (a circular bight leading to the narrow entrance channel). When transiting the entrance channel, favor the south side to avoid the mid-channel rock, covered 1 fathom, located in the narrowest part. Onshore, a 30-minute hike leads to Sagar Lake where warm water swimming and a spectacular red sand beach can be enjoyed.

An interesting side trip is to proceed north in Fisher Channel then follow Cousins Inlet branching to the west ending at **Ocean Falls.** This pulp-producing company town was active until 1980 when the supply of cheap logs ran out, the operation terminated and Ocean Falls became a ghost town. Few inhabitants remain, but the dam constructed for power production still creates an impressive backdrop to the community. Moorage can be taken on a long dock.   Take a walk through the town's remains or a mile to the west where a bar and grocery store overlook the water.

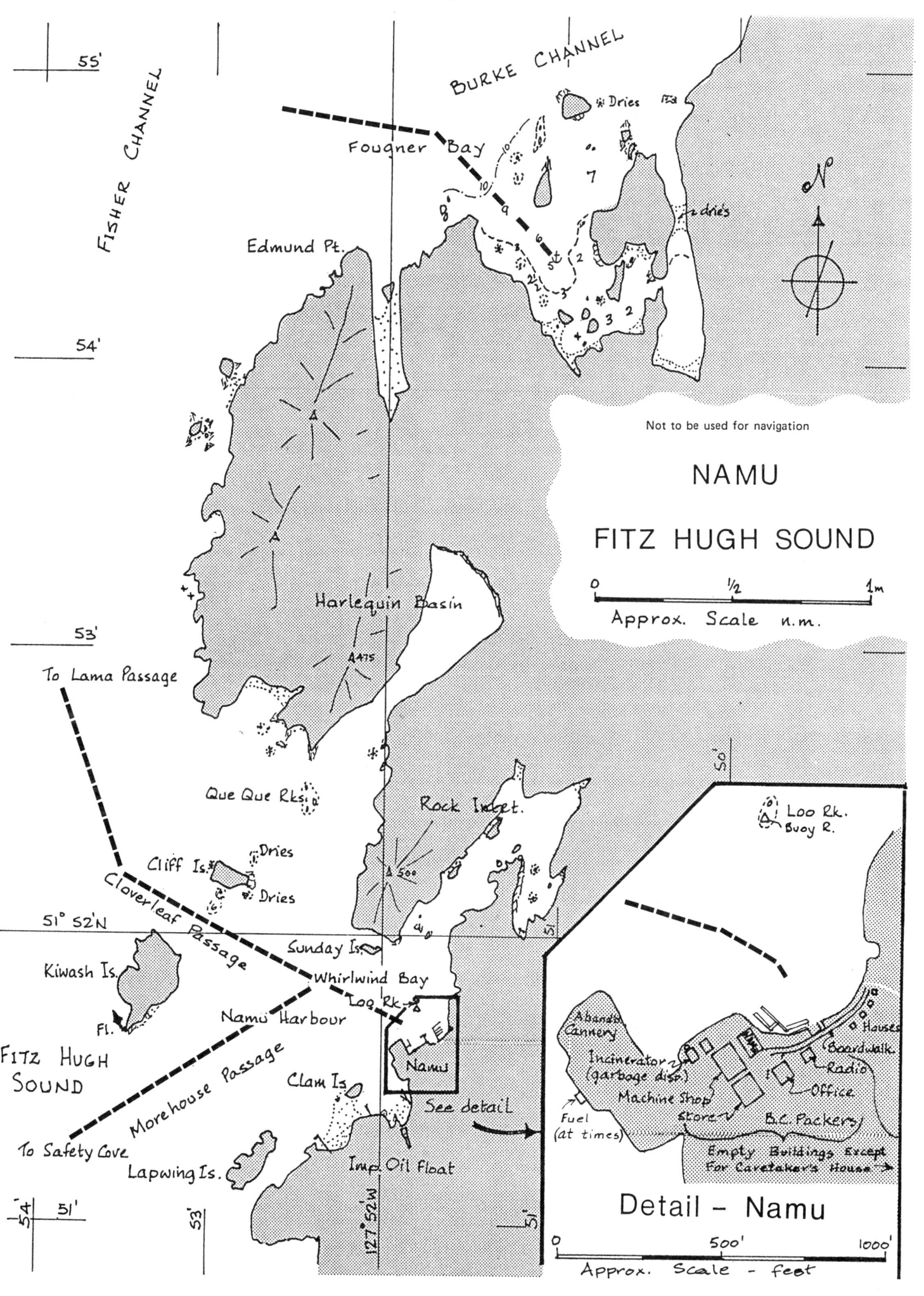

BURKE CHANNEL

FISHER CHANNEL

55'

Fougner Bay

Dries

7

dries

N

Edmund Pt.

54'

Not to be used for navigation

NAMU

FITZ HUGH SOUND

0   ½   1m

Approx. Scale n.m.

Harlequin Basin

△475

53'

To Lama Passage

Rock Inlet.

50'

Loo Rk.
Buoy R.

△500

Que Que Rks.

Dries

Cliff Is.

Dries

51° 52'N

Cloverleaf Passage

Sunday Is.

Whirlwind Bay

Kiwash Is.

Log Rk.

Namu Harbour

Fl.

FITZ HUGH
SOUND

Namu

See detail

Abandoned Cannery

Incinerator
(garbage disp.)

Houses

Boardwalk

Radio

Machine Shop

Office

store

B.C. Packers

Fuel
(at times)

Clam Is.

Morehouse Passage

To Safety Cove

Lapwing Is.

Imp Oil float

Empty Buildings Except
For Caretaker's House

Detail - Namu

127° 52'W

54' 51'

53'

0   500'   1000'

Approx. Scale - feet

BELLA BELLA and SHEARWATER

Lama Passage leads westward between Hunter Island and Denny Island for about 7 miles, then turns northward. There are some coves on the south shore in Cooper Inlet, just before the junction with Hunter Channel. There are many rocks in their entrances, but a small vessel can find a passage into **Lizzie Cove** or **Jane Cove** for a snug anchorage.

The narrowing channel of Lama Passage leads north past the ferry terminal at McLaughlin Bay to the small town of **New Bella Bella**. The fuel dock (open from 8 am to 5 pm sharp) is prominent on the waterfront. Care is needed when tying up, for metal projections on the docks can damage and mark a hull ·particularly when wash from passing vessels causes your boat to move. Limited, rolly moorage is available at the adjacent government dock. At the head of the pier is a liquor store, grocery/general store, hotel, bank and post office. A modern hospital is a couple of blocks to the south. Many fishing vessels moor at the public docks at the north end of town where the entrance is marked by a light. Rafting is necessary because it is usually crowded.

There is little activity at the old town of Bella Bella across Lama Passage. However, around the point and past Spirit Island there is the large bay of Kliktsoatli Harbor where the **Shearwater Marina** and **Fishermans Inn** are located. To enter, take a mid-channel course through Clayton Pass between Shearwater Island and Denny Island.

Moorage is available at the elongated dock, and beyond that a dilapidated floating wharf is used by local craft. Registration and payment for moorage is done at the cash register in the restaurant which overlooks the bay. A grocery store, laundromat and shower facilities are behind the restaurant. A marine supply store adjoins the slipway and workshops where boat repairs are done. A fuel dock is prominent on the little peninsula to the southeast behind which is a ferry dock. A scheduled Air BC service operates from the resort, as does a water taxi service to and from Bella Bella. A small public wharf is found in the little cove beyond the shipyard float, but most transient vessels moor at the resort or anchor in the bay.

Kakushdish Harbour is SE of Cypress Island and secure, quiet anchorage can be taken in 5 fathoms, mud. A shallow bar in the channel has a least depth of about 1.5 fathoms and beyond is a large bay bordered by shoals and swamps, home to millions of mosquitoes.

Lama Passage continues northward, passing between Campbell and Saunders Islands, the western of three channels, into Seaforth Channel. A buoy off the south point of Saunders Islands marks a shoal. The channel is about 300 m (1,000 feet) wide at its narrowest point, and the meeting of the tides seems to collect logs and debris here. The ferries and cruise ships in the Inside Passage use this pass, and at such times it can become crowded. Dryad Point Lighthouse on the northern point is an important reporting station. Once in Seaforth Channel the route turns northwest to pass Dall and Regatta Rocks before heading westward toward Ivory Island, Reid Passage, and Milbanke Sound.

Gunboat Passage continues east from Dryad Point and is a narrow and delightfully scenic route leading into Fisher Channel. This is the shortest route to Ocean Falls from Shearwater or Seaforth Channel. The route is well marked and careful attention to ranges and markers brings a vessel through in comfort.

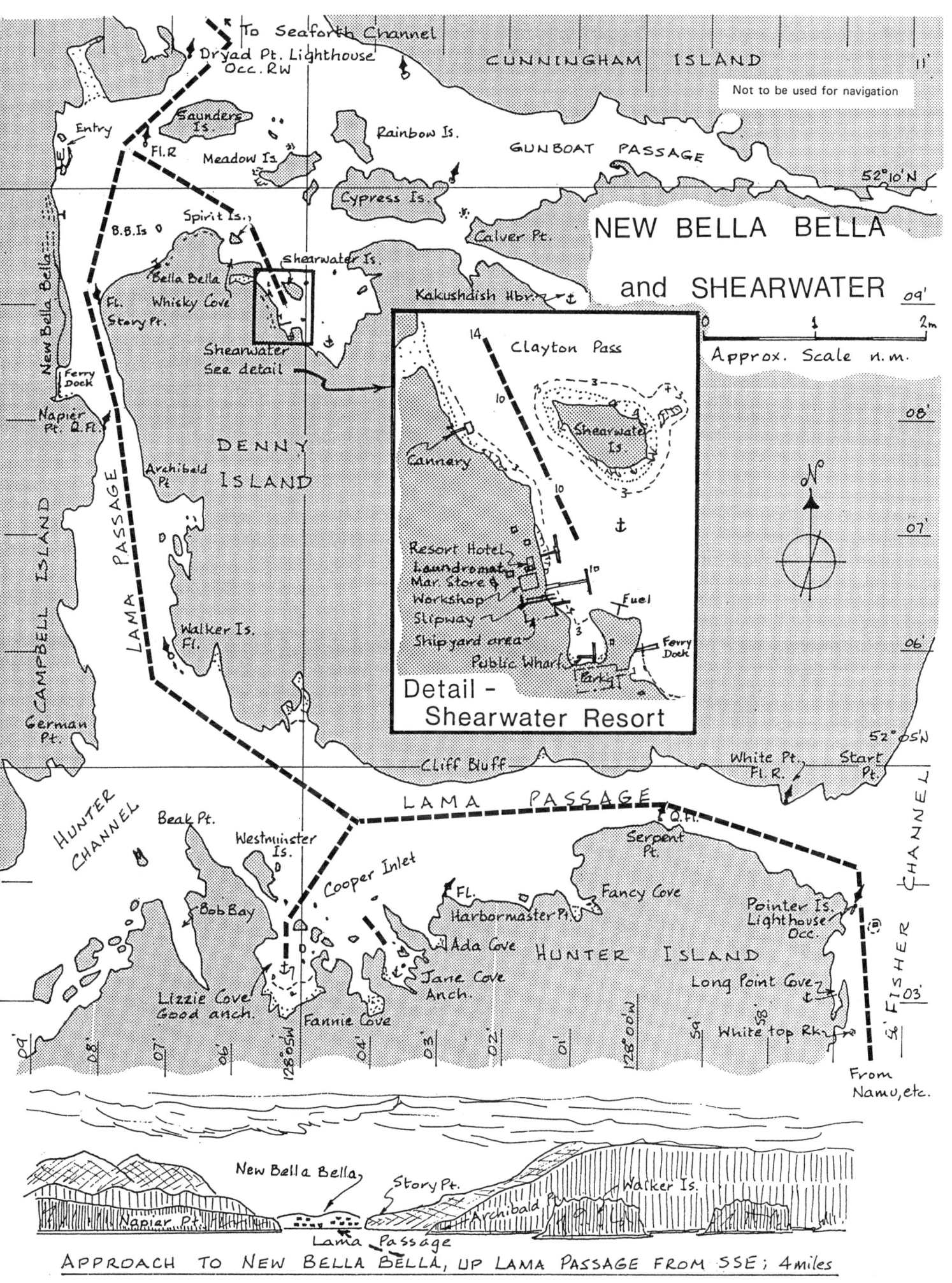

Not to be used for navigation

To Seaforth Channel
Dryad Pt. Lighthouse
Occ. RW
CUNNINGHAM ISLAND   11'

Entry
Saunders Is.   Rainbow Is.
Fl. R
Meadow Is.   GUNBOAT PASSAGE   52°10'N

B.B. Is   Spirit Is.
Bella Bella   Calver Pt.
Whisky Cove
Fl.
Story Pt.   Shearwater Is
Shearwater   Kakushdish Hbr.

NEW BELLA BELLA
and SHEARWATER   09'

0   1   2m
Approx. Scale n.m.

Detail -
Shearwater Resort

Clayton Pass
14
10
Cannery
10
Shearwater Is.
Resort Hotel
Laundromat
Mar. Store
Workshop
Slipway
Shipyard area
Public Wharf
Fuel
Ferry Dock
Ferry

08'

07'

06'

DENNY
ISLAND

Napier
Pt. Q. Fl.
Archibald
Pt.
Walker Is.
Fl.
German
Pt.

CAMPBELL ISLAND

LAMA PASSAGE

Cliff Bluff   White Pt.   Start
Fl. R.   Pt.
52°05'N

LAMA   PASSAGE
Q. Fl.

HUNTER
CHANNEL
Beak Pt.
Westminster
Is.
Cooper Inlet
Bob Bay
Serpent
Pt.
Fancy Cove
Harbormaster Pt.
Ada Cove
HUNTER ISLAND
Jane Cove
Anch.
Pointer Is.
Lighthouse
Occ.
Long Point Cove

Lizzie Cove
Good anch.
Fannie Cove
128°05'W
128°00'W
Sa
White top Rk.
03'

From
Namu, etc.

New Bella Bella
Story Pt.
Walker Is.
Napier Pt.   Archibald Pt.
Lama Passage

APPROACH TO NEW BELLA BELLA, UP LAMA PASSAGE FROM SSE; 4 miles

REID PASSAGE and OLIVER COVE

As Captain Vancouver's survey teams once found, this little passage offers a route to dodge the seas and weather in Milbanke Sound and to take a protected route into the lower part of Mathieson Channel. The route proceeds northward to cross via Oscar Passage into Finlayson Channel, or north to Kynoch Inlet for a side-trip visit to Fiordland Recreational Area.

Seaforth Channel becomes wider and more open to the sea as you approach Ivory Island. A major reporting lighthouse is at the southwestern end of Ivory Island, on Robb Point. In strong northwesterlies choppy seas develop which come into Seaforth Channel. The outside route through Milbanke Sound into Finlayson Channel may be uncomfortable at such times. East of Ivory Island, in the rock-strewn area between it and Harmston and Watch Islands there is a passage (marked by a light and red buoy) leading up to Reid Passage.

There are many large and small drying rocks in Blair Inlet and Powell Anchorage, but most are visible, especially near low water. From the red buoy a course set directly to the entrance of Reid Passage passes comfortably clear of these scattered rocks.

Carne Rock, with a light on it, lies in the middle of the passage. A shoal lies about 300 m (1,000 feet) SSW of Carne Rock, so favor the east side to pass these dangers. The least depth in this passage is about 4 fathoms.

Oliver Cove is a Marine Park on the eastern side near the northern end of Reid Inlet. A reef projects some distance from the southern point and there rocks fringing the northern point where the Marine Park sign is set. A dangerous rock, covered about .5 fathom lies in the middle of the opening of the bay. Entry to the bay is clear in the northern third of the entrance and anchorage may be taken in 5 - 6 fathoms, good holding mud. Two small, treed islands block the northern section but good anchorage can be taken in the south side. The remains of two old log cabins can be seen in the trees behind, as well as the posts and beams of what was a barn. They lie on the ground as they were assembled, and second-growth trees grow up through them. The head of the cove shoals to grass-covered mud flats.

The north end of Reid Passage can be exited by passing near the southern tip of Leighton Island before setting a course towards the southern end of Martha Island in Perceval Narrows. This route should clear the intimidating and extensive field of Lizzie Rocks at the southern tip of Lake Island. A course can then be set up Perceval Narrows into the broad opening of Mathieson Channel. When southbound, the approach to the north end of Reid Passage must be carefully plotted, for the islands and islets are confusing in their similarity.

Even in fog a slow, careful passage could be made through this section unless conditions make it absolutely inadvisable to travel. Do not attempt Lady Trutch Passage which is blocked with rocks. Moss Passage and Oscar Passage are discussed in the next page.

In calm weather the shortest route from Seaforth Channel to Finlayson Channel is via Milbanke Sound. Courses should be laid to clear the dangers off the coast, passing to the east of Vancouver Rock, before standing up into Finlayson Channel. However, between Ivory Island and Klemtu only 7 miles are saved, so that whatever the weather one might prefer the more interesting route via Reid Passage and Mathieson Channel.

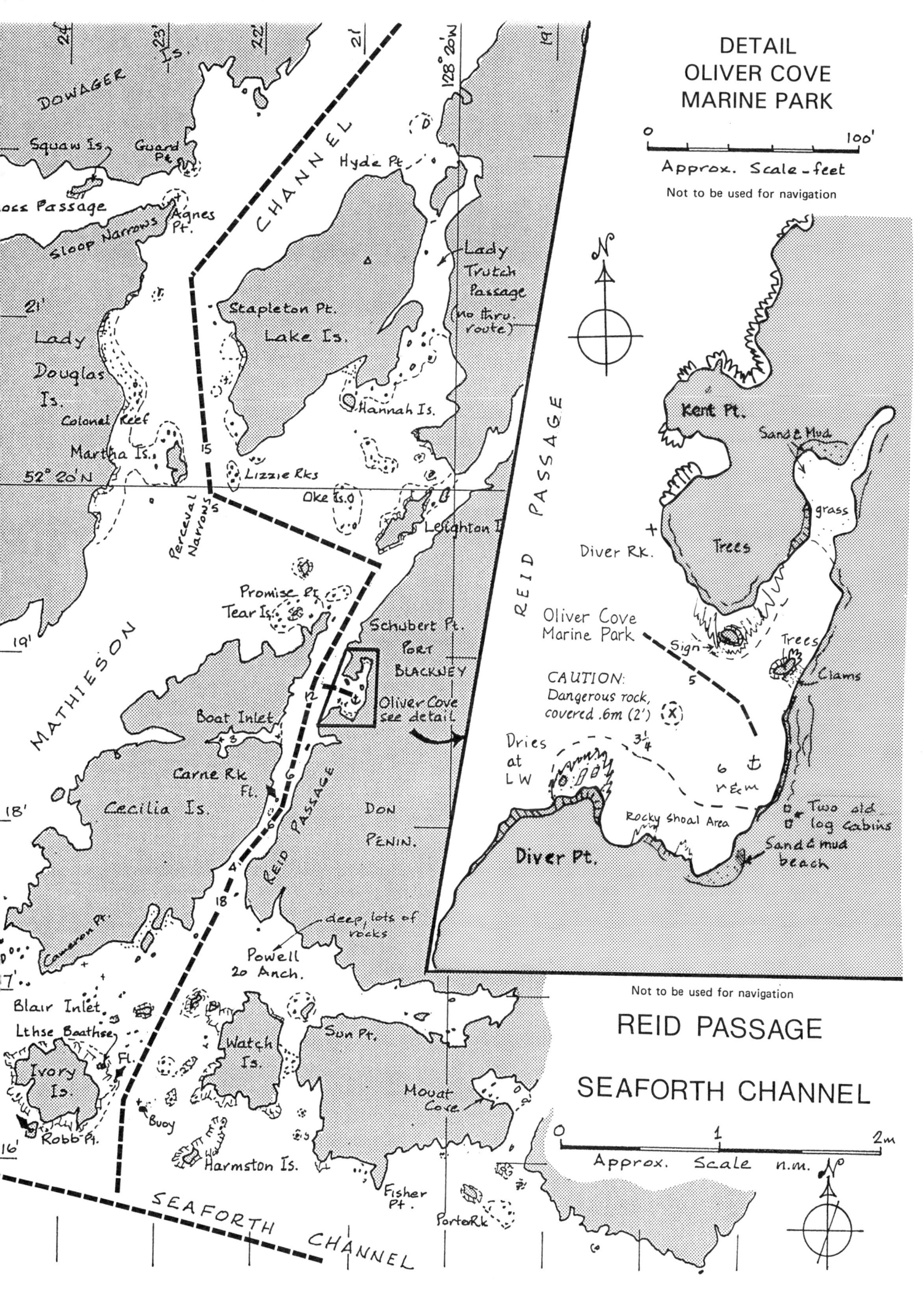

DETAIL
OLIVER COVE
MARINE PARK

0 _____ 100'

Approx. Scale - feet

Not to be used for navigation

Map labels (left map):

DOWAGER
24   23'   22'   CHANNEL   21'   128°20'W   19'
Squaw Is.   Guard Pt.
oss Passage   Agnes Pt.
Sloop Narrows
21'
Lady Douglas Is.
Colonel Reef
Martha Is.
52°20'N
15
Perceval Narrows
Lizzie Rks
Oke Is.
Leighton I.
Hyde Pt.
Stapleton Pt.   Lake Is.
Hannah Is.
Lady Trutch Passage (no thru route)

MATHIESON
Promise Pt.   Tear Is.
Schubert Pt.   PORT BLACKNEY
Oliver Cove see detail
Boat Inlet   8
Carne Rk. Ft.
Cecilia Is.   6
19'   6
DON PENIN.
18'
REID PASSAGE
4
18
deep, lots of rocks
Cameron Pt.
7'   Powell 20 Anch.
Blair Inlet
Lthse Boathse
Ft.
Ivory Is.   Watch Is.   Sun Pt.
Buoy
16'   Robb Pt.   Harmston Is.   Mouat Cove
Fisher Pt.
Porter Rk.
SEAFORTH CHANNEL

Right detail map labels:

N

Kent Pt.
Sand & Mud
grass
Diver Rk.
Trees
Oliver Cove Marine Park
Sign →
Trees
Clams
CAUTION: Dangerous rock, covered .6m (2')   (X)
5
Dries at LW
3½ 4
6   r & m
Rocky Shoal Area
Two old log cabins
Diver Pt.
Sand & mud beach

Not to be used for navigation

REID PASSAGE

SEAFORTH CHANNEL

0 _____ 1 _____ 2m

Approx. Scale   n.m.

OSCAR PASSAGE and NEARBY ANCHORAGES

There are several routes which cross from Mathieson Channel to Finlayson Channel. Jackson Passage, separating Susan and Roderick Islands, is about .25 mile wide throughout and narrows even more at the eastern end where it passes through Jackson Narrows. Here it is barely 180 m (600 feet) wide and the channel has many rocks. While this passage offers much of interest, it is challenging and should be attempted only at or near high water slack. The eastern end of Jackson Narrows is a small undeveloped Marine Park.

Oscar Passage is the southern route, separating Dowager and Susan Islands. It is wide, deep, and free from dangers. Even when Finlayson Channel and part of Mathieson are foggy, Oscar Passage may be clear. The steep shores, particularly on the north side make the trip similar to transiting a canal.

There are two handy anchorages about 1.5 miles south of the eastern entrance of Oscar Passage. A cove with two lobes indents Dowager Island, and **Arthur Island** lies in front of them. The approach to the anchorages may be made on either side of Arthur Island, the southern channel being the wider of the two. At low tide the reefs that extend from the points near the eastern entrance reduce the width to about 60 m (200 ft.); as this entrance is deep (15 fathoms) a mid-channel course is satisfactory. The west cove is larger than the east cove, but a little more exposed to southerly winds blowing through the opening between Arthur and Dowager Islands. The head of the cove is shoal and dries; thus it should not be approached too closely. Anchor in 7 to 10 fathoms, stone and mud bottom. This cove can accommodate several boats.

The east cove is separated from the other by a short, rocky point. It is considerably narrower and smaller and is sheltered by the bulk of Arthur Island lying before it. There are rocky outcrops along each side—leaving is room for only one or two boats. The bottom is rock and mud and varies from 6 to 8 fathoms.

Tom Bay in the southern end of Mathieson Channel, extending south from Symonds Point, provides anchorage in 8 to 10 fathoms; some kelp is found. An anchorage across Mathieson Channel N of De Freitas Islets is **Salmon Bay** which is entered between Carmichael Point and Ursus Point. The head of the bay is shoal, so anchor well off in 10 fathoms, soft mud.

The best anchorage in the vicinity is immediately before the eastern entrance to Jackson Narrows, in **Rescue Bay**. Rocky islands and shoals limit the width at the entrance but a mid-channel course is free of dangers. Drying rocks and shoals line the bay, particularly its western shore, but good anchorage is available for many vessels in mid-bay. Watch for a drying rock about .1 mile from the head. This attractive spot provides excellent protection and is strategically located for a stop-over to break the passage of Mathieson Channel or when waiting for the proper time to pass through Jackson Narrows.

Moss Passage at the southern end of Dowager Island (and Mathieson Channel) is a narrow passage leading to Finlayson Sound. At its eastern end it contracts to only 90 m (300 feet) at Sloop Narrows, where tidal currents are strong. Pass well south of the drying rock south of Guard Point, and continue to stay south of Squaw Island in the Narrows. Though Moss Passage widens at its western end there are many rocks, islands and kelp patches to be avoided, and extra care is needed for safe passage. During foggy weather this passage is inadvisable.

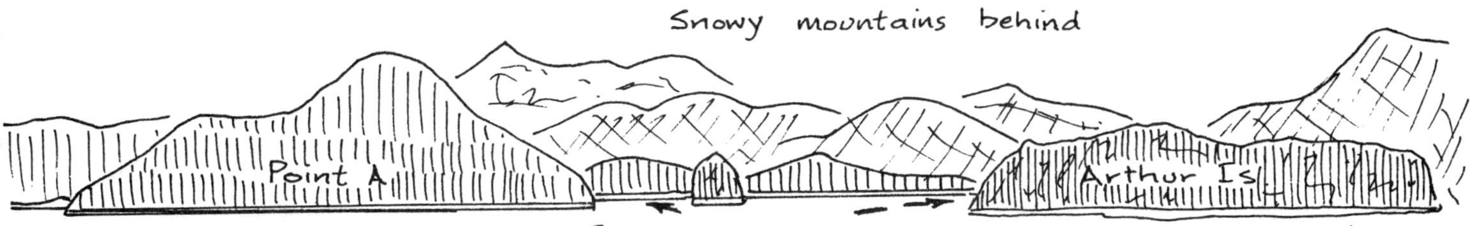

Snowy mountains behind

Point A   Arthur Is.

APPROACHING ARTHUR IS. ANCHORAGES FROM SE, distant abt. 1½ miles

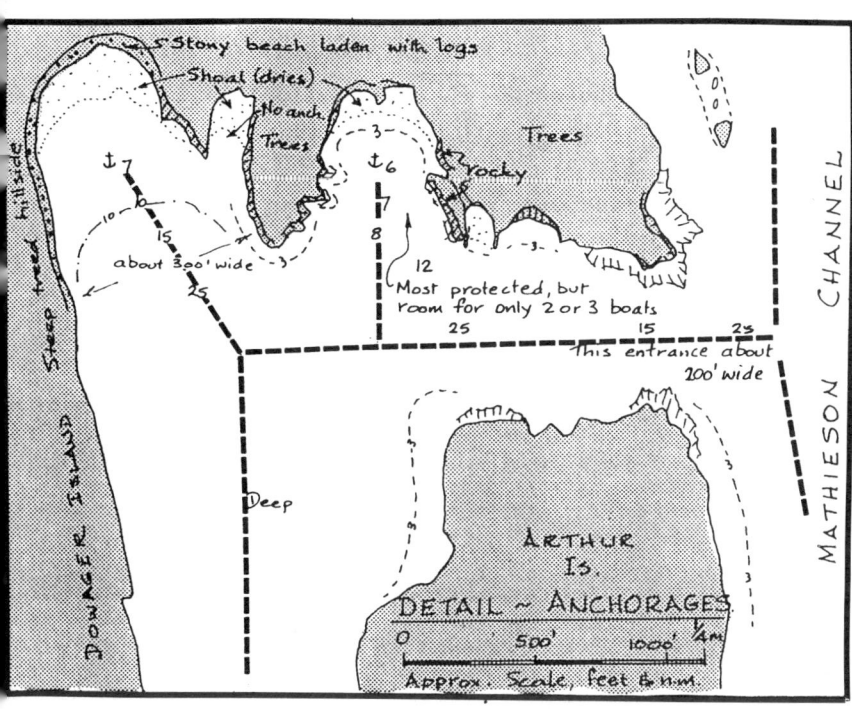

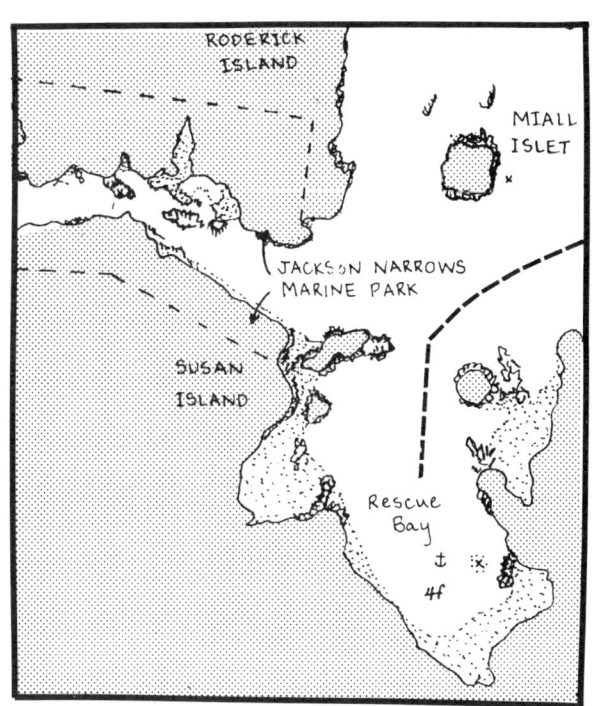

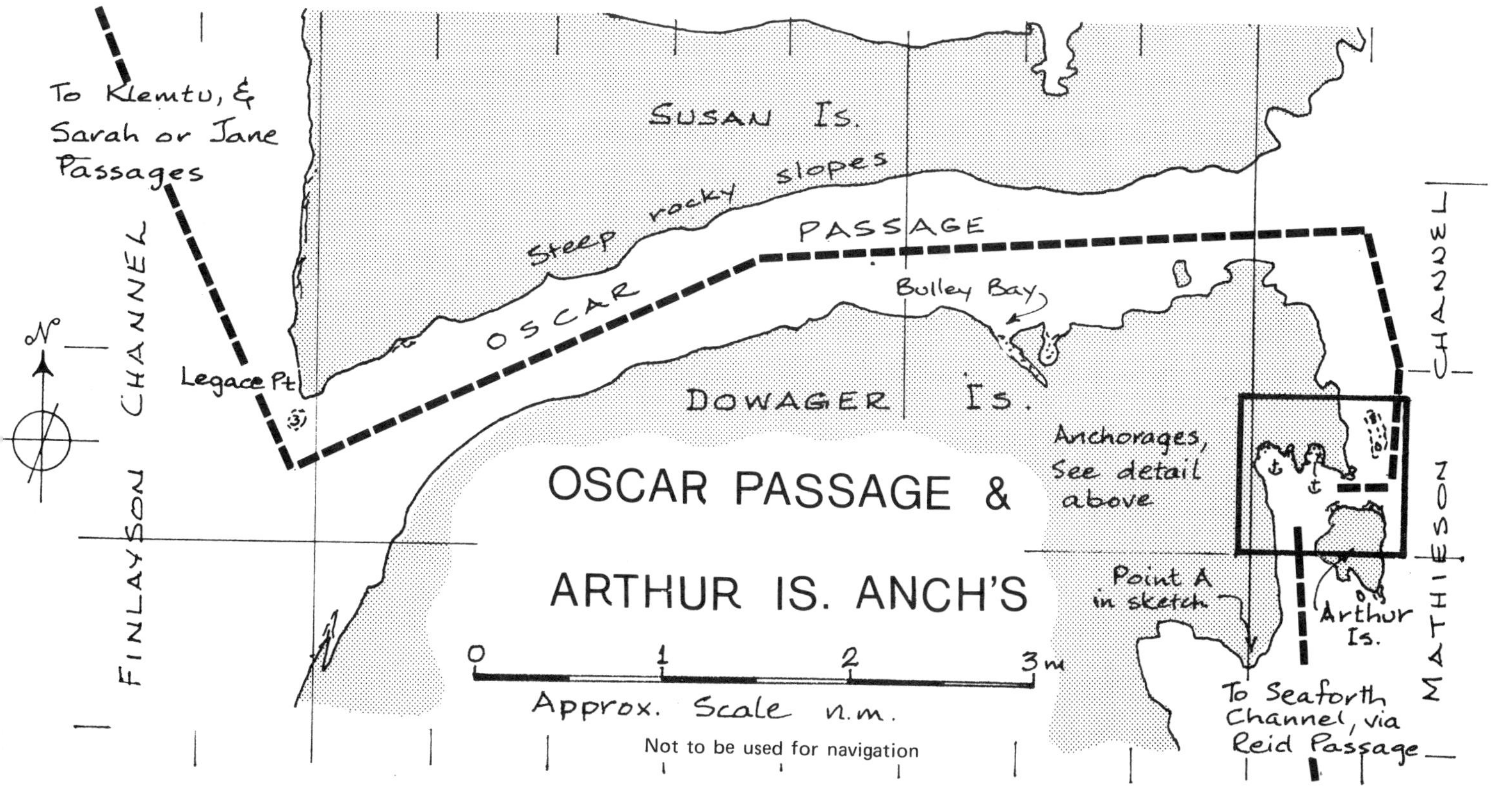

To Klemtu, &
Sarah or Jane
Passages

FINLAYSON CHANNEL

SUSAN IS.

Steep rocky slopes

OSCAR   PASSAGE

Bulley Bay

N

Legace Pt
③

DOWAGER   Is.

MATHIESON CHANNEL

Anchorages,
See detail
above

Arthur Is.

OSCAR PASSAGE &
ARTHUR IS. ANCH'S

Point A
in sketch

To Seaforth
Channel, via
Reid Passage

0   1   2   3 m

Approx. Scale n.m.

Not to be used for navigation

KLEMTU

This pretty village lies behind aptly named Cone Island on the west side of Finlayson Channel. At the north end of Cone Island two important passages, Jane Passage and Sarah Passage, connect Finlayson with Tolmie Channel. In turn, Tolmie Channel runs north alongside Sarah Island to join Graham Reach and continue the Inside Passage. Finlayson and Tolmie Channels are also joined at the north end of Sarah Island by Hiekish Narrows, where the passage is clear except for Hewitt Rock. A shoal extending 300 m (1,000 ft.) from the rock is marked by a light at its SE end. Transit of Heikish Narrows within an hour or two of slack water is trouble-free even for low-powered vessels.

Klemtu is well placed as a stop along the Inside Passage. The village is in Trout Bay, on the west side of Klemtu Passage about one mile south of the northern end of Cone Island. There is easy access to fuel and water on the dock adjacent to the ferry terminal at the northern edge of the village. If the fuel dock manager is not around he can be called on CB Ch 14, call sign 44. Two stores selling groceries, fishing gear and general goods serve the community. Near the ferry dock is the Kitasoo Band Store and coffee shop. Open six days a week the store also offers banking services. On the south side of the bay is another store, open all week, 9 to 5 and 6:30 to 10 p.m.

There is a government dock and a seaplane landing float at the middle of the cove in the western shore. This dock is usually filled with local fishboats and rafting is necessary if you want temporary moorage. The dock in the southern part of the cove is used by local fishermen for repairing their nets; this area is shoal. While shopping, you can sometimes tie for a short period at the end of the fuel dock.

Anchorage within Trout Bay is not recommended because of the shoals and regular traffic. Anchorage can be found in the middle part of **Clothes Bay**. Anchor off the passage behind the drying rocks in about 5 fathoms. Wash from channel traffic discourages anchorage in Trout Bay.

Fog rolls up Finlayson Channel and into Klemtu Passage, most often in the summer and fall though sometimes in the spring. Klemtu Passage is narrow but deep. Both Jane and Sarah Passage have hazards that limit their width, but are otherwise deep and free of problems. On the north (inside) point of Sarah Passage is Boat Bluff crowned by an attractive and photogenic lighthouse.

Further up Tolmie Channel where it passes Split Head at the top of Swindle Island is a well marked passage, just past a mid-channel shoal called Parry Patch. By slightly favoring either shore the patch is easily passed and weak tidal swirls cause no difficulty.

There are three anchorages in the area on the east side of Finlayson Channel. **Nowish Cove** is about 5.5 miles SE of Klemtu. Enter from north of Nowish Island and use plenty of scope as the water is deep (10 -15 fathoms) and an eddy current is evident. **Mary Cove** is about 5 miles north of Nowish Cove. Anchor in 10 fathoms at the head of the basin. The best is **Bottleneck Inlet,** 1.2 miles north of Howay Point. The 90m (300 ft.) wide entrance is difficult to identify until you are close to it and the channel has a least depth of 3 m (10 ft.). The elongated channel leads to a wider part followed by the basin at the head of the bay, where anchorage can be taken anywhere. This secluded and peaceful hideaway is the epitome of a perfect all-weather anchorage: calm, beautiful and large enough to hold many vessels. **Work Bay,** located on the west side of Finlayson Channel west of Adze Point, provides good anchorage in the northeastern end of the bay in 7 fathoms. **Cougar Bay,** 10 miles N, on the west side of Tolmie Channel, has a poor reputation for dragging but you could try the small cove on the E side of the bay in 10 fathoms.

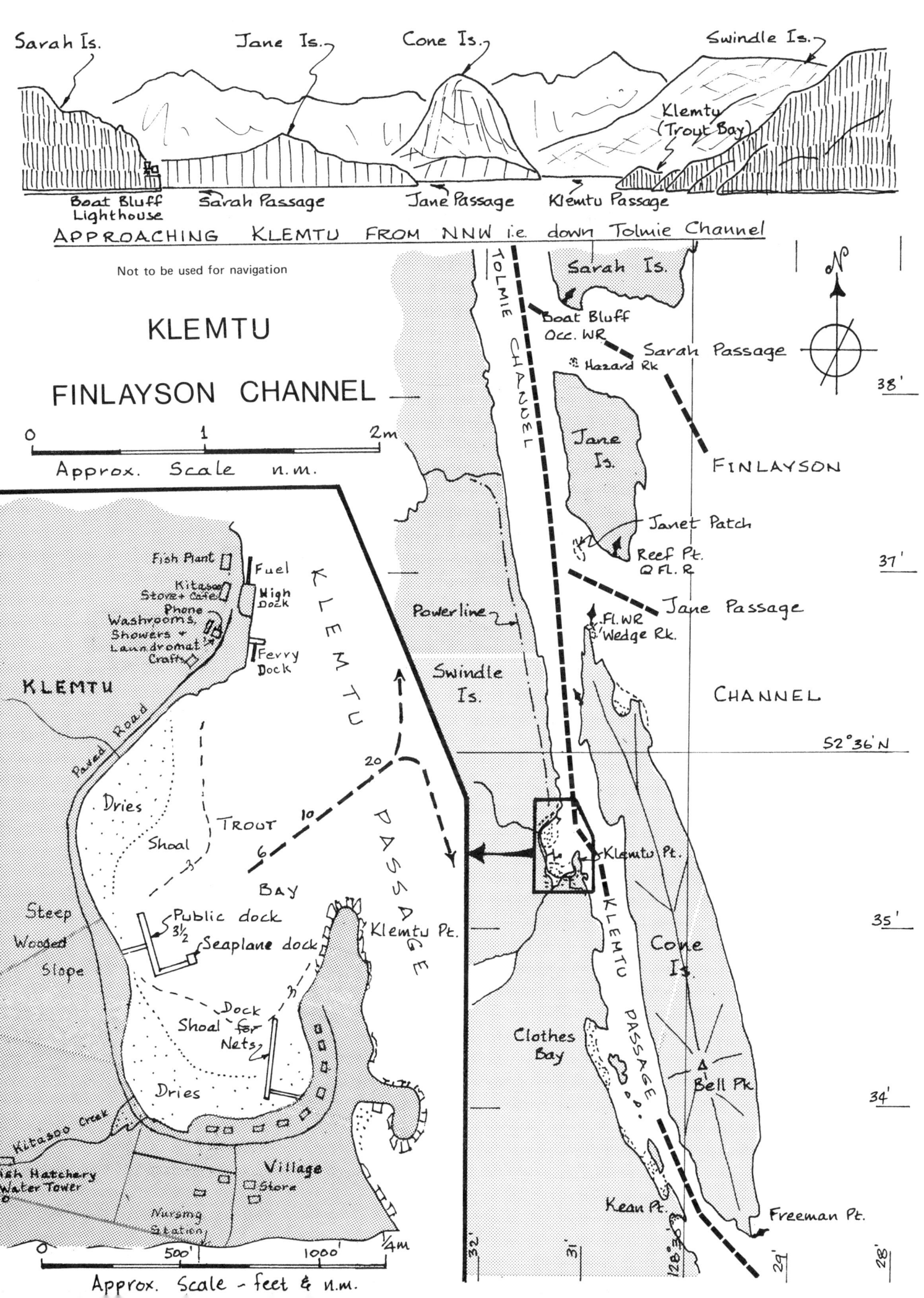

APPROACHING KLEMTU FROM NNW i.e. down Tolmie Channel

Sarah Is. Jane Is. Cone Is. Swindle Is.

Klemtu (Trout Bay)

Boat Bluff Lighthouse   Sarah Passage   Jane Passage   Klemtu Passage

Not to be used for navigation

KLEMTU

FINLAYSON CHANNEL

0   1   2m

Approx. Scale n.m.

Tolmie Channel

Sarah Is.

Boat Bluff Occ. WR

Hazard Rk

Sarah Passage

38'

Jane Is.

FINLAYSON

Janet Patch

Reef Pt. Q Fl. R

37'

Jane Passage

Fl. WR Wedge Rk.

CHANNEL

Powerline

Swindle Is.

52°36'N

Fish Plant

Kitasoo Stove + Cafe   Fuel High Dock

Phone Washrooms, Showers + Laundromat Crafts

Ferry Dock

KLEMTU

Paved Road

KLEMTU PASSAGE

20

Dries

Shoal

TROUT   10

6

BAY   3

Steep Wooded Slope

Public dock   3½

Seaplane dock

Klemtu Pt.

35'

Klemtu Pt.

Dock Shoal for Nets   3

Cone Is.

Dries

Clothes Bay

KLEMTU PASSAGE

Bell Pk

34'

Kitasoo Creek

Fish Hatchery Water Tower

Village

Store

Nursing Station

Kean Pt.

Freeman Pt.

0   500'   1000'   4m

Approx. Scale - feet & n.m.

32'   31'   128°30'   29'   28'

Green Inlet on the east side of Tolmie Channel across from Princess Royal Island is the northernmost B.C. Marine Park. Located 1.5 miles NNE of Quarry Point, the entrance is north of Netherby Point. Snug anchorage can be taken in **Horsefly Cove** on the north side of the inlet, .6 mile inside the entrance. A stern line to trees or snags on shore assists holding since secure anchorage using only one anchor can be difficult to obtain. This is a well-named cove for the size, appetite and number of horseflies and deer flies in this spot are beyond description. Four miles past the entrance is Baffle Point where tidal rapids make exploration of the tidal lagoon possible by dinghy at high water slack. Another spot where anchorage may be taken is reported to be off the green flats on the south side of the entrance channel.

Swanson Bay is a wide bight on the east side of Graham Reach north of Green Inlet. A rather narrow shelf off the SE side of the bay provides tolerable anchorage in 3 to 4 fathoms with limited swinging. Watch the state of the tide and check for sunken logs which line parts of the shore. The best spot is in the northern part of the bay slightly west of a blunt knob jutting into the bay. Avoid the large sand and grass shoal off the beach. An interesting walk can be taken around the ruins of a sawmill and pulp mill where a tall brick smokestack remains standing.

COMMON HERRING GULL

Looking down Fraser Reach towards Butedale

Pleasure craft are in a minority at Prince Rupert

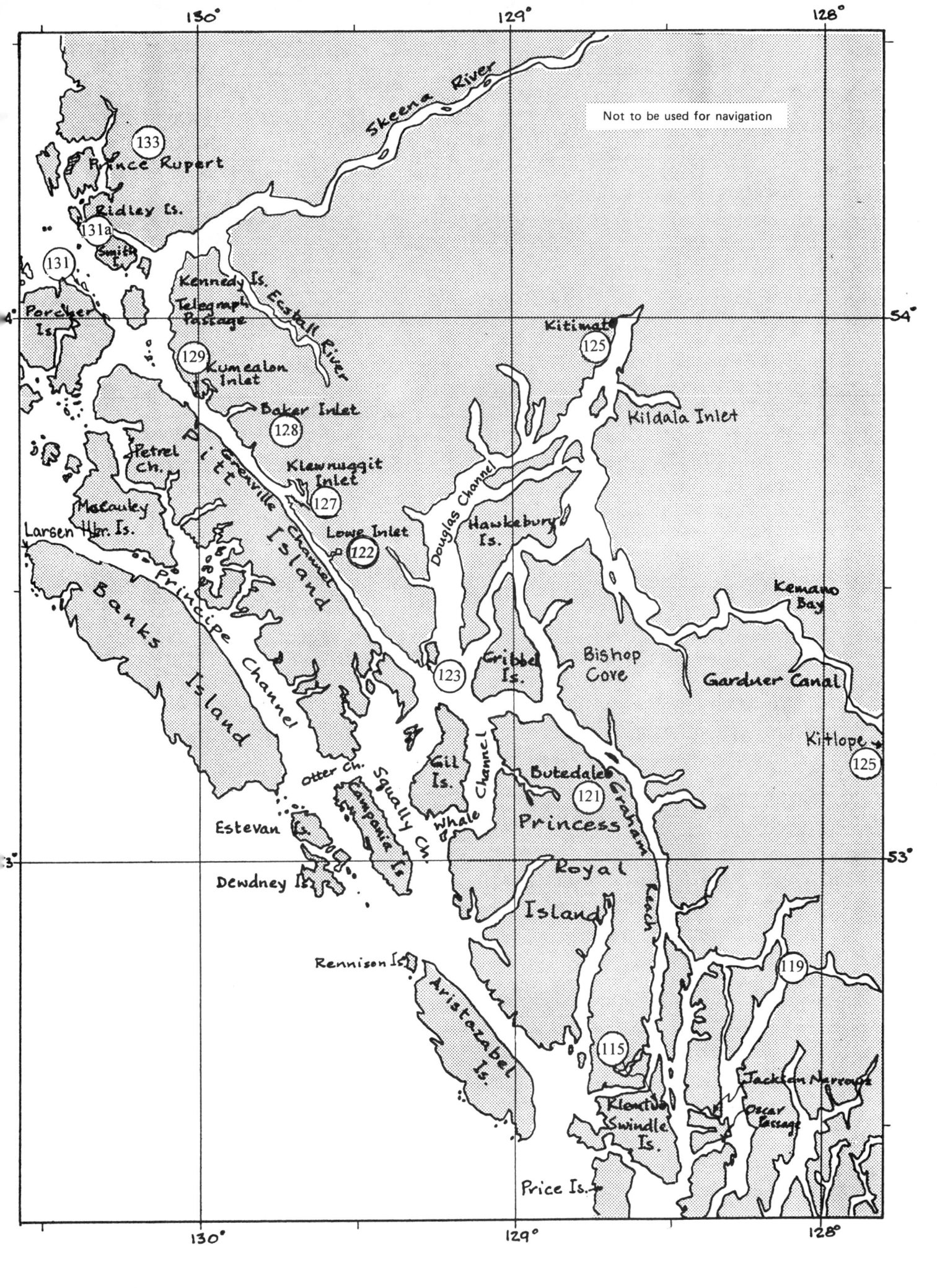

FIORDLAND RECREATIONAL AREA

An alternative route to traveling from Mathieson Channel to Finlayson Channel via Oscar Passage, Jackson Passage, or Moss Passage, is one which proceeds northward in Mathieson Channel. After exiting at Mathieson Narrows the route continues west in Sheep Passage until reaching the upper end of Finlayson Channel where Hiekish Narrows leads to the junction of Tolmie Channel and Graham Reach in Princess Royal Channel.

By proceeding north in Mathieson Channel until reaching the junction with Kynock Inlet you can visit **Fiordland Recreational Area.** This huge park covers 225,000 acres, encompassing the land surrounding all of Kynock and Mussel Inlets, land bordering part of the northern end of Mathieson Channel and part of Pooley Island. It is well named for the steep, precipitous granite cliffs rising more than 1,000 m (3,200 feet) are as spectacular as any found in the world. The sheer mountain faces are laced with waterfalls, particularly following a shower, making this one of the most beautiful areas on the B.C. coast. McAlpin and Lizette Falls in Mussel Inlet are worth seeing.

The most spectacular part of this park is **Kynock Inlet,** an 8.5-mile long inlet which joins Mathieson Channel about 15 miles north of the junction of Jackson Passage. It is entered between Kynoch Point on the south, and Garvey Point on the north. About 1.5 miles north of Garvey Point is a conspicuous waterfall followed by Desbrisay Bay (Big Bay) which is too deep for anchoring. Clouds and rain often obscure the scenery but if you can outlast the weather it is indeed worth the wait. Though it can be breezy, the only anchorage is clear of the drying flat and shoals extending from the head of the inlet. Anchor in 6 to 8 fathoms, sand, after checking that the vessel is well clear of the extensive shoals.

The eastern end of the inlet terminates in Culpepper Lagoon which can only be entered at slack high water. This is a fascinating spot to explore by dinghy though some venturesome sailors enter at high water slack and anchor just inside the lagoon or further up in 10 to 15 fathoms off the large shoal which extends from the head of the bay.

Two other anchorages found in adjacent waters are:

Windy Bay is located in the southeastern curve of Sheep Passage. The entrance is to the west of the treed islet near the east entrance point. Foul, rocky ground separates the islet from the shore. The best all-weather anchorage is off the steep-to drying flat about .3 mile from the head of the bay in 10 12 fathoms. This bay is well named for when southeasterly winds blow in Mathieson Channel the Venturi effect accelerates the winds as they pass through the low part of the mountains south of the bay, resulting in gusty blasts which sweep the bay and create a considerable chop.

During settled weather anchorage can be taken southeast of the islet in 6 to 8 fathoms, mud. This location provides a ring-side seat for viewing the antics of a congregation of seals living in the vicinity. As the tide falls, a large flat rock provides a hauling-out and rest area where the largest bulls preempt the best spot before it is even visible. As the tide falls and more of the rock is above the waterline, the rest of the herd congregate until 30 or more pile on, arguing and growling until the tide rises, their rock gradually submerges and they slide into the water to fish for the next meal.

Bolin Bay is 3 miles north of Windy Bay and is almost due west of Mathieson Narrows. With good protection in all but easterly winds, this little niche is tucked below towering mountains. Shoals at the head of the bay shelve rapidly; anchor in 10 - 12 fathoms, mud.

FIORDLAND RECREATIONAL AREA

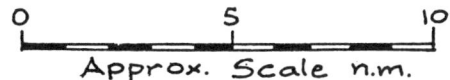

0   5   10

Approx. Scale n.m.

Not to be used for navigation

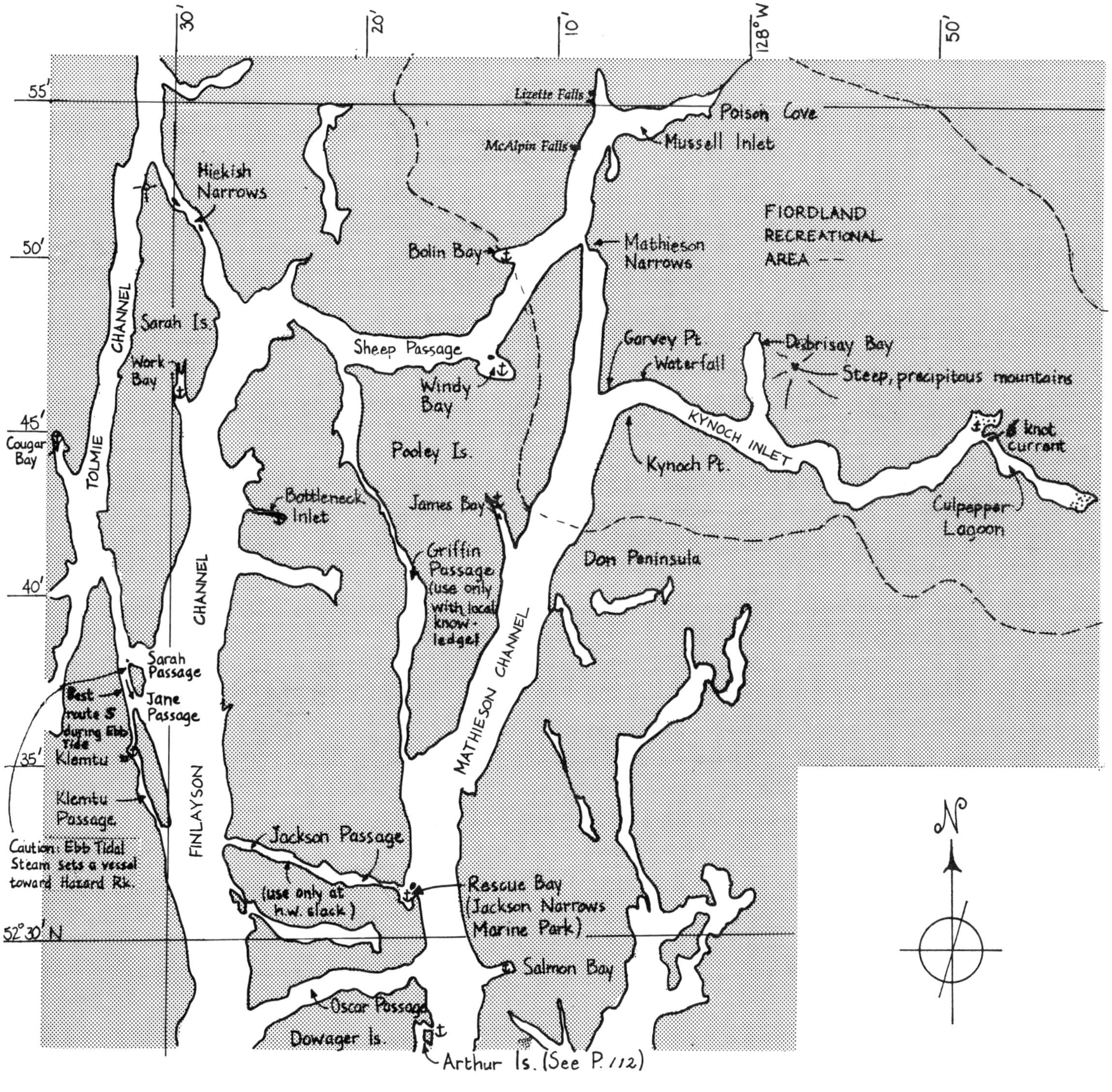

30'   20'   10'   128°W   50'

55'
Lizette Falls
Poison Cove
McAlpin Falls
Mussell Inlet

Hiekish Narrows

FIORDLAND
RECREATIONAL
AREA ---

Bolin Bay

50'
Mathieson Narrows

Sarah Is.

Debrisay Bay

Sheep Passage

Garvey Pt.
Waterfall

Steep, precipitous mountains

Work Bay

Windy Bay

45'
Cougar Bay

Pooley Is.

KYNOCH INLET

knot current

Kynoch Pt.

Culpepper Lagoon

Bottleneck Inlet

James Bay

TOLMIE CHANNEL

Don Peninsula

40'
Griffin Passage (use only with local knowledge)

FINLAYSON CHANNEL

Sarah Passage

Best route S during Ebb Tide
Klemtu

35'
Jane Passage

MATHIESON CHANNEL

Klemtu Passage

Caution: Ebb Tidal Steam sets a vessel toward Hazard Rk.

Jackson Passage

(use only at h.w. slack)

Rescue Bay (Jackson Narrows Marine Park)

52°30'N

Salmon Bay

N

Oscar Passage

Dowager Is.

Arthur Is. (See P.112)

KHUTZE INLET and BUTEDALE

The entrance to Khutze Inlet (on the east shore of Graham Reach) is almost 13 miles north of Hiekish Narrows. The mile-wide entrance to the inlet is between Griffin Point on the south and Asher Point on the north. Steep, sometimes precipitous, mountains surround the inlet except for Khutze River mud flats which are over a mile long and block the half-mile wide head of the inlet. When entering the inlet favor the north shore to pass Green Spit, which extends from the southern shore and leaves a clear passage (about 300 m/1,000 ft.) wide about 1.5 miles east of Asher Point. Anchorage east of the inner end of the spit may be taken in about 6 - 8 fathoms, good holding mud. Fishing is productive near the spit.

By proceeding 3.5 miles past the end of the spit and favoring the southern shore you pass Pardoe Point to arrive at an anchorage area near a spectacular waterfall. Anchor close to shore west of the waterfall in 6 - 8 fathoms, sticky mud. Very shallow shoals off the waterfall drop off quickly and must be given plenty of clearance to avoid grounding when the tide falls or tidal currents cause the vessel to swing. If you anchor at high tide the nearest land to the east is over a mile distant and it is easy to assume you have plenty of swinging space, but when the tide falls the heavy odor of rich clam mud tells you the soft shoals are <u>very</u> close at hand. The calls of waterfowl and the constant sound of the lovely waterfall make this an unforgettable spot.

Graham Reach continues about 5 miles to the north before joining Butedale Passage at Redcliff Point, marked by a light. Two miles west of the Point at the south end of Fraser Reach is a bight. **Butedale*** is at the head of the bight and north of the buildings is a spectacular waterfall. Here, torrents of water tumble down even in late summer when many of the other falls have almost dried up. The docks and buildings are in ruins and the entire area is a shambles. Although several people have proposed developing this prime location it continues to deteriorate with only a watchman to oversee the dilapidated remains. A path leads to a large lake where fishing is good, but the mosquitoes are ravenous. An Indian summer village was located here long before the arrival of Europeans when it became a busy fish cannery and then a popular stop for vessels traveling the inside Passage. Now, it is a reminder of the vagaries of time.

When winds are light or from the southeast, passable anchorage may be taken on the narrow shelf midway into the bay, though it is open to wash from ferries and cruise ships rushing up and down the channel and there is risk that the anchor could foul on logging debris. Some vessels tie between the rotting pilings at the south end of the bay. In the southeast corner is an unstable log dock where one or two boats may tie if permission is obtained from the caretaker.

In the spring the waterfalls along Graham and Fraser Reaches are among the most appealing attractions of travel along the Inside Passage. They appear in all shapes and sizes from single large falls to tiny threads and multiple cascades. Fraser Reach has the better of Graham Reach in the variety and beauty of its waterfalls.

*Butedale is on Princess Royal Island, one of the few areas inhabited by the rare Spirit or Kermode Bear but without regard for this endangered species the Provincial government has given permission to Interfor Corp. to log the island. International pressure is mounting to declare the Island a protected area.

APPROACHING BUTEDALE FROM 120 WNW, i.e. down Fraser Reach

KHUTZE INLET & BUTEDALE

Approx. Scale n.m.

0 1 2 3 4 5

Not to be used for navigation

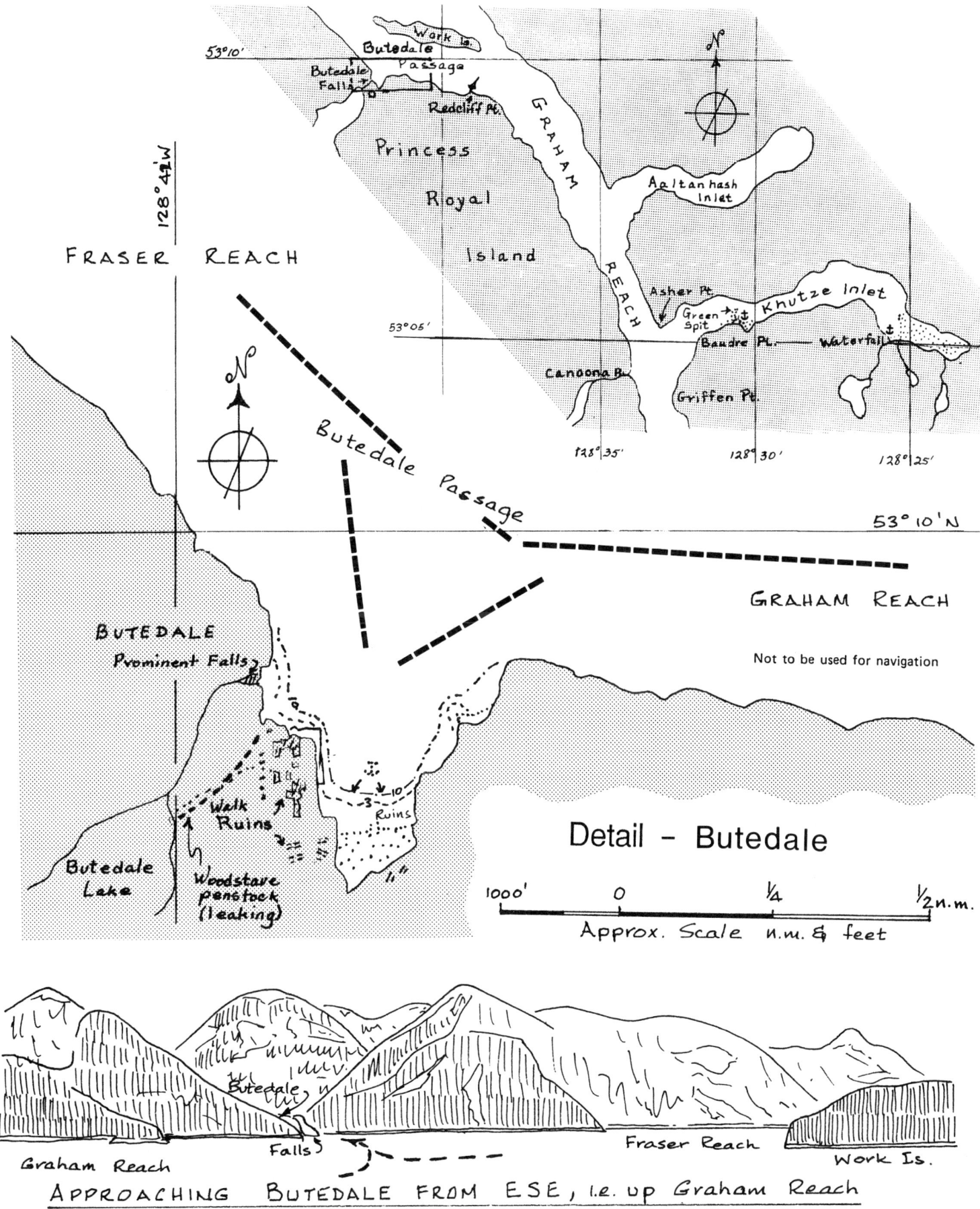

53°10'
Butedale
Work Is.
Butedale Passage
Butedale Falls
Redcliff Pt.

Princess Royal Island

128°42'W

FRASER REACH

GRAHAM REACH

Aaltanhash Inlet

Asher Pt.
Green Spit
Khutze Inlet
Baudre Pt.
Waterfall

Canoona R.
Griffen Pt.

53°05'

128°35'   128°30'   128°25'

Butedale Passage

53°10'N

GRAHAM REACH

Not to be used for navigation

BUTEDALE
Prominent Falls

10
3
Walk
Ruins
Ruins

Butedale Lake
Woodstave penstock (leaking)

Detail – Butedale

1000'   0   ¼   ½ n.m.

Approx. Scale n.m. & feet

Butedale

Graham Reach   Falls   Fraser Reach   Work Is.

APPROACHING BUTEDALE FROM ESE, i.e. up Graham Reach

COGHLAN ANCHORAGE and HARTLEY BAY

Coghlan Anchorage lies in the channel between Promise Island and the mainland at the southern entrance into Grenville Channel. Promise Island is dome-shaped with two peaks and stands out before the mountains in the background.

Enter the anchorage from the south, past Thom Point on Promise Island. Harbor Rock in the center of the passage is marked by a light. The anchorage lies beyond, on the shelf off a mud and stone beach, opposite Brodie Point. Holding is good on the shelf but exposed to the SE.

Opposite the anchorage are two buoys of white painted tires belonging to local fishermen who return to them nightly. The channel turns eastward around the top of Promise Island at Stewart Narrows. A short distance beyond is the Indian village of **Hartley Bay** where fuel, water and basic provisions are available. The fuel dock attendant monitors VHF Ch 06 and 14. The first-aid post up the hill has a nurse in attendance. A heli-pad is located here and float plane service also serves the community. The friendly people of the village are very helpful and happy to share local information with cruisers. No liquor is sold in this 'dry' village.

Grenville Channel leads northwestward from Wright Sound to Arthur Passage where it opens into Chatham Sound, thence to Prince Rupert. The south entrance is at Sainty Point, where a light is located. A bay adjacent to the light has no anchorage, being deep close inshore. Grenville Channel appears dead ended, for it narrows and has a slight jog that gives this impression. This 45-mile long, almost straight, and narrow passage, with steep mountains on both sides is one of the most unique parts of the Inside Passage. The succession of steep points off the mountains receding into the distance tends to make the channel look even narrower; huge cruise ships dwarfed by the landscape give perspective to the scene.

Several inlets indent the east side of Grenville Channel and anchorage can be found in Lowe, Klewnuggit, Baker, and Kumealon Inlets. Waterfalls are not as numerous as along Fraser Reach.

Lowe Inlet, a Marine Park about 14.5 miles from Sainty Point, is the first anchorage available when traveling from the south. The entrance is between James Point and Hepburn Point. A light on a small island in Grenville Channel is located about .25 mile NW of James Point. A short distance after turning into the inlet there is a 6-fathom bank on the south side between Hepburn and Don Points on which a vessel may anchor. The channel then narrows to .25 mile and the inlet extends for about 1.75 miles towards the northeast.

A prettier anchorage is at the far end of Lowe Inlet in **Nettle Basin**. It is reached by passing through the narrows between the peninsula of Pike Point and Mark Bluff. Anchor behind Pike Point on the southern side of spectacular Verney Falls in about 12 - 15 fathoms. Some current is felt from the falls so extra scope should be allowed. Salmon jump the falls in season and a trail on the north side of the falls provides a nice hike to a second falls.

Tides enter both ends of Grenville Channel, meeting at about Evening Point. In the narrow sections of the channel the current can attain some speed so it is advantageous to start through on the last of the flood and benefit from ebbing currents when the tide changes. However, most vessels proceed through at all stages of the tide.

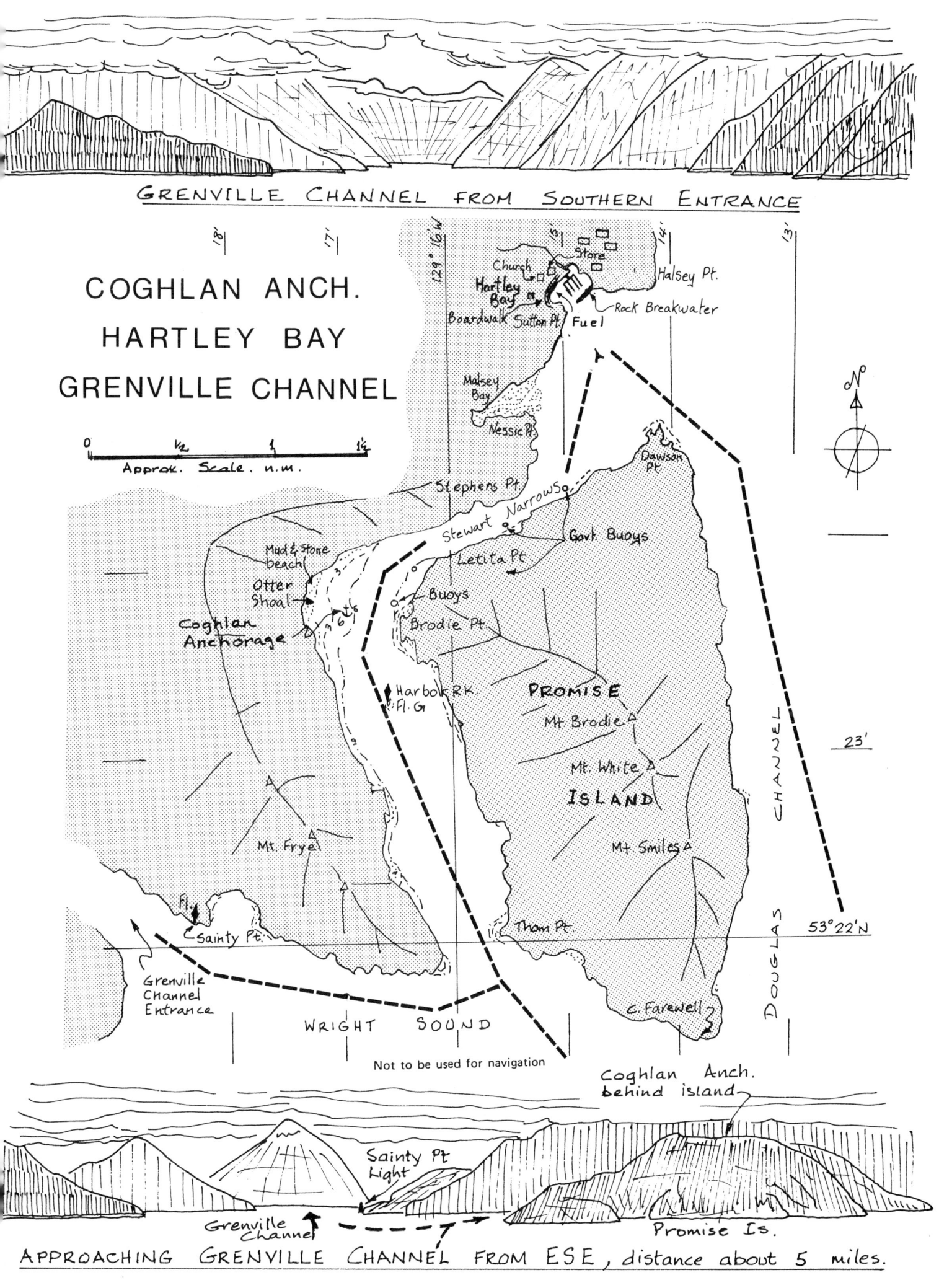

GRENVILLE CHANNEL FROM SOUTHERN ENTRANCE

COGHLAN ANCH.
HARTLEY BAY
GRENVILLE CHANNEL

Approx. Scale. n.m.

129° 16′ W

18′   17′   16′   15′   14′   13′

Store
Church
Hartley Bay
Boardwalk Sutton Pt. Fuel
Halsey Pt.
Rock Breakwater

Matsey Bay
Nessic Pt.

Dawson Pt.

Stephens Pt.
Stewart Narrows
Govt. Buoys
Letita Pt.

Mud & Stone beach
Otter Shoal
Coghlan Anchorage

Buoys
Brodie Pt.

Harbok RK.
Fl. G.

PROMISE

Mt. Brodie △

Mt. White △

ISLAND

23′

Mt. Smiles △

Mt. Frye △

Tham Pt.

53°22′N

DOUGLAS CHANNEL

Fl.
Sainty Pt.

Grenville Channel Entrance

WRIGHT   SOUND

Not to be used for navigation

C. Farewell

Coghlan Anch. behind island

Sainty Pt Light

Grenville Channel

Promise Is.

APPROACHING GRENVILLE CHANNEL FROM ESE, distance about 5 miles.

KITIMAT and the KITLOPE

This cruising area with its many anchorages, a town for provisioning, good fishing and beautiful scenery can be a side-trip on your return from Alaska, or can be a destination in itself. It can be approached either by continuing north of Hartley Bay in Douglas Channel or by way of Ursula Channel. Weather forecasts for Douglas Channel cover this area.

The Inside Passage proceeds north in Fraser Reach to turn west in McKay Reach before transiting Wright Sound and then entering Grenville Channel. At the east end of McKay Reach a 10-mile side-trip north in Ursula Channel leads to the entrance to **Bishop Bay** where the first of several hotsprings in the area are located. The Kitimat Y.C. maintains a short dock and two mooring buoys in the bay, or anchorage can be taken in 8 to 12 fathoms, sand and mud. A walkway leads to the refreshing hotsprings, where two basins are arranged for a choice of covered or outside bathing.

By following Ursula Channel to Verney Passage you can proceed north through Devastation Channel and then Douglas Channel to **Kitimat. Kitsaway Anchorage** is a beautiful anchorage off Devastation Channel west of Kitsaway Island. It provides excellent protection for many vessels is in 2 - 3 fathoms, mud and shells. Crabs and clams are outnumbered only by the multitude of horseflies and deer flies.

Continuing northward, **Weewanie Hotsprings** are about 6 miles distant on the east shore of the channel. Avoid the drying rock 18 m (60 ft.) off the south point. Two buoys provide moorage and a ladder provides assistance in reaching the unenhanced springs. Where Devastation Channel joins Douglas Channel there can be a marked increase in wind velocity if southerly winds are blowing. An excellent refuge from rough conditions can be found by anchoring at the head of **Eagle Bay** (southwest of Coste Island) in 6 - 8 fathoms. Though wind gusts can sweep through the gap at the head of the bay, the holding is good and the water is fairly calm.

The town of **Kitimat** has an economy centered on the huge Alcan Aluminum smelter. Moorage is available in three places. The small dock marked "Public" on the chart is usually filled with local fishboats, but you can raft up. A stop here is "a must" to visit the gallery of renowned Haisla carver and artist, Sammy Robinson, whose studio is near the head of the ramp. A short distance to the north is **MK Bay Marina**, a full-service marina with all the amenities. On the opposite side of the bay is **Moon Bay Marina** which also has fuel, water and moorage. Transportation to Kitimat is by taxi, hitch-hiking or bus (a walk of about .5 miles to the bus stop). The town has shopping centers, a liquor store, banks post office and a hospital.

Gardner Canal should be traveled during settled, sunny weather to view the spectacular colors in the rocky precipices, along with waterfalls and glimpses of glaciers. Unfortunately the views are marred in places by clear cuts. You must stop at Europa Hotsprings to enjoy their unique, natural setting. During stormy weather this trip should be avoided for gusty winds are magnified in the convoluted passages and the scenic mountains are hidden by clouds and fog. The Alcan Company town of Kemano is being terminated and the future of the Kemano Y.C. docks is presently unknown, but anchorage can be taken outside the harbor. By continuing to the end of Gardner Canal where the **Kitlope River** delta fans out for a considerable distance you reach the edge of a huge ecological reserves which is the largest temperate coastal watershed in the world. Check the depthsounder regularly, for shoals extend well off the mouth of the river and the cloudy water gives no indication of depth. Anchorage may be taken in **Chief Mathews Bay** where the Haisla Indians have constructed a longhouse.

KITIMAT and the KITLOPE

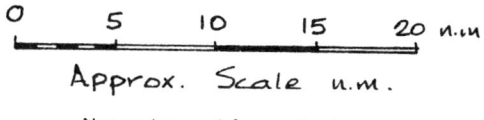

0   5   10   15   20 n.m.

Approx. Scale n.m.

Not to be used for navigation

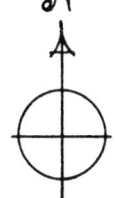

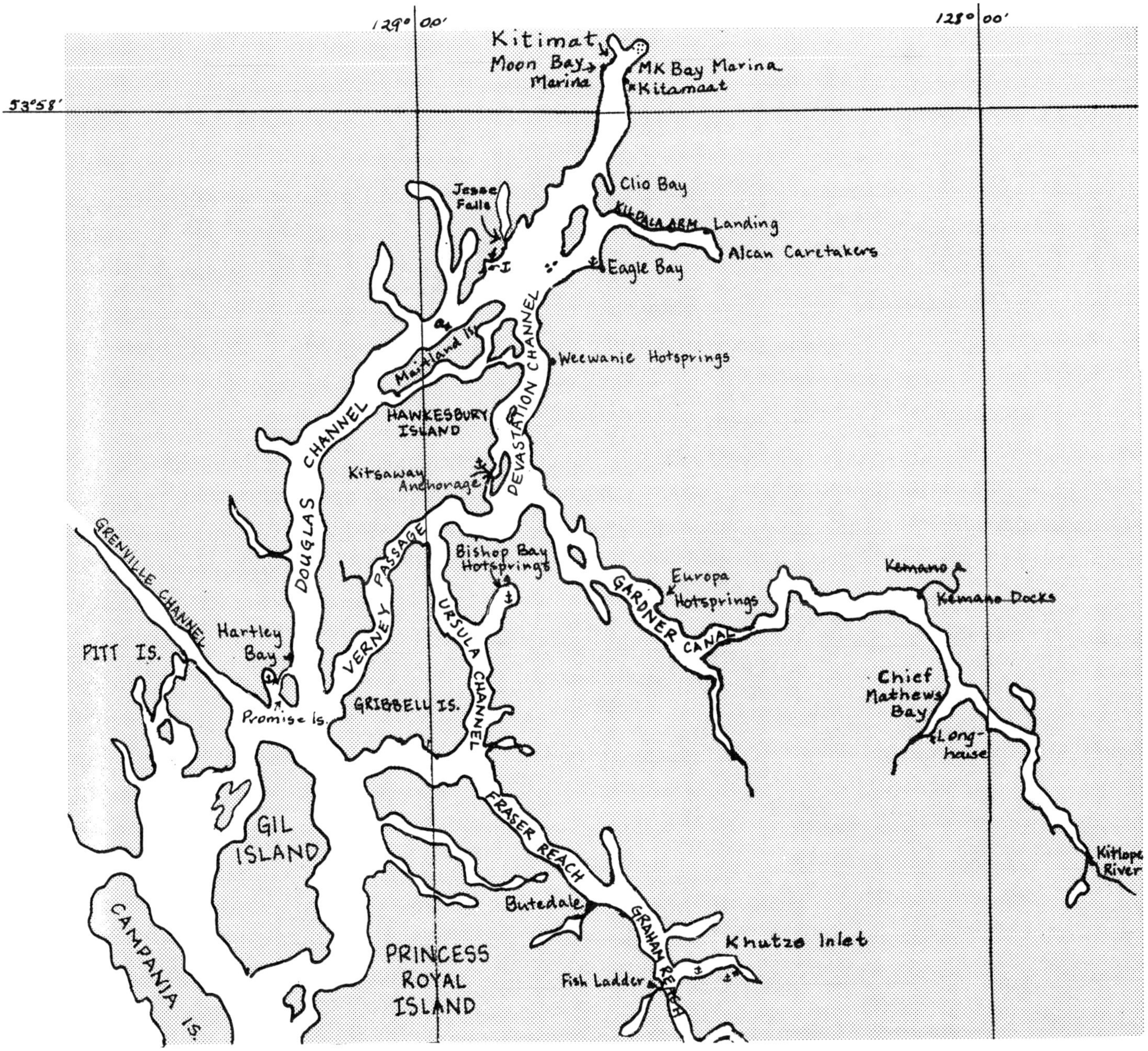

129° 00'

125° 00'

53°58'

Kitimat

Moon Bay
Marina

MK Bay Marina

*Kitamaat

Clio Bay

KILDALA ARM Landing

Alcan Caretakers

Jesse
Falls

Eagle Bay

Maitland I.

Weewanie Hotsprings

DOUGLAS CHANNEL

DEVASTATION CHANNEL

HAWKESBURY ISLAND

Kitsaway
Anchorage

GRENVILLE CHANNEL

VERNEY PASSAGE

Bishop Bay
Hotsprings

URSULA CHANNEL

GARDNER CANAL

Europa
Hotsprings

Kemano

Kemano Docks

PITT IS.

Hartley
Bay

GRIBBELL IS.

Chief
Mathews
Bay

Promise Is.

Long-
house

Kitlope
River

FRASER REACH

GIL
ISLAND

CAMPANIA IS.

Butedale

GRAHAM REACH

Khutze Inlet

PRINCESS
ROYAL
ISLAND

Fish Ladder

KLEWNUGGIT INLET

This is a very beautiful anchorage, isolated and secure, but a long way in from Grenville Channel. Klewnuggit Inlet Marine Park includes East inlet, Brodie Lake, Freda Lake (lightly indicated on the sketch) and the surrounding land. It is well worth the effort to visit this area, for the scenery is magnificent.

When turning in to the wide entrance of the inlet give a safe clearance to Morning Reef, marked by a light. A partially drying, submerged reef runs between Evening Point and the light. Do not turn in until the inlet is well abeam and a route into the center of the inlet can be taken.

APPROACHING KLEWNUGGIT INLET FROM SE, up Grenville Ch.

A deep anchorage lies between Harriot Island and the long peninsula which projects southward into the Inlet. However, for small boats, better anchorage is around this peninsula in the northwestern inner bay of **East Inlet**. This spacious anchorage is seldom visited by more than one or two boats at a time. In this protected bay, surrounded by forested slopes and rocky peaks you are truly isolated from the outer world. Crabbing is excellent. The head of the bay is shoal.

Exposed Inlet, the southern portion of Klewnuggit is exposed to winds coming through gaps in the mountains, but during settled weather or southerly winds anchorage may be taken. Drying flats at the head of the bay lie off a large swamp.

ENTRANCE INTO KLEWNUGGIT INLET

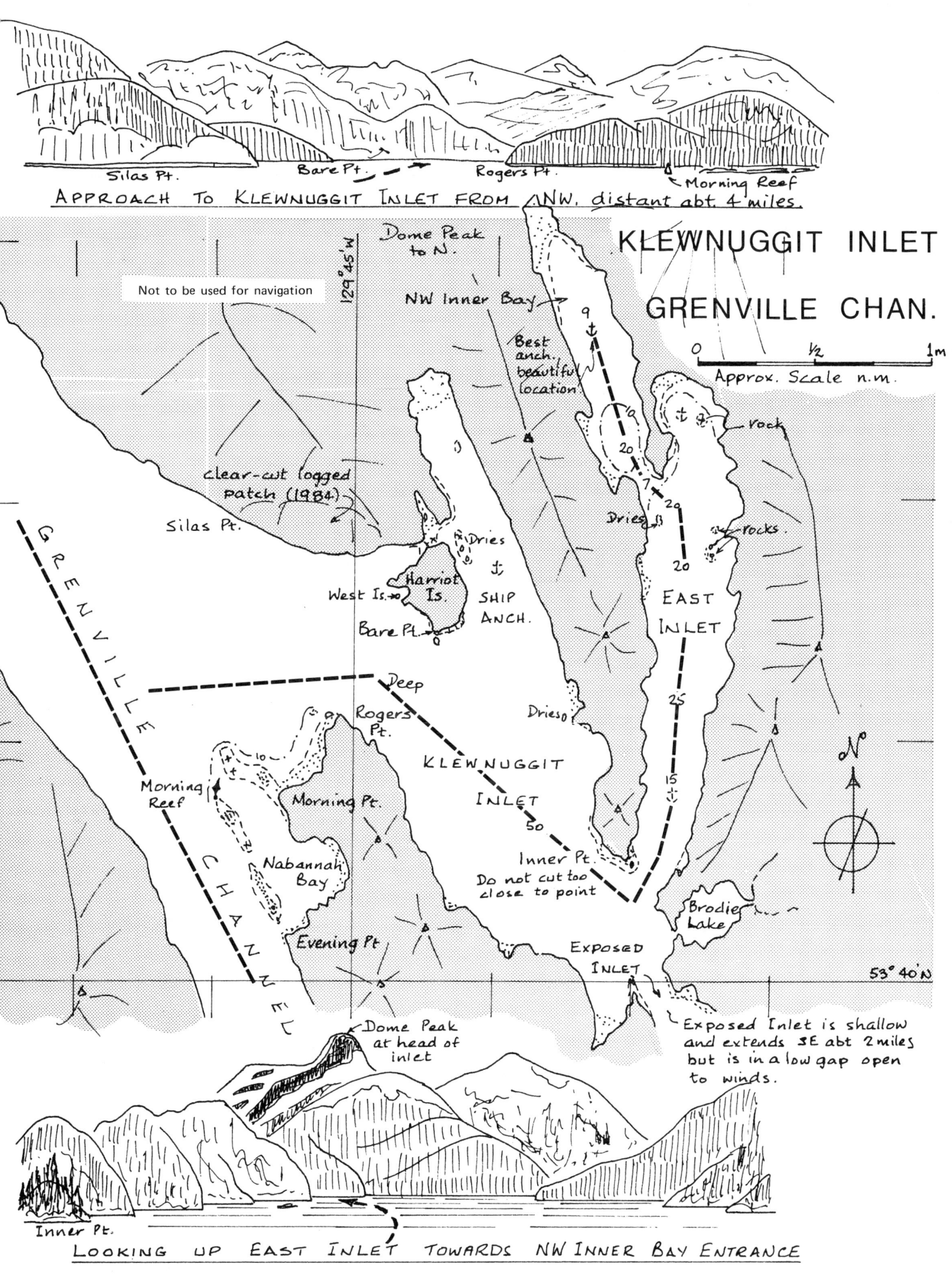

Silas Pt.   Bare Pt.   Rogers Pt.   Morning Reef

APPROACH TO KLEWNUGGIT INLET FROM NW. distant abt. 4 miles.

KLEWNUGGIT INLET

GRENVILLE CHAN.

Not to be used for navigation

Dome Peak to N.

NW Inner Bay

129°45'W

0   ½   1m
Approx. Scale n.m.

clear-cut logged patch (1984)

Silas Pt.

Best anch, beautiful location

20

9

7

20

Dries

20

rock

rocks

EAST INLET

Dries J.

West Is.   Harriot Is.   SHIP ANCH.

Bare Pt.

GRENVILLE

Deep

Rogers Pt.

10

Morning Reef

Morning Pt.

Nabannah Bay

KLEWNUGGIT INLET

50

Dries

25

15

N°

CHANNEL

Inner Pt.
Do not cut too close to point

Brodier Lake

Evening Pt

5

6

Dome Peak at head of inlet

EXPOSED INLET

53°40'N

Exposed Inlet is shallow and extends SE abt 2 miles but is in a low gap open to winds.

Inner Pt.

LOOKING UP EAST INLET TOWARDS NW INNER BAY ENTRANCE

BAKER INLET and KUMEALON INLET

Baker Inlet, 10 miles further north on the eastern shore of Grenville Channel, provides anchorage at the eastern end. The entrance through Watts Narrows (60 m/ 200 feet wide) is deep but has strong currents; use Prince Rupert slack water times when entering. When traveling north the entrance is easy to miss in spite of the light on the south side of the entrance. A white house at Po-aae River on the west side of Grenville Channel indicates the location of the Narrows.

Three miles north of Baker Inlet, on the northeastern side of Grenville Channel is Kumealon Inlet. The 450 m (1,500-foot) wide entrance is between Lerwicke and McMurray Points. Give a safe clearance to foul ground located .2 mile offshore south of McMurray Point. There is a logging camp in the small bay beyond the entrance, with a small float in front¬depth unknown.

The main anchorage lies further up at the head of the inlet. Stay about 60 m (200 feet) off the north shore to pass the rocky patch extending into mid-channel from the southern shore. Beyond the rocky area the eastern end of the inlet forms a basin, where anchorage in 10 - 12 fathoms can be taken. At the north side of the basin a narrow, rock encumbered channel with tidal falls leads from Kumealon Lagoon. It cannot be entered except by dinghy at slack water.

A smaller but more convenient anchorage lies at the entrance, west of Lerwick Point. There is room for only two or three boats here.

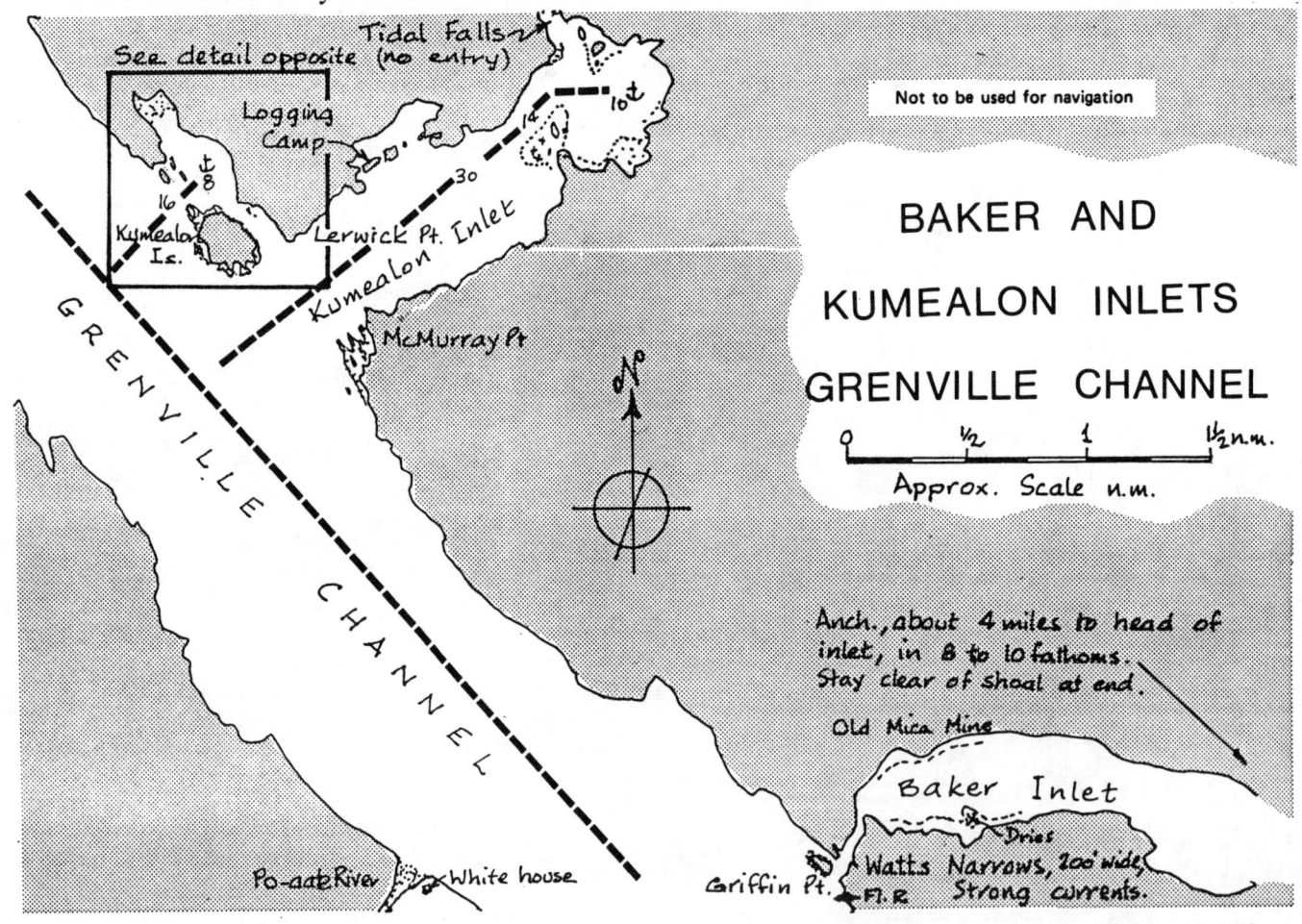

See detail opposite
Tidal Falls (no entry)
Logging Camp
Kumealon Is.
Lerwick Pt. Inlet
Kumealon
McMurray Pt
GRENVILLE CHANNEL
Po-aae River   White house
Griffin Pt.   Fl. R

Not to be used for navigation

BAKER AND

KUMEALON INLETS

GRENVILLE CHANNEL

0   ½   1   1½ n.m.

Approx. Scale n.m.

Anch., about 4 miles to head of inlet, in 8 to 10 fathoms. Stay clear of shoal at end.
Old Mica Mine
Baker Inlet
Dries
Watts Narrows, 200' wide, Strong currents.

ENTRANCE TO KUMEALON IS. ANCHORAGE

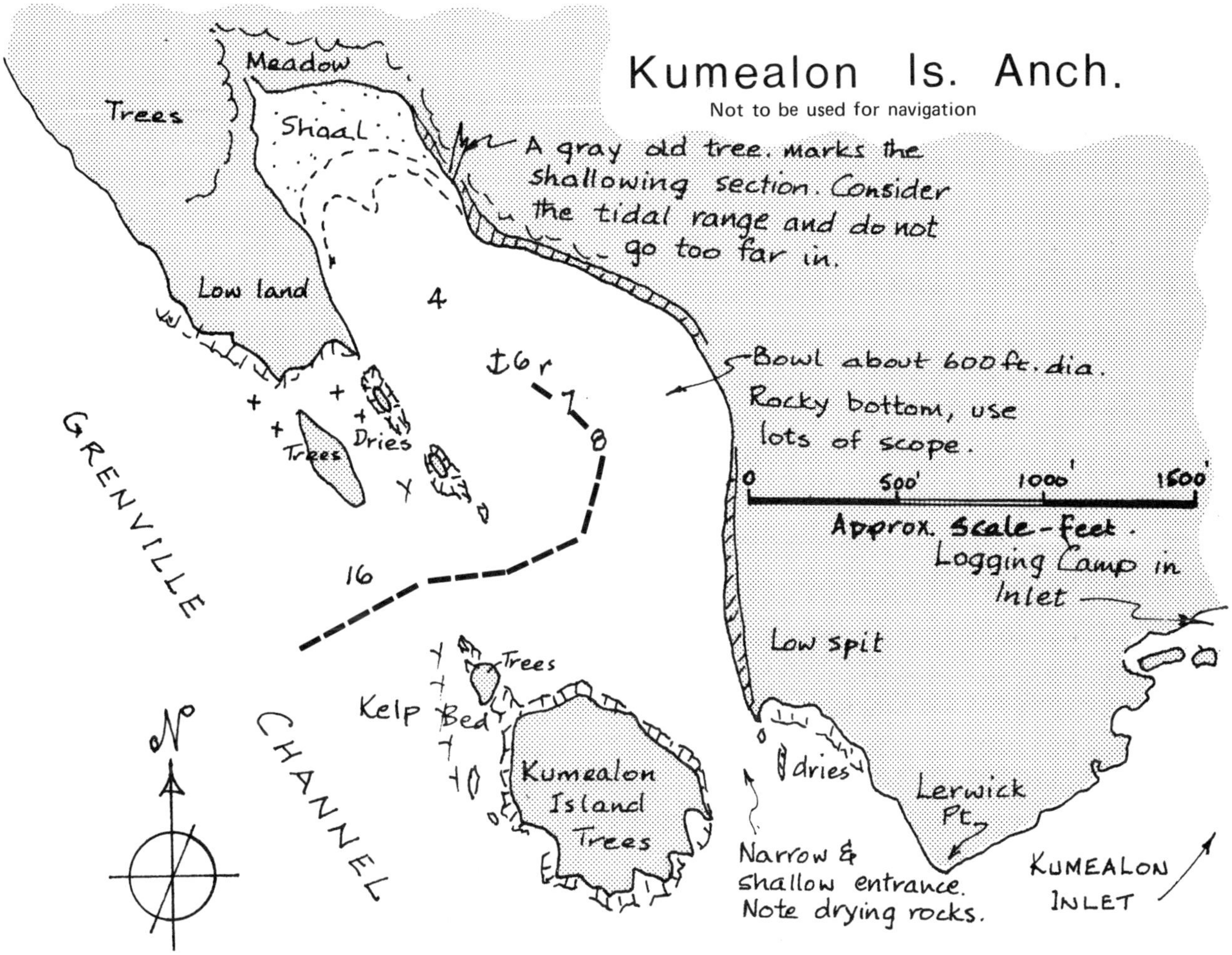

Kumealon Is. Anch.
Not to be used for navigation

Meadow

Trees

Shoal

Low land

4

‡6r

7

8

16

A gray old tree marks the
shallowing section. Consider
the tidal range and do not
go too far in.

Bowl about 600 ft. dia.
Rocky bottom, use
lots of scope.

0   500'   1000'   1500'

Approx. Scale - Feet

Logging Camp in
Inlet

Low spit

GRENVILLE CHANNEL

N

Trees

Dries

Trees

Kelp Bed

Kumealon
Island
Trees

dries

Lerwick
Pt.

Narrow &
shallow entrance.
Note drying rocks.

KUMEALON
INLET

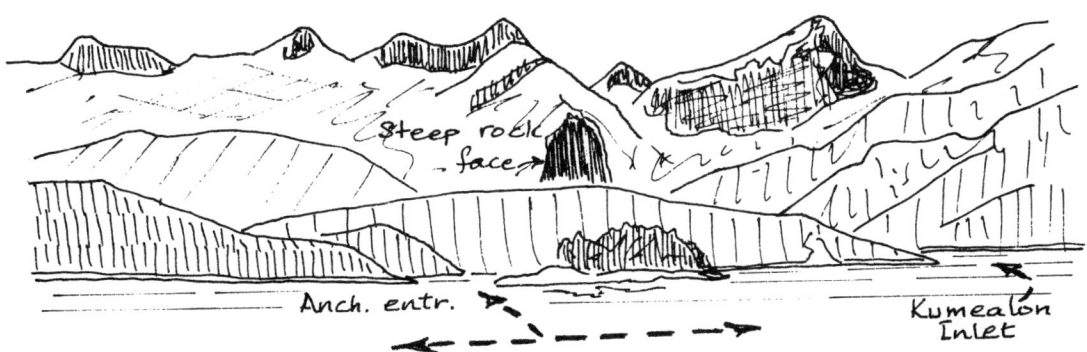

Steep rock
face

Anch. entr.

Kumealon
Inlet

APPROACH TO KUMEALON INLET ANCHORAGE FROM W.

McMICKING ANCHORAGES

From the northern end of Grenville Channel the Inside Passage continues through Arthur Passage and Malacca Passage to Chatham Sound and the approaches to Prince Rupert. Anchorages in this area are the closest ones south of Prince Rupert and can be used as a resting place or to await reasonable weather and sea conditions for approaching the city.

McMicking, Elliott and Lewis Islands are on the western side of Arthur Passage. Chismore and Kelp Passages are narrower channels that separate the three islands on their western sides from the shore of Porcher Island. Kelp Passage is constricted with rock and shoal and should not be attempted.

Lawson Harbor lies in a bight on Lewis Island and is marked by a beach on the southern shore where some ruins remain. Avoid the rock off the north end of Break Island. By anchoring in the middle of the basin you should clear the rocks in the SE corner. The holding is good though there is exposure to the north and the effect of passing cruise ships is felt. For a more spacious anchorage continue through Bloxam Pass (currents of about 1 knot are normal) to enter the basin south of Cocktail Point.

Chismore Passage forms a basin south of Elliott Islands which provides good anchorage on the Lewis Island side. Approach this basin using a mid-channel course through Bloxam Passage, between Elliott and Lewis Islands. When northbound in Arthur Passage pass well clear of Herbert Reefs, which are marked by a concrete post and light.

Porcher Island Cannery, south of Ada Islands on the northeastern tip, and Hunt Inlet on the north side of Porcher Island can also be used as a refuge. Both have narrow entrances, with rocky ledges near the approaches.

The crossing of the southeastern part of Chatham Sound to Prince Rupert is well marked with lights and buoys on all rocks, shoals and islands. From Herbert Reefs the flashing green lit buoy off Cecil Patch can be passed on its east side; then the light on Genn Islands passed on its west. This clears the sand and shoal areas of the Skeena River entrances. The course from Genn Islands must clear the Horsey and Agnew Bank buoys south of Ridley Island. The coal terminal and grain elevator of the deep sea port (marked by strobe lights) are visible even in daylight, a sure sign that Prince Rupert is near.

APPROACHING PRINCE RUPERT FROM SE, i.e. from near Genn Is. Light

McMICKING IS. ANCH.

ARTHUR PASSAGE

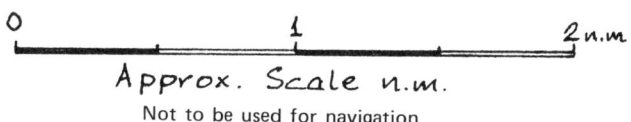

0   1   2 n.m.

Approx. Scale n.m.

Not to be used for navigation

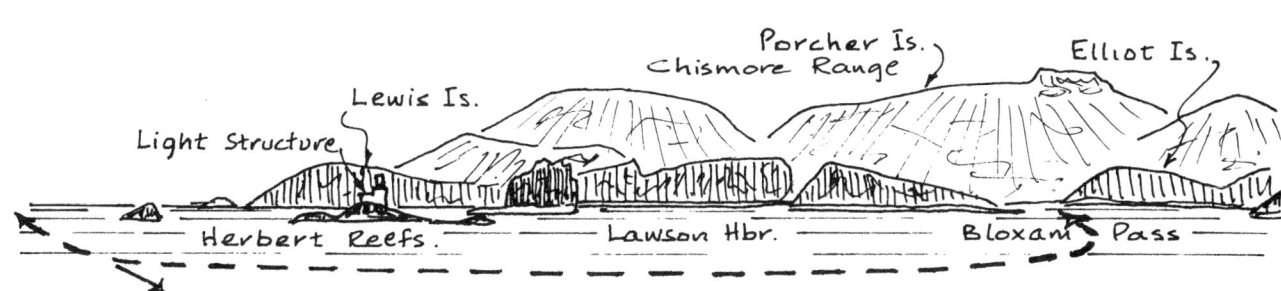

Light Structure — Lewis Is. — Chismore Range — Porcher Is. — Elliot Is.

Herbert Reefs. — Lawson Hbr. — Bloxam Pass

APPROACHING McMICKING ISLANDS ANCHORAGE FROM N

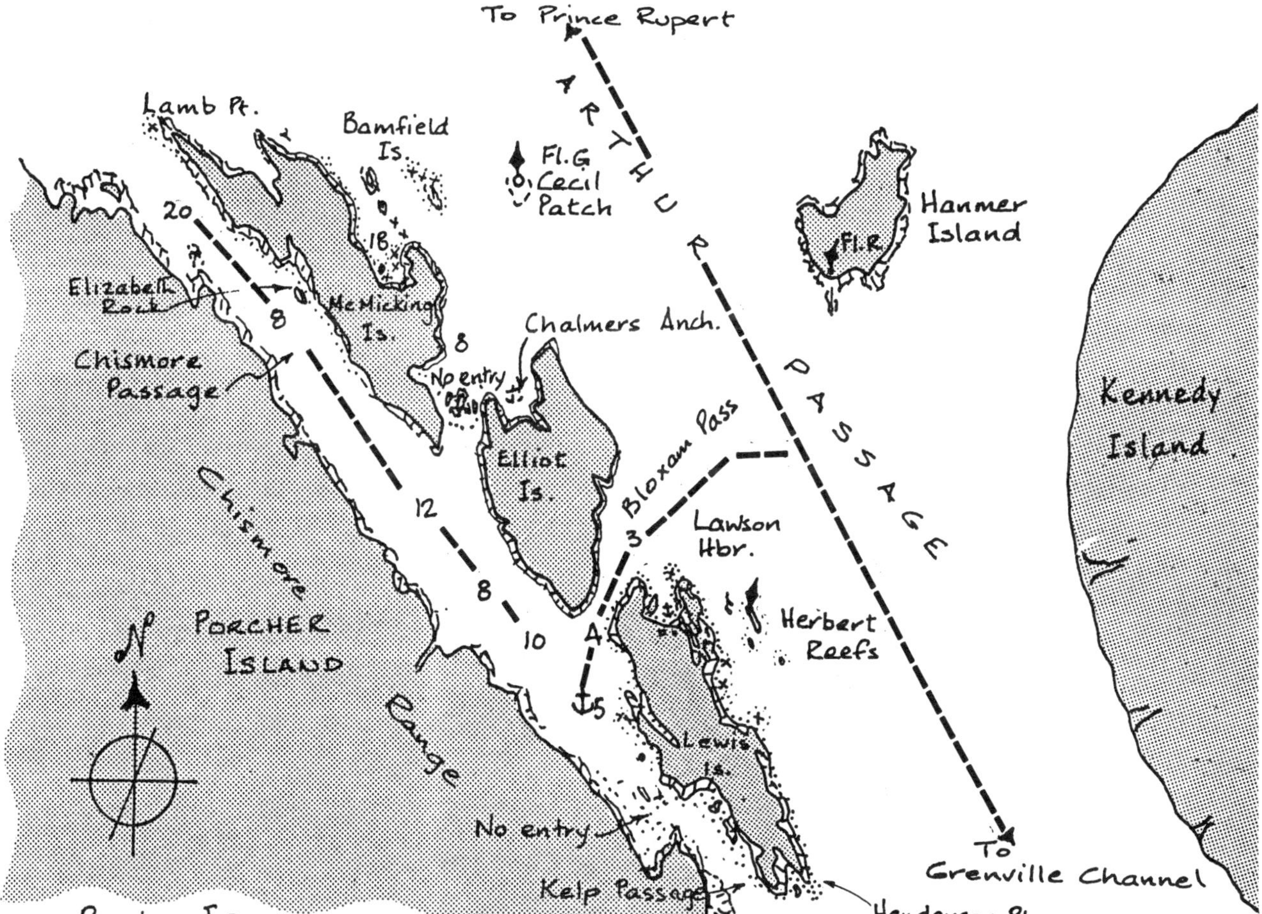

To Prince Rupert

ARTHUR

Lamb Pt.   Bamfield Is.

Fl.G Cecil Patch   Hanmer Island   Fl.R.

20   McMicking Is.   18   Chalmers Anch.   PASSAGE

Elizabeth Rock

8   No entry   Kennedy Island

Chismore Passage   8

12   Elliot Is.   Bloxam Pass   Lawson Hbr.

Chismore   3

N   PORCHER ISLAND   8   A   Herbert Reefs

10   A   To Grenville Channel

Range   5   Lewis

No entry

Kelp Passage   Henderson Pt.

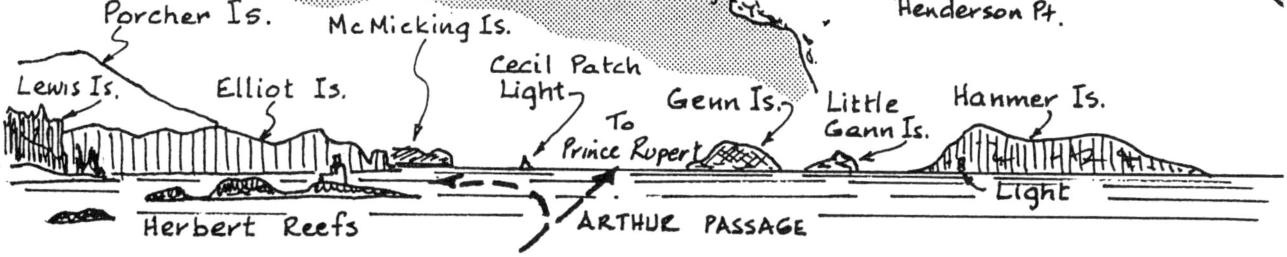

Porcher Is.   McMicking Is.   Cecil Patch Light   Gann Is.   Little Gann Is.   Hanmer Is.

Lewis Is.   Elliot Is.   To Prince Rupert   Light

Herbert Reefs   ARTHUR PASSAGE

APPROACHING McMICKING ISLANDS ANCHORAGE FROM SE

PORT EDWARD in PORPOISE CHANNEL

Until recently the facilities in Port Edward were available only to private vessels and fishboats but this facility now has moorage space available and welcomes transient cruising vessels. This quiet little village is a convenient spot to stop, particularly if winds in Chatham Sound create beam seas which make travel uncomfortable for the approach to Prince Rupert Harbour. Similarly, when vessels are returning from Alaskan waters this provides a suitable spot to stop, since it reduces the following day's southbound travel exposed to beam seas. An early start the next morning can be done in relative comfort before the westerlies pick up in Brown Passage.

This harbor may be approached from the south or from the northwest. At low tide Flora Bank becomes evident as it dries, and with any wind, breakers mark Agnew Bank and other shoal waters. From the <u>south</u> you will find the turn into the Porpoise Channel fairway marked by Agnew Bank light and bell buoy "D24." The Porpoise Harbour Entrance range and port and starboard hand buoys lead to the entrance to the Channel. From the <u>northwest</u> follow the deeper (15 fathoms) waters of the channel, where waters are less disturbed, to avoid the shoal areas and drying reefs. Caution is advised when transiting Porpoise Channel for tidal streams at the entrance can reach 2 knots and there is a strong northward set to tidal currents at the northeast end of the channel during a falling tide. A mid-channel course takes you past commercial structures lining the shores until the moorage facilities come into view.

The Harbour Authority located at Port Edward has control of moorage facilities here and in Prince Rupert (Fairview and Rushbrook). Moorage is on a first-come, first-served basis; vessels tie to the docks and then register at the harbor office. Showers, restrooms and a laundromat are available and docks have water and power (110V, some with 220V). Plans are in the works to establish a fuel facility but at present the nearest source of fuel is in Prince Rupert at the Fairview dock. Moore's Boatworks can provide mechanical and electrical services and the boatyard can repair wood, fiberglass and aluminum vessels. The travelift has a 15-ton capacity. There is a post office, laundromat, general store and bank in the town and bus service connects the community to Prince Rupert. The eating establishments offer take-out food but for restaurant dining you must go to Prince Rupert.

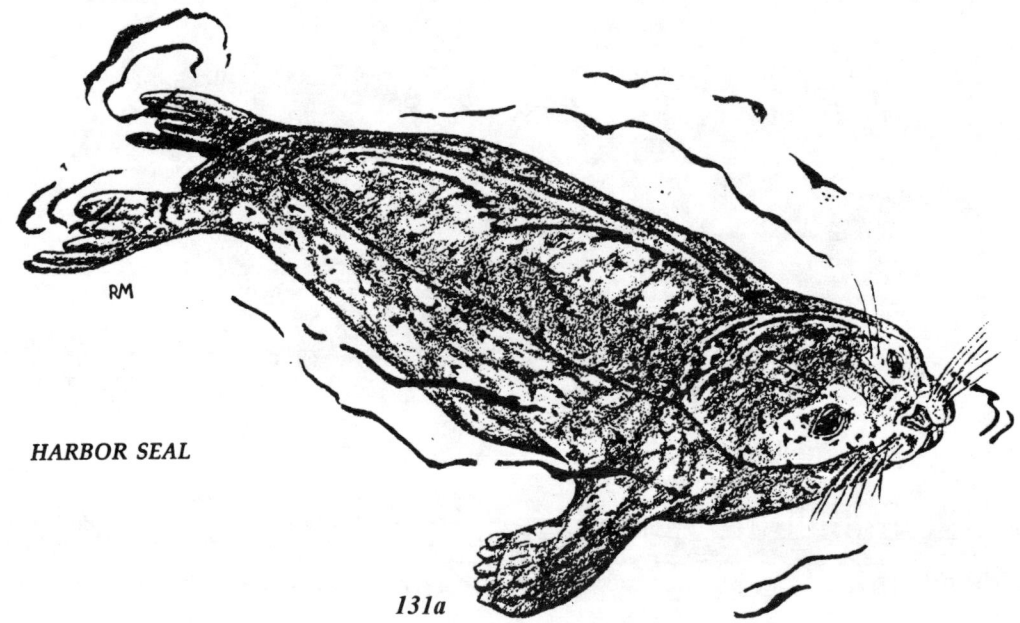

HARBOR SEAL

131a

Details

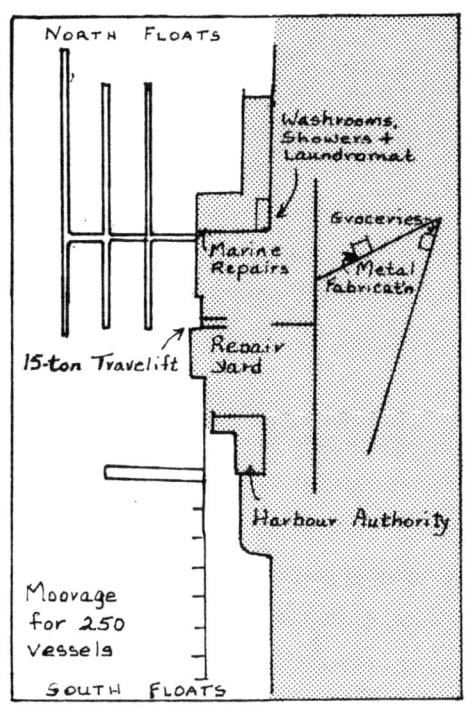

North Floats

Washrooms, Showers + Laundromat

Groceries

Marine Repairs

Metal Fabricatn

15-ton Travelift

Repair Yard

Harbour Authority

Moorage for 250 vessels

South Floats

Port Edward

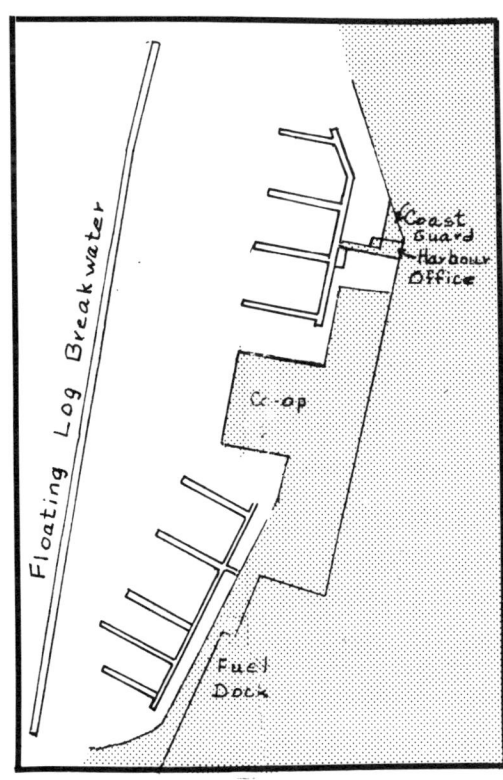

Floating Log Breakwater

Coast Guard

Harbour Office

Co-op

Fuel Dock

Fairview

PORT EDWARD
Porpoise Harbour

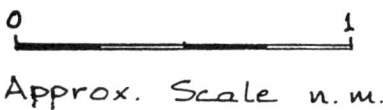

Approx. Scale n.m.

Not to be used for navigation

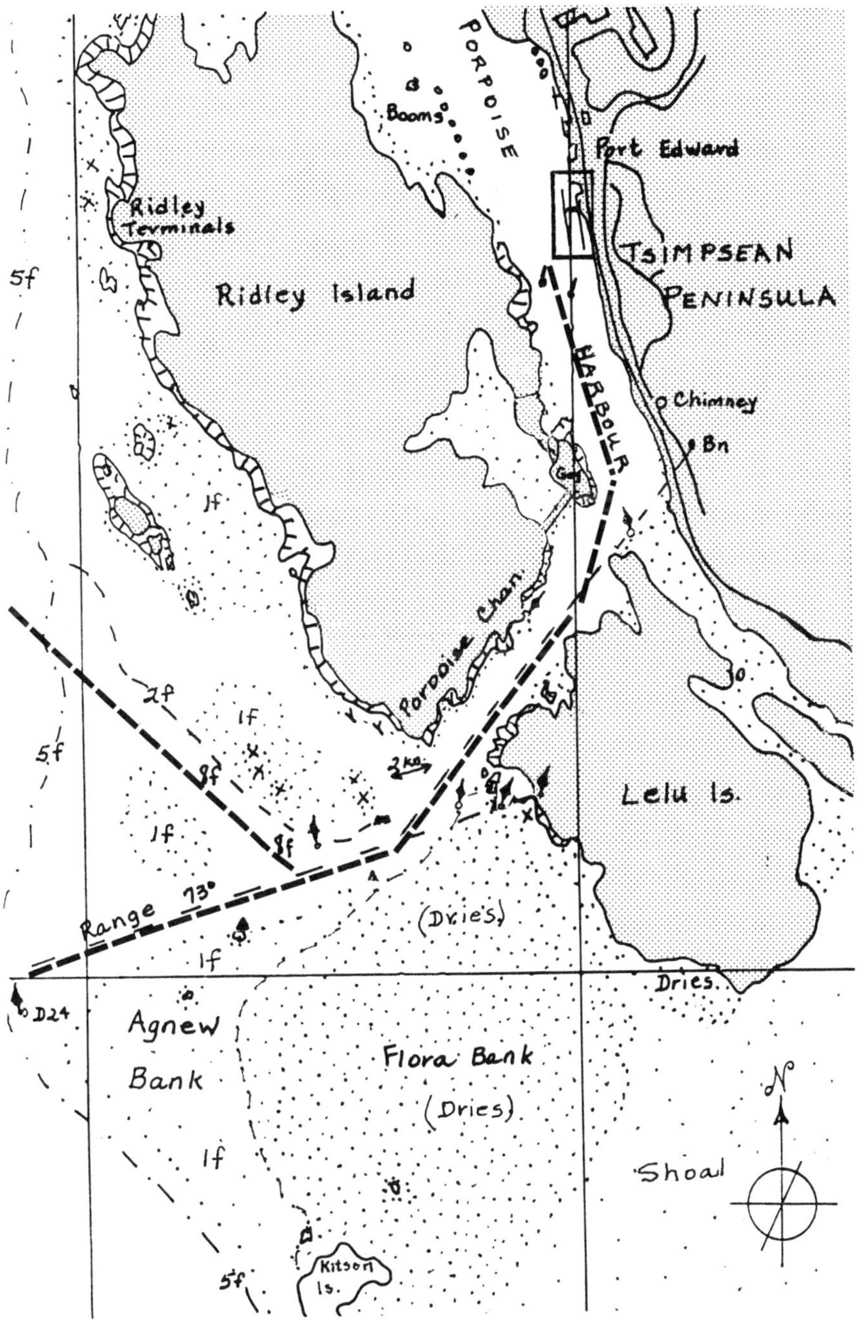

Booms

PORPOISE

Port Edward

Ridley Terminals

Ridley Island

TSIMPSEAN PENINSULA

Chimney

Bn

5f

HARBOUR

Porpoise Chan.

Lelu Is.

2f

1f

5f

1f

1f

2kn

1f

Range 73°

(Dries)

Dries.

1f

D24

Agnew Bank

Flora Bank (Dries)

Shoal

1f

5f

Kitson Is.

PRINCE RUPERT

This attractive, busy city is the northernmost population center of B.C. It bustles with activity for much of the summer as the fishing fleet uses the large harbor as a home base and many cruising vessels stop in to rest, re-stock, and enjoy eating out. It is also a **Port of Entry**, where you must report when returning from Alaska.

The harbor is a magnificent natural basin, protected from seaward by Digby Island. It has deep water and plenty of space for expansion. Prince Rupert lies on the flat part of Kaien Island, overlooked by the high, steep bulk of Mount Hays. When approaching from the south the Ridley Island Deep Sea Terminal and some of the industrial mills on Port Edward in front of Mount Hayes are visible from a distance.

The approach from Ketchikan passes inside the screen of Dundas and Melville Islands along Chatham Sound to the buoy at Petrel Rock (Fl.G, #D.39), then turns south of bell buoy D33 before entering the harbor. From seaward (i.e. Dixon Entrance) pick up the lighthouses and buoys of Brown Passage, 16 miles WNW of Petrel Rock. See the sketch on page 217.

The harbor entrance between Kaien and Digby Islands is well marked at the various ledges and shoals, and is wide enough to accommodate the heavy traffic of a busy deep sea port. Much driftwood collects here with the tidal flow and a careful lookout is needed.

Prince Rupert's facilities lie on the east side of the harbor. On the west side of the harbor a narrow, buoyed channel which can be used only at high water, leads through Venn Passage to the village of Metlakatla, then out through the bay into Chatham Strait. This channel shortens the trip northward and the detail chart 3955 must be used.

When entering the harbor the deep sea terminals are passed, followed by the Fishermen's Co-op and **Fairview Public Floats** behind a breakwater. These are usually filled with fishing vessels; a detailed sketch of them is on the previous page. The B.C. and Alaska Ferry Terminals are next. The harbor front turns northwesterly after the Railway Barge Terminal and the downtown part of Prince Rupert is visible. The Atlin Docks are designed to accommodate small cruise ships and mega-yachts. To arrange moorage at all docks (except at the Yacht Club) call (250) 628-9220. Beyond the cruise ship dock are the Prince Rupert Yacht Club floats, a good place to moor when space is available. Protected by a floating breakwater, it is somewhat affected by wash in the channel.

Transients can usually find moorage at **Rushbrook Public Floats** located near the top of the harbor. A floating log breakwater protects the floats and the entrance is at the northern end. It may be necessary to raft up during the summer months. After tying up, report to the harbormaster who is an excellent source of local information. Water is available on the floats and garbage disposal is at the head of the pier.

Rushbrook is about a mile out of the main city center. While taxis are available, walking is commonplace. On the way in you will pass Smiles Seafood, a highly recommended eating place. The waterfront road joins the Prince Rupert downtown core near the Courthouse and the Visitor's Bureau and Museum. Shopping centers, craft shops and the Post Office are along 1st, 2nd, and 3rd Avenues. A laundromat is on McBride, just up from the Courthouse. For a nominal charge showers can be had at the Pioneer Rooms on 3rd Avenue in an old, but clean boarding house. The Esso fuel dock also has a shower which usually has a queue.

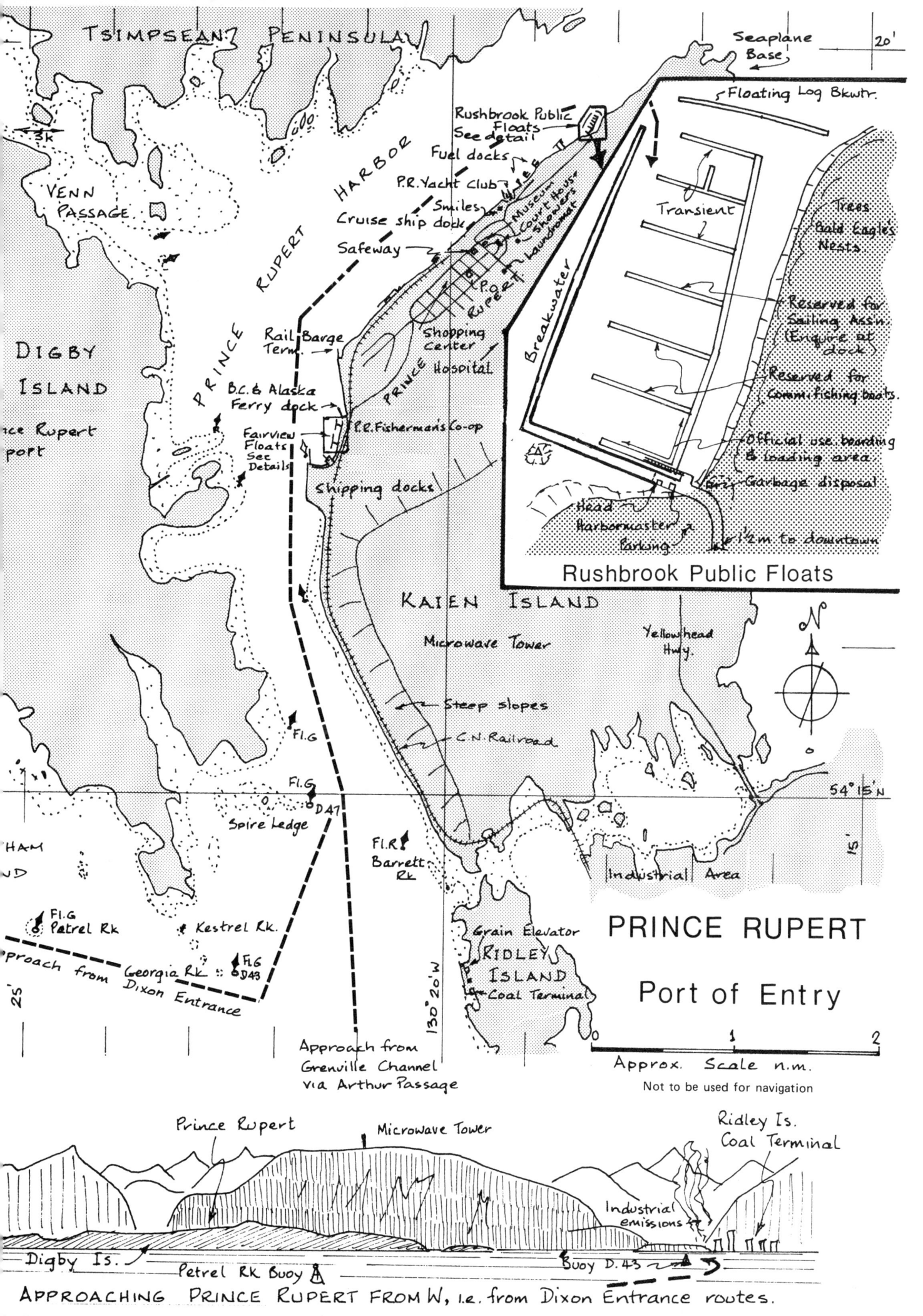

TSIMPSEAN? PENINSULA

VENN PASSAGE

3k

DIGBY ISLAND

ce Rupert
port

PRINCE RUPERT HARBOR

Rushbrook Public Floats
See detail

Fuel docks

P.R. Yacht Club

Smiles

Cruise ship dock

Safeway

Rail Barge Term.

B.C. & Alaska Ferry dock

Fairview Floats See Details

Shipping docks

Museum
Court House
Showers
Laundromat

P.o.e.
P. Rupert

Shopping Center

Hospital

P.R. Fisherman's Co-op

Seaplane Base

20'

Floating Log Bkwtr.

Transient

Breakwater

Trees Bald Eagles Nests

Reserved for Sailing Ass'n (Enquire at dock)

Reserved for Comm. fishing boats.

Official use boarding & loading area

Garbage disposal

Head Harbormaster Parking

1½m to downtown

Rushbrook Public Floats

KAIEN ISLAND

Microwave Tower

Steep slopes

C.N. Railroad

Yellowhead Hwy.

N

54° 15' N

15'

Fl.G

Fl.G

D 47

Spire Ledge

Fl.R
Barrett Rk

Industrial Area

Fl.G
Petrel Rk

Kestrel Rk.

Fl.G
D 43

HAM
ND

25'

Approach from Dixon Entrance

Georgia Rk.

Approach from Grenville Channel via Arthur Passage

130° 20' W

Grain Elevator

RIDLEY ISLAND

Coal Terminal

PRINCE RUPERT

Port of Entry

0   1   2

Approx. Scale n.m.

Not to be used for navigation

Prince Rupert

Microwave Tower

Ridley Is. Coal Terminal

Industrial emissions

Digby Is.

Petrel Rk Buoy

Buoy D. 43

APPROACHING PRINCE RUPERT FROM W, i.e. from Dixon Entrance routes.

Bar Point Basin at Ketchikan

Vixen Harbor

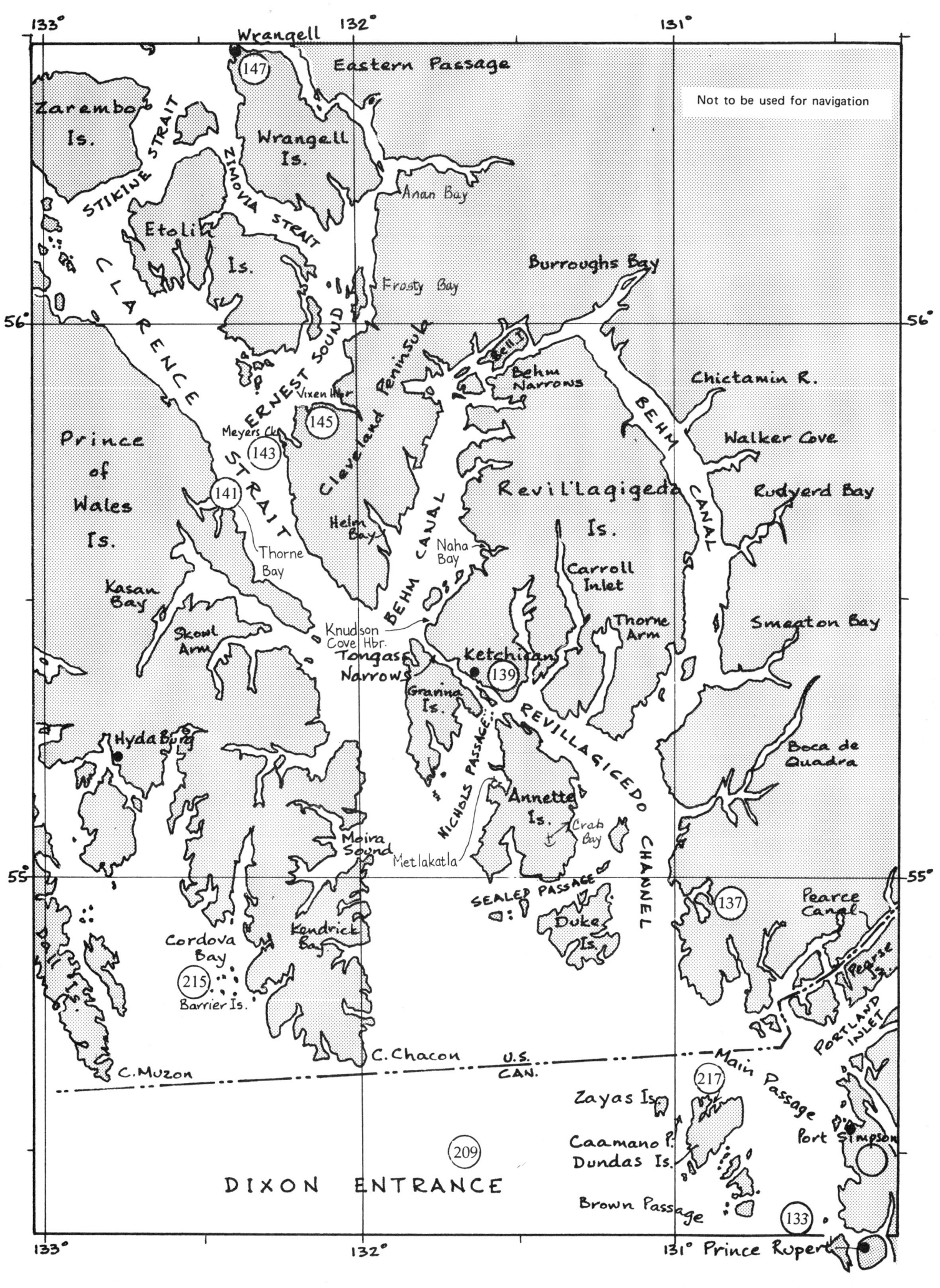

FOGGY BAY

The distance between the Ports of Entry of Prince Rupert and Ketchikan is about 90 miles; between them lies Dixon Entrance. This is more than a normal day's travel for the average yacht though use of Venn Passage eliminates quite a few miles and one must use Charts 3955 and 3957. Foggy Bay and Brundige Inlet on Dundas Island are anchorages that will help to break the distance to be covered into convenient stages. One method would be to use Brundige Inlet for the voyage north, and Foggy Bay for the trip south. However, the crossing of Dixon Entrance is a major step and a skipper might prefer to cross when he can. If Foggy Bay is to be used on the northbound trip, then it is advisable that U.S. Customs in Ketchikan be called (907-225-2254) from Prince Rupert for permission to stop in Foggy Bay before entering Ketchikan the next day

The initial portion of the crossing is in Chatham Sound, in the lee of Dundas Island. It is after passing Green Island Lighthouse and the light on Holiday Island at the northwestern tip of Dundas Island that the yacht faces the 10 miles of the actual crossing of Dixon Entrance. Tree Point Lighthouse in Alaska is a welcome sight indicating the crossing is completed, but the swell still crashes on the lee shore as you travel up into Revillagigedo Channel. Seven miles from Tree Point is Foggy Point and the entrance into Foggy Bay. The swell marks the reefs and rocks that surround the bay, and can present an intimidating sight when the seas are high.

It is preferable to enter anchorages Foggy Bay anchorages during the lower part of the tide when the various rocks, reefs, and shoals are clearly visible. When turning into **Foggy Bay (Inner Cove),** clear the reefs that extend about .5 mile north of Foggy Point, then steer to pass south of the submerged reefs that extend about .75 mile south and southeast of DeLong Islands. Ahead, on the east side of the bay an obvious opening leads into Very Inlet. The approach to an excellent anchorage lies south of this opening, behind a large, wooded island. As you close the shore the entrance becomes clearer, but never obvious because the land behind appears to enclose it. Stay clear of the reefs in the entrance, until the channel leading behind the island is visible. Though narrow, a mid-channel route leads easily into the wider basin where secure anchorage can be taken in 5 to 6 fathoms, mud. The southern openings into the basin at the south end of the large island are shallow, drying at low water. They give a view into the outer bay where swell marks the reef.

Somewhat exposed anchorage can be taken in the outer cove of Foggy Bay about 1.5 miles south of the approach to the inner cove. Here, a pipeline from a spring gives good water. Anchorage can be taken in Very Inlet, but it can only be entered at high water slack because of the rapids at the narrows, hence it is not useful for a transient vessel.

There are additional anchorages in this area. **Kah Shakes Cove** is about 5 miles north of Foggy Bay. **Ray Anchorage** and **Morse Cove** on Duke Island can be used. The latter anchorage has a narrow entrance with a drying rock near mid-channel and thus should be entered at low water, but since there are many rocks in this area it is not a recommended choice. In Canadian waters anchorage can be taken in **Brundige Inlet** on Dundas Island. For sketch see page 216.

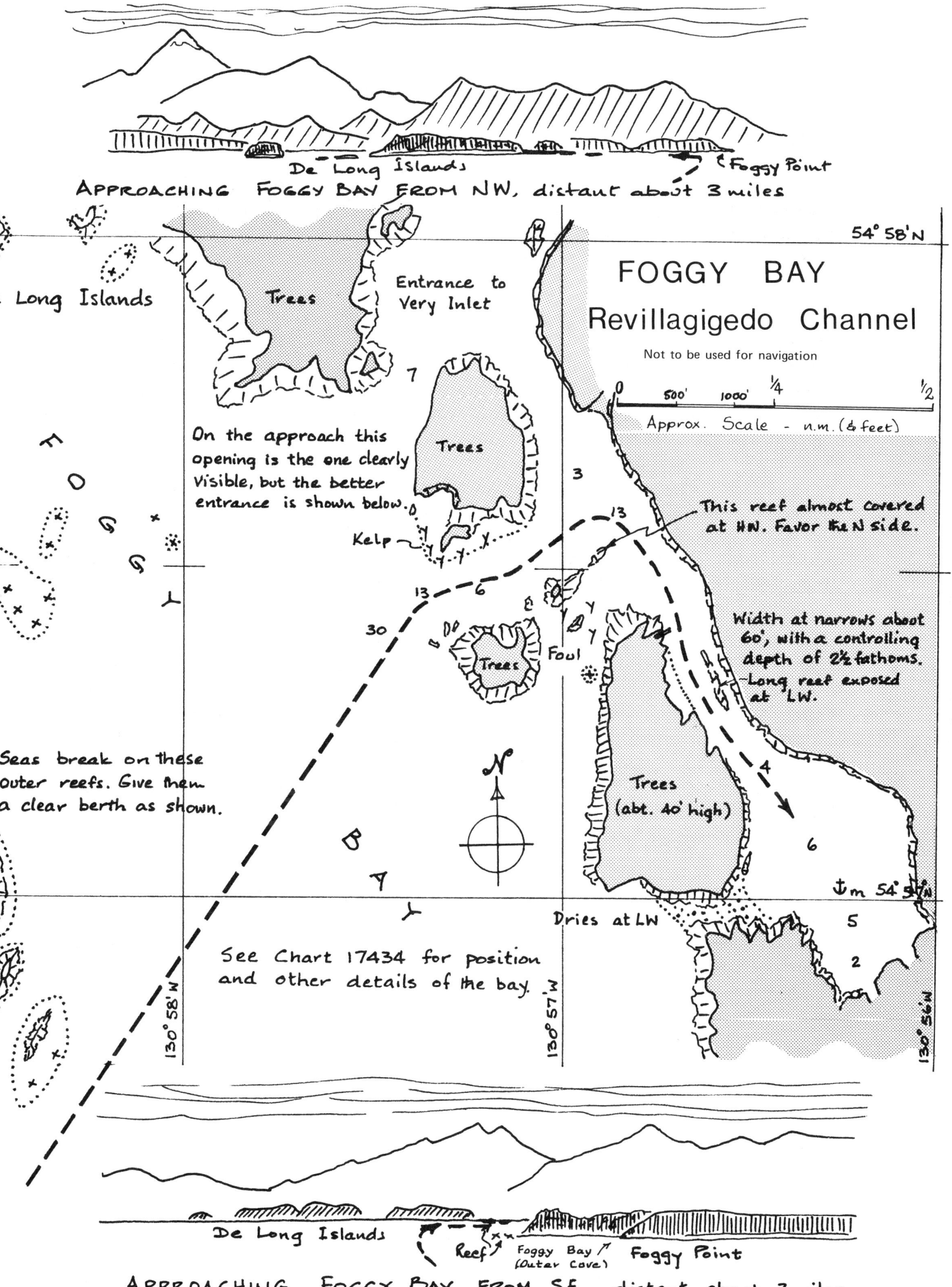

APPROACHING FOGGY BAY FROM NW, distant about 3 miles

De Long Islands

Foggy Point

54° 58'N

FOGGY BAY
Revillagigedo Channel

Not to be used for navigation

0   500'   1000'   ¼   ½

Approx. Scale - n.m. (& feet)

Long Islands

Trees

Entrance to
Very Inlet

7

Trees

3

On the approach this
opening is the one clearly
visible, but the better
entrance is shown below.

Kelp

13

This reef almost covered
at HW. Favor the N side.

13   6

30

Trees

Foul

Width at narrows about
60', with a controlling
depth of 2½ fathoms.
Long reef exposed
at LW.

4

F O G G Y

Seas break on these
outer reefs. Give them
a clear berth as shown.

B A Y

N

Trees
(abt. 40' high)

6

⌘m 54° 57'N

5

130° 58'W

130° 57'W

130° 56'W

Dries at LW

2

See Chart 17434 for position
and other details of the bay.

De Long Islands

Reef

Foggy Bay
(Outer Cove)

Foggy Point

APPROACHING FOGGY BAY FROM SE, distant about 3 miles

METLAKATLA

This Tsimshian village on a Federal Native Reserve is located on Annette Island about 50 miles from the Brundige Inlet anchorage on Dundas Island and approximately 16 miles south of Ketchikan. It not only provides moorage for transient vessels but it is the first fuel stop in Alaska. It important to obtain permission from the Customs office in Ketchikan before stopping here.

Nichols Passage branches off from Clarence Strait and separates Gravina Island from Annette Island. The entrance to the Passage is between Hid Reef on the southeastern end of the Passage and Point McCartey to the northwest. This is the edge of an extensive field of rocks clustered at the southern tip of Gravina Island and is marked by light shown from a skeleton tower with a red and white diamond-shaped daymark. Another rock, marked by a buoy, which uncovers .6 m (2 ft.) is about .3 mile ESE from Point McCartey. The Micro Tower in the cove south of Cedar Point is prominent and a lovely white sand beach is seen at the northern end of the cove. Close approach is unwise for numerous rocks line Cedar Point and the coast to the north. Rock patches on both sides of Port Chester leading to the village of Metlakatla are marked by buoys. About 1.5 miles south of the village is Yellow Hill, composed of several bare, rounded knolls. Flood currents in the Passage set north as much as 2.8 knots on the flood and is strongest in the vicinity of Walden Rocks, at the NE end of Nichols Passage where it meets Tongass Narrows.

Metlakatla has a number of commercial wharves and is also a State ferry terminal. There is regular seaplane service to Ketchikan. Two small craft basins (controlling depth 3 m/10 ft.) with a capacity for over 50 vessels are located in the town about .5 mile from the town center. Transient moorage with power is provided, but water is not available on the docks. The harbormaster monitors VHF 16 or can be reached by telephone at (907) 8864646. The fueling station is on the same ramp as the northerly airplane dock. To arrange for propane or fuel call Annette Island Gas at (907) 886-7851 or give them a call on VHF Ch 72. Tidal currents affect the line-ups waiting to take on fuel as there is no fuel float and the vessel must be tied to pilings. One of the crew must then climb up the ladder to the top of the pier in order to hand down the fuel hose.

*An Indian reserve about 5 miles from Prince Rupert, B.C. has the same name and should not be confused with its Alaskan namesake. It was from this location that the ancestors of natives in the Alaskan reserve moved in 1887 as a result of a power struggle within the Anglican Church hierarchy.

METLAKATLA

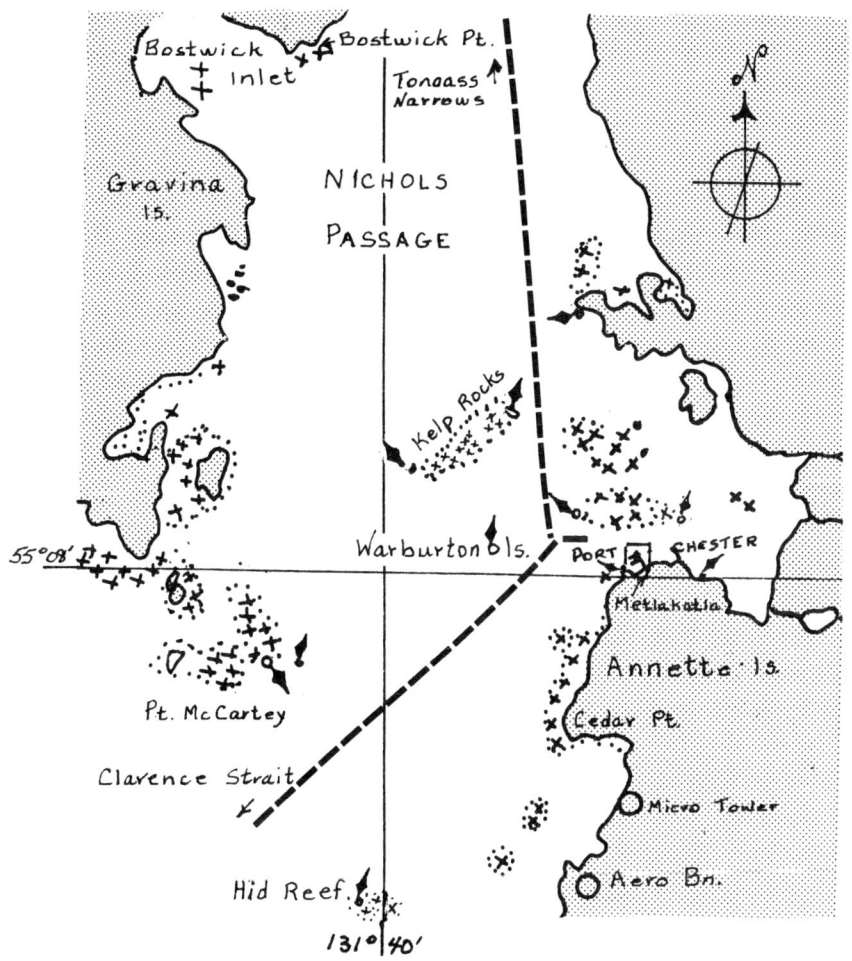

Approx. Scale n. m.

RM

DETAIL

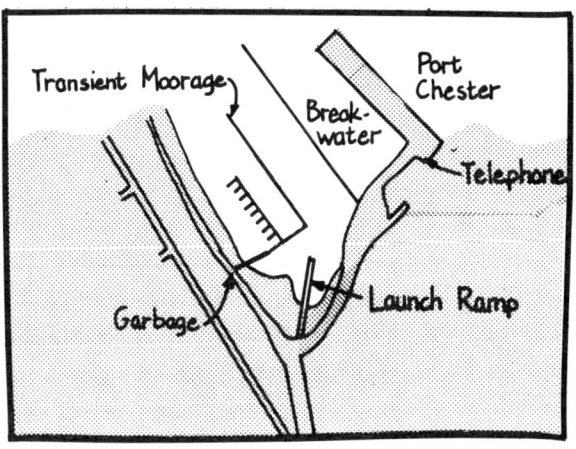

Metlakatla Harbor

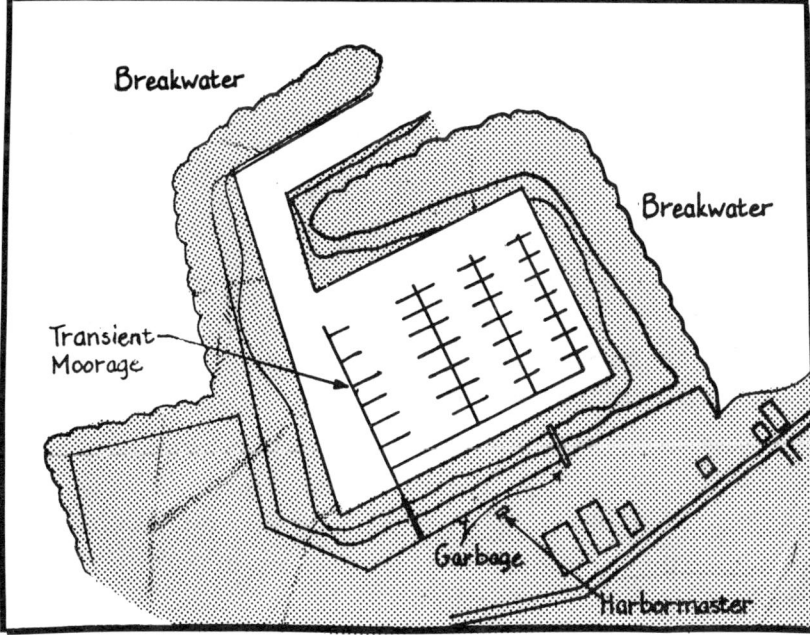

Breakwater

Breakwater

Transient Moorage

Garbage

Harbormaster

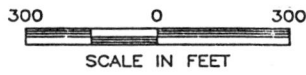

300   0   300

SCALE IN FEET

City Float

Transient Moorage

Port Chester

Breakwater

Telephone

Garbage

Launch Ramp

200   0   200

SCALE IN FEET

KETCHIKAN

The southernmost **Port of Entry** in Alaska, Ketchikan is a growing and active city. Its facilities sprawl along the east bank of Tongass Narrows. The approach and entry to Ketchikan is straightforward—one merely continues up Revillagigedo Channel into Tongass Narrows.

There are three mooring areas in the vicinity. Approaching from the south, the first is **Thomas Basin**. The entrance lies between a rock breakwater and a floating log boom protector. Transient moorage areas are shown on the sketch, but they are usually filled, so you normally take a vacant berth while checking in. The advantage of Thomas Basin is that it is close to the downtown area of Ketchikan. There is a good market close by on Stedman Street while the Customs Office is about .25 mile away on Main Street. At present Customs Officers require the skipper to come ashore to the office to report in; they do not come to the boat as in some Ports of Entry.

A telephone booth at the creek near the float walkway allows you to contact the Harbormaster whose office is at Bar Point Basin. He can also be called on VHF Ch. 16 or by phone at (907) 228-5632. Since most berths in the Ketchikan area are rented, the harbormaster will inform the skipper which berths are temporarily empty and may be used.

The next moorage is at the **City Floats.** They are at the downtown waterfront, and even if space is available the wash from harbor activity creates an uncomfortable moorage. Better moorage is available in **Bar Harbor** about one mile northwest, where concrete and rock breakwaters protect the floats. Washrooms, shower and laundromat facilities are in the Highliner facility at the south end of Bar Harbor South. Though this basin lies about a mile from the downtown area, all facilities such as supermarkets, restaurants, bars, etc. can be found along the way.

The fuel docks are south of Thomas Basin, just northwest of the Coast Guard base which is passed when entering the harbor. The Alaska State Ferry dock, as well as the local ferry to the airport (located across Tongass Narrows) are northwest of the Bar Harbor Basin.

Ketchikan is a lively and interesting place. The downtown area has the usual tourist attractions, shops and marine stores. Creek Street, once a red light district, is now a tourist area with many small specialty stores. Several walks can be taken to explore the city and its immediate environs. Brochures describing these walks can be obtained at the Ketchikan Visitors' Bureau on Front Street. The Totem Heritage Center is of special interest for restored totems and a display of other native crafts. About 3 miles south of Ketchikan is a large collection of totem poles at the Saxman Totem Park. Another collection, with a replica of a community house is 10 miles north at Totem Bight State Historic Park.

Misty Fiords National Monument lies a short distance to the east. The scenery is spectacular and if time permits it is well worth visiting. On a clear day, an aerial view is spectacular. However, Ketchikan and Misty Fiords lie in the 'wet' belt, and have up to 410 cm (162 inches) of rain per year. Cloudy days are the norm for more than two-thirds of the year so if you experience a sunny day with blue skies you are indeed fortunate!

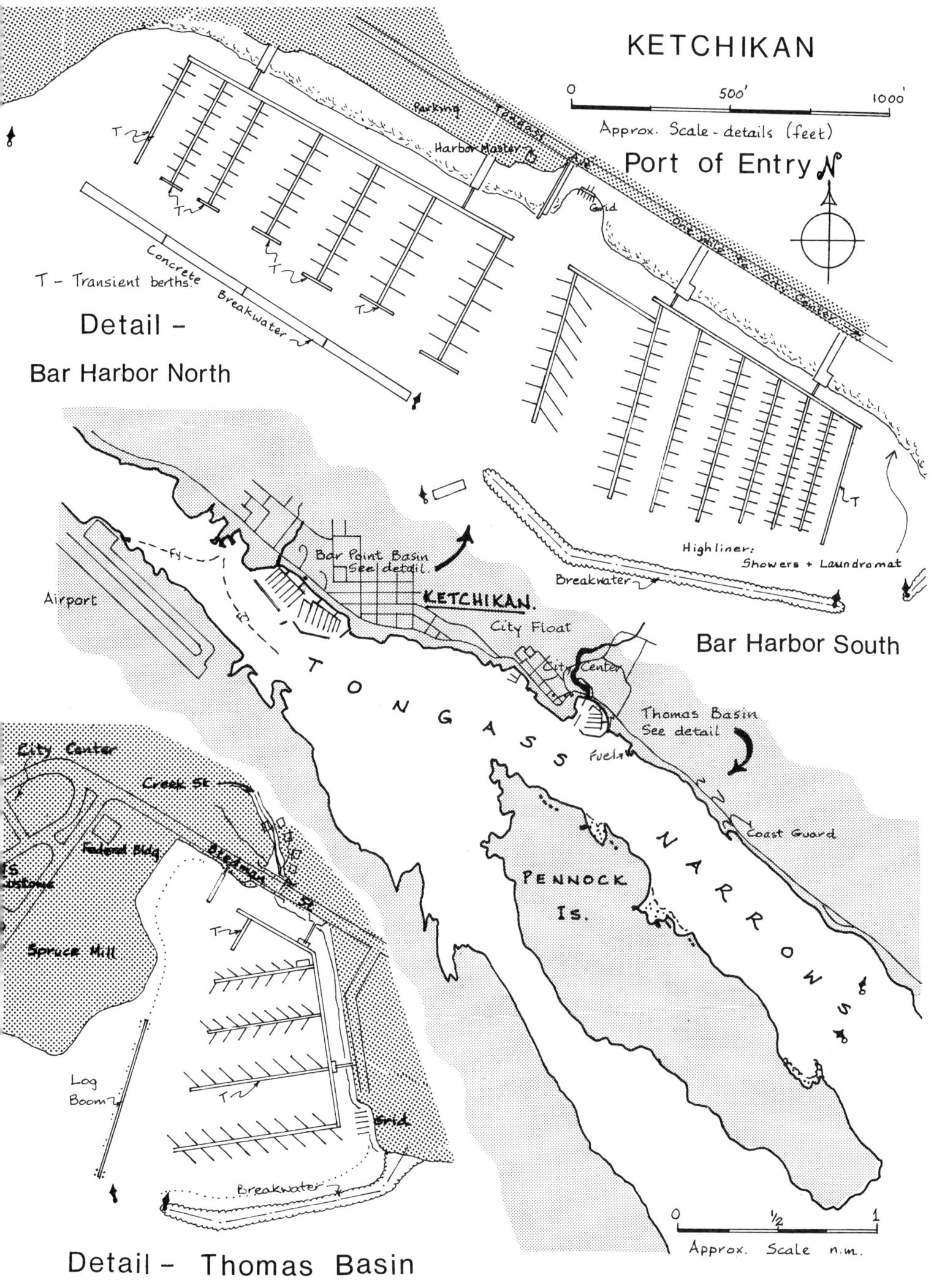

KETCHIKAN

0   500'   1000'

Approx. Scale - details (feet)

Port of Entry N

Parking

Tongass

Harbor Master

Ave.

Grid

T

T - Transient berths.

Concrete

Breakwater

Detail –
Bar Harbor North

Highliner:
Showers + Laundromat

Breakwater

T

Airport

Bar Point Basin
See detail

KETCHIKAN.

City Float

City Center

Bar Harbor South

Fuel

Thomas Basin
See detail

T O N G A S S   N A R R O W S

Coast Guard

City Center

Creek St.

Federal Bldg

Stedman St.

Is.

ustoms

Spruce Mill

T

PENNOCK
Is.

Log
Boom

T

Grid

Breakwater

0   ½   1

Approx. Scale n.m.

Detail – Thomas Basin

THORNE BAY

Thorne Bay is a convenient stop-over and fueling station as it is strategically located approximately 50 miles north of Ketchikan and 60 miles southwest of Wrangell. It is situated about half way up the eastern coast of Prince of Wales Island, southwest of the junction of Ernest Sound and Clarence Strait.

A large island almost blocks the mouth of the entrance to the bay which is 2.5 miles west of Tolstoi Point. When approaching from the east look for the sharpest indention in the horizon to pin-point the entrance. The featureless, tree-covered rolling hills on the coast make the entrance difficult to identify until the 6 m (20 foot) light on the island south of Thorne Head comes into view.

Entrance to the bay should be made only at slack water, to avoid the eddies and rips occurring in the narrow channel when the current is running. A shoal area close to the north shore of the channel, north of the large island, extends over half way into the channel. This part of the channel has thick kelp which is towed under when the current runs strong. Follow a mid-channel course until reaching the western part of the channel where the bay begins to open. At the western end of the channel, off the southern tip of the northern shore a shoal extends in a southerly direction about two-thirds the distance across the channel. To avoid this shoal favor the southern side until well into the bay. NOAA Charts 17420 and 17423 must be used when approaching the bay.

The "city" of Thorne Bay has a population of about 650 and is a community whose economy is centered around logging and sportsfishing. An effort has been made to increase tourism with the construction of marine facilities. Vessels up to 15 m (50 feet) can find moorage in the slips, with space for larger vessels along the breakwater float. Water and power are available on the docks. Two fuel docks are available and a pump-out station is being constructed. Groceries, liquor, postal services, a restaurant and a laundromat are available in town. Propane is available at Island Tire and Prince of Wales Gas.

Thorne Bay is connected to the rest of Prince of Wales Island by an extensive system of roads originally built by logging companies which have operated on the island for many years. At one time Thorne Bay was the largest logging camp in the U.S. and it was from those temporary beginnings that the community evolved. Both float-plane and ferry service link the town to Ketchikan.

Lyman Anchorage is another handy stop-over on the southwestern shore of Clarence Strait about 28 miles south of Thorne Bay and 6.5 miles northwest of Streets Island. Its outer part is an open bight about 1 mile wide at its entrance with and inner harbor extending another .6 mile to the southwest. Entrance can only be done at high water, for the entrance has a controlling depth of .5 fathom. Excellent protection can be enjoyed here with good holding in 4 to 5 fathoms, mud.

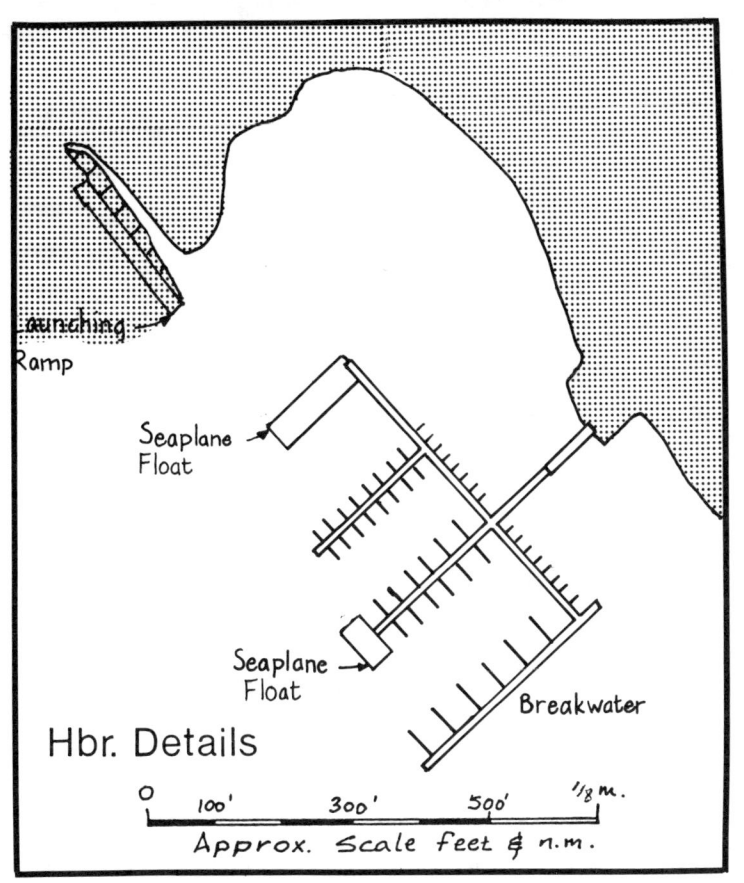

Launching
Ramp
Seaplane
Float
Seaplane
Float
Breakwater
Hbr. Details
0
100'
300'
500'
1/8 m.
Approx. Scale feet & n.m.

THORNE BAY

PRINCE OF WALES IS.

0 ½ 1 1½ n.m.

Approx. Scale n.m.

Not to be used for navigation

132°30'W
Log
Booms
See Detail Above
Shoal
3½f
3f
THORNE BAY
5f
Log
Boom
3f
7f
6f
7f
3f
20f
Fl. R 6 sec. "2" 4m
11f
3f
Thorne
Head
Local knowledge
needed for safe
entry to Snug
Anchorage
55°40'N
Prince of Wales Is.
N

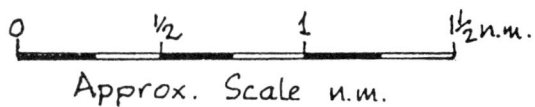

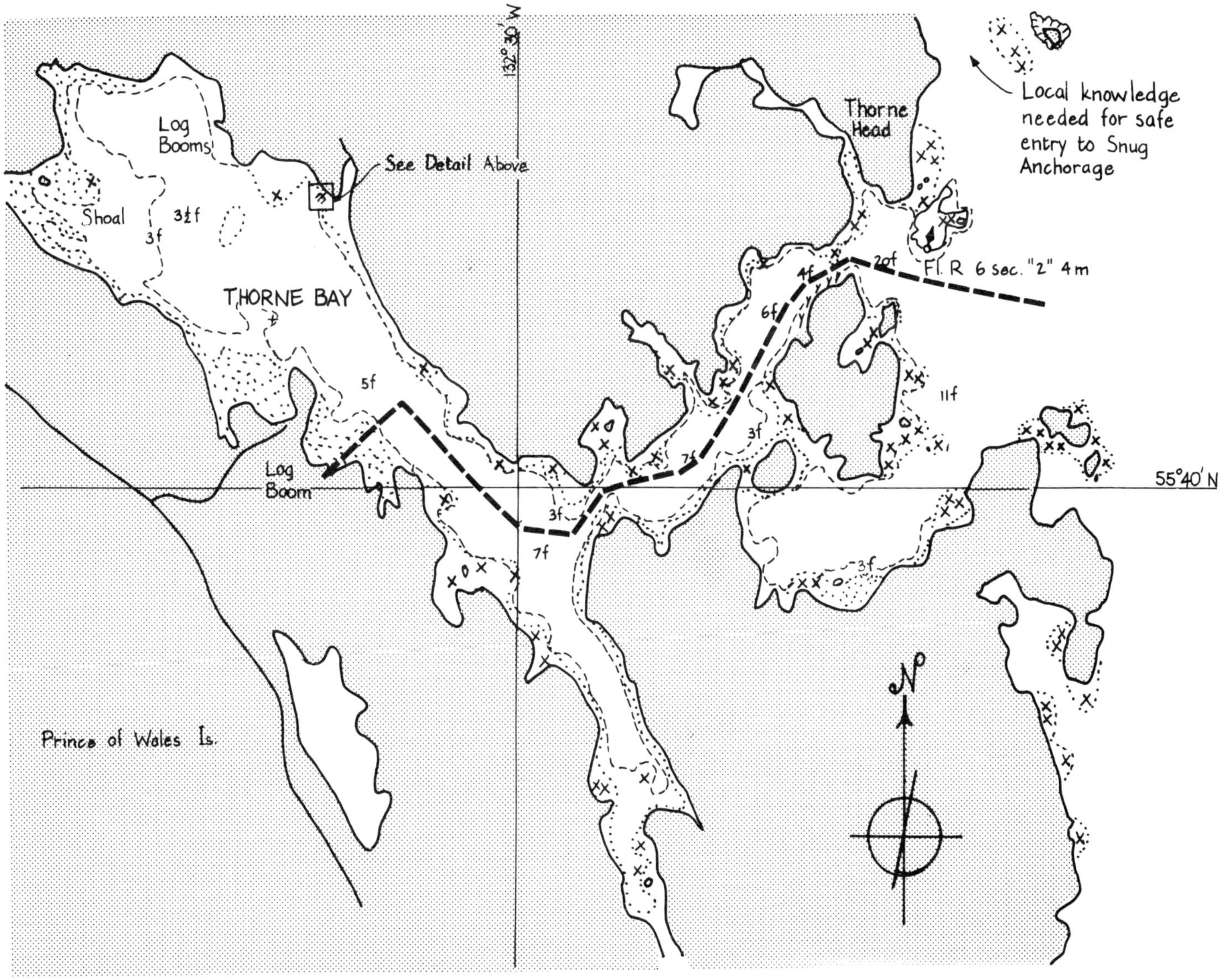

MEYERS CHUCK

Proceeding north from Ketchikan, the exit from Tongass Narrows is marked by the Guard Island Lighthouse. Here there is a choice of several directions to follow: northeast up the Behm Canal to traverse the Misty Fiords; west across Clarence Strait to Kasaan Bay and Kasaan, or north towards Wrangell. When going north the course lies along the west coast of Cleveland Peninsula. Ernest Sound opens from Clarence Strait at Lemesurier Point; about 1.5 miles southeast of the point is Meyers Chuck.

This is a small, convenient harbor to use to split the distance from Ketchikan to Wrangell but if fuel is required it must be taken on in Thorne Bay, described on the previous page. Meyers Chuck is formed by the protection given by Meyers Island and a screen of smaller islands against the side of Lemesurier Point. As you approach the harbor from Clarence Strait the microwave tower (visible above the trees) pinpoints the location of the settlement. Meyers Island lies north of the tower. The entrance to the harbor lies between the northern end of Meyers Island where a light is displayed, and a buoy marking the reefs of the small islands north of the light.

Misery Island (the large island lying .5 mile northwest of Meyers Chuck) has rocks awash at its southern end which are indicated by a green marker. When entering, approach the entrance from due west, south of the green marker to avoid the reefs that lie about 120 m (400 feet) off the northwestern corner of Meyers Island. Do not approach Meyers Island closer than .3 mile until the entrance is clear. At the entrance the depths reduce sharply to about 3 fathoms but the opening is clear midway between the buoy and the light. After turning into the small harbor, you will find the State-operated public float in the northeast corner. A seaplane float extends northwesterly, near the gangway. A reef that dries at low water lies further east of the seaplane float. The main floats are open to transient moorage.

This settlement is devoted primarily to fishing. There is a small store with limited supplies and a Post Office from which mail is picked up weekly. The post office is open on Tuesday from 11 am to 2 pm and on Wednesday for one hour after the mail plane arrives. The closest fuel docks are across Clarence Strait in Thorne Bay. The southwestern corner of the harbor has pilings and is used by fishermen for their nets. A wind generator is on an island to the west.

Anchorage can be taken in the harbor if moorage is not available, but the bottom is rocky. Anchorage can also be taken in the narrow arm beyond the small islands forming the eastern side of the harbor. It is necessary to go out of the entrance and around to enter it. This area ices up during the winter.

Lemesurier Pt.   Misery Is.   Microwave Tower

APPROACHING MEYERS CHUCK FROM SSE, distant about 3 miles

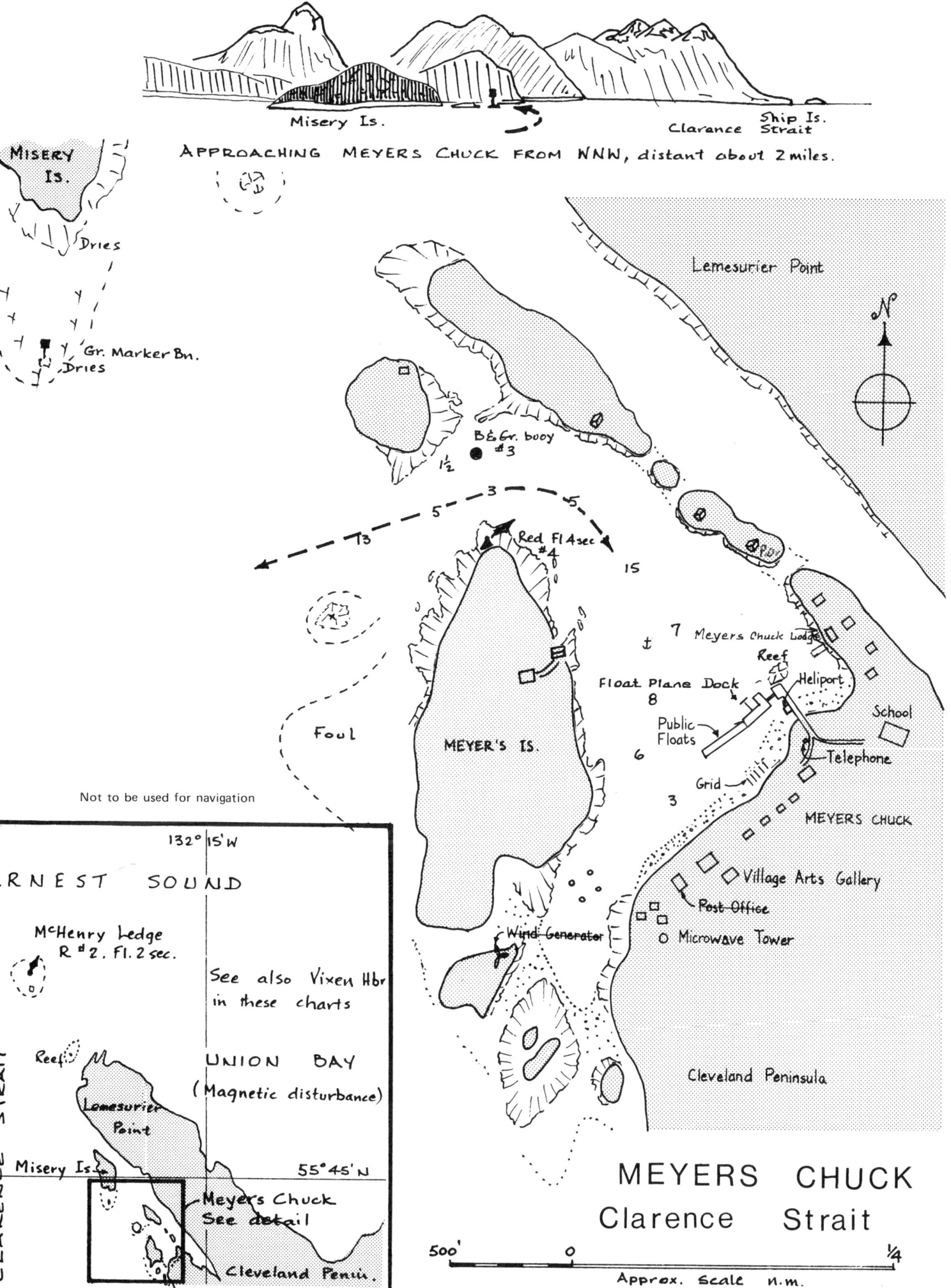

APPROACHING MEYERS CHUCK FROM WNW, distant about 2 miles.

Misery Is.

Clarance   Ship Is.
            Strait

MISERY Is.

Dries

Gr. Marker Bn.
Dries

Lemesurier Point

N

B & Gr. buoy #3

1½

5   3   5

13   5

15

Red Fl 4 sec #4

7   Meyers Chuck Lodge

Reef

Float Plane Dock

Heliport

8

Public Floats

School

Foul

6

MEYER'S IS.

Telephone

Grid

3

MEYERS CHUCK

Not to be used for navigation

Village Arts Gallery

Post Office

Wind Generator

Microwave Tower

132° 15' W

ERNEST   SOUND

McHenry Ledge
R #2. Fl. 2 sec.

See also Vixen Hbr
in these charts

UNION BAY
(Magnetic disturbance)

Reef

Lemesurier
Point

55° 45' N

Misery Is.

Meyers Chuck
See detail

Cleveland Penin.

Cleveland Peninsula

MEYERS CHUCK
Clarence Strait

500'   0   ¼

Approx. Scale   n.m.

VIXEN HARBOR

If you travel to Wrangell by the scenic route which uses Ernest Sound and Zimovia Strait then Vixen Harbor is a very pretty anchorage to use either after Meyers Chuck or as an alternative to it. The entrance is narrow and not obvious until it is carefully lined up, but it is a well sheltered anchorage backed by a beautiful mountain.

At Lemesurier Point (the southern point at the entrance to Ernest Sound) several dangers lie offshore. Lemly Rocks are about .25 mile off the point while McHenry Ledge is about .75 mile east. Strong magnetic disturbances occur between Lemesurier and Union Points—as much as 30 degrees was noticed at the time of writing. Since compass courses cannot be relied on, good visibility is needed to be certain of the vessel's course and location. This is especially true in this area as the current sets towards Union Point.

It is necessary to proceed about .25 to .5 mile off the coast until the entrance into Vixen Harbor can be ascertained. The shallow southern entrance is more obvious at first. However, even though it is more evident, do not attempt the southern entrance for shoals reduce it far more than the main entrance. Line up the northern entrance from offshore and steer carefully through using a mid-channel course. The pilot indicates a width of 30 m (100 yards) but this may be the distance between high water shorelines. At low tide, reefs extending out from both sides reduce the actual channel width to about 18m (60 feet), but the depth is at least 1.5 fathoms.

Once past the islands the harbor opens up nicely. Anchorage can be taken in about 4.5 fathoms, mud. The view of the mountains to the southeast is spectacular and the anchorage is peaceful.

On leaving, clear the entrance and set a visual course until well clear of the magnetic effects of the area before relying on the compass. Other anchorages in the area include the cove behind **Magnetic Point** and a smaller cove behind the nearby islands where houses have been erected.

Zimovia Strait is a pretty, much used route to Wrangell. The Narrows are clearly marked and are interesting to traverse. Whaletail Cove looks inviting as an anchorage, but is unusable since the entrance is shoal.

Other anchorages in the area include **Ratz Harbor**, about 10 miles north of the entrance to **Thorne Bay** on Prince of Wales Island and across from it on Etolin island is **McHenry Anchorage**.

Union Pt. House Magnetic Pt. UNION BAY

APPROACH TO VIXEN HBR. FROM SW, i.e. across Union Bay

Shallow S. entrance is
more evident on approach.   Main N. entrance   Union Pt. (note ledges)

APPROACHING VIXEN HBR. FROM NNE (ZIMOVIA STR.), distant 1 mile.

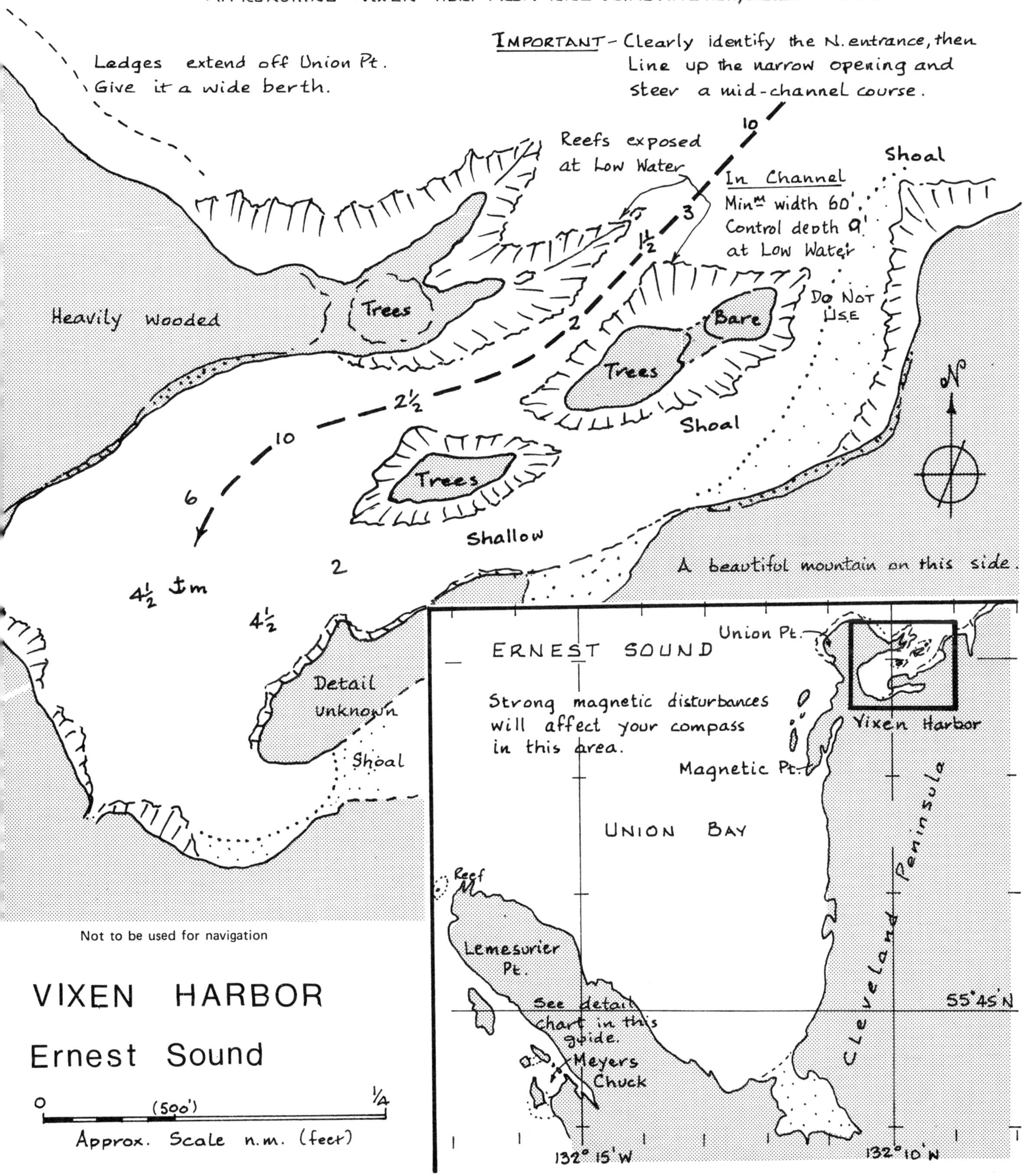

Ledges extend off Union Pt.
Give it a wide berth.

<u>IMPORTANT</u> – Clearly identify the N. entrance, then
line up the narrow opening and
steer a mid-channel course.

Reefs exposed
at Low Water

Shoal

10

In Channel
Min^m width 60'
Control depth 9'
at Low Water

3

1½

Do Not
Use

Heavily Wooded

Trees

2

Bare

Trees

Shoal

2½

10

Trees

Shoal

6

A beautiful mountain on this side.

4½ ‡m

2

4½

Detail
Unknown

Shoal

ERNEST SOUND

Union Pt.

Strong magnetic disturbances
will affect your compass
in this area.

Magnetic Pt.

Vixen Harbor

Cleveland Peninsula

UNION BAY

Not to be used for navigation

Reef

Lemesurier
Pt.

55° 45' N

VIXEN HARBOR

Ernest Sound

See detail
chart in this
guide.

Meyers
Chuck

0   (500')   ¼

Approx. Scale n.m. (feet)

132° 15' W   132° 10' N

WRANGELL

Wrangell lies near the north end of Wrangell Island. It may be approached from Clarence and Stikine Straits, up Zimovia Strait, or up Eastern Passage and around the northern tip of the island. The combination of the magnificent backdrop of the Stikine Mountains and the town's frontier appearance draws many cruise ships to the area.

After passing the cruise ship terminal the main harbor extends along the shore, but the small craft harbor is in a bight behind Point Skekesti, where a wooden breakwater extends partly across the entrance to provide shelter in the southern cove. This cove is divided into an outer and inner harbor. In the outer harbor the floats on the western side are used by commercial vessels. Fuel docks are also on this side. The long floats on the eastern side have transient moorage which is almost always filled—you can expect to raft up. The harbormaster's office is at the head of the walkway with a shrimp cannery lying behind it. (Phew!)

The inner harbor is approached through a connecting channel having about 2 fathoms, marked by day beacons. Here the floats cater to small craft and power boats with very reasonable moorage fees. Limited turning room makes this area awkward for large sailing vessels.

The harbormaster at Wrangell also controls **Shoemaker Boat Harbor** which lies about 3.5 miles SSE, near Wrangell Institute. The breakwater of the harbor is visible when approaching Wrangell, and although it is a cleaner area, its distance from the town is a disadvantage.

Wrangell was originally located at the mouth of the Stikine River because it controlled the route into the interior. Its history is varied, for Russian, British and American flags have flown over the town and it was an important trading point for the Tlingit Indians. On Shakes Island are several totem poles and Chief Shakes Community House, which can be approached by following a wooden walkway near the harbormaster's office. The old false front business houses along Front Street and other buildings in the streets behind give evidence of the age of the town. The Visitors' Bureau (near the cruise ship terminal at the northern end of the town) can provide information on petroglyph locations and other points of interest.

THE STIKINE PEAKS BEHIND WRANGELL FROM WORONKOFSKI IS.

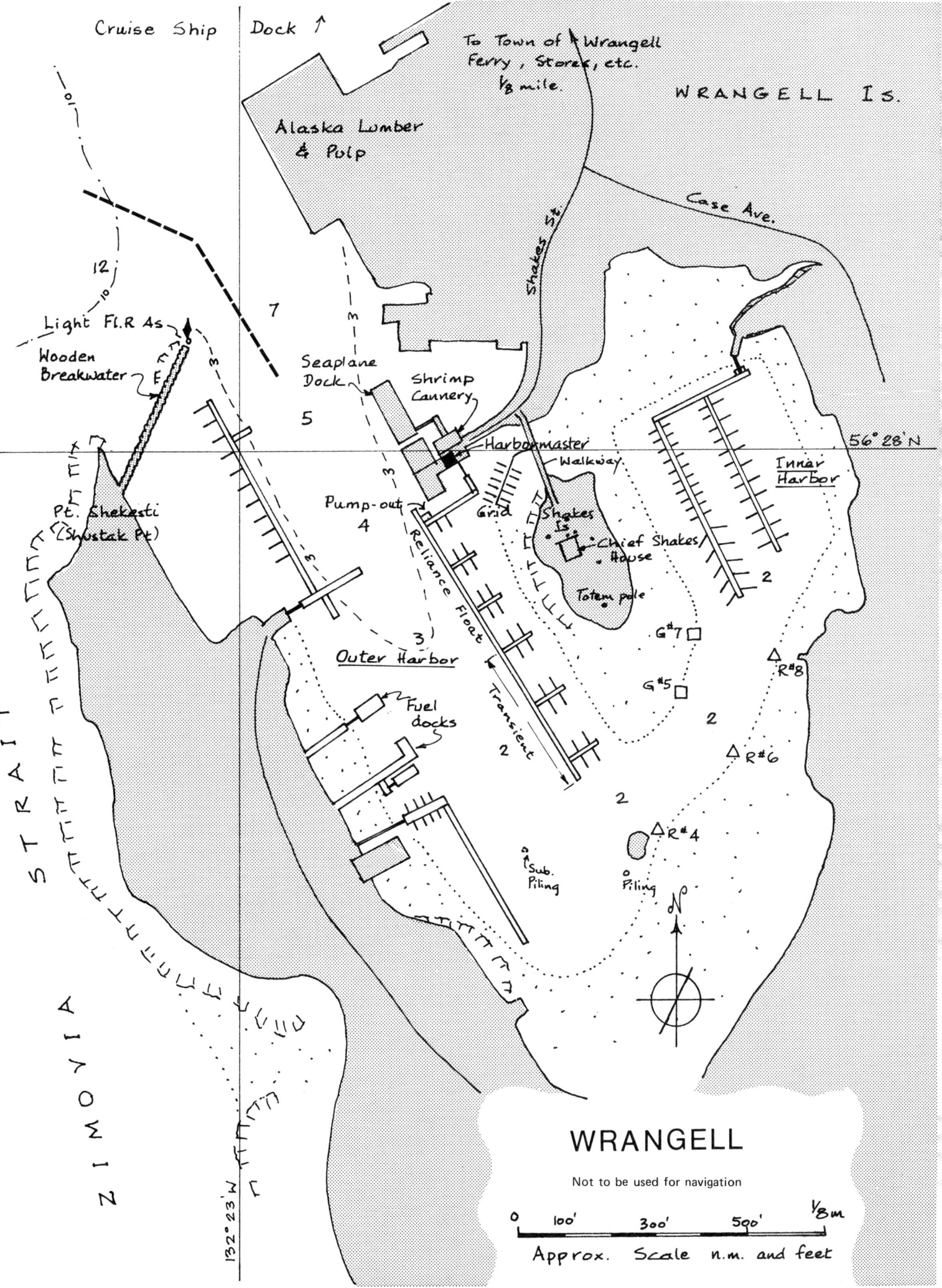

Cruise Ship Dock ↑

To Town of Wrangell
Ferry, Stores, etc.
⅛ mile.

WRANGELL Is.

Alaska Lumber & Pulp

Case Ave.

Shakes St.

12

Light Fl.R 4s

Wooden Breakwater

7

Seaplane Dock

Shrimp Cannery

5

Harbormaster

Walkway

Inner Harbor

56° 28' N

Pt. Shekesti (Shustak Pt)

Pump-out

4

Grid

Shakes Is.

Chief Shakes House

Reliance Float

3

Outer Harbor

Totem pole

2

G #7

G #5

R #8

Fuel docks

Transient

2

R #6

2

Sub. Piling

R #4

Piling

N

132° 23' W

STRAIT

ZIMOVIA

WRANGELL

Not to be used for navigation

0   100'   300'   500'   ⅛m

Approx. Scale n.m. and feet

Additional views found in this section:

One of The Twins   Pt. Hughes (distant, across the sound)   Sunset Is.   Pt. Windham   N. Point of Hobart Bay

VIEW NW UP STEPHENS PASSAGE ON LEAVING HOBART BAY, OUT 1½ MILES.

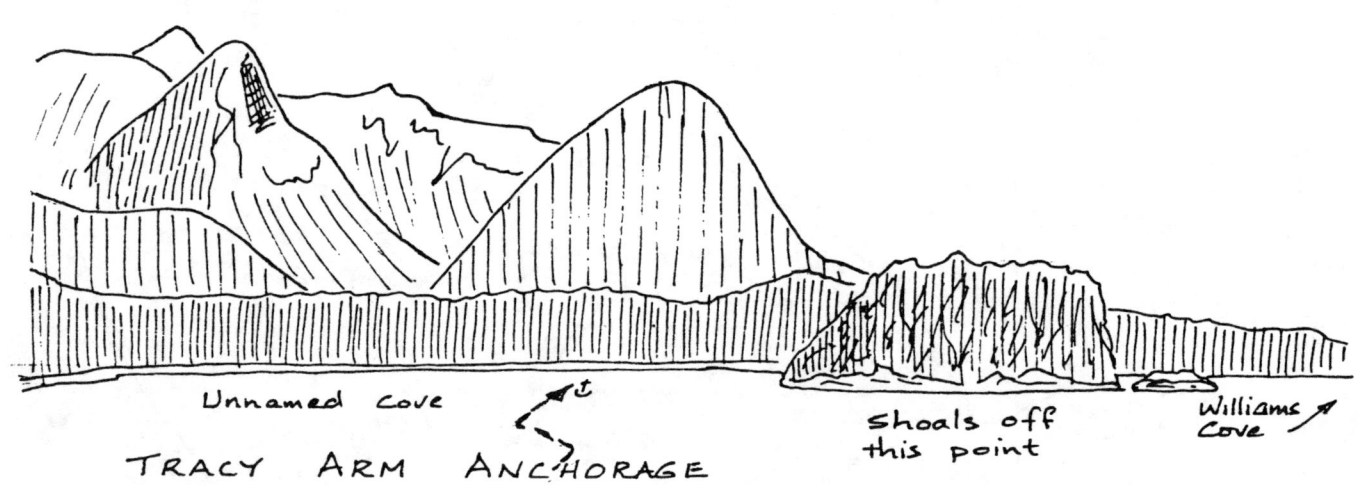

Unnamed Cove   Shoals off this point   Williams Cove

TRACY ARM ANCHORAGE

Devil's Thumb, a spectacular peak near Petersburg

In Tracy Arm

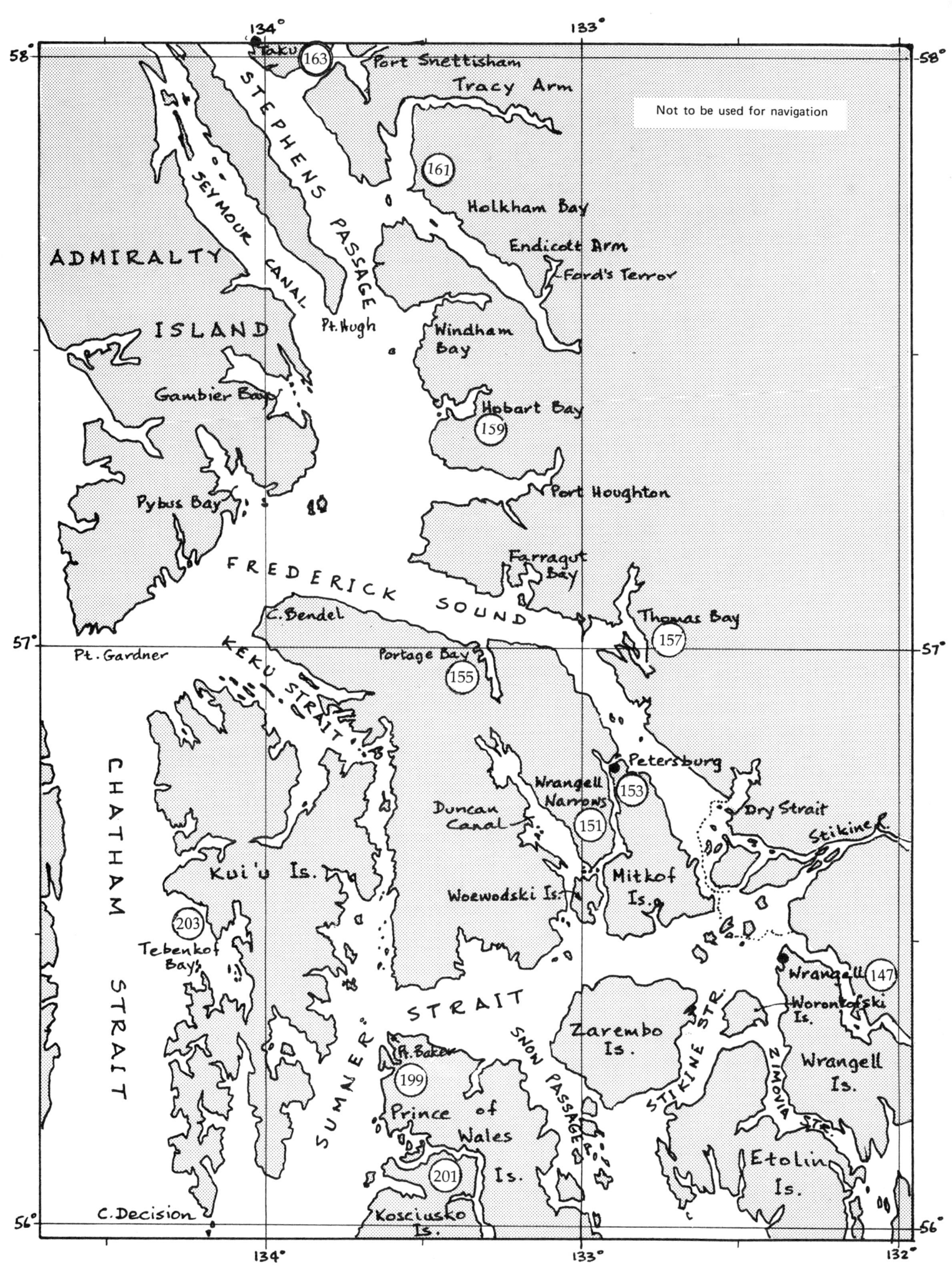

Not to be used for navigation

58°

134°   133°

'Taku   (163)
Port Snettisham
Tracy Arm

(161)

STEPHENS PASSAGE

Holkham Bay

Endicott Arm
Ford's Terror

ADMIRALTY

SEYMOUR CANAL

ISLAND   Pt. Hugh   Windham
                                        Bay

Gambier Bay   Hobart Bay
                                        (159)

Pybus Bay   Port Houghton

                        FREDERICK   Farragut
                                        Bay
                   C. Bendel   SOUND
57°
Pt. Gardner   KEKU STRAIT   Portage Bay   Thomas Bay
                                        (155)   (157)

                                                             Petersburg
                                        Wrangell   (153)
CHATHAM   Duncan   Narrows
                  Canal   (151)   Dry Strait
                                                             Stikine
         Kui'u Is.
                                        Woewodski Is.   Mitkof
STRAIT   Is.

(203)

Tebenkof
Bay   SUMNER   STRAIT   STIKINE STR.

                    R. Baker   Zarembo   Wrangell (147)
                    (199)   SNOW   Is.   Woronkofski
                                                                Is.
                  Prince of   PASSAGE   ZIMOVIA STR.
                         Wales   Wrangell
                                                               Is.
                  (201)   Is.   Etolin
                                                               Is.
56°
C. Decision   Kosciusko
                   Is.

134°   133°   132°

WRANGELL NARROWS

This waterway, the shortest route between Wrangell and Petersburg,. is a well known and exciting part of the trip which also provides the southern entrance at Point Alexander on Mitkof Island (off Sumner Strait) is about 20 miles west of Wrangell. The Narrows consist of 21 miles of waterway with more than 66 navigation markers, leading to Petersburg in the north, where it opens on to Frederick Sound. At night, with its myriad of flashing red and green lights it is easy to understand its nickname of "Christmas Tree Lane."

It is not possible with the small charts and brief comments of this guide to describe the many details of the Narrows, nor is it intended. This guide merely describes significant and interesting aspects of the passage.

The ship channel narrows in places to 90 m (300 feet) wide, and though the major section the controlling depth is 6 m (19 feet). Any larger vessels that might be encountered are most likely to be the Alaska State Ferries, which use the narrows at high tide.

For small boat use when navigating the channel it is recommended that NOAA Chart #17375 (which divides the Narrows into two sections printed side by side) be cut along the vertical division; then match and tape the two sections together in a long continuous chart of the waterway. By folding this into four it gives a handy and useful chart size reference at the helm for the actual transit. It will assist navigation if a check mark is placed as each odd (or even) beacon is passed. This will not only determine position but will also allow a skipper to make a quick decision as to whether he can move off the channel (and to which side) if a large vessel is met in the Narrows. With the aid of the chart the passage can be taken easily by all small craft. High-speed powered vessels should slow down to reduce the turbulence of the wake they create.

For most slow-speed small craft going either way, the passage should be commenced on the last part of the flood. The currents enter Wrangell Narrows from both ends to meet at about Green Point (9 miles from Petersburg and 12 miles from the southern entrance). Thus, a prudent skipper will arrange his entry to carry a favorable current all the way through.

In foggy weather it is strongly recommended that the passage be delayed until it is clear, even if the vessel is equipped with radar. If fog is encountered when in the passage it is wise to haul well off the channel at the first opportunity to anchor and wait for clearing. Though yachts can do this at several places the best site is at **Halfmoon Anchorage** (about 8.5 miles from the southern entrance), where depths are 2 to 3 fathoms, mud. Other areas off the channel may have hard or rocky bottoms and kelp,

Dry Strait appears to be an apparent alternative route north from Wrangell, but it should not be attempted without local knowledge. Considerable shoaling and muddy water with strong currents can put a stranger in difficulties. Keku Strait, further west of the Narrows cannot be used, as navigation markers have been removed. The only alternative to the Narrows is to proceed through Sumner Strait, around Cape Decision and up Chatham Strait.

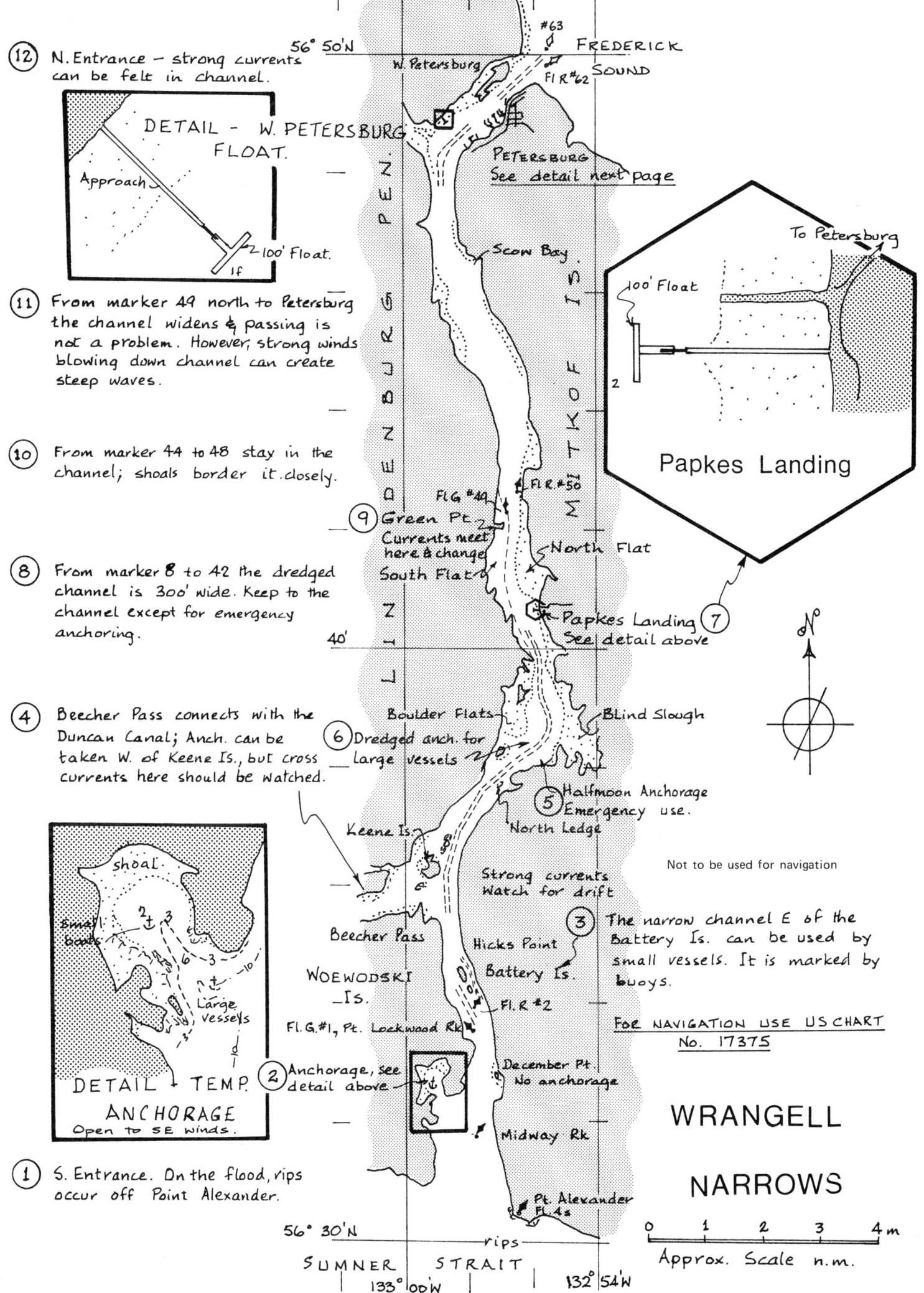

(12) N. Entrance – strong currents can be felt in channel.

DETAIL – W. PETERSBURG FLOAT.

Approach

100' Float.

1f

(11) From marker 49 north to Petersburg the channel widens & passing is not a problem. However, strong winds blowing down channel can create steep waves.

(10) From marker 44 to 48 stay in the channel; shoals border it closely.

(8) From marker 8 to 42 the dredged channel is 300' wide. Keep to the channel except for emergency anchoring.

(4) Beecher Pass connects with the Duncan Canal; Anch. can be taken W. of Keene Is., but cross currents here should be watched.

shoal

small boats

2 ⚓ 3

6 — 3 — -10

⚓ Large vessels

d

DETAIL – TEMP. ANCHORAGE Open to SE winds.

(1) S. Entrance. On the flood, rips occur off Point Alexander.

56° 50'N

#63

FREDERICK

W. Petersburg

Fl R #62   SOUND

PETERSBURG
See detail next page

Scow Bay

Fl R #50

Fl G #49

(9) Green Pt.
Currents meet here & change

North Flat

South Flat

Papkes Landing
See detail above   **(7)**

Boulder Flats

Blind Slough

(6) Dredged anch. for large vessels

Halfmoon Anchorage
(5) Emergency use.

Keene Is.

North Ledge

Strong currents
Watch for drift

Beecher Pass

Hicks Point

Battery Is.

WOEWODSKI
Is.

Fl R #2

Fl. G. #1, Pt. Lockwood Rk

(2) Anchorage, see detail above

December Pt
No anchorage

Midway Rk

Pt. Alexander
Fl 4s

56° 30'N   rips

SUMNER   STRAIT

133° 00'W   132° 54'W

To Petersburg

100' Float

2

Papkes Landing

N

Not to be used for navigation

(3) The narrow channel E of the Battery Is. can be used by small vessels. It is marked by buoys.

FOR NAVIGATION USE US CHART
No. 17375

WRANGELL

NARROWS

0   1   2   3   4 m
Approx. Scale n.m.

PETERSBURG

The charming town of Petersburg lies at the northern end of Wrangell Narrows, on the tip of Mitkof Island. This busy town is more concerned with fishing and lumbering than with tourists. This refreshing attitude is reflected in the prosperity of the people, the expanded boat harbors, and in the number of large seiners and fishboats. The Norwegian heritage of many of the inhabitants is celebrated each May 17 (Norwegian Independence Day) during the annual "Little Norway Festival." Other signs of this pride are seen in the rosemaling on building fronts and the replica Viking vessel in the harbor.

There are three major boat harbors in Petersburg, but the main transient accommodation is the northernmost, between the Whitney-Fidalgo Seafoods pier and the Petersburg Fisheries Cannery docks. The harbormaster's office is at the head of the dock or he may be reached by calling VHF Ch. 16 or CB Ch. 9. A reasonable mooring charge is assessed, and depending on the location, electrical power may be available. A water tap is on the transient dock. The people of Petersburg are very friendly and helpful.

In the same building as the harbormaster's office are restrooms and a large coin-operated stainless steel shower. Although it often has a queue when the fishing boats come in, it's worth the wait! Adjacent to the showers is the Visitor Center where maps and guides can be obtained. A grid is just below the walkway. Garbage and waste oil disposal facilities are nearby.

Main Street is half a block from the dock. There are two major grocery and hardware stores, The Trading Union and Hammer & Wikan. Also within walking distance are a hospital, post office and an intriguing little museum.

If the budget is tight, there is open mooring at the West Petersburg Public Float, across Wrangell Narrows in the community of Kupreanof. However, there is no public transportation back and forth to Petersburg.

The weather is dominated by rain; with an annual average of 2.7 m (106 inches). Heavy weather gear and boots are right in style for everyday wear in Petersburg. In fact when rain is pounding on the deck you will likely hear the local radio announcer cheerfully reporting, "Today we'll have a few sprinkles!"

Exiting the Narrows from Petersburg brings you to Frederick Sound where icebergs from the glacier can often be seen. The spectacular mountain view behind Petersburg is highlighted by a granite rock pinnacle, the Devil's Thumb. Just 25 miles southeast is Le Conte Glacier, the southernmost tidewater glacier. It is well worth visiting, but shoaling at the entrance to the bay makes entry difficult without local information.

A cruising destination for boaters from Petersburg is Tebenkof Bay, about 50 miles distant. This popular bay with its numerous anchorages is described on page 202.

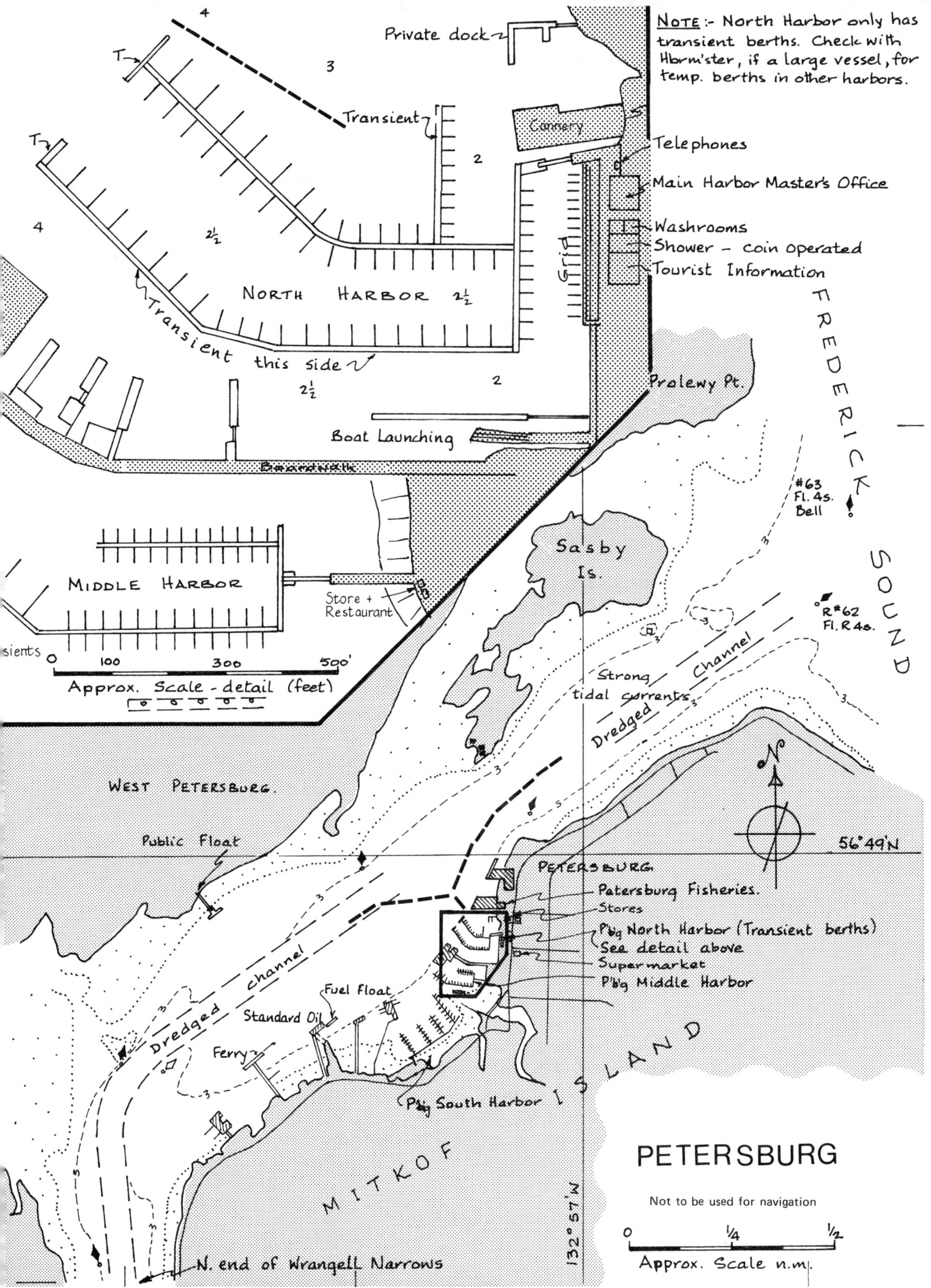

4

Private dock

NOTE:- North Harbor only has
transient berths. Check with
Hbrm'ster, if a large vessel, for
temp. berths in other harbors.

3

Transient

2

Cannery

Telephones

Main Harbor Master's Office

Washrooms

Shower - coin operated

Tourist Information

T

T

Grid

NORTH HARBOR 2½

2½

Transient this side

2½

2

Prolewy Pt.

4

FREDERICK SOUND

Boat Launching

Boardwalk

Sasby Is.

#63
Fl. 4s.
Bell

R #62
Fl. R 4s.

MIDDLE HARBOR

Store +
Restaurant

Strong
tidal currents

Dredged Channel

sients

0   100   300   500'

Approx. Scale - detail (feet)

WEST PETERSBURG.

Public Float

N

PETERSBURG

56°49'N

Patersburg Fisheries.

Stores

P'b'g North Harbor (Transient berths)
See detail above

Supermarket

P'b'g Middle Harbor

Dredged channel

Fuel Float

Standard Oil

Ferry

P'b'g South Harbor

MITKOF ISLAND

PETERSBURG

Not to be used for navigation

0   ¼   ½

Approx. Scale n.m.

N. end of Wrangell Narrows

132°57'W

PORTAGE BAY

This protected and very pleasant anchorage lies on the south side of Frederick Sound, indenting Kupreanof Island. It is very different from the bays that lie on the other side of the Sound, with their glaciers coming down to sea level. Portage Bay provides a good stop for vessels proceeding along Frederick Sound to or from Petersburg.

The low points that lie each side of the entrance are marked by the two small Portage Islets roughly .75 of a mile west of the entrance. On the east side the mountains of the Missionary Range rise between the bay and Petersburg, with some snow usually remaining on them throughout the year.

Stay about a mile offshore, and when the entrance is clear begin the approach. Both East and West Points project into the opening with shoals that reduce the useful passage to about 150 m (500 feet). The tidal flow into and out of the fairly long bay can attain considerable velocity at times. However, except at the maximum tides vessels can enter and usually use a natural range to guide the vessel into the channel.

East Point has a light on a tower with a green daymark. The tip of the grassy verge should be aligned on Hook Point (with a gap in the trees and a hut now hidden in undergrowth), and on a low peak behind—as shown in the sketch. Follow this bearing till at the entrance, first round West Point, then East Point, staying about mid-channel. West Point has a red daybeacon on it. Once in the bay past East Point, a large shoal bay lies to the west and a booming ground to the east. You can anchor in about 5 fathoms in the area of the booming ground, but a better anchorage is found further in.

A prominent logging camp lies on the east side about a mile and half into the inlet. Anchor in the middle of the bay, slightly beyond the camp, in about 4 to 6 fathoms. Do not go too close to the shoreline. The main part of the bay is large enough to accommodate many boats.

Further into the bay Stop Island marks the beginning of shoaling, and this area is called Goose Bay. Harrington Rock is about .25 mile north of Stop Island.

KAKE

The village of Kake is about 12 miles west of Point Gardner at the entrance to Frederick Sound, and about 15 miles west of Portage Bay. Kake has public floats, stores, lodges, and other services. It also has a tall totem pole which is visible from well offshore. The village is at the entrance to Keku Strait, but the use of this dangerous route is not recommended. All navigational markers have been removed by the Coast Guard to discourage its use.

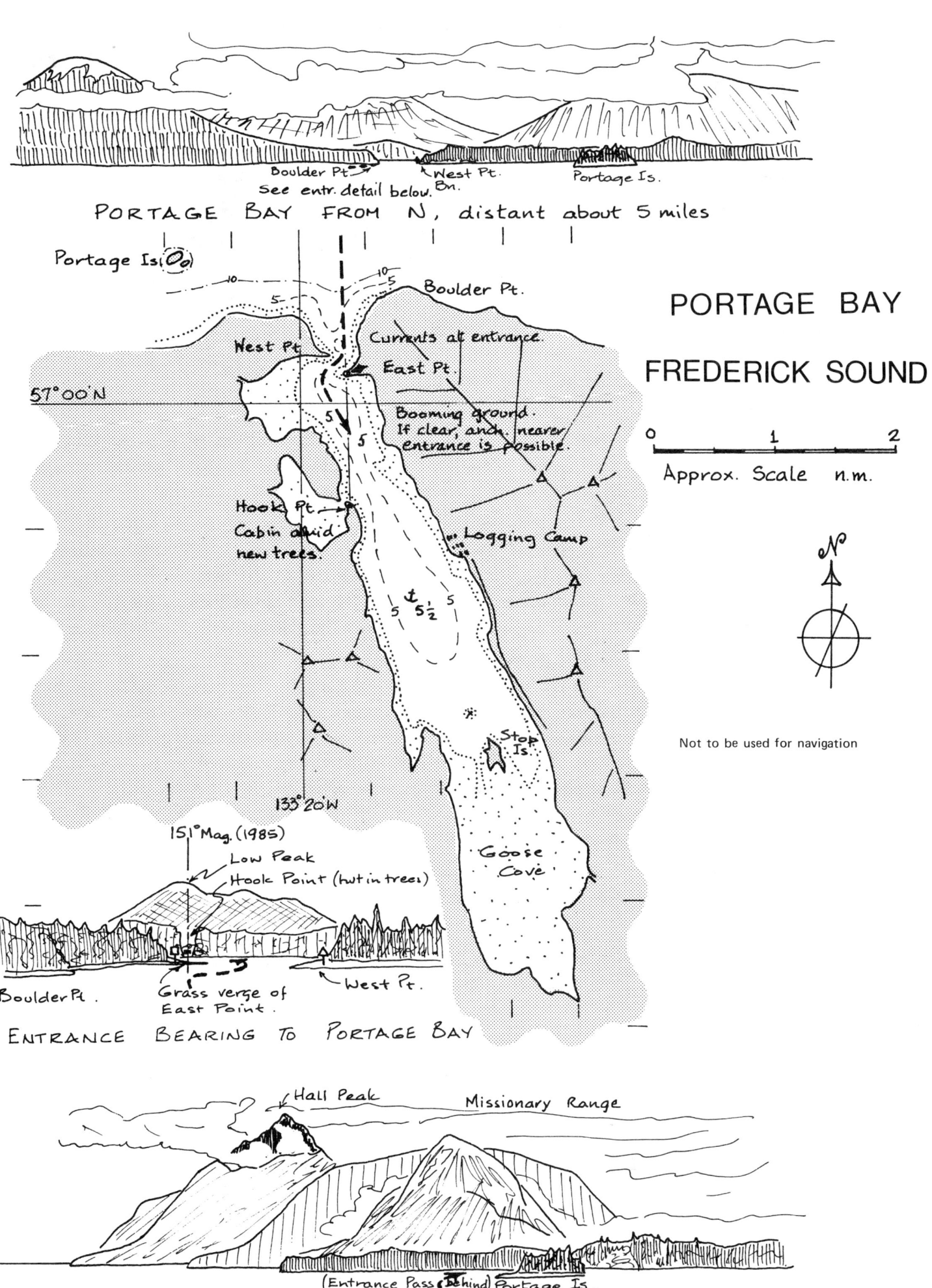

PORTAGE BAY FROM N, distant about 5 miles

Boulder Pt.
See entr. detail below.
West Pt.
Bn.
Portage Is.

Portage Is.

PORTAGE BAY

FREDERICK SOUND

Boulder Pt.

West Pt.

Currents at entrance.

East Pt.

57°00'N

Booming ground.
If clear, anch. nearer
entrance is possible.

0 ——— 1 ——— 2

Approx. Scale n.m.

Hook Pt.
Cabin amid
new trees.

Logging Camp

N

5 5½ 5

Not to be used for navigation

Stop
Is.

133°20'W

Goose
Cove

151° Mag. (1985)
Low Peak
Hook Point (hut in trees)

Boulder Pt.

Grass verge of
East Point.

West Pt.

ENTRANCE BEARING TO PORTAGE BAY

Hall Peak   Missionary Range

(Entrance Pass behind) Portage Is.

APPROACHING PORTAGE BAY FROM W, distant about 2 miles.

THOMAS BAY

Ten miles north of the buoys at the Petersburg entrance to Wrangell Narrows, and across Frederick Sound is the entrance to Thomas Bay. This is the first opportunity to see a glacier fairly closely. The entrance to Thomas Bay lies between Point Vandeput in the northwest and Wood Point in the southeast. Although the two points are about 2.25 miles apart, shoaling and reefs at the mouth of the bay are extensive, thus reducing the opening to a narrow buoyed entrance. Depending on the state of the tide, considerable turbulence and swirls may be encountered at the entrance, but by watching the course and drift with care there is no difficulty in entering.

Puffin

The water here is noticeably milky with glacial silt. The shape of the bay may be likened to a lazy T, resting on its side. The east side of the cross arm of the T is a range of peaks, whose flanks descend in steep sides to the water. Several landslides mark the tree-clad slopes, and numerous waterfalls can be seen.

The northern arm ends at Baird Glacier. Though not a tidewater glacier at this time, it is not very far back from the water's edge, and apart from the lack of ice discharged into the bay it provides very scenic views. Do not approach the end of the inlet closer than half a mile, for considerable shoaling occurs due to the discharge of silt down the glacial river.

Near the end of the northern arm, a narrow steep-walled inlet leads off to the east. This is **Scenery Cove**, a small version of Fords Terror. Almost overhanging walls hem the sides, which shoal quickly at the head. In very settled weather it is possible to anchor on a 9-fathom shelf extending off the northern entrance point of the cove. Anchor off a prominent scar on the face. You can then take a dinghy to the flats below the face of the glacier and walk up to explore it. However, a better and safer anchorage is available in the south arm of Thomas Bay. **Ruth Island** lies roughly north/south and on its southeastern side are two coves. Both can be used as anchorages, though the southern one is preferable.

Anchorage is also possible close to the shore south of a prominent cascade behind Spray Island. But like Scenery Cove, this anchorage has very limited shelf area close to a steep mountainside.

The southern arm of Thomas Bay has the terminal river of Patterson Glacier, which has receded so far back that its only visible remains are the moraines.

APPROACHING RUTH IS. ANCH. FROM W

Ruth Is.

To Glacier

Anch.

2nd Cove   To exit

THOMAS BAY

FREDERICK SOUND

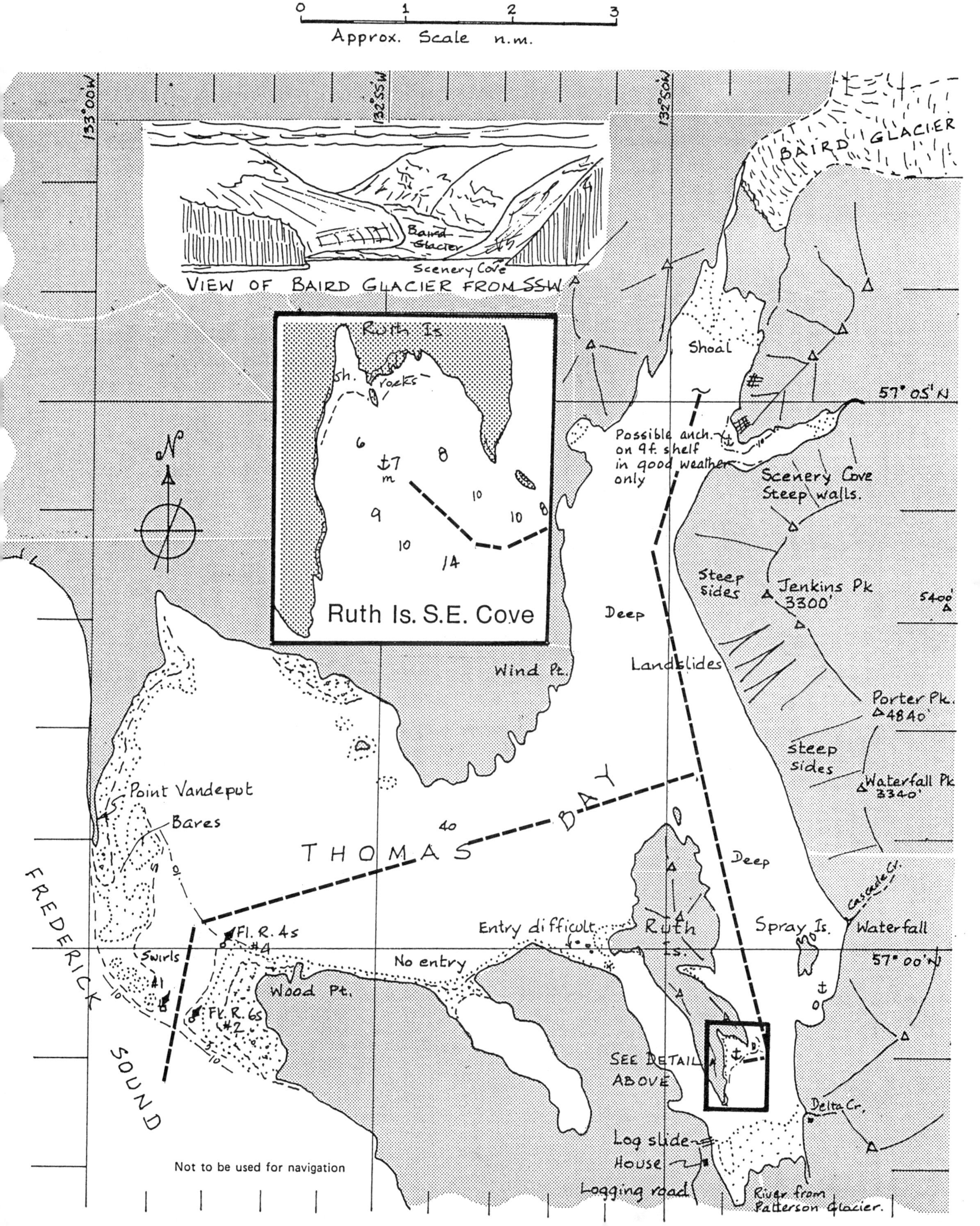

0   1   2   3

Approx. Scale   n.m.

133° 00'W

132° 55'W

132° 50'W

Baird
Glacier

Scenery Cove

VIEW OF BAIRD GLACIER FROM SSW

BAIRD GLACIER

N

Ruth Is.

Sh. rocks

6

‡7
m

8

9

10

10

10

10   8

14

Ruth Is. S.E. Cove

Wind Pt.

Shoal

57° 05' N

Possible anch.
on 9 ft. shelf
in good weather
only

Scenery Cove
Steep walls.

Deep

Landslides

Steep
sides

Jenkins Pk
3300'

5400'

Porter Pk.
△ 4840'

steep
sides

Waterfall Pk
3340'

THOMAS   BAY

40

Point Vandeput

Bares

Deep

Cascade Cr.

Entry difficult

Ruth
Is.

Spray Is.

Waterfall

57° 00' N

FREDERICK

Fl. R. 4s
#4

No entry

Swirls
#1

Wood Pt.

Fl. R. 6s
#2

SEE DETAIL
ABOVE

‡

Delta Cr.

SOUND

Log slide
House

Logging road

River from
Patterson Glacier.

Not to be used for navigation

HOBART BAY

Cape Fanshawe marks the point where Stephens Passage opens northward off Frederick Sound. These are wide stretches of sea, where weather conditions can create rough water. There is an anchorage near the Cape in Cleveland Passage behind Whitney Island. It is in 6 to 8 fathoms at the southeastern end, tucked east of East Spit (a rocky shoal awash at low water which projects out from the mainland). While the pilot recommends entry from the north around Whitney Island, small vessels can enter from the south by keeping a mid-channel course and allowing for a clear berth of East Spit. However, this anchorage is relatively open; swell affects it and gusty southeast winds often blow down the nearby mountains.

The course northward passes Five Fingers Islets, on which is a lighthouse often mentioned in local weather reports. This is useful for reckoning the weather in Stephens Passage. Port Houghton is the first large bay on the mainland, but it is too deep for anchoring.

Hobart Bay opens into the mainland about 5 miles further, and at first appears to be a shallow indentation. It is marked by small islands, The Twins, two miles west and by the larger Sunset Island, about 5 miles north.

Entrance Island lies in the center of the entrance to Hobart Bay. Behind it a long, high arm projects outwards, almost closing the opening into the inner part of Hobart Bay. A stand pipe and several houses mark a large logging operation, with snow-clad peaks in the background.

The anchorage and moorage lie in a small L-shaped inlet on the southern side of **Entrance Island**. As you approach the island from either direction a large fault becomes visible. On the rocky south shore there is a small niche with a house behind the stony beach. This is seen before the true opening is visible. Turn into the small inlet, where the State maintains a 30 m (100 foot) float in the western niche. It is unconnected to the shore, except for two underwater cables that affect the ability of all but very small vessels to use the south side of the float. The house previously seen on the approach is on the neck of land behind the float. This is a quiet and restful spot, used primarily as a weather lay-over by vessels traveling these waters.

It is possible to enter the remainder of Hobart Bay through the narrow, rock-strewn entrance, and to find other anchorage immediately northwest of the entry. But the currents and multitude of rocks discourage such exploration, especially when the quiet moorage at Entrance Island is available.

There are two other anchorages in this area. The best one is **Cannery Cove** in Pybus Bay located on the west side of, and across Stephens Passage. When anchoring in **Windham Bay** you should anchor in a niche near the entrance or proceed far into the bay and anchor at the head.

APPROACHING HOBART BAY FROM SSE, distant about 5 miles

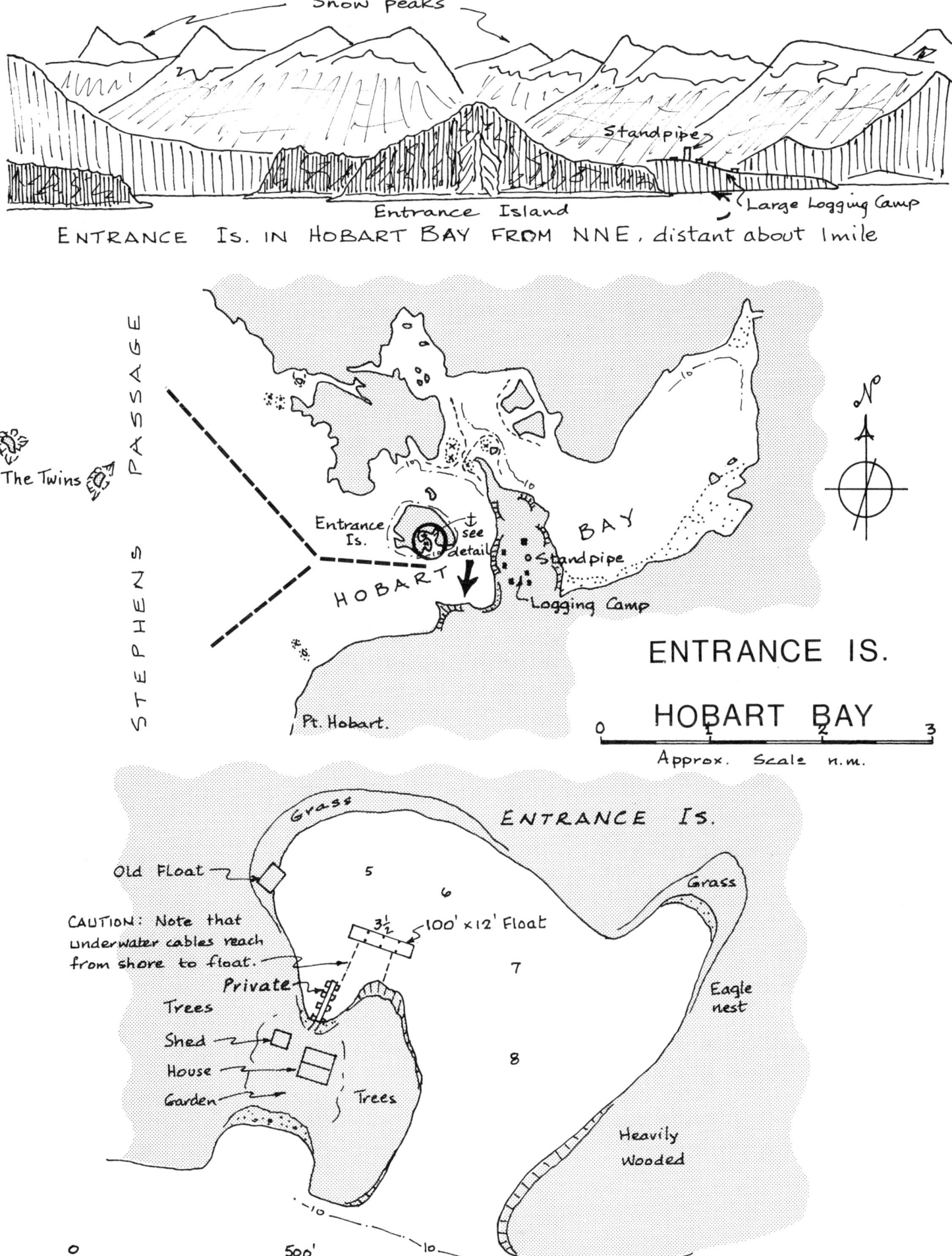

Snow peaks

Standpipe

Entrance Island

Large Logging Camp

ENTRANCE Is. IN HOBART BAY FROM NNE, distant about 1 mile

The Twins

STEPHENS PASSAGE

Entrance
Is.

see
detail

HOBART

Standpipe

BAY

Logging Camp

Pt. Hobart.

N°

ENTRANCE IS.

HOBART BAY

0   1   2   3

Approx. Scale n.m.

ENTRANCE Is.

Grass

Old Float

5

6

Grass

$3\frac{1}{2}$ — 100'×12' Float

7

Eagle
nest

CAUTION: Note that
underwater cables reach
from shore to float.

Private

Trees

Shed

House

Garden

Trees

8

Heavily
Wooded

0   500'

Approx. Scale - feet

Not to be used for navigation

HOLKAM BAY

Holkam Bay has a 5-mile wide opening between Point Coke in the north and Point Astley in the south. Harbor Island along with several smaller islands stretch across the bay toward Wood Spit and its extension of tidal flats and islands. Tracy Arm and Endicott Arm are two long fiords that extend roughly north and southeast respectively from the bay. High, snow-clad mountains and glaciers form the backdrop for these arms.

This is a spectacular and very scenic area, with long fiords and calving tidewater glaciers. Though there are few secure anchorages, a visit to this area is truly worthwhile. Tourists are brought high-speed craft from as far away as Juneau.

Tracy Arm

Enter Tracy Arm by going around the north point of Harbor Island to pick up the unlit range on Harbor Island that leads through the shoal areas at the mouth. A day beacon is located on the opposite shore. Currents can be up to 4 knots, and swirls and tidal effects will be encountered in the entrance. For entering the Arm use the detailed information on Chart 17360.

Tracy Arm extends north for about 9 miles before turning east in a sinuous passage between steep, Yosemite-like cliffs for 13 miles to its head. Here the North and South Sawyer Glaciers discharge into the sea. Icebergs are encountered throughout the passage, becoming more numerous as you come closer to the glaciers; the South Sawyer Glacier is the more active of the two. Approach to the glaciers depends on ice conditions which can vary from year to year. The water in Tracy Arm is very deep and the only anchorage possible is near the entrance taking care to avoid the rocky shoal at the east point of the entrance. Though this anchorage is of reasonable depth and protection, it is open to the southeast; in bad weather it would be better to retreat to Taku or elsewhere.

Endicott Arm

This Arm can be entered from the north by passing behind Harbor Island, or from a point 1 mile north of Point Astley you can steer for prominent Sumdum Glacier in order to reach the entrance. Wood Spit Light marks the southern part of this half-mile wide entrance which is more easily entered than Tracy Arm. Swirls will be encountered here. It is about 27 miles along the Arm to Dawes Glacier which discharges ice directly into the sea.

About 5 miles into Endicott Arm is an anchorage at **Sanford Cove** on the south side, abreast of Sumdum Island. It is an indifferent anchorage, deep and on a narrow shelf. The anchorage in Tracy Arm is preferred as a base, even with the few additional miles involved.

Fords Terror is a spectacular, narrow, steep-walled inlet about 5 miles long. It is on the north side of Endicott Arm and about 13 miles from Sumdum Island. About 1.25 miles into this inlet it narrows and shallows considerably. Since currents run up to 15 knots, accompanied with overfalls, entry is possible only at high water slack. This occurs about 20 minutes after high tide in Juneau. The best spot to anchor is in the west arm, off a waterfall in the northwest corner.

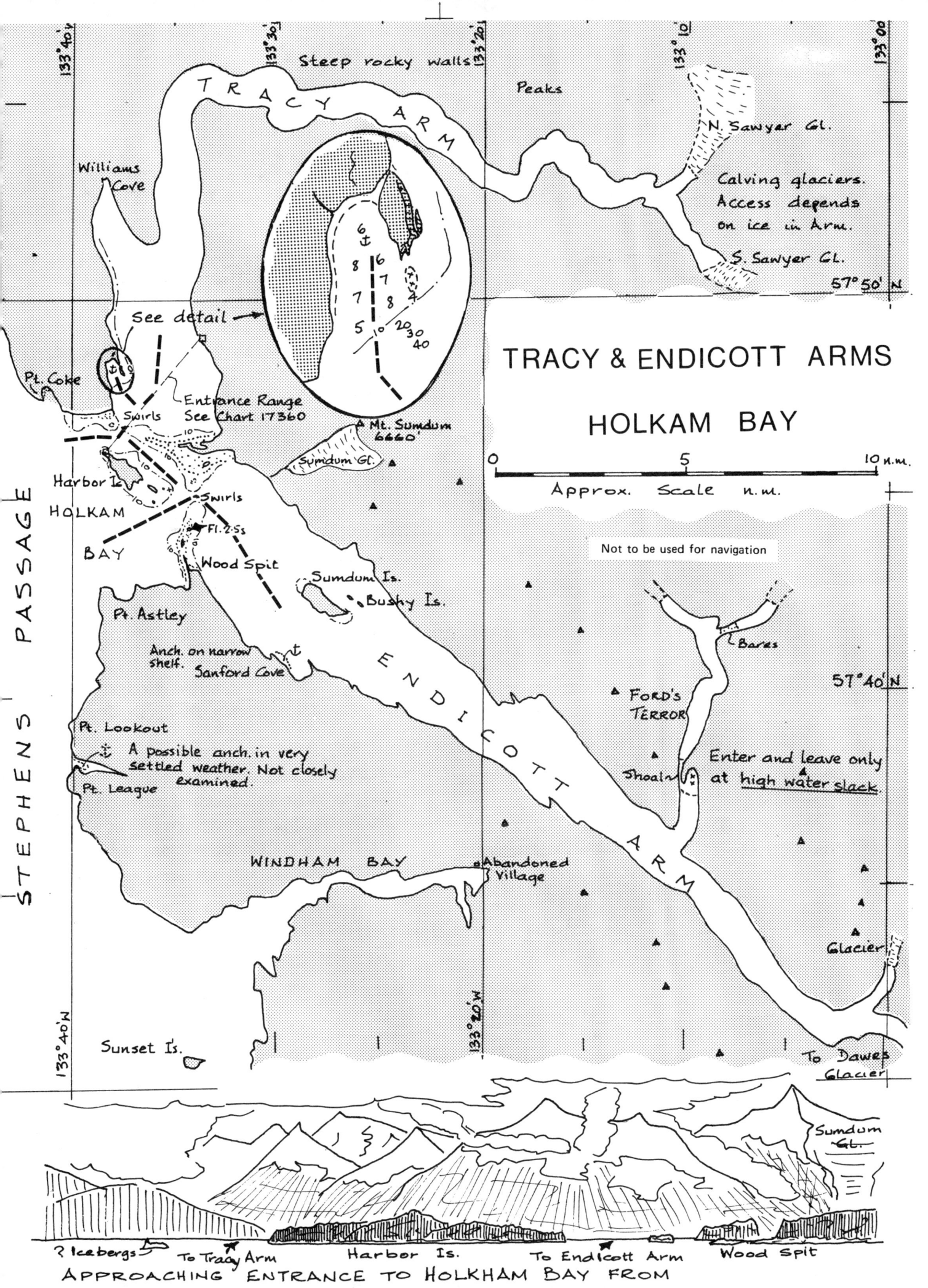

TRACY & ENDICOTT ARMS

HOLKAM BAY

Steep rocky walls

TRACY ARM

Peaks

N. Sawyer Gl.

Calving glaciers.
Access depends
on ice in Arm.

S. Sawyer Gl.

57° 50' N

Williams Cove

See detail

Pt. Coke

Swirls

Entrance Range
See Chart 17360

Harbor Is.

HOLKAM

BAY

Swirls

Fl. 2·5s

Wood Spit

Mt. Sumdum
6660

Sumdum Gl.

Sumdum Is.

Bushy Is.

0   5   10 n.m.

Approx. Scale n.m.

Not to be used for navigation

Bares

57° 40' N

FORD'S
TERROR

Shoal

Enter and leave only
at high water slack.

Pt. Astley

Anch. on narrow
shelf.
Sanford Cove

Pt. Lookout

A possible anch. in very
settled weather. Not closely
examined.

Pt. League

WINDHAM BAY

Abandoned
Village

ENDICOTT ARM

Glacier

Sunset Is.

To Dawes
Glacier

STEPHENS PASSAGE

Sumdum
Gl.

? Icebergs   To Tracy Arm   Harbor Is.   To Endicott Arm   Wood Spit

APPROACHING ENTRANCE TO HOLKHAM BAY FROM

TAKU

This harbor is within 20 miles of Juneau. One would not normally make so short a run near one of the major ports of a trip, but it has one inestimable benefit in providing a safe harbor if strong winds are blowing down Taku Inlet.

Taku Inlet is 15 miles long and opens into the east side of Stephens Passage just beyond Taku Harbor. It has a spectacular backdrop of glaciers and peaks. Taku Glacier is advancing and producing sediments which make the upper part of the Inlet shoal. Stephens Passage is well known for the strength and bone-chilling temperatures of the winds that funnel down from the icefields above. While passage in summer is never as bad as in winter (when icing is an additional problem) it can be a rough and uncomfortable trip. In such cases it is wise to retreat to the security of Taku Harbor and wait for calmer weather before proceeding.

Taku Mountain (640 m/2,100 feet) is a prominent, conical landmark rising to the north of the entrance to the bay. There is a light is on Grave Point at the southern tip of Taku Mountain. Stockade Point, off a low, forested peninsula marks the southern boundary of the entrance. The entrance itself is wide and deep and has no difficulties.

The ruins of a large cannery wharf are near the northeastern corner of the protected harbor. About 200 m (600 feet) south are the T-shaped public floats having a 60 m (200-foot) face and a 30 m (100-foot) cross arm, which are connected to the boardwalk on shore by a float (walkway). The main floats have at least 2 fathoms or more alongside. No facilities are available, but Juneau is close by. Watch for old pilings when maneuvering in the dock area.

The harbor is shoal both at its northern head and in the southern section. Anchorage is possible in the southeastern part in 7 to 9 fathoms, soft bottom. Some minor current effects may be noticed. Winds can swirl off the mountains around the harbor, but the harbor itself is secure.

Limestone Inlet, the narrow opening less than 2 miles south of Taku Harbor, is an ecological research area and has no anchorage.

Slocum Inlet, about 5 miles north of Taku Harbor, is shoal and does not provide an anchorage. On the south shore is Butler Peak an even more conical peak than Taku Mountain, but half its size. All of these shores are steep and heavily wooded. The power line route is evident along the coast.

Grand Isle, in the middle of Stephens Passage, is prominent from the south and has steep slopes. Though it can be passed on either side the usual route passes it on the east.

Apart from the discomfort of the winds down Taku Inlet, the trip can be enjoyed for its scenery and to savor the approach to Juneau. From Juneau excursion flights can be taken over the glaciers and icefields. Taku Glacier Lodge, where overnight accommodation and guided tours can be arranged, is situated at the head of the inlet. Information on these facilities can be obtained at the Visitor Information Center or by inquiring at the Merchants Wharf in Juneau.

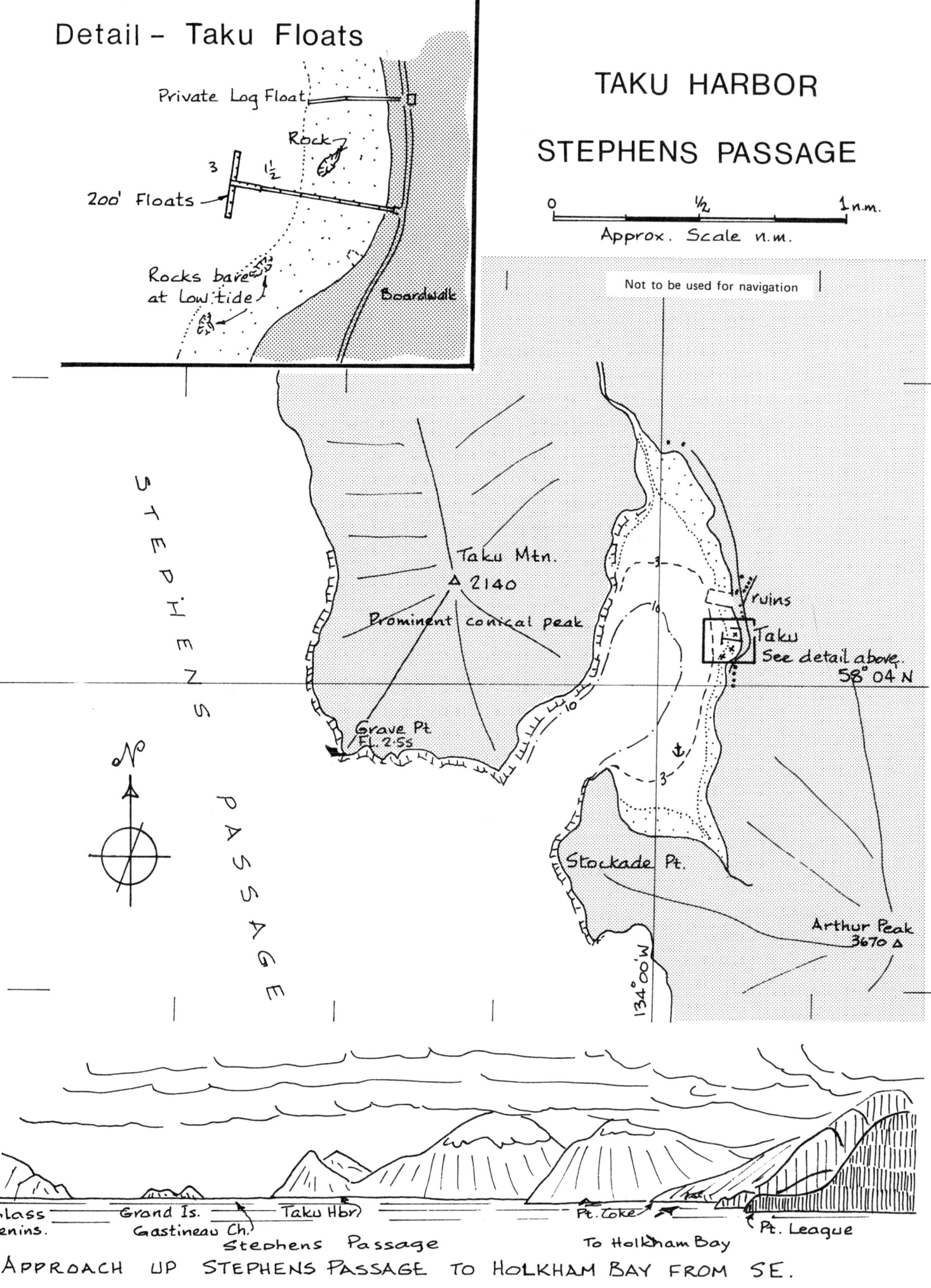

Detail - Taku Floats

Private Log Float

Rock

3   1½

200' Floats

Rocks bare
at Low tide

Boardwalk

TAKU HARBOR

STEPHENS PASSAGE

0   ½   1 n.m.

Approx. Scale n.m.

Not to be used for navigation

S T E P H E N S

P A S S A G E

Taku Mtn.
△ 2140
Prominent conical peak

3

10

Grave Pt
Fl. 2·5s

ruins

Taku
See detail above.
58° 04 N

N

Stockade Pt.

3

Arthur Peak
3670 △

134° 00'W

Glass
Penins.
Grand Is.
Gastineau Ch.
Taku Hbr.
Stephens Passage
Pt. Coke
To Holkham Bay
Pt. League

APPROACH UP STEPHENS PASSAGE TO HOLKHAM BAY FROM SE.

SECTION 7 - Juneau to Glacier Bay to Sitka

Additional views found in this section:

Douglas & West Juneau — Green Bn. — To Aurora & Harris Harbors — Cruise ship area — R&W Steel Tower — Microwave Twr.

JUNEAU HARBOR

Douglas Boat Basin.

DOUGLAS HARBOR

Blue Mouse Cove

In the ice pack before Muir Glacier

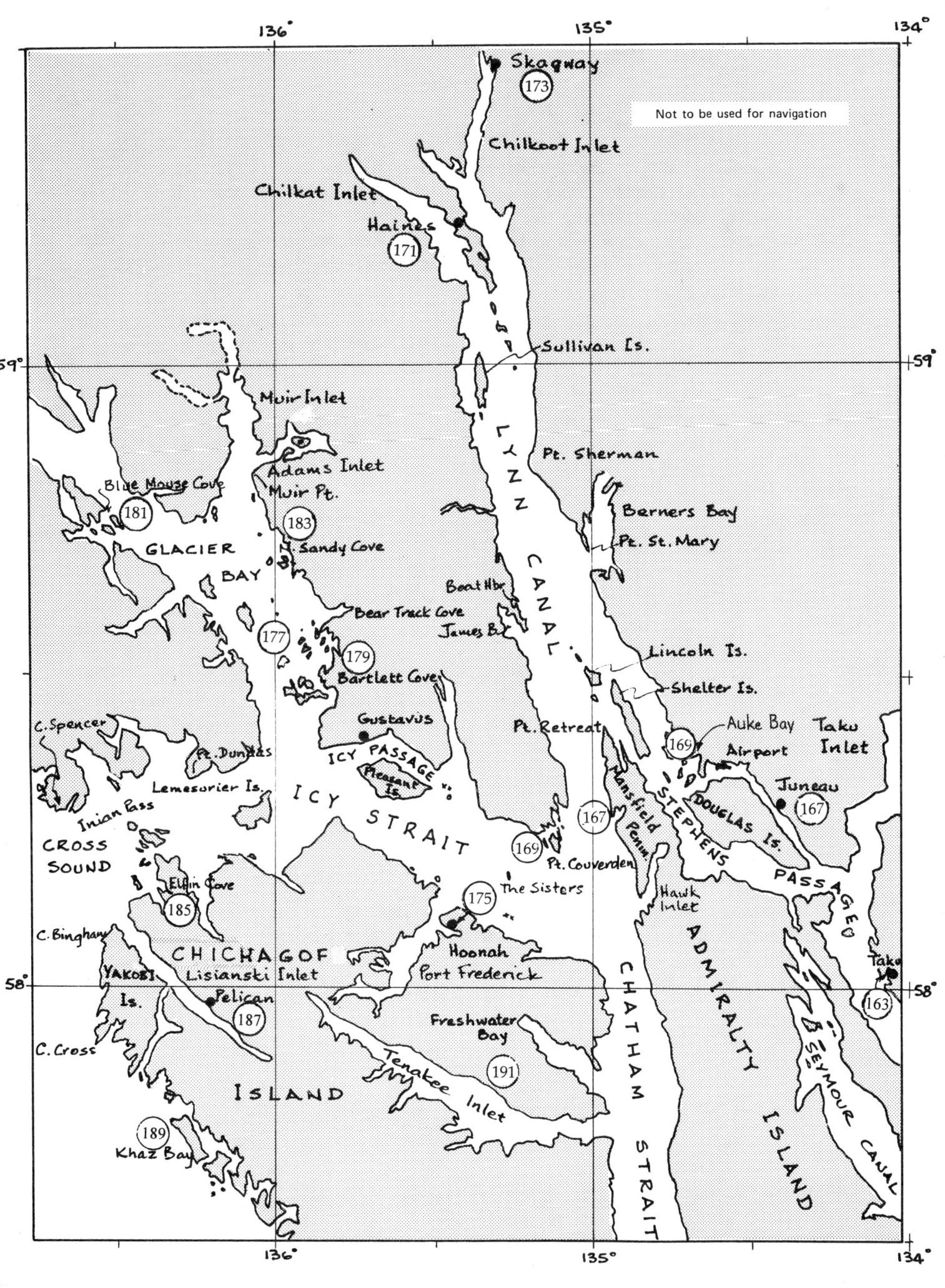

Not to be used for navigation

Skagway 173

Chilkoot Inlet

Chilkat Inlet

Haines 171

Sullivan Is.

LYNN CANAL

Pt. Sherman

Muir Inlet

Adams Inlet
Muir Pt.

Blue Mouse Cove 181

Berners Bay
Pt. St. Mary

183

N. Sandy Cove

GLACIER

BAY

Boat Hbr.

Bear Track Cove

James B.

177

Lincoln Is.

179

Shelter Is.

Bartlett Cove

C. Spencer

Gustavus

Pt. Retreat

Auke Bay
Airport

Taku
Inlet

169

Pt. Dundas

ICY PASSAGE

Pleasant
Is.

Lemesurier Is.

ICY   STRAIT

167

Juneau 167

Inian Pass

169

Mansfield Penin.

STEPHENS

Douglas Is.

CROSS

Pt. Couverden

SOUND

Elfin Cove

The Sisters

175

Hawk
Inlet

PASSAGE

C. Binghang

CHICHAGOF

Hoonah

Taku

YAKOBI

Lisianski Inlet

Port Frederick

ADMIRALTY

163

Is.

Pelican 187

Freshwater
Bay

C. Cross

ISLAND

191

ISLAND

CHATHAM   STRAIT

189

Tenakee   Inlet

SEYMOUR   CANAL

Khaz Bay

JUNEAU

This is the state Capital and the largest city of the Southeast. The city lies along the west bank of Gastineau Channel beneath the steep flanks of Mount Juneau, and it extends northwesterly to Mendenhall Valley and Auke Bay. The town of Douglas is across the channel. The main port area is a cruise ship anchorage, while facilities for yachts are beyond the bridge joining the communities of Douglas and Juneau. The bridge has a clearance of 15 m (51 ft.).

Some transient moorage is available at the Juneau **City Floats** near the ferry terminal, but the main transient moorage facilities are at **Harris** and **Aurora Harbors** immediately beyond the bridge. The harbormaster's office is on the southeast corner of Aurora Basin and he controls all transient moorage. Report to him on arrival, either by calling on VHF Channel 16 (working Ch. 73) or checking into his office. If all transient slips are filled, you may have to take a vacant slip until directed elsewhere and be prepared to move if your are staying for an extended period of time. Harbor Washboard (with a dry-cleaner and laundry at the back) is the nearest shower and laundry facility, about 1.5 blocks south of Harris Harbor on the road leading to the bridge. A bank is nearby..

It is about .5 mile from Aurora to downtown Juneau; half that from Harris. The walk downtown along the street one block inland from the freeway goes past a supermarket, stores, restaurants, the post office, the Alaska State Museum and Centennial Hall. Both of the latter places are well worth a visit to learn about this part of Alaska.

The town of Douglas lies beyond Juneau in the Gastineau Channel. Operated by the City of Juneau, the **Douglas Boat Harbor** is located about 3 miles from the center of Juneau. Transient moorage is available on the first (of three) floats seen when entering the basin. Power and water are available on the float and there is no time limit on length of stay. Grocery stores and a restaurant are close by but fuel, repairs and any other services can only be obtained in Juneau.

Juneau is a tourist-oriented city. There seems to be a cruise ship or two docked almost all the time. There are many tourist shops in the downtown area. Perhaps because of this regular tourist parade and the winter's legislative period (marked by an influx of elected officials, staffs, and lobbyists) this city loses its friendliness when compared with other communities of the Southeast.

A visit to Mendenhall Glacier can be accomplished by city bus or rented car. Maps of hiking trails are found at the Center. The new community areas of Mendenhall Valley are served by a large shopping center which rivals the selection of goods found in Juneau. The airport is also located here.

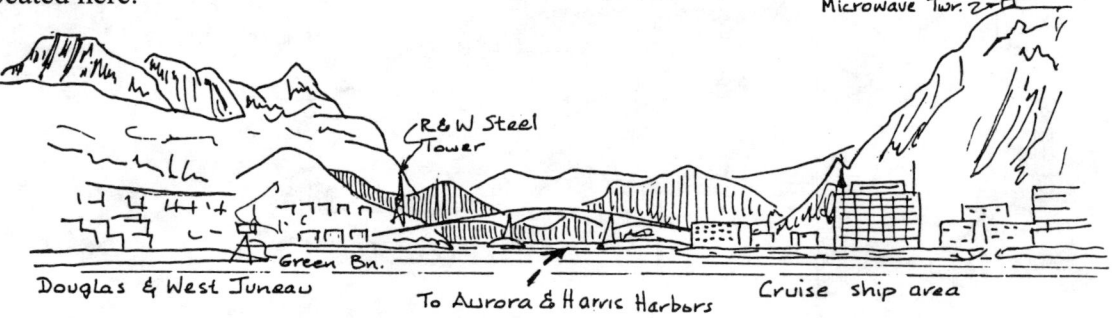

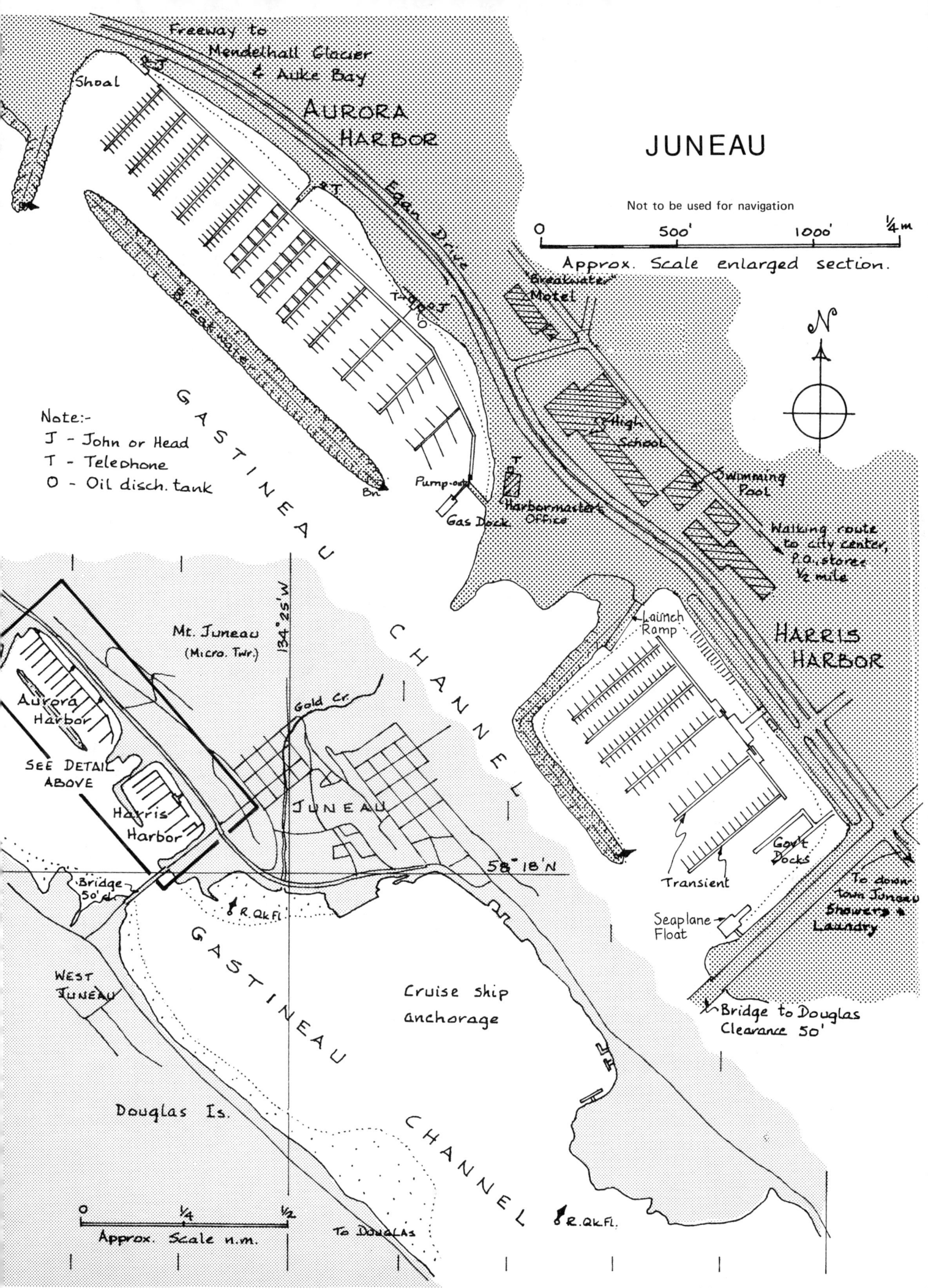

AUKE BAY

This handy starting point for the next stage of the cruise is off Stephens Passage, facing Favorite and Saginaw Channels. Coghlan Island is on the SW side of Auke Bay, about 1 mile NW of Spuhn Island. Point Louisa and Indian Point are on the north shore of the bay, about 1.2 miles NW and .6 mile N, respectively, of the northern extremity of Coghlan Island. Fairhaven is on the shore of the bay between these two points. After passing .2 miles S and E of Coghlan Island, enter the bay on a NE course as indicated on the sketch.

Since this is the only deep-draft facility in the area it is the site of the Alaska State Ferry Terminal, the National Marine Fisheries Service and the National Parks Service Pier. The pleasure craft facilities which cater to both transient vessels and local boats are located in the northeastern part of the bay.

Auke Bay Public Float is about 300 m (330 yards) north of the National Marine Fisheries Service Float. There are over 50 transient berths which can accommodate vessels up to 18 m (60 feet) in length on a first-come, first-served basis with the maximum allowable stay being 72 hours. The Juneau harbormaster controls the public floats and the 14 m (45-foot) grid which is just to the north of the floats. The harbormaster monitors VHF Ch. 16 (working channel 73) and can be reached by phone at (907) 789-0819. Water and power is available on some floats. The two private marinas are filled with local vessels and do not have space for transients. Fuel, marine supplies and minor repairs are available at both marinas. A travelift is available at Dehart's Marina.

A store with groceries, liquor and sundry items and a restaurant are one block up the hill and there is a telephone and a weather forecast device at the top of the gangway. Restrooms, waste oil receptacles, pump-out facilities and garbage collection facilities are available as shown on the sketch.

Juneau may be reached by a 33-mile trip around Douglas Island and up Gastineau Channel which is marked by lights, buoys, and daybeacons. An alternate route crossing Mendenhall Bar should be taken only by vessels having a fairly shallow draft and after a thorough and careful investigation of current tide and bar conditions. A generous allowance must be made for the fact that the actual height of high tide can differ markedly from the predicted high tide, with actual height usually less than the predicted height. A free diagram of the channel across Mendenhall Bar is available from the Aids to Navigation Branch of Coast Guard District office in Juneau or by writing to: Commander, 17th Coast Guard District, Federal Bldg., Box 25517, Juneau, AK 99802-5517. The channel is marked, but at low water the markers rest on the bars so current knowledge of the channel is essential before using this route.

Glacier Highway connects Auke Bay to the Juneau Airport (about 2 miles distant) and Juneau which is about 10 miles further. If a major reprovisioning is needed it would be more convenient and economical to shop in Juneau.

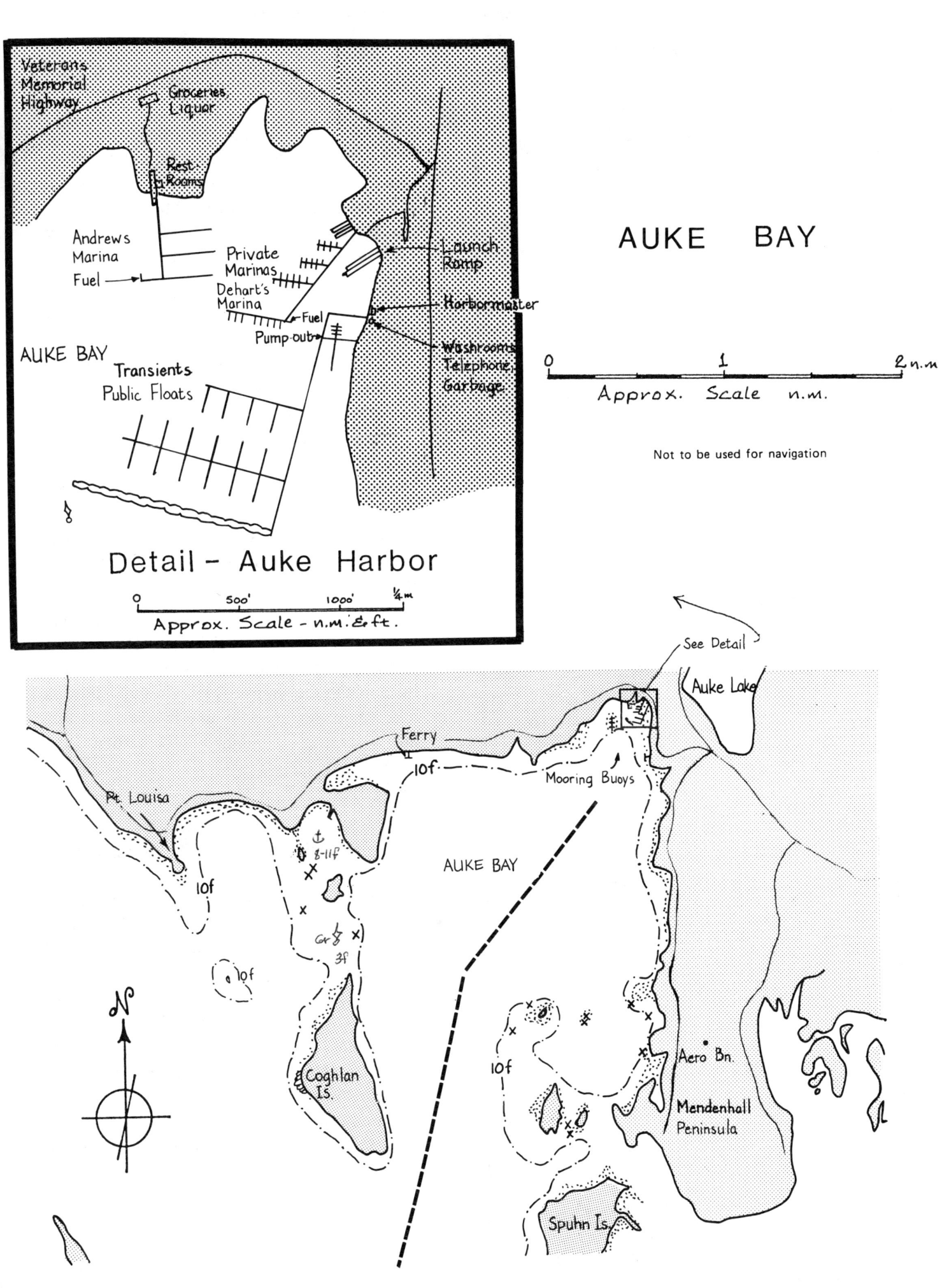

AUKE BAY

Approx. Scale n.m.

0   1   2 n.m.

Not to be used for navigation

Detail - Auke Harbor

Approx. Scale - n.m. & ft.

0   500'   1000'   ¼ m

Veterans Memorial Highway

Groceries Liquor

Rest Rooms

Andrews Marina

Fuel

Private Marinas

Dehart's Marina

Fuel

Pump-out

AUKE BAY

Transients Public Floats

Launch Ramp

Harbormaster

Washrooms Telephone Garbage

See Detail

Auke Lake

Ferry

10f

Mooring Buoys

Pt. Louisa

10f

8-11f

Gr   3f

10f

10f

AUKE BAY

Coghlan Is.

Spuhn Is.

Aero Bn.

Mendenhall Peninsula

N

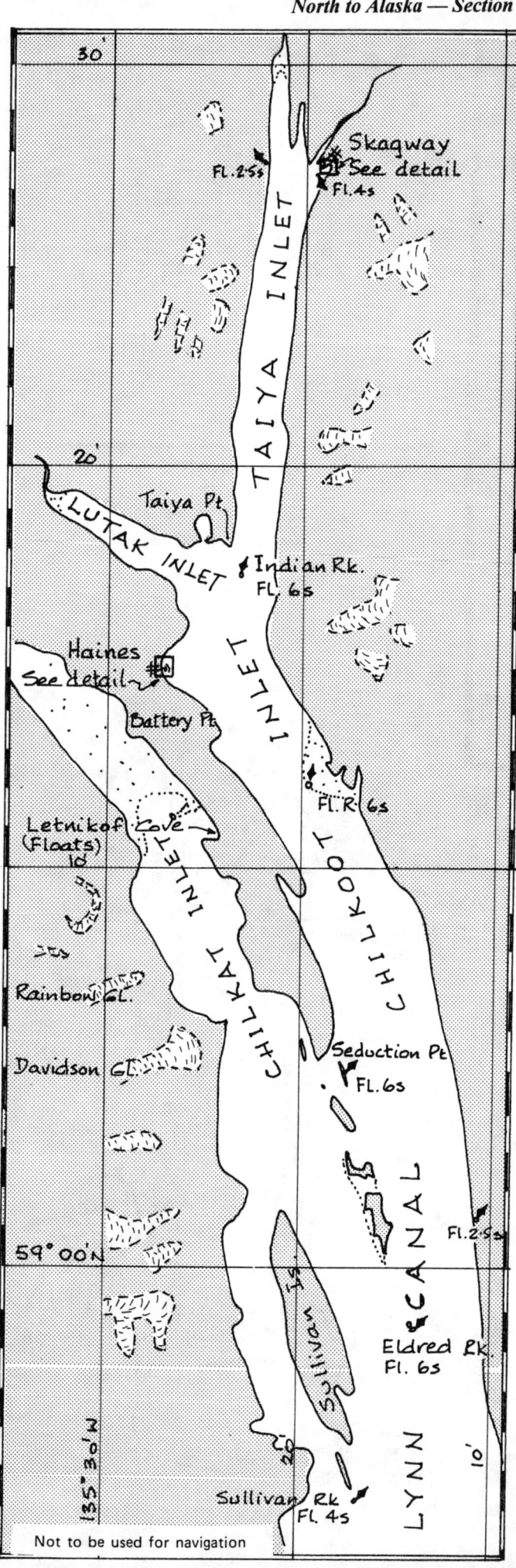

LYNN CANAL

This long and beautiful inlet and its arms reach about 85 miles NNW from the junction of Chatham and Icy Straits. It is deep and varies in width from 3 to 6 miles. Lined on both sides by glaciers and peaks, this can be a very scenic trip.

Haines

On the west side of Chilkoot Inlet in Portage Bay, this town of has a spectacular backdrop composed of the Cathedral Peaks. The small boat harbor is protected by a rock breakwater and entry should be made via the southern entrance. The harbormaster controls berths in the harbor. The ferry terminal is at Lutak Inlet a few miles out of town. The Haines Highway gives year-round access to the Alaska Highway.

The Chilkat Dancers give evening performances at Fort William H. Seward. Local Indian arts and crafts are readily available in the shops. A laundromat, showers and restaurants are available in town and fuel and water may be obtained in the harbor.

Skagway

Skagway lies near the end of Taiya Inlet off Chilkoot Inlet. The population of 2,000 is greatly reduced from the infamous city of 30,000 in the days of Soapy Smith. However, it celebrates its gold rush history by maintaining the atmosphere with unchanged store fronts and locals in period costumes. A highway gives access in summer to the Alaska Highway. With the closing of the mines the White Pass and Yukon Railway no longer operates. The small boat harbor is protected by a breakwater and lies adjacent to the ferry terminal and the railway. Fuel can be obtained at a float in the southern end of the harbor.

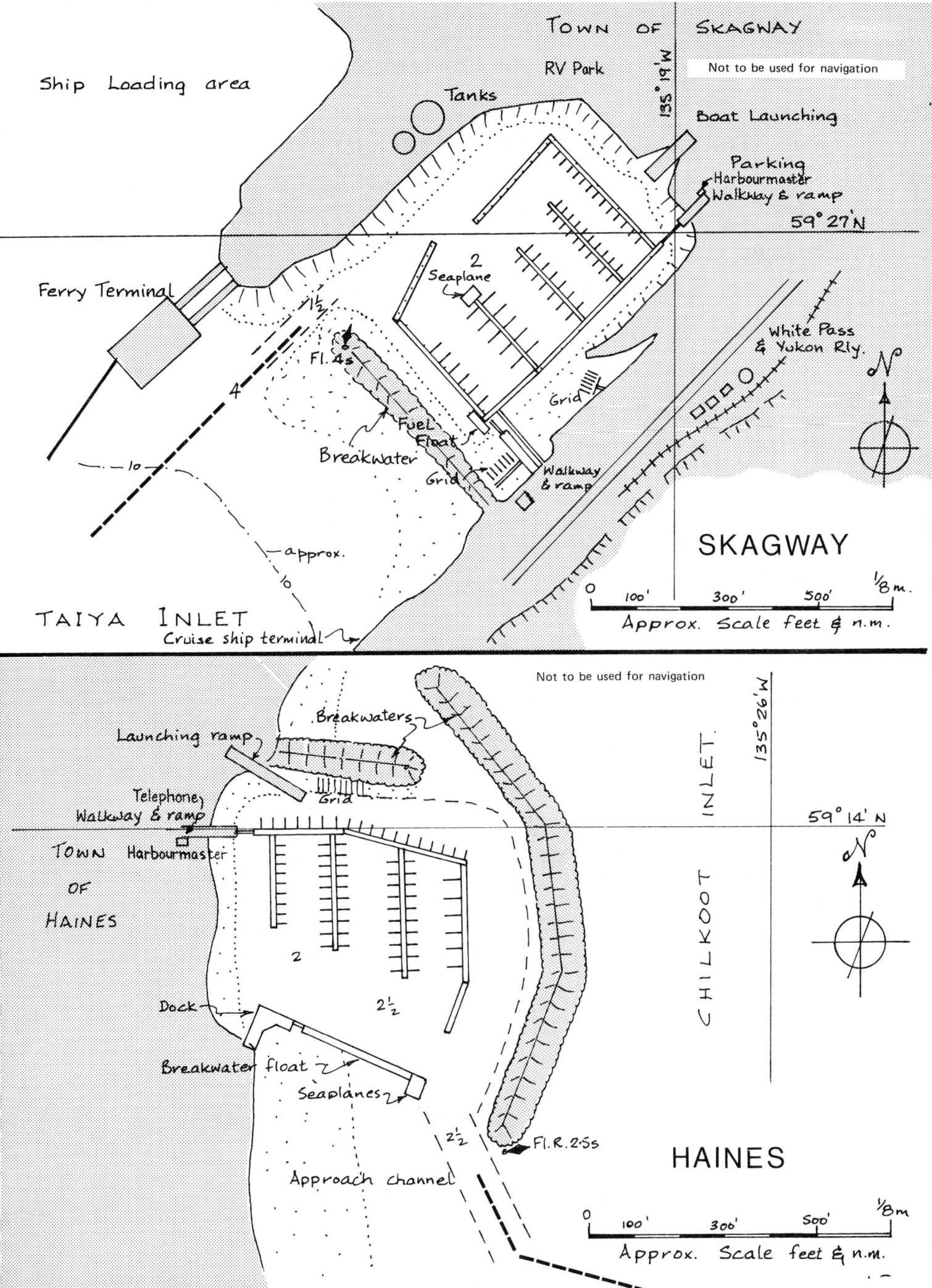

Ship Loading area

Town of Skagway

RV Park

Not to be used for navigation

Tanks

Boat Launching

Parking
Harbourmaster
Walkway & ramp

59°27'N

135°19'W

Ferry Terminal

2
Seaplane

Fl. 4s

White Pass
& Yukon Rly.

N

4

Fuel
Float

Breakwater

Grid

Grid

Walkway
& ramp

SKAGWAY

10

approx.

10

TAIYA INLET

Cruise ship terminal

0   100'   300'   500'   ⅛ m.

Approx. Scale feet & n.m.

Not to be used for navigation

Breakwaters

Launching ramp

Telephone
Walkway & ramp

CHILKOOT INLET.

135°26'W

59°14'N

Town
OF
HAINES

Harbourmaster

Grid

N

2

Dock

2½

Breakwater float

Seaplanes

2½

Fl.R.2·5s

HAINES

Approach channel

0   100'   300'   500'   ⅛ m.

Approx. Scale feet & n.m.

ANCHORAGES AT THE SOUTH END OF LYNN CANAL

The junction of Lynn Canal, Chatham, and Icy Straits is a crossroads for yachts bound to or from Glacier Bay or Juneau. There are two very good anchorages in this area.

Funter Bay

Mansfield Peninsula projects NNW off Admiralty Island with Lynn Canal on its west side. Funter Bay is on the west side, about 10 miles south of Point Retreat (the tip of Mansfield Peninsula). It is a fairly large bay with several islands near the entrance.

On a northern approach Naked Island (with a light on it) and the pair of smaller islands called the "Kittens" should be passed on their west side. The northern point of the entrance to Funter Bay is Clear Point (with a light on it). There is a wide opening to the group of islands off the southern point of the entrance, Rat Island, Station Island and two smaller islets.

Roughly east of Clear Point Light and against the southeastern side of the bay is a 45 m (150-foot) State operated float, unconnected to the shore. Another State-operated 30 m (100-foot) float can be found at the ruins of the cannery wharf in the northern part of the bay, between Coot and Crab Coves. Caution is needed in this area due to the ruins of the wharf and a rocky ledge nearby.

Swanson Harbor

Across Lynn Canal from Funter Bay is Swanson Harbor, formed by a group of islands lying off the land. Less than a mile off the southern tip of Couverden Island is Rocky Island, a prominent, rounded, grass-topped rock with a light. Set a course to enter the channel between Point Couverden and Rocky Island. Leaving Rocky Island astern, proceed northwesterly, follow along the southwest shore of Couverden Island, then take a mid-channel course between it and Entrance and Ansley Islands successively. Around the northwestern tip of Couverden Island is a bight with drying flats and a small island to the west. Here a 45 m (150-foot) State operated float is located, unconnected to the shore. Boats can moor on both sides.

At high tide the scenic mountains behind Juneau and Auke Bay can be seen from the float. When it is calm the float has many annoying deer flies but with a breeze they are not in evidence.

Alternate anchorage can be taken off the stony beach on **Ansley Island** at the side of the harbor on the shelf close to shore. Large vessels could anchor in the bight at the head. The gap between Ansley and Entrance Islands has rocks and reefs that discourage use. From Rocky Island courses may be set down Chatham or Icy Straits.

Mt. Robert Barron

Clear Point behind) — Naked Is. — Station Is.

APPROACHING FUNTER BAY FROM NNE, distant about 2 miles

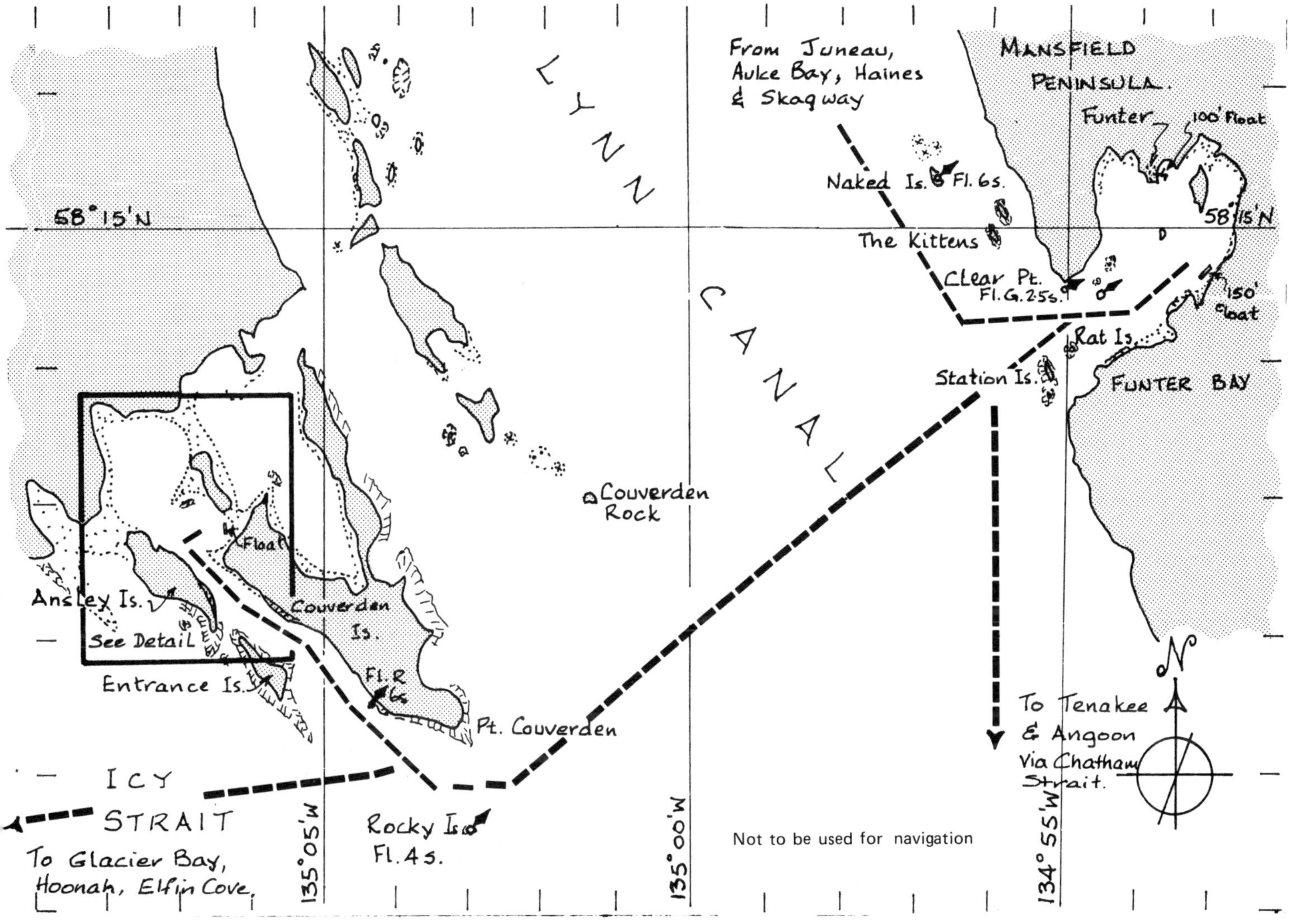

From Juneau,
Aulke Bay, Haines
& Skaqway

MANSFIELD PENINSULA.

Funter 100' Float

Naked Is. Fl. 6s.

58°15'N 58°15'N

The Kittens

Clear Pt.
Fl.G.2.5s. 150' Float

Rat Is.

Station Is. FUNTER BAY

LYNN CANAL

Couverden Rock

To Tenakee
& Angoon
Via Chatham
Strait.

N

Ansley Is.

See Detail Float

Entrance Is. Couverden Is.
Fl.R

Pt. Couverden

ICY STRAIT

To Glacier Bay,
Hoonah, Elfin Cove.

Rocky Is.
Fl.4s.

Not to be used for navigation

135°05'W 135°00'W 134°55'W

ANCHS. AT THE S. END OF LYNN CANAL

0 1 2 3
Approx. Scale n.m.

Snow Peaks

Old cannery

Clear Point
Lynn Canal

Bare Is

Green buoy

Float

Rat Is.

Station Is.

ABOUT ONE MILE OUT FROM THE ENTRANCE TO FUNTER BAY

HOONAH

This is the largest Tlingit community of the South East. The original Tlingit name of "huna" means "Place where the north wind doesn't blow." and warm ocean currents usually keep minimum temperatures just below freezing. The village lies on the east side of Port Frederick, which is an inlet on Chicagof Island, on the south side of Icy Strait.

Enter Port Frederick after passing the light at Inner Point Sophia. The fish plant facilities just behind the point are the Excursion Inlet Packing Corporation docks. Continue past them for about 1.5 miles to Hoonah, entering the small boat harbor southeast of Pitt Island. Pass east of Pitt Island and between the two breakwaters with lights. The transient float, operated by the town, is at the north end of the basin. Fuel can be obtained at the docks; water and power are available at the floats. Shower and laundry facilities are next to the harbormaster's office. The docks are very busy during summer months and reservations are recommended; contact the harbormaster at (907) 945-3670 or Fax (907) 945-3445.

A walk along the gravel shore road brings you to the store, cafe and gift shops. The cultural center has interesting local exhibits. The State ferry makes regular stops at Hoonah.

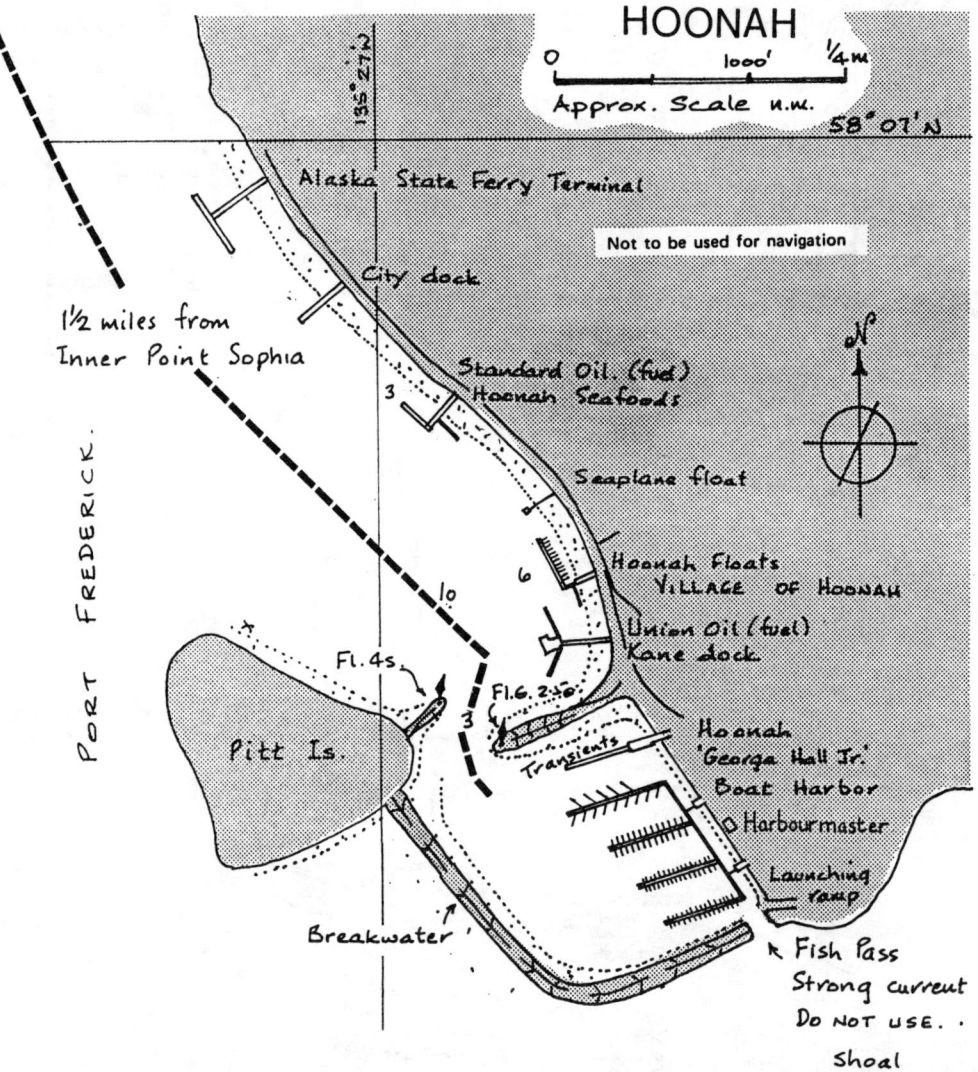

174

Entrance Is. — Ansley Is. — Couverden Is. —

Float behind →

NEARING THE TURN TO SWANSON HARBOR FLOAT.

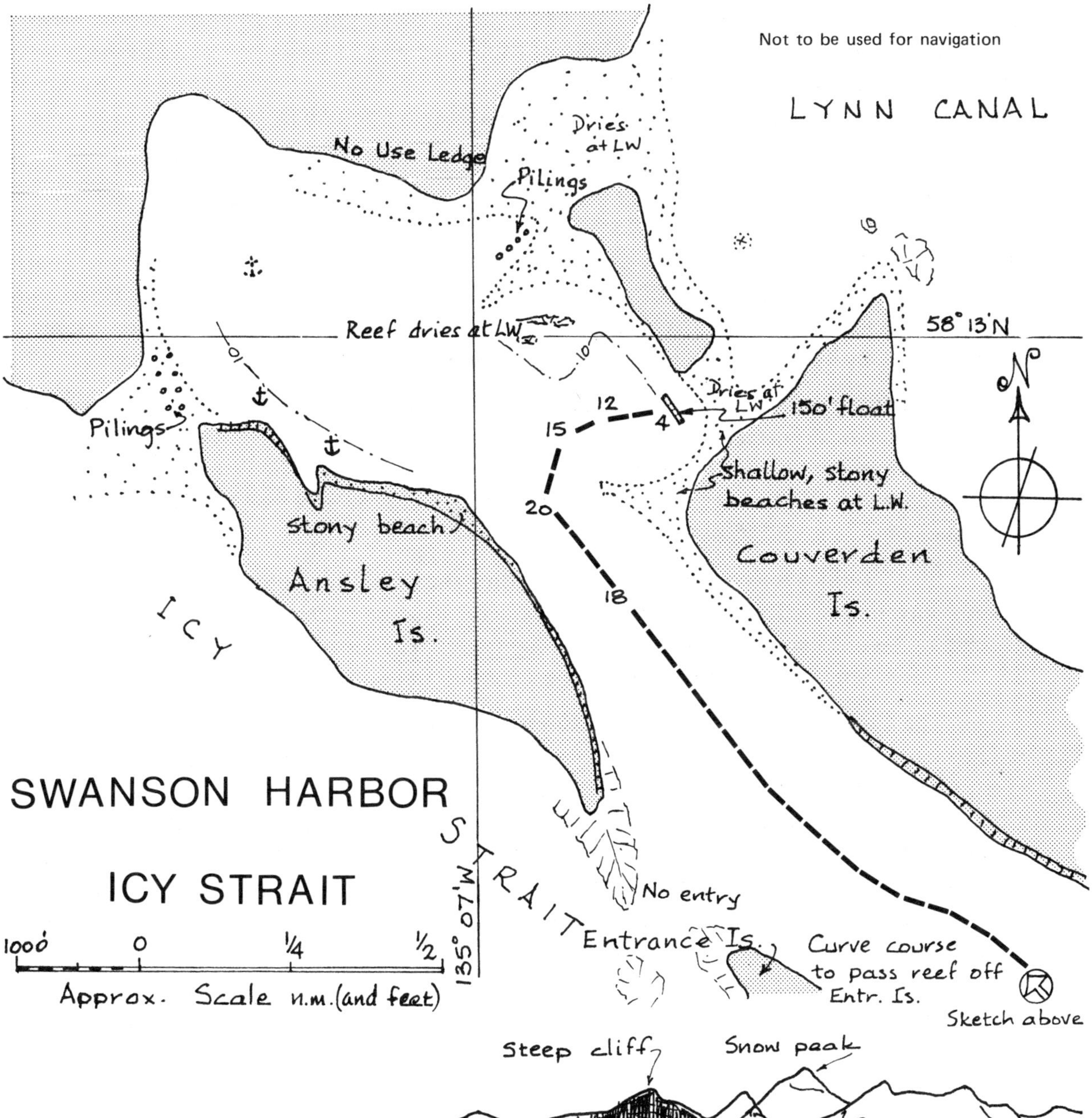

Not to be used for navigation

LYNN CANAL

No Use Ledge

Dries at LW

Pilings

Reef dries at LW

58° 13'N

N

Pilings

12

15

4

Dries at LW

150' float

20

Shallow, stony beaches at L.W.

stony beach

Ansley Is.

18

Couverden Is.

ICY

SWANSON HARBOR

ICY STRAIT

STRAIT

135° 07' W

No entry

Entrance Is.

Curve course to pass reef off Entr. Is.

1000'   0   ¼   ½

Approx. Scale n.m. (and feet)

Sketch above

Steep cliff

Snow peak

Ansley Is.

light. Fl. R. 6s.

Entrance Is. — Sharpe Ledge — Couverden Is. —

ENTERING SWANSON HARBOR, LEAVING ROCKY IS. ASTERN ½ MILE

GLACIER BAY

This magnificent area with its high, permanently snow-clad peaks and over 20 large and many smaller glaciers (12 of which reach the sea) is included in the 4,400 square miles of Glacier Bay National Monument. Yachts, local tour boats and cruise ships bring many visitors to the Bay. Entry is controlled by the National Park Service and special restrictions regarding entry are enforced as noted below.

The entrance to Glacier Bay is north off Icy Strait, and lies between Point Gustavus on the east and Point Carolus on the west. The bay is large, of varying width and extends in two major arms. It is about 45 miles north to the head of Muir Inlet and 54 miles northwest to the head of Tarr or John Hopkins Inlets. The western portion of the Park includes the peaks of the Fairweather range culminating in the wedge-shaped peak of Mount Fairweather (4,650 m/15,300 feet).

The National Park Service regulations aim at minimizing the disturbance of humpback whales, an endangered species which feed in Glacier Bay. Thus the number of powered vessels entering the Park in the period from June 1 to August 31 is limited. Pleasure boats are controlled by entry permits to ensure that no more than 25 private vessels, two cruise ships and 3 tour boats are in the Bay at any one time. No vessel can enter the Park, even to proceed to Bartlett Cove, without a permit or permission given by telephone or VHF in lieu of a permit. Thus, if early or just arriving in the area other anchorages must be found while waiting.

Requests for applications for permits and information about the park should be addressed to: The Superintendent, Glacier Bay National Park, P. O. Box 140,Gustavus, Alaska 99826-0140. You may get permission to enter by phoning 907-697-2627 or by VHF Ch 12 or16 to KWM20 Bartlett Cove when within VHF range. Additional information can be accessed at www.nps.gov/glba/ and the e-mail address is GLBA_Administration@nps.gov.

Since applications are not accepted earlier than 60 days before the entry date requested vessels traveling from distant ports are adversely affected. Permits are not needed for visits concluding before June 1 or beginning after August 31. The most heavily booked period is July 4 to 15, the time when local vessels as well as boats coming from the south are in the area.

The application requires the following: vessel's name and number, skipper's name, address, phone number, the number of people on board, a description of the boat, the proposed date of entry (first, second, and third choices), and the duration of one's visit (a maximum of 7 days is allowed). Once in the Park an extension of up to 7 days may be requested provided that unused permits are available. Even with a permit, confirmation is required just before entry by calling the Park Office by telephone on VHF within 48 hours of the scheduled entry (no later than 10 a.m. on the day of entry. Note that this fixes your date of entry; if you are either too early or too late you are back to square one and have lost any benefit of early application. If this happens, it is worthwhile to contact the Park Office on a daily basis to see if a cancellation has occurred that makes a space available to you. Entry occurs when you cross the line between Point Gustavus and Point Carolus.

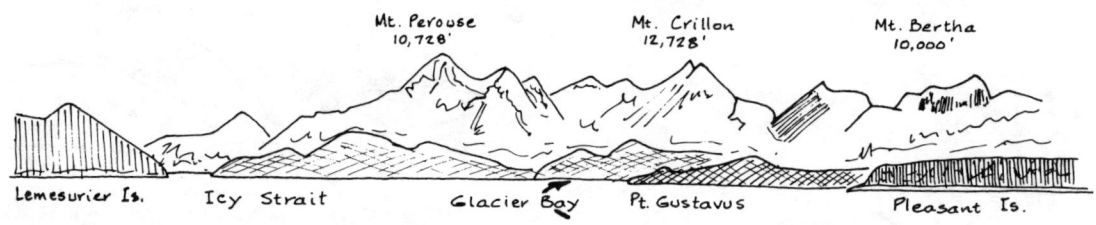

THE APPROACH TO GLACIER BAY FROM ESE, distant about 20 miles

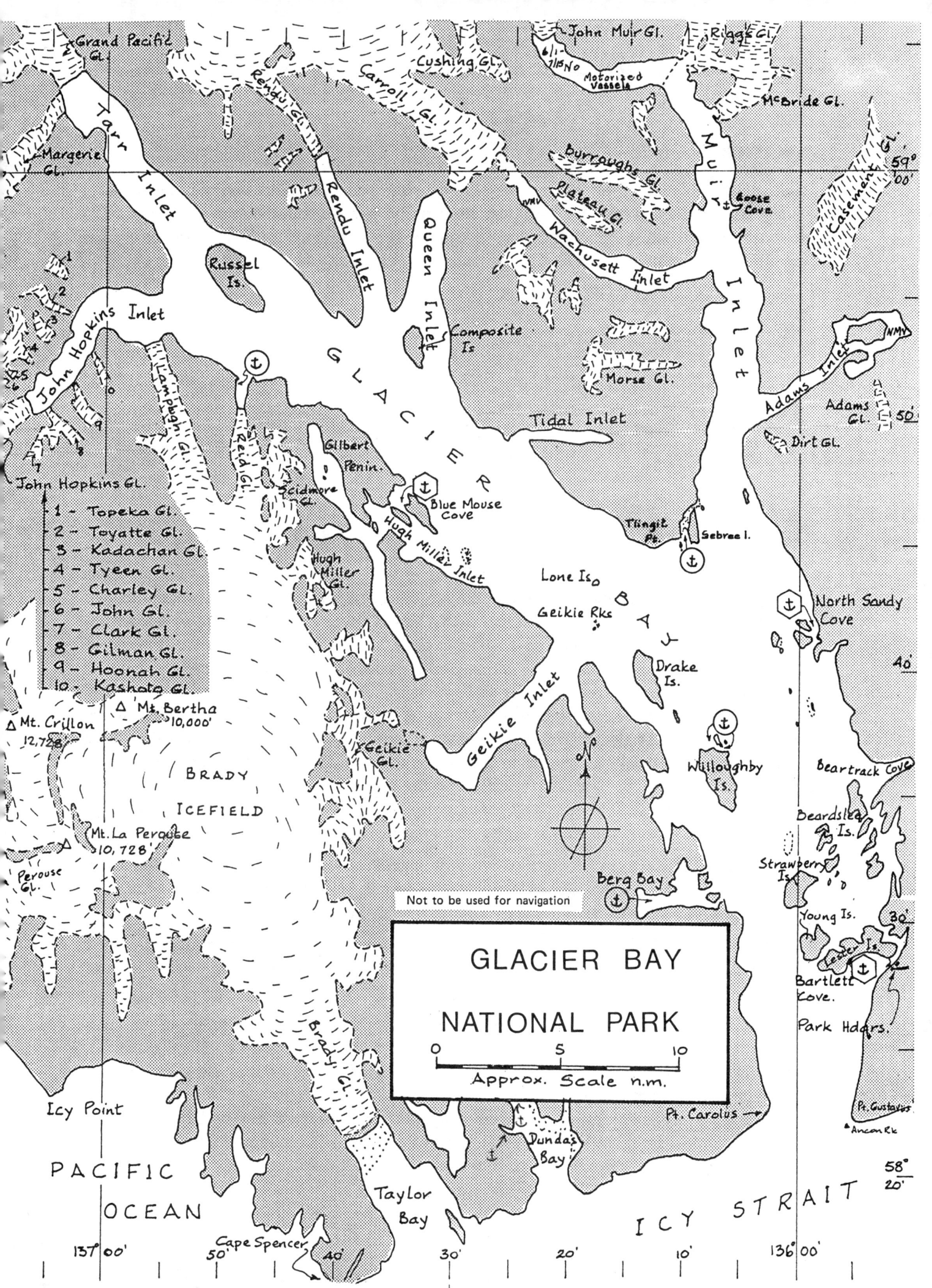

GLACIER BAY

NATIONAL PARK

Not to be used for navigation

Approx. Scale n.m.

0   5   10

John Hopkins Gl.

1 - Topeka Gl.
2 - Toyatte Gl.
3 - Kadachan Gl.
4 - Tyeen Gl.
5 - Charley Gl.
6 - John Gl.
7 - Clark Gl.
8 - Gilman Gl.
9 - Hoonah Gl.
10 - Kashoto Gl.

Grand Pacific Gl.
Margerie Gl.
Tarr Inlet
John Muir Gl.
Riggs Gl.
Cushing Gl.
Carroll Gl.
No Motorized Vessels
McBride Gl.
Rendu Gl.
Queen Inlet
Burroughs Gl.
Plateau Gl.
Wachusett Inlet
Muir Inlet
Casement
Goose Cove
Russel Is.
Rendu Inlet
Composite Is
Morse Gl.
Adams Inlet
Adams Gl.
GLACIER
Tidal Inlet
Dirt Gl.
Lamplugh Gl.
Reid Gl.
Scidmore Gl.
Gilbert Penin.
Blue Mouse Cove
Hugh Miller Inlet
Tlingit Pt.
Sebree I.
Hugh Miller Gl.
Lone Is.
Geikie Rks
North Sandy Cove
BAY
Mt. Crillon 12,728'
Mt. Bertha 10,000'
Drake Is.
Geikie Inlet
Geikie Gl.
Willoughby Is.
Beartrack Cove
BRADY
ICEFIELD
Mt. La Perouse 10,728'
Berg Bay
Beardslee Is.
Strawberry Is.
Young Is.
Perouse Gl.
Bartlett Cove.
Park Hdqrs.
Icy Point
Pt. Carolus
Pt. Gustavus
Ancon Rk
PACIFIC
OCEAN
Dundas Bay
Taylor Bay
ICY STRAIT
Brady Gl.
Cape Spencer

137°00'   50'   40'   30'   20'   10'   136°00'

59°00'
50'
40'
30'
58°20'

GLACIER BAY Cont'd.

Other regulations apply to your vessel in the park, and a pamphlet outlining them is sent with any communication from the Park Service. Briefly, you are required to stay more than .25 mile from a whale and to travel mid-channel courses at less than 10 knots in designated areas (presently from the entrance to Strawberry Islands and/or Bartlett Cove).

ENTRANCE TO GLACIER BAY FROM S, distant about 2 miles

BARTLETT COVE

Located on the east side of the bay and 4 miles from the entrance, this cove is the main Park Service Ranger Office and Entry Station. A large lodge is located here and the Park Service maintains a pier, small craft floats and a fuel float. Vessels over 9 m (30 feet) must anchor out and may use the floats on a first-come, first-serve basis for not more than 8 hours in every 48 hours. Anchorage may be taken in the quadrant north to northeast of the pier in about 7 fathoms. Tour boats dock at the pier so allow for their passage. A seaplane landing area marked by seasonal buoys, is northeast of the pier where anchoring is prohibited. Dinghies and skiffs can be moored at the rear of the floats. Water is available at the floats but is so highly treated as to be almost unsuitable for drinking. Although supplies are unavailable, there is a garbage disposal station where trash must be sorted into recyclable containers made of <u>any</u> material, compostables (food waste), trash (waxed/plastic-coated paper, snack wrappers, tissues and disposable diapers). Batteries and biohazard wastes such as syringes and bandages must be clearly marked.

The Park Rangers provide information as to anchorages, ice conditions, regulations, etc. Not all areas are open to traffic. For example, Marble Islands are closed to foot traffic because of the sea birds. Other areas sometimes have restrictions related to bears.

Strong rips and tidal currents occur in the Narrows approaching Strawberry Island. Either channel past Willoughby Island may be taken, but the current is evident on both sides. Above Willoughby less current is evident.

Under certain conditions in summer, outflow winds of great velocity pour out the inlets that lead from the mountain and glacier massifs on the west. They whip up steep waves for varying distances downwind across Glacier Bay. Such winds scream out of Berg Bay, Geikie Inlet, Hugh Miller Inlet and Reid Inlet. These winds can make entering these inlets very difficult, and the anchorages in or near them dangerous. Keep this in mind when using these inlets. Fog and mist are frequent in the colder parts of the Bay in late summer. The Park Service broadcasts weather forecasts on VHF Ch. 16/09 at 8:45 a.m. and 5:45 p.m.

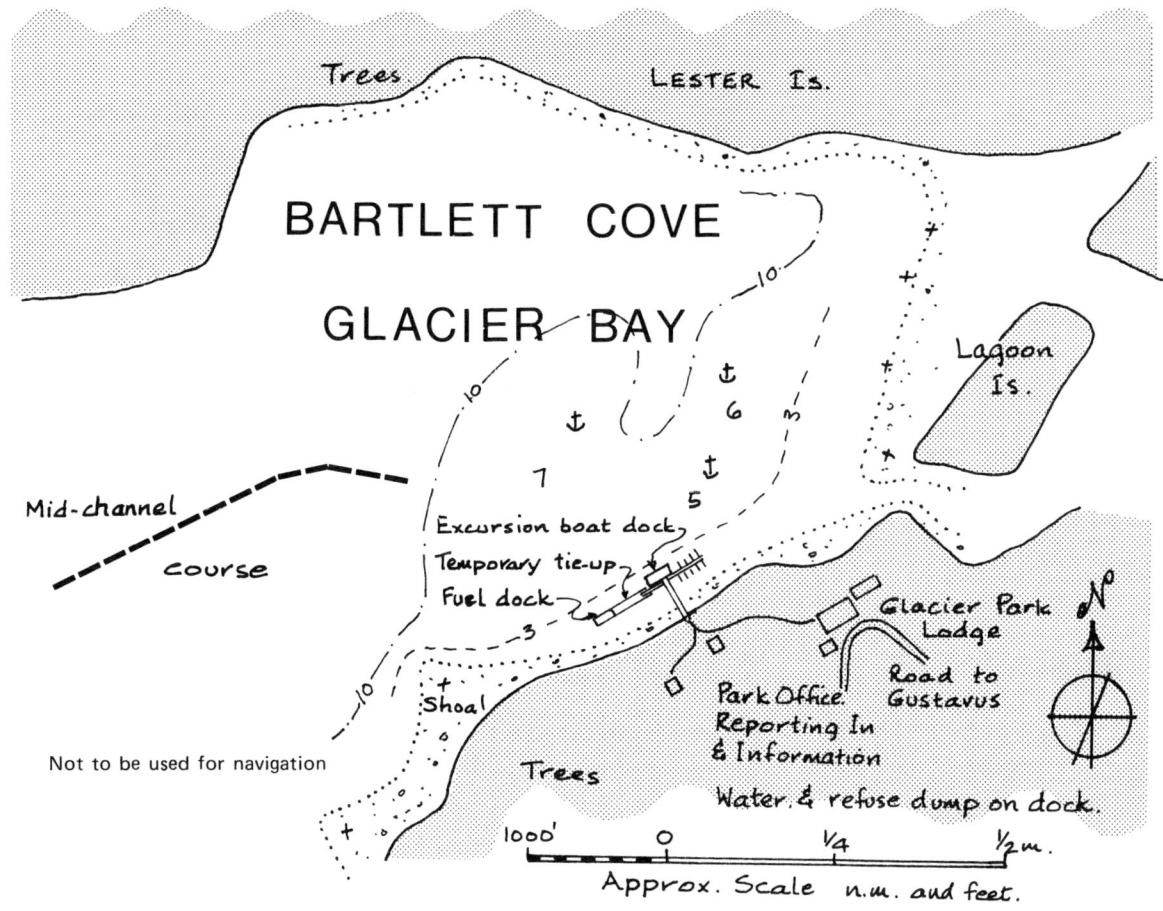

One method to explore Glacier Bay is to move out of Bartlett Cove as soon as practicable to an advance base anchorage. Depending on the weather this will allow for exploration and return from the ice-filled arms where passage may be slow and sometimes difficult and stressful. **Blue Mouse Cove** is a good base for visiting Tarr and John Hopkins Inlets, with **Reid Inlet** a further advance base to use in good weather.

Other anchorages in the Bay, with their own attractions include the following: Berg Bay (care is needed because of the many rocks in the entrance; anchor on the north side of the west arm), North and South Sandy Cove, Tidal Inlet, Russell Island, Goose Cove Adams Inlet, North and South Fingers Bay, Beardslee, Entrance, Johnson Cove, Willoughby Island (north end), Shag Cove (in Geikie Inlet), and Sebree Cove (between Tlinglit Point and the southern part of Sebree Island).

Peak –	Mt. Perouse	Mt. Crillon	Mt. Bertha	Mt. Fairweather
Height –	10,728'	12,728'	10,000'	15,300'
Distance –	43 miles	49 miles	45 miles	67 miles

VIEW OF GLACIER BAY NATIONAL PARK PEAKS FROM BARTLETT COVE

BLUE MOUSE COVE

This is an excellent anchorage to use as a base for exploring the northwestern arms of Glacier Bay. It is a well protected cove at the end of Gilbert Peninsula about 29 miles from Bartlett Cove. Anchorage can be taken on two 8-fathom patches on the south and southwestern sides of the cove. A smaller but shallower anchorage is in a niche on the north side.

The west side of the cove looks out over Hugh Miller Inlet to a truly beautiful mountain scene. Winds can blow down the peaks and inlets behind the cove, but it provides better protection than any other nearby anchorage.

Ice is not a concern in Blue Mouse Cove though an occasional berg may ground on the shoals near the entrance. Access to the glaciers in John Hopkins and Tarr Inlets depends on the time of year and on the amount of glacial calving which has occurred. If John Hopkins Glacier has been active small vessels rarely get further than Lamplugh Glacier. Grand Pacific and Margerie Glaciers in Tarr Inlet have tended to be easier to approach. However, year to year conditions differ so greatly that you must take things as they come.

REID INLET

This advanced base has its own tidewater glacier, and anchoring here gives a very special feeling. However this should be considered as an anchorage to be used only during settled, fair weather. (Note the remark on outflow winds made earlier.) There is a shallow bar across the entrance. Suitable anchorage may be taken on the west side tucked in behind the drying area and the island. Park regulations prohibit the operation of generators in the inlet between the hours of 10 p.m. and 6 a.m.

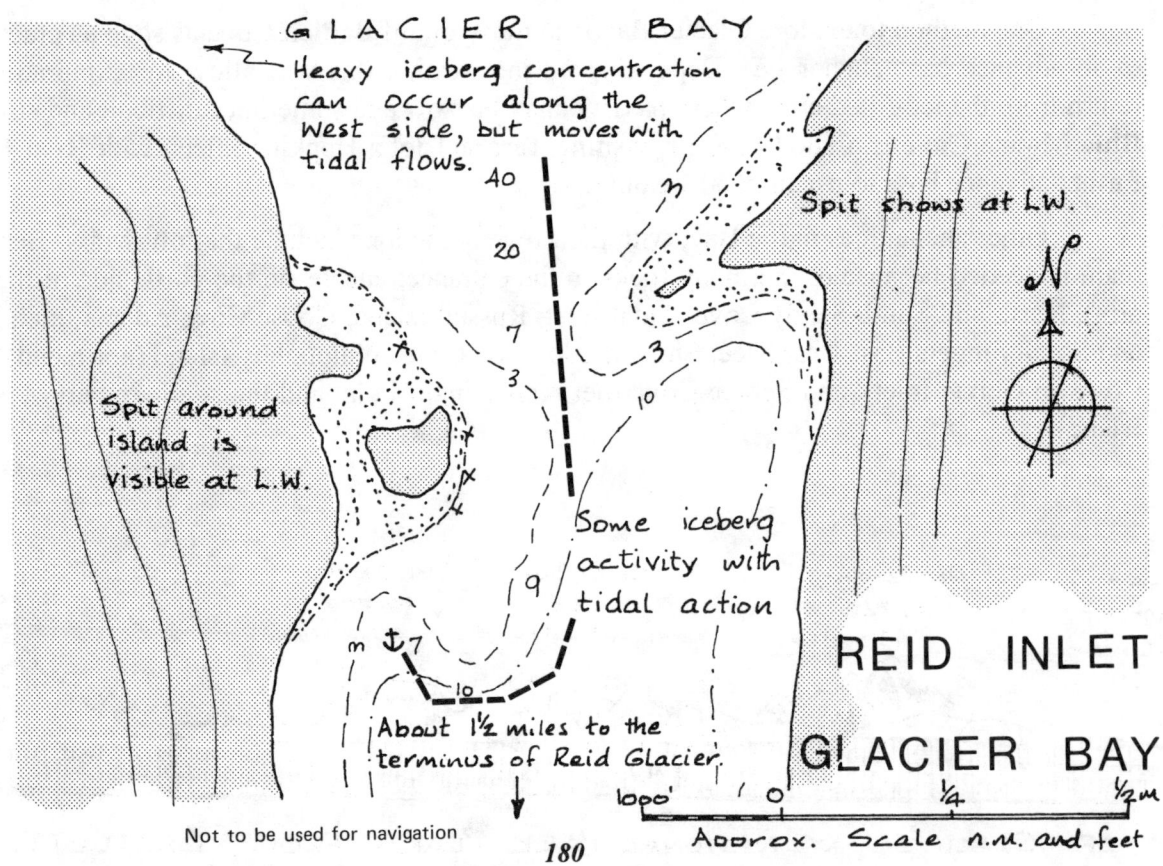

Not to be used for navigation

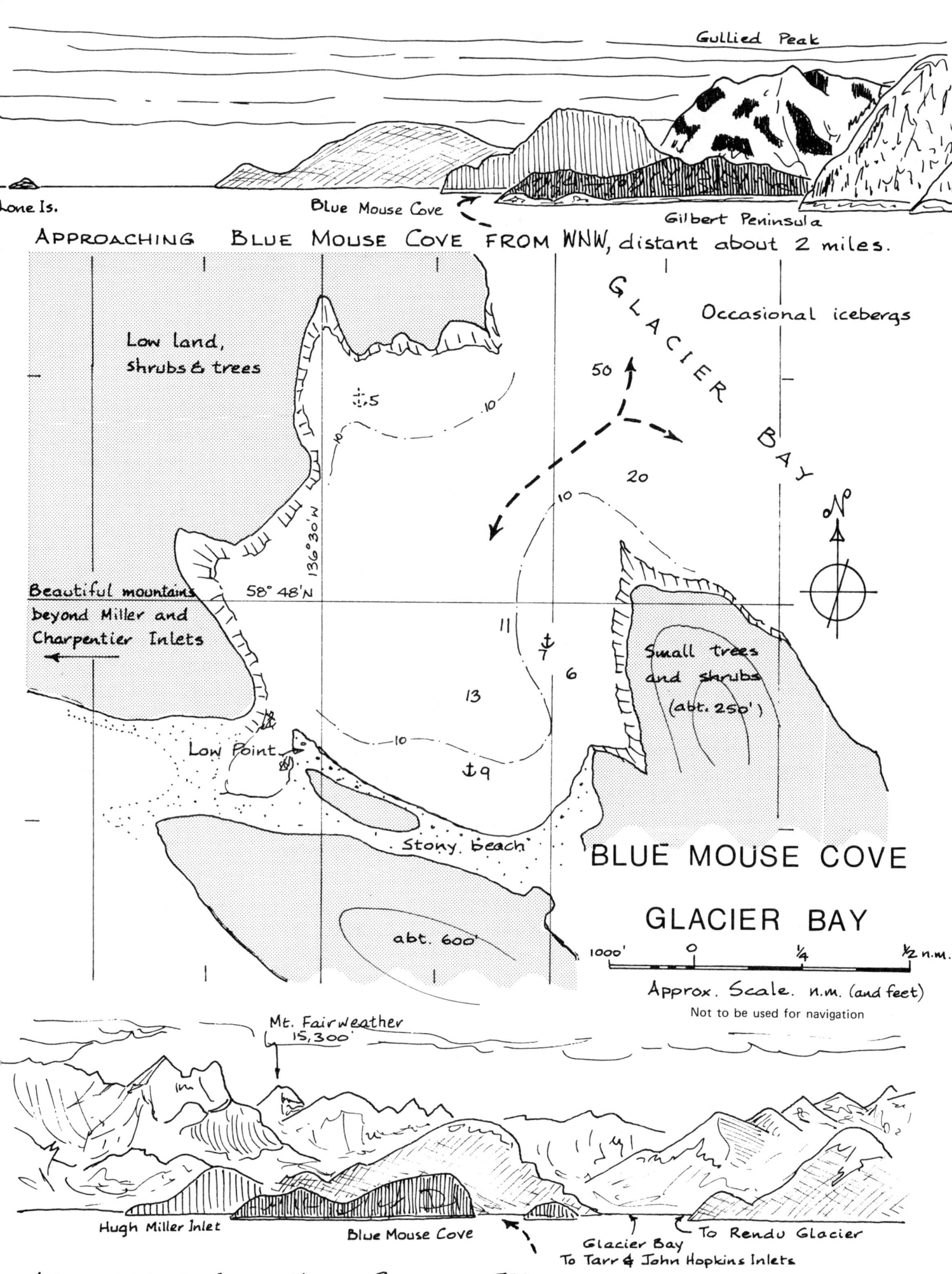

Gullied Peak

Lone Is. Blue Mouse Cove Gilbert Peninsula

APPROACHING BLUE MOUSE COVE FROM WNW, distant about 2 miles.

Low land,
shrubs & trees

Occasional icebergs

GLACIER BAY

50

Low land,
shrubs & trees

10

20

10

Beautiful mountains
beyond Miller and
Charpentier Inlets

58° 48'N 136° 30'W

11

⚓
7 6

Small trees
and shrubs
(abt. 250')

13

10

⚓9

Low Point

Stony beach

abt. 600'

N

BLUE MOUSE COVE

GLACIER BAY

1000'   0   ¼   ½ n.m.

Approx. Scale. n.m. (and feet)

Not to be used for navigation

Mt. Fairweather
15,300'

Hugh Miller Inlet   Blue Mouse Cove   Glacier Bay   To Rendu Glacier
To Tarr & John Hopkins Inlets

APPROACHING BLUE MOUSE COVE FROM ESE, distant about 3 miles

An alternative anchorage on the other side may be available but as the movement of ice varies from year to year current ice conditions determine the preferred anchorage spots.

When the bergy bits in the inlet are not numerous, the vessel can be taken to within 2.5 mile of the glacier. It is not difficult to land on the shores of the inlet near the anchorage and hike over an easy trail to the face of the glacier. Rumbling, creaking sounds give evidence of the movement of the glacier, advising caution near the glacier's face, as immense slabs of ice may break away (calve) with little or no warning. Since the tidal range is very high in these latitudes the dinghy should be secured above the high water line to avoid a cold, bone-chilling retrieval when the tide comes in.

NORTH SANDY COVE

This anchorage provides a base for exploring Muir Inlet, and lies about 20 miles from Bartlett Cove. The cove can be approached from the northwest via either channel past Puffin Island. The best anchorages are along the southern shores. No-see-ums are prevalent here, and they can be annoying if one is anchored close to the shore. Another anchorage, though exposed to the south, is at Sebree Cove, between Tlingit Point and the southern end of Sebree Island. Give safe clearance to Tlingit Point to avoid the rock south of the islet off the point.

The inner recesses of Adams inlet, Wachusett Inlet and Muir Inlet can only be visited by motorized vessels before June 1 and after July 15. During this period seals are birthing their offspring which they leave on ice floes while they search for food. It is essential that the young seals not be disturbed for they slip into the water and become lost, resulting in their death. Consequently only canoe and kayaks are allowed in these areas during this critical period when the young are so vulnerable. Canoes and kayaks can be rented at the Glacier Bay Lodge, just to the north of the Park Headquarters in Bartlett Cove.

It is about 20 miles from North Sandy Cove to the restricted area of Muir Inlet where Muir Glacier which has receded so much that it is no longer a tidewater glacier. Adams Inlet, about 8 miles along, has strong tidal currents at the entrance which is strewn with rocks. Seven miles further brings you to Sealers Island, a small island close to the east shore of Muir Inlet. East of the island is shoal and narrow Goose Cove, where anchorage may be taken. A Park Ranger is stationed here.

Though there are fewer glaciers along Muir Inlet it is an exceptionally interesting and revealing journey. The rapid retreat of Muir Glacier over the last few decades has exposed the whole spectrum of development of glaciated land. Near North Sandy Cove the steep mountainsides are covered with timber and other vegetation. But as you travel further into the inlet the terrain becomes steeper and more barren. Proceeding on from Riggs and McBride Glaciers (which can be easily reached), the land is raw and stark. Glacial streams and moraines mark the sides. Since Muir Glacier has receded so much in recent years that it is no longer a tidewater glacier, bergy bits are not as prevalent as they once were.

An additional attraction of this area is that the cruise ships do not come up this narrow, inlet. This area is favored by campers and kayakers who often camp on the flat area near McBride Glacier.

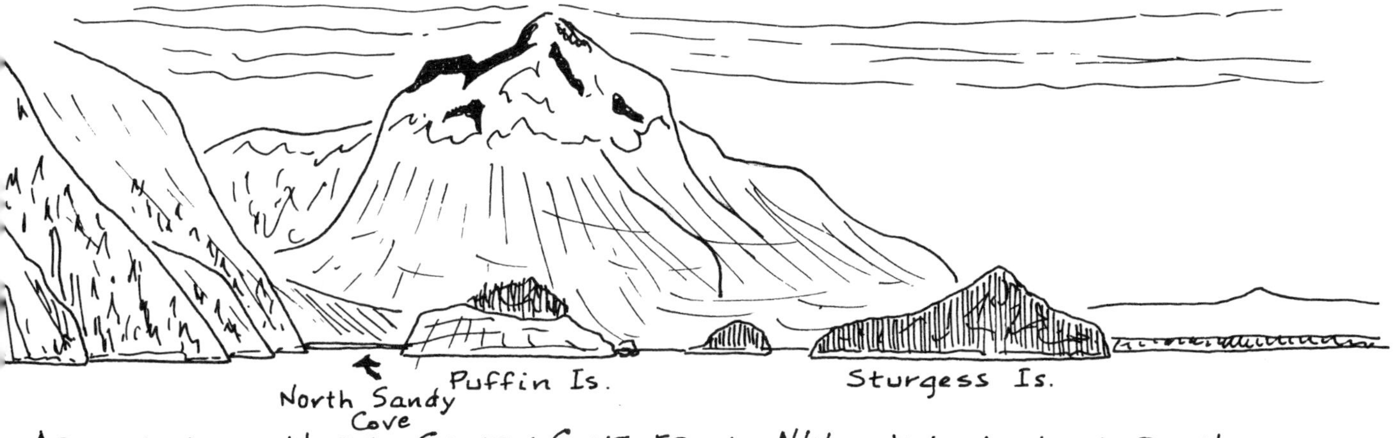
North Sandy Cove
Puffin Is.
Sturgess Is.

APPROACHING NORTH SANDY COVE FROM NW, distant about 3 miles.

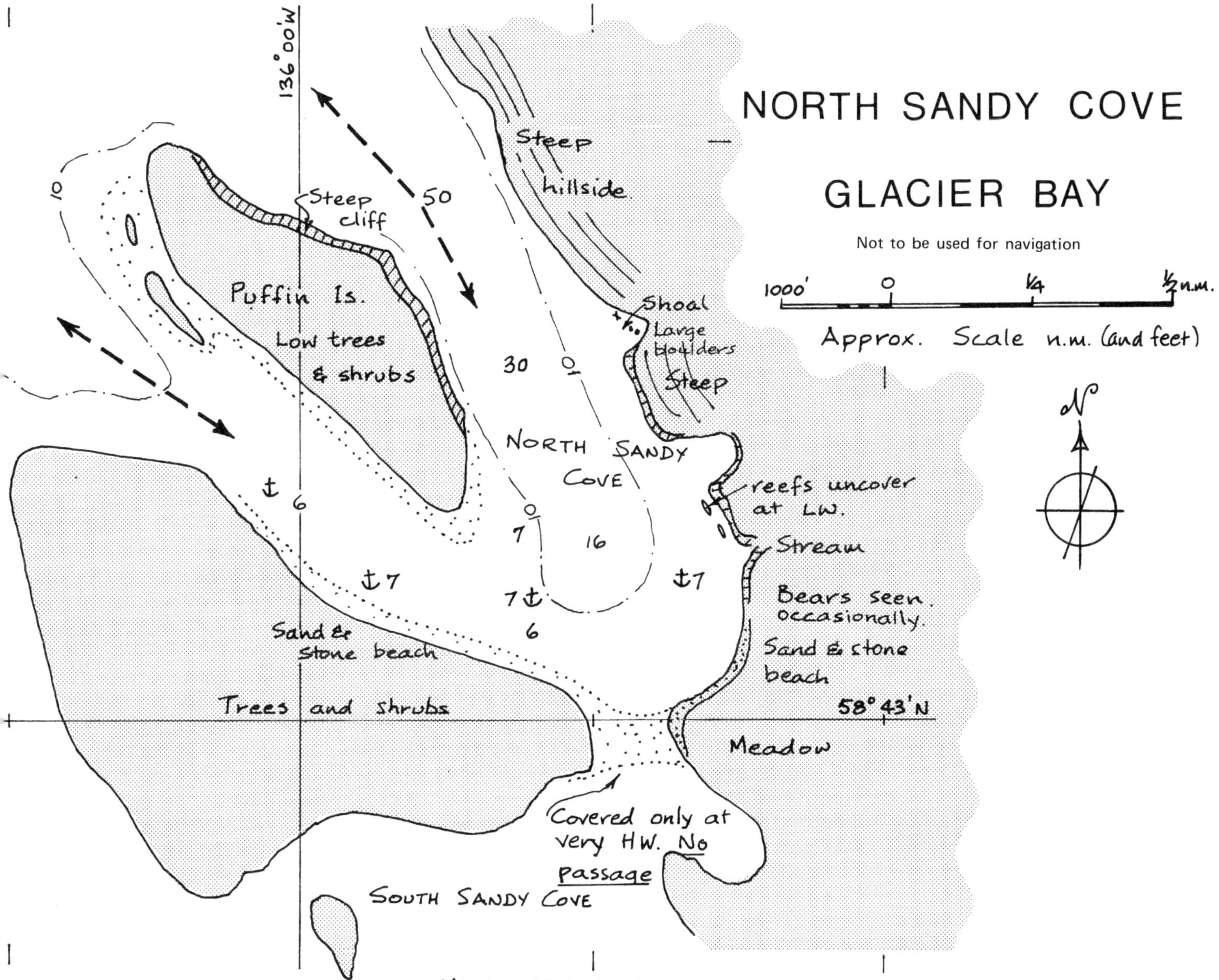
NORTH SANDY COVE
GLACIER BAY
Not to be used for navigation
1000' 0 1/4 1/2 n.m.
Approx. Scale n.m. (and feet)
N
136°00'W
58°43'N
Steep cliff
Steep hillside
50
10
30
Puffin Is.
Low trees & shrubs
Shoal
Large boulders
Steep
NORTH SANDY COVE
reefs uncover at LW.
Stream
6
7
16
7
7
7
6
Bears seen occasionally.
Sand & stone beach
Sand & stone beach
Trees and shrubs
Meadow
Covered only at very HW. No passage
SOUTH SANDY COVE

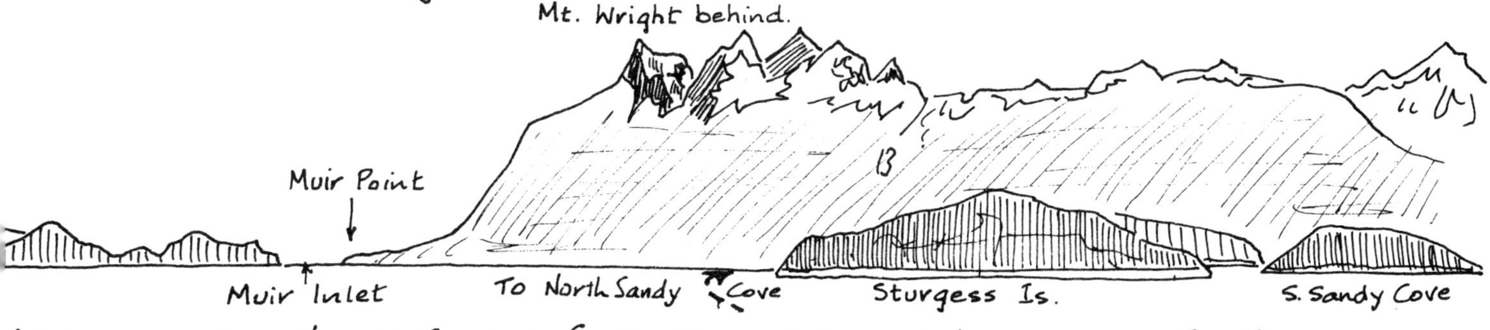
Mt. Wright behind.
Muir Point
Muir Inlet
To North Sandy Cove
Sturgess Is.
S. Sandy Cove

APPROACHING NORTH SANDY COVE FROM SE, distant about 3 miles.

ELFIN COVE

The small village of Elfin Cove lies in a beautiful setting on the south side of Cross Sound and is well worth visiting if Glacier Bay is on your itinerary. Both North and South Inian Pass connect Icy Strait to Cross Sound. The route through North Inian Pass is longer but with less current than South Inian Pass. A good anchorage, **Inian Cove**, is on the north side of the Inian Islands. Anchor in the wide end of the cove, where a mooring buoy and dolphins are in place. A prominent light, North Inian Pass Light, is on the northwest point of the next small island to the west.

South Inian Pass is the shorter and more attractive route to Elfin Cove. It should be traversed near slack, for the current can be strong (approaching 9 knots on the ebb), and when a westerly wind opposes the ebb severe tidal rips and steep waves and swirls occur at the western end of the pass. At times this may make the passage extremely difficult.

Point Lavinia, marked by a light, is the southerly point of the western entrance to South Inian Pass. Elfin Cove is in a small inlet in the north shore of the Inian Peninsula south of Point Lavinia. A large island, with a couple of smaller ones nearby, lies at the entrance to the cove. Passage is possible on either side of the large island. The eastern entrance leads directly into the outer harbor of Elfin Cove where most transient vessels lie. Rafting may be necessary as the float is only 60 m (200 ft.) long, with vessels mooring on either side. A seaplane landing is at the tip and a long wharf connects the float to the shore. Apart from water, no facilities are available.

Another dock is to the west, behind the large island, where fuel may be obtained. Fish buyers transact business at this dock. Beyond this float a route via a narrow dredged channel (the Gut) leads into the inner harbor. Most of the fishing vessels berth here. The channel should be entered at or near high water as it is only 12m (40') wide and has a controlling depth of 2.4m (8'). Markers indicate the route.

The village of **Elfin Cove** clusters around the edge of the harbors. The Post Office, general store, laundry and most of the houses are close to the boardwalk which is built up along the steep, rocky edges of the cove. Some vacation homes are also around the boardwalk. The permanent summer population is less than 50, which is augmented by fishing boats based here, and other transient visitors. However, in winter life in the cove reverts to an isolated, inward-looking existence where there is little contact with the outside world for the few hardy souls remaining.

When one sits at the end of the dock and looks across to Brady Glacier beneath the tall peaks of Glacier Bay, the lure that takes people north and draws some to stay seems all too clear.

Outer Harbor   To Inner Harbor   George Is.

APPROACHING ELFIN COVE FROM N
distant about 2 miles

ELFIN COVE

CROSS SOUND

Approx. Scale n.m.

0 1 2 3 n.m.

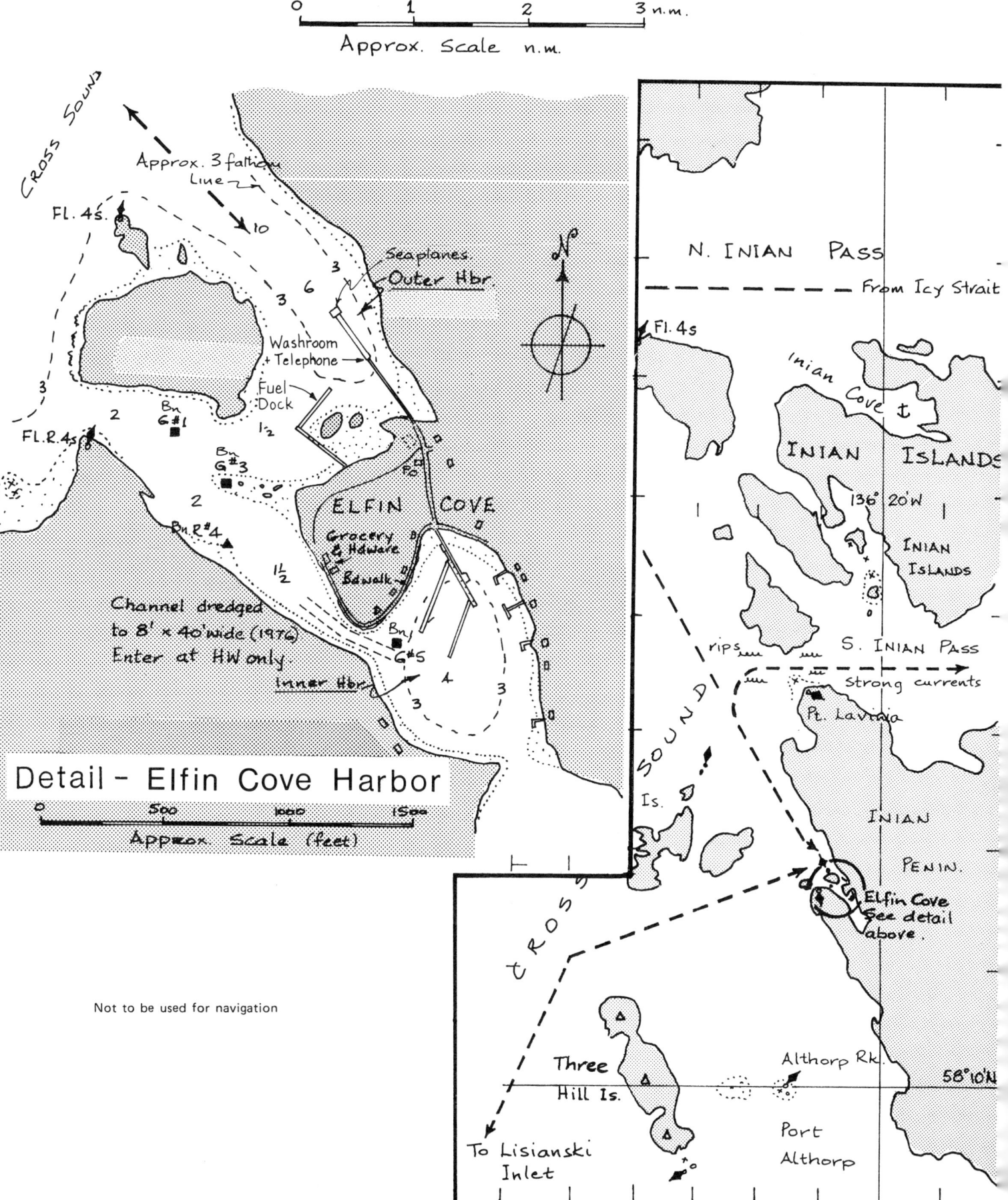

Cross Sound

Approx. 3 fathom Line

Fl. 4s.

10

3 6 3

Seaplanes
Outer Hbr.

N

Washroom
+ Telephone

Fuel
Dock

3

3

2

Bn
G #1

Fl. R. 4s.

1½

Bn
G #3

2

ELFIN   COVE

Bn. R #4

1½

Grocery
& Hdware

Bdwalk

Channel dredged
to 8' x 40' wide (1976)
Enter at HW only.

Bn
G #5

Inner Hbr.

4

3

3

Detail - Elfin Cove Harbor

Approx. Scale (feet)

0 500 1000 1500

Not to be used for navigation

N. INIAN   PASS

From Icy Strait

Fl. 4s

Inian Cove

INIAN   ISLANDS

136° 20'W

INIAN
ISLANDS

S. INIAN PASS

rips

Strong currents

Pt. Lavinia

INIAN

CROSS   SOUND

Is.

PENIN.

Elfin Cove
See detail
above.

Three
Hill Is.

Althorp Rk.

58° 10'N

Port
Althorp

To Lisianski
Inlet

PELICAN, LISIANSKI INLET and LISIANSKI STRAIT

The open Pacific Ocean lies beyond Cape Spencer and Cape Bingham at the entrance to Cross Sound. The direct, open sea route can be avoided by passing to the south of George Island and north of Three Hill Island to reach the entrance to Lisianski Inlet. This 21-mile long inlet extends southeasterly and is lined by pretty,snow-covered peaks. The first 6 miles lie between two very large islands, Chichagof Island on the east and Yakobi Island on the west.

The small port of **Pelican** lies about 11 miles inside Lisianski Inlet, on the northern shore. It is mainly a fishing town and in season hums with activity. Public floats operated by the city are in the center, north of the Alaska Ferry dock. A general store, post office and laundromat are along the boardwalk near the fuel dock where water is available. Rosies Bar is the center of activity in the evenings.

Lisianski Strait enters Lisianski Inlet about 4.5 miles northwest of Pelican (6.5 miles from the entrance). Miner Island, wooded and surrounded by kelp, lies off the northern point. A narrow passage separates the north point of Miner Island from Yakobi Island, but should not be attempted.

Southeast of Miner Island, and about a mile south is Junction Island, small, wooded, and marked by a quick flashing light. Between Miner and Junction Island (closer to the latter) there are rocky patches covered with only a few feet of water. For vessels that are not going to Pelican but are turning into Lisianski Strait the turn can be by staying about 300 m (1,000 feet) off Miner Island. There are tidal rips and swirls here, for the currents coming down Lisianski Inlet meet those coming through Lisianski Strait.

Almost as soon as one passes Miner Island the Strait begins to narrow. About a mile from the junction the channel passes between Yakobi Island and a shoal area with two small islands marked by a flashing red light at its southern end. Just beyond, a daybeacon marks a shoal near a small float and the buildings of a nickel exploration camp at Bohemia Creek. Four miles further on, the opening to Stag Bay is passed.

The opening to the ocean is encumbered with rocks on both sides, making the actual channel narrower than it appears. On the south side is Esther Island which has a flashing red light with a red triangular day mark. A course can be laid passing between the rocky patches at the entrance and south of the seasonal bell buoy off Star Rock. Swell, surge and breaking waves may be encountered, depending on the external sea conditions.

Sea otters are well established here and may be seen in the Strait or around the entrance.

EXIT FROM LISIANSKI STRAIT TO GULF OF ALASKA, VIEW N'WARD

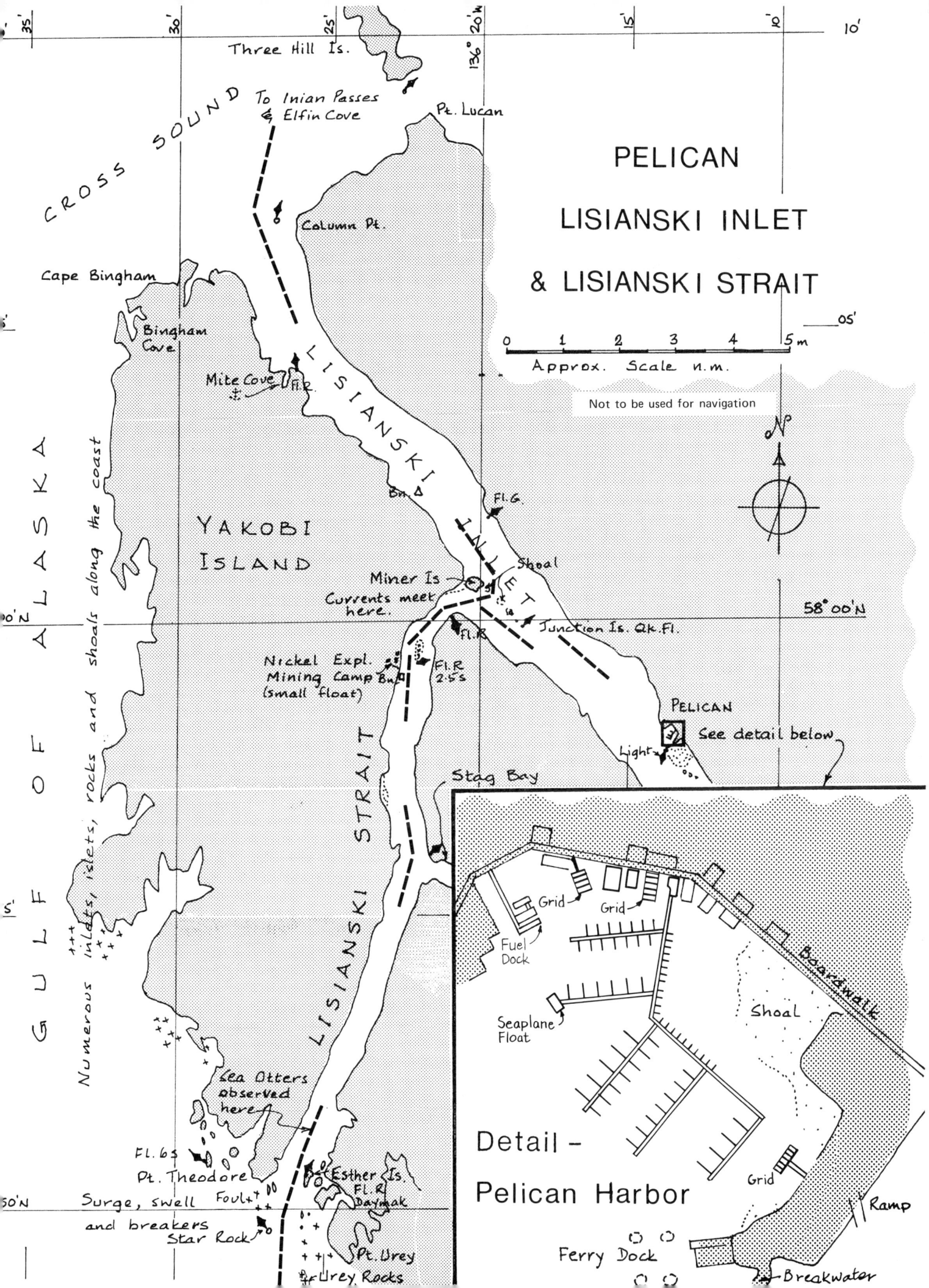

PELICAN

LISIANSKI INLET

& LISIANSKI STRAIT

Approx. Scale n.m.

0 1 2 3 4 5 m

Not to be used for navigation

CROSS SOUND

Three Hill Is.

To Inian Passes
& Elfin Cove

Pt. Lucan

Column Pt.

Cape Bingham

Bingham
Cove

Mite Cove
Fl.R.

LISIANSKI

ALASKA

Numerous inlets, islets, rocks and shoals along the coast

YAKOBI
ISLAND

Bn

Fl.G.

Shoal

INLET

Miner Is
Currents meet
here.

Junction Is. Qk.Fl.

58° 00'N

Fl.R.

Nickel Expl.
Mining Camp Bn
(small float)

Fl.R
2.5s

PELICAN

See detail below

Light

GULF OF

LISIANSKI STRAIT

Stag Bay

Sea Otters
observed
here

Fl.6s

Pt. Theodore

Surge, swell
and breakers

Esther Is.
Fl.R
Daymak

Foul

Star Rock

Pt. Urey

Urey Rocks

Detail –

Pelican Harbor

Grid

Grid

Fuel
Dock

Seaplane
Float

Shoal

Boardwalk

Grid

Ramp

Ferry Dock

Breakwater

LISIANSKI STRAIT to KHAZ BAY

The west coast of Chichagof Island is full of interest and spectacular scenery. From Star Rock bell buoy set a course to clear Porcupine Rock, a prominent, bare offshore rock 3 miles south. In good weather Ilas Bay to the east can be entered and a route threaded carefully into **Porcupine Bay**, where anchorage is available in 8 fathoms, mud. From this location a visit can be made to the hot springs at White Sulphur Springs, first by boat to the west arm of Bertha Bay about a mile south, then over a half mile trail to the two buildings at the springs. Bertha Bay is full of rocks. Use US chart 17321 when entering.

From Porcupine Rock a course can be taken for 6 miles to enter Imperial Passage between Hill and Hogan Islands. Though there are many rocks and islands off the points on each side, the passage is wide and leads into the expanse of Portlock Harbor. South Passage is an equally good entrance. Within Portlock Harbor the effect of the swell and wind are not felt, and an inner route can be threaded through Surveyor and Ogden Passages. **Didrickson Bay**, on the east side of Portlock Harbor, has anchorage toward the head of the bay in sight of the waterfall in about 10 fathoms, soft mud. The bay shoals for some distance before the waterfall.

A more protected anchorage can be taken in **Kimshan Cove** at the junction of Surveyor and Ogden Passages (just before reaching the #3 green day beacon near Fitz Island). Enter in the middle of the opening to the cove, taking care to avoid the crab traps that are scattered about, and anchor on the east side. On the southern shore there are the pilings and ruins of a wharf as well as buildings belonging to a gold-mining venture on Dooth Mountain.

Leaving Kimshan Cove be careful to pass at least 90 m (300 feet) away from the green day beacon near Fitz Island to avoid the reef which extends south of the marker. Ogden Passage leads behind a screen of islands towards Smooth Channel, which is the best outlet to the sea through Khaz Bay.

Entry to the anchorages in **Klag Bay** is marked by a day beacon and an unlit range leading roughly northwesterly into The Gate. Use US Charts 17321 and 17322 when navigating in this area. From The Gate the route passes through the scattered rocks of Elbow Passage, then past the east side of Klag Island to the head of Klag Bay. Anchorage can be found anywhere in the bay, or off the largely abandoned mining town of Chicagof near the head. The mine is kept active and work sometimes proceeds. Enter Klag Bay just at or past low water slack when the many rocks can be clearly seen and the currents are reduced.

Guide Rocks, which are bare and noticeable, and a lighted buoy mark the exit from Smooth Channel leading towards Khaz Breakers and the open sea. A lighted whistle buoy marks Khaz Breakers, but in almost any swell breakers can be seen over the rocks. There are many rocks and breakers, but as long as the buoys and Khaz Breakers are identified the route passes through deep, clear water. This is no place to attempt to enter or leave in bad weather or fog.

There are other anchorages along Slocum Arm in **Waterfall Cove** or in Ford Arm at **Elf Cove**, which are worth visiting if time permits. A short-cut sometimes used by local boats through Piehle Passage close westerly of Khaz Point should not be taken for it is very complicated and has many rocks.

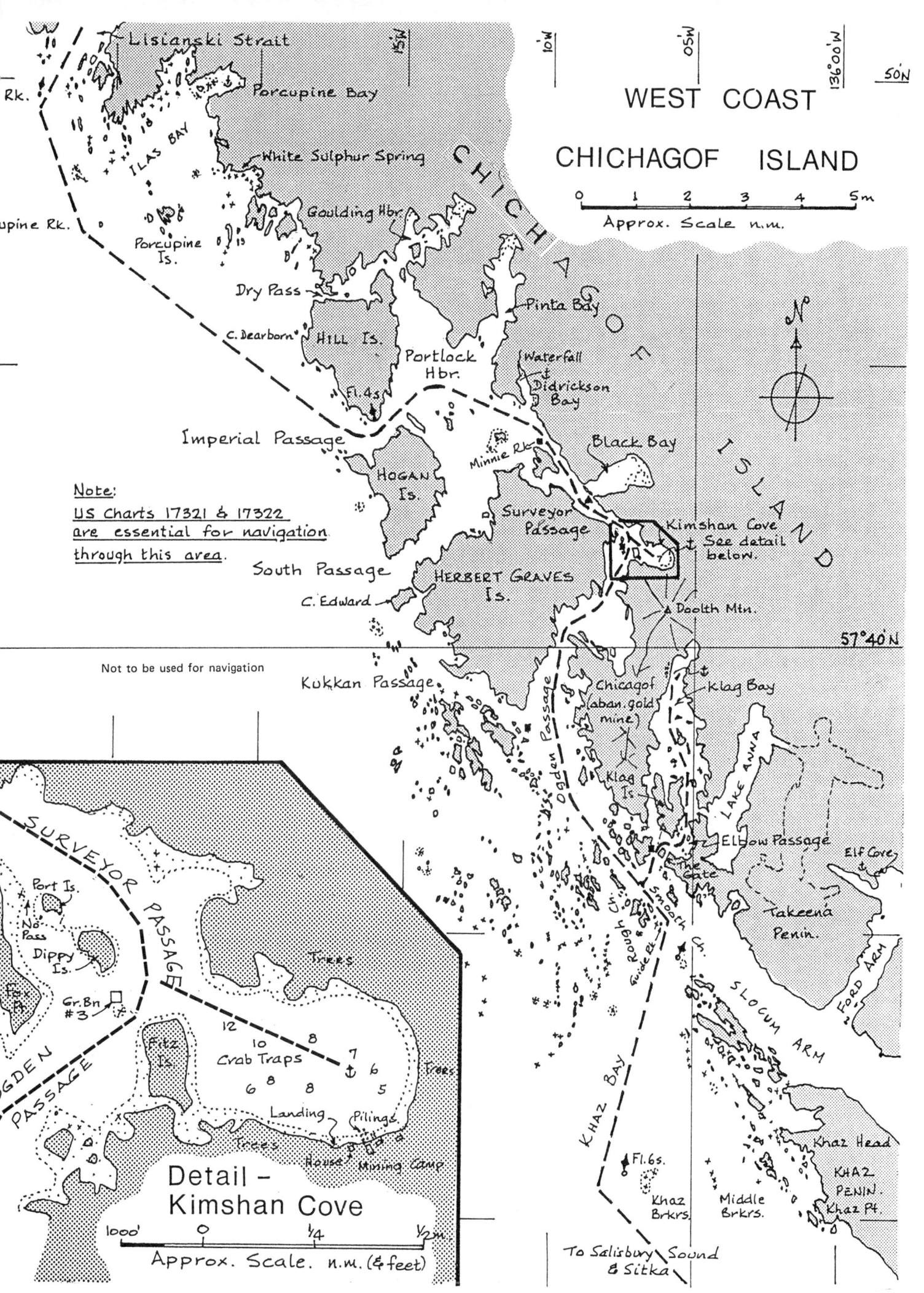

Lisianski Strait

Rk.

Porcupine Bay

White Sulphur Spring

ILAS BAY

Goulding Hbr.

CHICHA

upine Rk.

Porcupine Is.

Pinta Bay

Dry Pass

C. Dearborn

HILL Is.

Portlock Hbr.

Waterfall

Didrickson Bay

GOF

Fl.4s.

Black Bay

Minnie Rk.

Imperial Passage

HOGAN Is.

Surveyor Passage

Kimshan Cove

See detail below.

ISLAND

Note:

US Charts 17321 & 17322 are essential for navigation through this area.

South Passage

HERBERT GRAVES Is.

Doolth Mtn.

C. Edward

57°40'N

Not to be used for navigation

Kukkan Passage

Chicagof (aban. gold mine)

Klag Bay

Ogden Passage

Klag Is.

LAKE ANNA

Elbow Passage

Elf Cove

The Gate

Takeena Penin.

SURVEYOR PASSAGE

Port Is.

No Pass

Dippy Is.

Fox Pt.

Gr.Bn #3

12

8

Trees

Smooth Ch.

Rough Ch.

Guide Rk.

Fitz Is.

10

7

Crab Traps

6

Trees

SLOCUM ARM

FORD ARM

6

8

8

5

OGDEN PASSAGE

Landing

Pilings

Trees

House

Mining Camp

KHAZ BAY

Khaz Head

KHAZ PENIN.

Khaz Pt.

Detail – Kimshan Cove

1000'   0   ¼   ½m

Approx. Scale. n.m. (& feet)

Fl.6s.

Khaz Brkrs.

Middle Brkrs.

To Salisbury Sound & Sitka

WEST COAST

CHICHAGOF ISLAND

0   1   2   3   4   5m

Approx. Scale n.m.

N°

57°40'N

PERIL STRAIT and the APPROACH to SITKA

The usual approach to Sitka is through Neva and Olga Straits. The straits are entered from the north, either via the offshore route into Salisbury Sound or via Peril Strait from the inside waters of Southeast Alaska. Salisbury Strait is open to the ocean on the west, while Peril Strait and Neva Strait lie on the western end of the sound. The straits are slightly protected while the sound is open to the prevailing wind and sea conditions.

The outer route leads south from Khaz Bay into Salisbury Sound. Make certain that the course is clear of the many rocks that lie off the coast, where heavy swell breaks to warn of danger. One such danger is Olga Rock which lies about 1.25 miles west of Klokachef Island. Once past Olga Rock and Klokachef Island the course can be altered to enter the sound. There are two anchorages that can be useful while waiting to enter Peril Strait.

Kalinin Bay is on the south side of Salisbury Sound and indents the north shore of Kruzof Island. The entrance is wide at first but the west side should be favored to avoid the rocks off Sinitsin Island. The inlet narrows and bends, and a mid-channel course should be followed from the bend. Rocks lie off the shores at the narrowest part of the bay but the opening is sufficiently large for small vessels. At half tide or less most rocks are visible; a float marks a submerged rock on the west side. The head of the bay offers a good anchorage.

Sukoi Inlet, at the entrance to Neva Strait, provides another anchorage, though you must go in about 3 miles. This inlet is actually a narrow strait between Kruzoff and Partofshikof Islands. The head of the inlet is shoal and very narrow. The sketch shows the position of the anchorage well out past the shoal area at the outlet of the small creek.

Peril Strait is the most frequented route to and from the inside waters and Sitka. It is about 39 miles from the entrance off Chatham Strait to Kakul Narrows and Salisbury Sound. The frequent twists in the channel and strong currents make it essential that proper navigational charts are used. Charts Nos. 17323 and 17324 cover Peril Strait, Neva, and Olga Straits for the route into Sitka. This passage is straightforward except for the short section at Whitestone Narrows where a range guides one through the dredged channel. Many lights and markers lead past Starrigaran Bay (where the ferry terminal is located) and Sitka Rocks, and on to Sitka.

For an easterly passage through Peril Strait, enter Kakul Narrows slightly before low water slack to arrive at Sergius Narrows (about 3.5 miles along) just at or before slack water. Passage through the narrows is simple except for heavy traffic; good judgment and a sharp lookout are essential. If you lack current tables, the tide turns from south to north about 1.75 hours before low water at Sitka, and from north to south about 2 hours before high water at Sitka. Though Kakul Narrows has tidal swirls it is easier to traverse than Sergius Narrows.

Anchorages on the east side of Sergius Narrows can be found at **Deep Bay** and a less suitable one in **Bear Bay**. Enter Deep Bay between the green day mark on Grass Top Rock and a big island northeast of it, keeping closer to Big Island. Thereafter use mid-channel and anchor about a mile past the entry marker, staying well clear of the shoal area that fills the head of the bay.

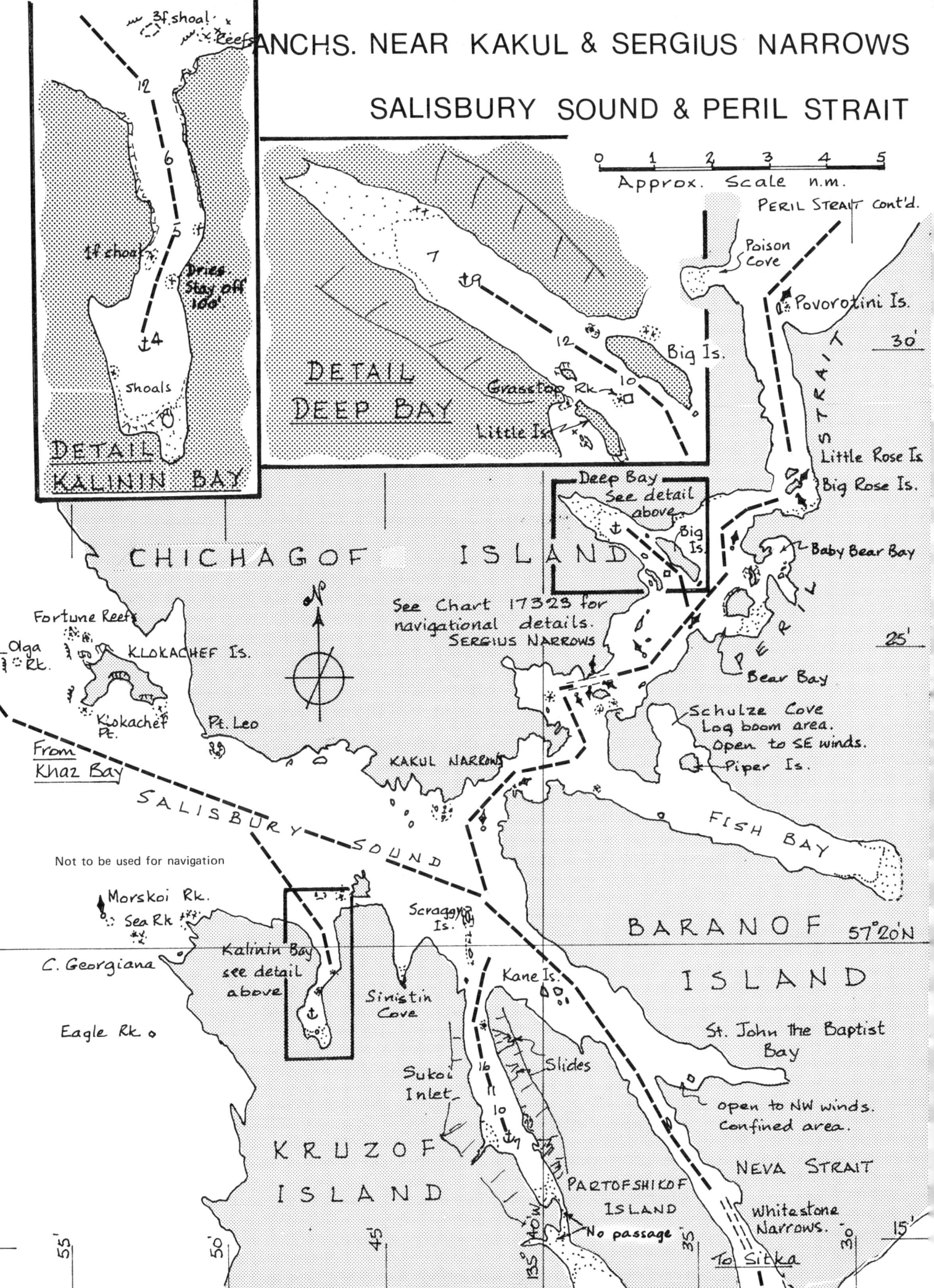

ANCHS. NEAR KAKUL & SERGIUS NARROWS

SALISBURY SOUND & PERIL STRAIT

DETAIL KALININ BAY

3f. shoal
Reefs
12
6
1f. shoal
Dries Stay off 100'
⊥4
shoals

DETAIL DEEP BAY

7
⊥9
12
10
Grasstop Rk.
Little Is.

Approx. Scale n.m.
0 1 2 3 4 5

PERIL STRAIT cont'd.

Poison Cove
Povorotini Is.
30'
Big Is.
Little Rose Is
Big Rose Is.
Baby Bear Bay
25'
Bear Bay
Schulze Cove
Log boom area.
Open to SE winds.
Piper Is.
FISH BAY

Deep Bay
See detail above.
Big Is.

CHICHAGOF ISLAND

See Chart 17323 for navigational details.
SERGIUS NARROWS

Fortune Reefs
Olga Rk.
KLOKACHEF Is.
Klokachef Pt.
Pt. Leo

N

From Khaz Bay

SALISBURY SOUND

KAKUL NARROWS

Not to be used for navigation

Morskoi Rk.
Sea Rk
C. Georgiana

Kalinin Bay see detail above

Sinistin Cove

Scraggy Is.

BARANOF 57°20'N

ISLAND

Kane Is.

St. John the Baptist Bay

Eagle Rk

Sukoi Inlet

16

Slides

10

open to NW winds.
Confined area.

KRUZOF ISLAND

PARTOFSHIKOF ISLAND
No passage

135°

NEVA STRAIT

Whitestone Narrows.

To Sitka

55' 50' 45' 35' 30' 15'

SITKA

This is a great place to visit and it is also one of the busiest fishing ports in the US. Sitka has natural beauty, a historic background, friendly people and the best gift and specialty shops in the South East. It is no accident that the cruise ships have discovered Sitka.

Sitka can be approached from the north as described, or from offshore via Sitka Sound, between Biorka Island and Cape Edgecumbe. The cape is an easily recognized cliff of black lava 30 m (100 feet) high, with the prominent landmark of Mount Edgecumbe behind it. When it isn't raining this 1,000m (3,271') volcanic mountain can be seen both from seaward and from Sitka. Its isolated position, crater-formed flat top, conical shape and snow-streaked gullies make it a good landmark. After entering the harbor through the opening in the breakwater you are in a NO WAKE area which must be adhered to.

There are five small boat harbors in Sitka, and the northernmost (**New Thomsen Harbor**) is the designated transient harbor. After passing through the opening in the breakwater it is the first facility seen and is adjacent to the **Old Thomsen Harbor**. The City **ANB Harbor** (opposite the government docks) is off Katlian Street, just north of downtown. The other two small craft harbors are at **Sealing Cove** and **Crescent Harbor**, neither harbor has moorage for transient vessels. Clearance at the bridge is 16 m (52 feet).

The harbormaster controls both moorage locations; his office is located next to the Old Thomsen Harbor. Office hours are 7 a.m. to 6 p.m. daily. Vessels approaching Sitka should call the harbormaster on VHF Ch. 16 or phone (907) 747-3439) to obtain directions for moorage. In the event you are assigned a slip on a "hot berth" basis you must be ready to move on short notice. Showers and a laundromat are at the head of the dock and a cafe is next door. A super-market is within walking distance of the harbor. Moorage charges are very reasonable and increase from the basic 28 cents per foot per day for vessels over 24 m (80 feet).

Fueling stations are at the Chevron station near the bridge and at the Texaco dock south of the Old Thomsen Harbor. There are three pump-out stations in the harbor.

This city offers many interesting things to see and do, all within easy walking distance. Tlingit artifacts and other Alaskan Indian, Inuit, and Aleut items can be seen at the Sheldon Jackson Museum as well as at the Visitor Center at the Sitka National Historic Park. At the latter there is a great collection of totem poles arranged along a lovely walk which leads to the site of the battle between the Tlingit and Russians. The Russian occupation period is featured in St. Michael's Cathedral, the Russian Bishop's House, the Russian cemetery, Castle Hill, and the Isabel Miller Museum in the Centennial Building.

Today's arts and crafts are well represented in the shops, featuring both native and Russian influences as well as modern artists; thus making this a fascinating place to explore. In June there is a summer chamber music festival and the All-Alaska Logging Championships, the conjunction well describing Sitka.

APPROACH TO SITKA FROM OLGA STRAIT. i.e. W. (Sitka still 10m. away)

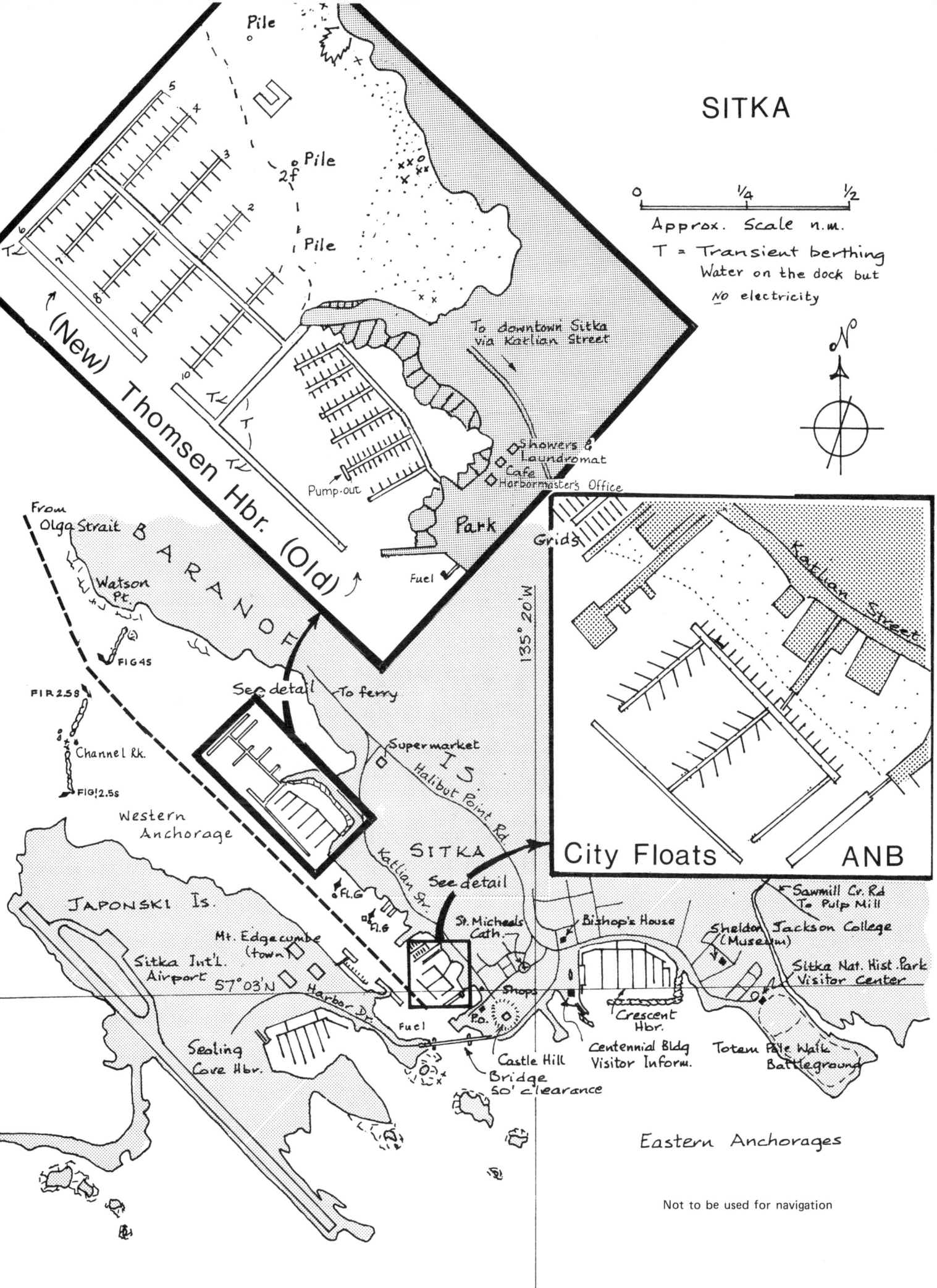

SITKA

Approx. Scale n.m.
0   1/4   1/2

T = Transient berthing
Water on the dock but **No** electricity

Pile

Pile

Pile

2f

(New) Thomsen Hbr. (Old)

To downtown Sitka
via Katlian Street

Pump-out

Showers &
Laundromat

Cafe

Harbormaster's Office

Park

Fuel

Grids

Katlian Street

City Floats   ANB

From
Olga Strait   BARANOF

Watson
Pt.

FIG4S

FIR2.5S

Channel Rk.

FIG!2.5s

Western
Anchorage

See detail

To ferry

Supermarket

Halibut Point Rd.

IS.

SITKA

See detail

135° 20' W

Sawmill Cr. Rd
To Pulp Mill

Sheldon Jackson College
(Museum)

St. Michaels
Cath.

Bishop's House

Sitka Nat. Hist. Park
Visitor Center

JAPONSKI Is.

Mt. Edgecumbe
(town)

Sitka Int'l.
Airport

57°03'N

Katlian St.

Fl.G

Fl.G

Harbor Dr.

Shops

P.O.

Fuel

Castle Hill
Bridge
50' clearance

Crescent
Hbr.

Centennial Bldg
Visitor Inform.

Totem Pole Walk
Battleground

Sealing
Cove Hbr.

Eastern Anchorages

Not to be used for navigation

Thomsen Boat Harbor, Sitka, with Mount Edgecumbe

El Capitan Passage

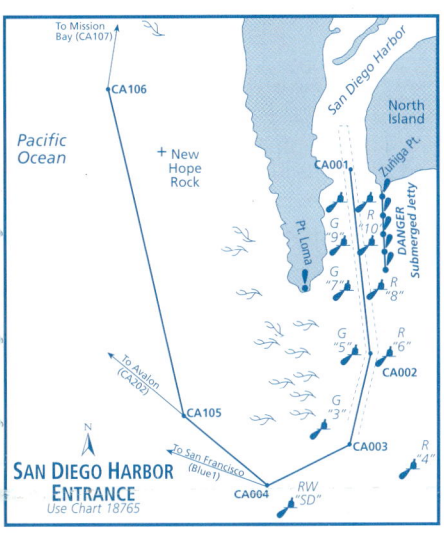

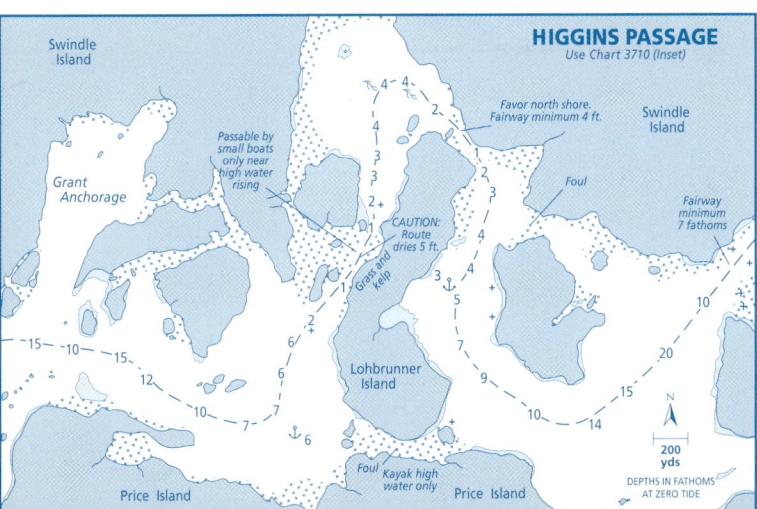

The acclaimed new generation of pilothouse guides

". . . Your [books] are like family whose advice we rely on daily..."—TOM AND PAT MOSES, "ADVENTURE"

Exploring Southeast Alaska
Dixon Entrance to Skagway—Details of Every Harbor and Cove

Don Douglass & Réanne Hemingway-Douglass

"This book is stunning. Nobody has given the cruising community what this book gives. You have just created a classic."—SEATTLE PUBLISHER

This completely all-new revision of the best-selling classic guidebook, *Exploring the Inside Passage to Alaska*, with an increased focus on virtually all places to anchor in Southeast Alaska, offers new anchor sites, expanded descriptions and additional waypoints to guide small craft sailors through one of the world's best cruising grounds. Almost completely protected, these waters give access to pristine wilderness of breathtaking beauty—thousands of islands, deeply-cut fjords, tidewater glaciers and icebergs. The Douglasses, who cruise to and from Alaska every year, supply skippers with all the up-to-date local knowledge they need.

View entire 576-page Exploring Southeast Alaska Free—Visit AlaskaOnLine© at www.FineEdge.com

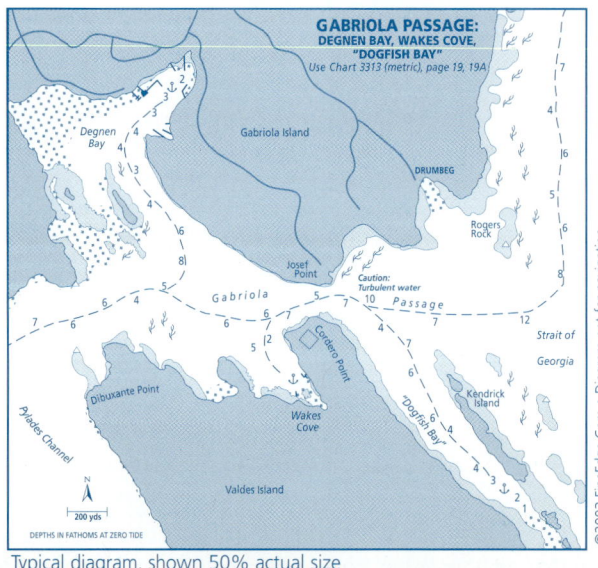

Typical diagram, shown 67% actual size

"The best resources are the Douglass's books on the Inside Passage."—BLUE WATER SAILING

Exploring the South Coast of British Columbia
Gulf Islands and Desolation Sound to Port Hardy and Blunden Harbour
SECOND EDITION

Don Douglass & Réanne Hemingway-Douglass

"Clearly the most thorough, best produced and most useful [guides] available . . . particularly well thought out and painstakingly researched."—NW YACHTING

Exploring the South Coast of British Columbia is designed by experts to give small boat skippers the kind of accurate, up-to-date information they need to set sail for the unmatched natural beauty of the Pacific Northwest. As with all of Fine Edge Productions' bestselling cruising guides, complete descriptions of routes and anchorages are based on the authors' personal experience of each location and on information from local skippers not available anywhere else. From the balmy Gulf Islands to the unspoiled fishing grounds off the north end of Vancouver Island, nautical adventurers can find hundreds of pristine coves and inlets to add to their cruising pleasure.

Typical diagram, shown 50% actual size

GPS Instant Navigation

Plotting, Selecting Waypoints and Routes, Electronic Charting

SECOND EDITION

Kevin Monahan and Don Douglass

"If you want the greatest possible benefit from GPS, I strongly recommend this book. Their illustrated techniques will save you time and clearly explain the system."
—JOHN NEAL, BLUEWATER SAILOR, MAHINA TIARE EXPEDITIONS

"Every GPS user should have this book on board!"—CAPTAIN JACK'S CATALOG

The Second Edition of this best-selling manual for GPS has been newly revised and expanded to help skippers plan route selection and plot waypoints and adapt them to electronic charting. Whether you are an experienced mariner, or a novice who needs the basics, this manual helps you solve classic piloting and navigational problems. Includes advanced techniques of error reduction, electronic charting and navigation software, as well as 150 detailed diagrams that graphically illustrate the many ways to use GPS. Monahan is a Canadian Coast Guard officer with over 20 years' experience cruising the Inside Passage. Douglass has logged over 150,000 miles cruising from 60°N to 56°S.

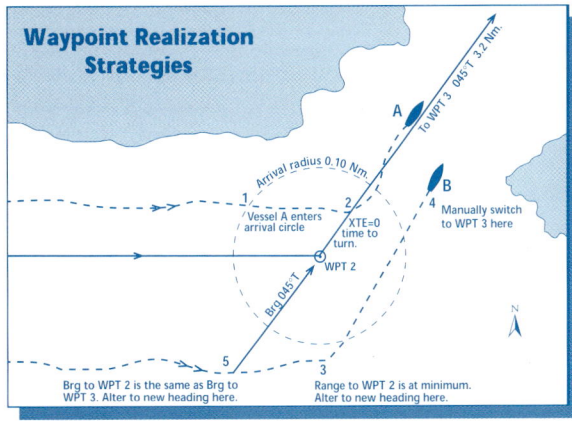

Typical diagrams, shown 64% actual size

New GPS Accuracy

EXPANDED 2ND EDITION

NEW GPS ACCURACY STANDARDS

GPS
Instant Navigation

From Basic Techniques to Electronic Charting

Kevin Monahan & Don Douglass

Featuring: 150 detailed diagrams • 6" x 9"
• ISBN 0-938665-76-6 • $29.95 • 336 pages

Arctic Odyssey

Dove III Masters the Northwest Passage
Len Sherman

Artist Len Sherman, the third crew member on the epic 1995 Northwest Passage voyage of the *Dove III*—one of the first west-to-east single-year passages on record—captures in wonderful pen and ink drawings and journal entries, the beauty and solitude of the far north, as well as its courageous, adventurous people.

Nonfiction • 180 pages • line drawings and hand drawn maps
• ISBN 0-938665-63-4 • $24.95

The Arctic to Antarctica

Cigra Circumnavigates the Americas
Mladen Sutej

The dramatic account of the first circumnavigation of the North and South American continents. After a successful transit of the Northwest Passage, this expedition continues around Cape Horn via Easter Island and then to Antarctica before returning to Europe. Told through the words of a notable circumnavigator with beautiful photographs throughout.

Nonfiction • 160 pages • photographs • maps
• ISBN 0-938665-65-0 • $19.95

The Final Voyage of the *Princess Sophia*

Did they all have to die?

Betty O'Keefe and Ian Macdonald

Seasoned writers of West Coast history and contemporary issues, O'Keefe and Macdonald tackle questions that still linger eighty years after the heroic efforts of those who answered the SOS in Lynn Canal between Skagway and Juneau, Alaska in 1918. Was the resulting inquiry a bureaucratic whitewash? Was the real cause of the wreck "peril of the sea?" With such a death toll, why was so little ever written about the sinking? Was it because, unlike the *Titanic*, there were no survivors of the *Princess Sophia*? Co-published with Heritage House, Vancouver, B.C.

Non-fiction • 224 pages • ISBN 0-938665-60-X • $12.95

Destination Cortez Island

A sailor's life along the BC Coast
June Cameron

A nostalgic memoir of the lives and times of coastal pioneers—the old timers and their boats—that were essential in the days when the ocean was the only highway. June Cameron has cruised the coast for over sixty years and is a regular contributor to *Pacific Yachting*. Co-published with Heritage House, Vancouver, B.C.

Non-fiction • 192 pages • ISBN 0-938665-61-8 • $12.95

Sea Stories of the Inside Passage

Iain Lawrence

Personal stories that capture the essence and flavor of the Inside Passage by the author of *Far-Away Places*, Prince Rupert resident Iain Lawrence. Readers will identify with Iain and his mate, Kristin, as they rescue a tiny orphaned seal, cheer for salmon struggling to reach their natal waters, meet a saintly old sailor, or shrink with embarrassment on hearing the tantrums of an arrogant skipper. The stories, written with sympathy, feeling, and humor, each stand alone.

Non-fiction • 168 pages • ISBN 0-938665-47-2 • $13.95

Trekka Round the World

John Guzzwell

"The stuff of dreams . . . John Guzzwell is an inspiration to all blue-water sailors."—MATTHEW P. MURPHY, EDITOR, WOODEN BOAT

"Only a few offshore sailors have earned a permanent place on the pantheon of voyagers . . . John Guzzwell is one of them."
—BLUE WATER SAILING

A new edition of John Guzzwell's, *Trekka Round the World*. Long out-of-print, this international classic is the story of John's circumnavigation on his 20-foot yawl *Trekka*. In a new epilogue Guzzwell recounts his experiences and sailing adventures since the book first appeared in the 1960s; included are previously unpublished photos and a foreword by bluewater sailor-author Hal Roth.

Non-fiction • 304 pages • ISBN 0-938665-56-1 • $18.95

State-of-the-Art Route Planning Maps now available

Select from dozens of routes and locate every route, harbor, and cove

The Pacific Coast Route Planning Maps are a perfect compliment to the new "Exploring the Pacific Coast" book featuring over 500 places to tie up or anchor a boat. All the great coves of the Channel Islands of Southern California, the public marinas, all the coastal ports, San Francisco Bay, the lower Sacramento River, the lower Columbia River, and Puget Sound are presented along with colorful topographic detail of the islands and inland areas. Unique to Pacific Coast maps are their Proven Cruising Routes©.

The Inside Passage to British Columbia and Alaska is one of the most sheltered and scenic waterways in the world. Our 24" x 60" maps include an index to all harbors and coves in this superb wilderness allowing you to customize your own routes. 4,000 place names are documented on the southern and northern portions of this beautiful two-map series. Descriptions include geographical locations, nautical chart numbers, and nearly 6,000 GPS waypoints to help you locate all the named places, as well as hundreds of other undiscovered and previously unnamed coves on each map. Also shown are hundreds of unique scenic and sheltered routes, as well as the more direct express routes. Now, you can plot your own custom itinerary and prepare your trip of a lifetime.

BOTH THE NORTH & SOUTH PORTIONS OF THE PACIFIC COAST ARE AVAILABLE IN:	BOTH THE NORTH & SOUTH PORTIONS OF THE INSIDE PASSAGE MAP ARE AVAILABLE IN:
LAMINATED AND INSERTED IN A PLASTIC TUBE:	**LAMINATED AND INSERTED IN A PLASTIC TUBE:**
South Portion—San Diego/Ensenada to Ft. Bragg: ISBN 0-938665-96-0 • $29.95	South Portion—Columbia River to Grenville, B.C.: ISBN 0-938665-85-5 • $29.95
North Portion—Ft. Bragg to Seattle/ Vancouver: ISBN 0-938665-97-9 • $29.95	North Portion—North B.C. and Southeast Alaska: ISBN 0-938665-87-1 • $29.95
ACCORDION-FOLD WITH 4-COLOR JACKET:	**ACCORDION-FOLD WITH 4-COLOR JACKET:**
South Portion: ISBN 0-938665-94-4 • $19.95	South Portion: ISBN 0-938665-88-X • $19.95
North Portion: ISBN 0-938665-95-2 • $19.95	North Portion: ISBN 0-938665-89-8 • $19.95

Exploring the Marquesas Islands

Joe Russell

Jumping off for the South Pacific, whether you sail from California or via Panama, the first landfall will be the Marquesas. Joe Russell, who has lived and sailed in the Marquesas, documents this beautiful little-known place. With volcanic tropical beauty and ease of navigation, the Marquesas provide one of the most interesting and dramatic cruising grounds in the world. The Marquesans, proud of their rich history, are the islands' greatest asset. This book includes history, a language guide, chart diagrams, mileage and heading tables, and information about recent archeology.

Expert Local Knowledge • Detailed anchor diagrams • Beautiful photographs
• Large format • ISBN 0-938665-64-2 • $39.95

Sailboat Buyer's Guide: *Conducting Your Own Survey*

Karel Doruyter

This practical guide, written by registered marine surveyor, Karel Doruyter, helps you purchase a used sailboat by learning what to look for PRIOR to making an offer. The author has 30 years' experience in offshore cruising and in designing, constructing and maintaining boats.

Complete buyer's checklist • Photographs & diagrams • ISBN 0-038665-72-3 • $14.95

Up the Lake with a Paddle

Volume 1: Sierra Foothills and Sacramento Region
Volume 2: Lake Tahoe & Sierra Lakes
Volume 3: Tahoe National Forest–West, Lakes within the Yuba River Drainage

William Van der Ven

"This book is a gift…for this and future generations."—JOHN SEALS, DAGGER CANOE & KAYAK

Up the Lake with a Paddle, Volumes 1, 2, and 3 are the first guidebooks to address the growing needs of canoeists and kayakers. User-friendly information on all the great places to paddle in the foothills and mountains of California's Sierra Nevada, how to get there and what to expect. Well-researched routes detail classic trips for families or solo paddlers.

Detailed diagrams, photographs: Vol. 1: ISBN 0-938665-54-5 • $18.95
Vol. 2: ISBN 0-938665-70-7 • $21.95 • Vol. 3: ISBN 0-938665-82-0 • $19.95

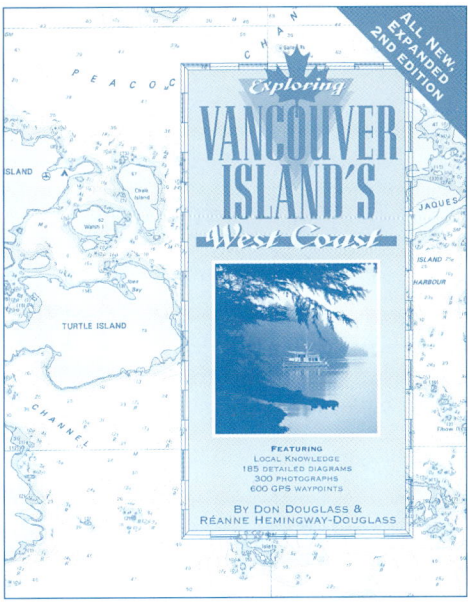
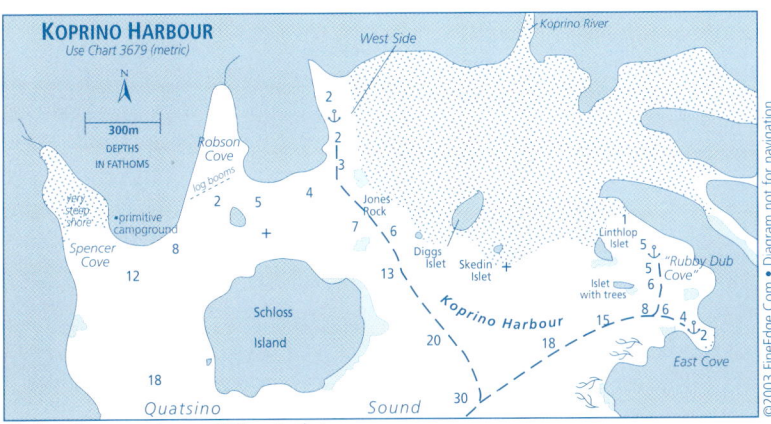
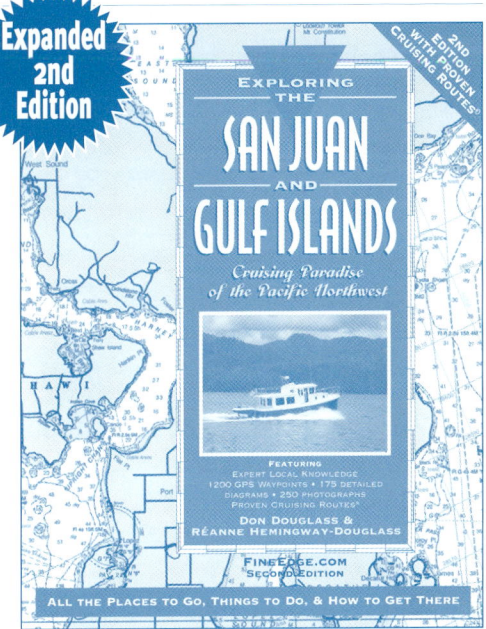
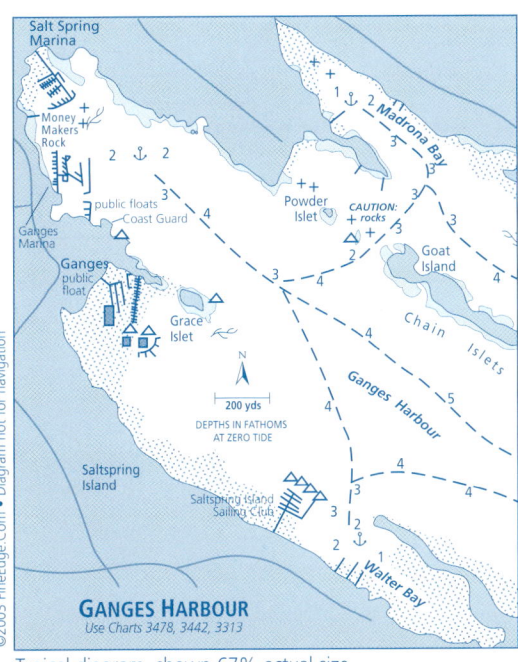

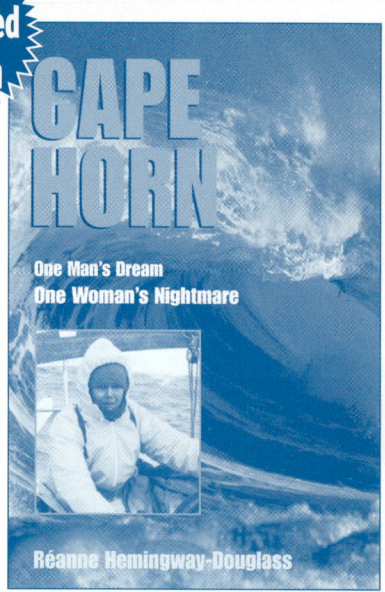

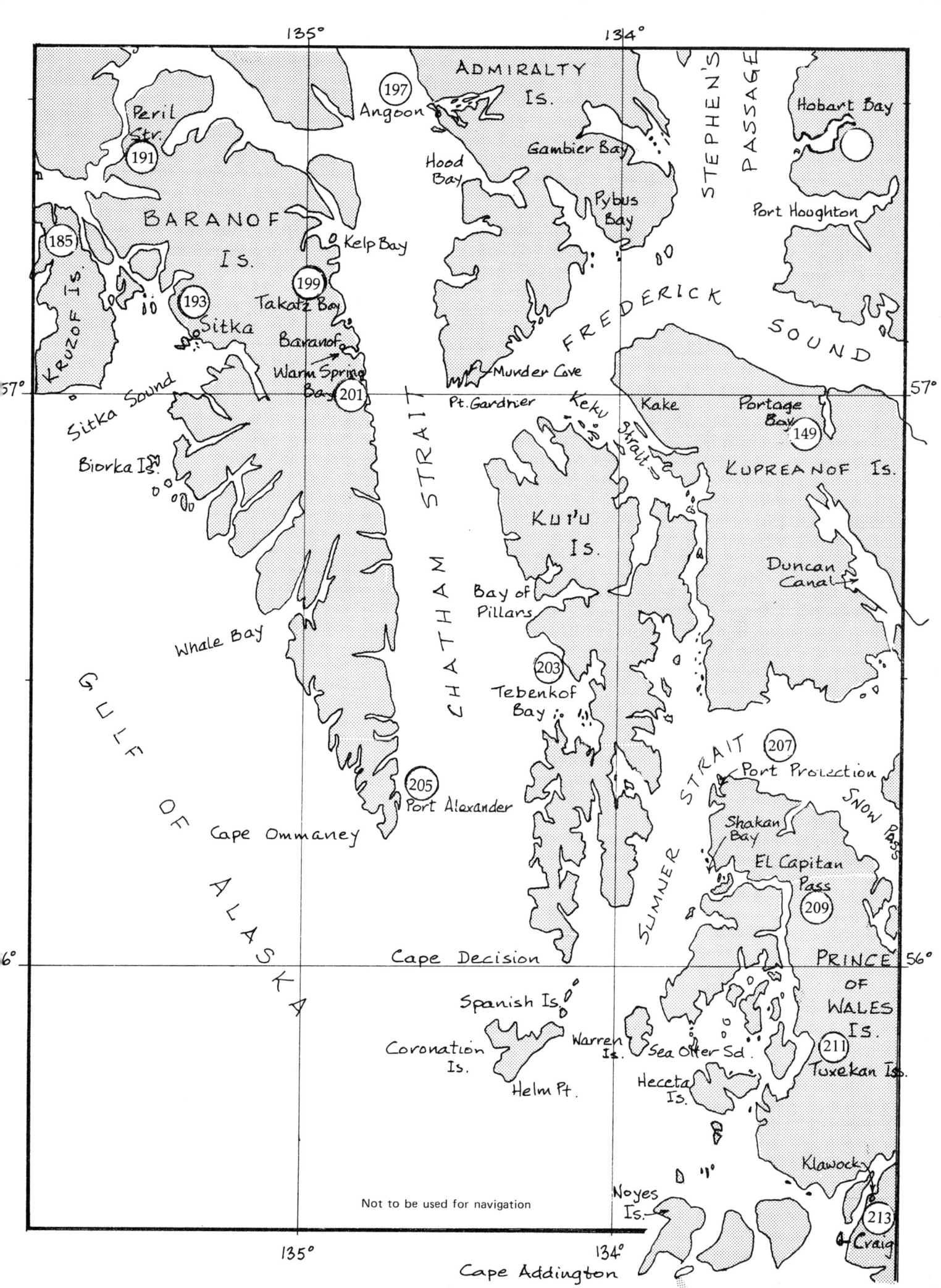

Not to be used for navigation

TENAKEE INLET and ANGOON

Tenakee Springs is a popular little village on the north shore of Tenakee Inlet, which enters the east side of Chichagof Island off Chatham Strait. It serves as a vacation home area for many of Juneau's residents, but is equally attractive for visiting cruisers because of its hot springs. A grassy track meanders along the shore, dotted with cabins along the way. No vehicles are allowed except for oil and fuel trucks. The state ferry dock is at the village where fuel is available. The state-maintained small craft basin is about .5 mile east of the village.

There are a store, cafe, and tavern are in the village. The green concrete bath house is the center of Tenakee and separate bathing hours are posted for men and women. Remove silver jewelry before entering the baths as there is sulfur in the water.

Crab Bay is 4 miles to the SW, on the south side of the inlet. There are mud shoals at the head of the bay and on the south side, but the north side is steep-to. Anchor in mid-bay in 5 - 10 fathoms, mud. A 2.5 fathom spot is east of the private mooring buoy.

Another spot is 3 miles northwest in **Saltery Bay** where good anchorage in the small inner basin can be taken in 5 - 10 fathoms, mud.

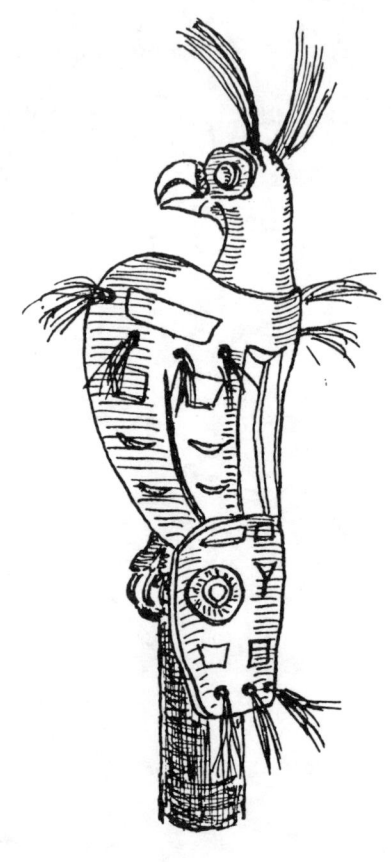

EAGLE
TOP OF CEREMONIAL STAFF
(Tlingit)

ANGOON

Angoon lies on the east side of Chatham Strait, about 20 miles south of Tenakee Inlet, and almost directly across from the exit of Peril Strait into Chatham Strait. This Tlinglit village, located in the Tongass National Forest, is the only permanent settlement in the wilderness of Admiralty Island. It lies on the narrow section of a peninsula behind which Kootznahoo Inlet enters Admiralty Island. Kootznahoo means, "Fortress of the Bears," a most appropriate name since Admiralty Island has the highest brown bear population of the Southeast, as well as the greatest number of bald eagles. A long pier extends into Chatham Strait. Fuel and water can be obtained at the dock but there is no moorage available for transients. There is a small store with limited supplies and local crafts are sold at Whaler's Cove Fishing Lodge.

The state-built, village-operated small craft floats are inside Kootznahoo Inlet in **Favorite Bay**. As the current is swift, and the passage is narrow, get local advice and information before entering at slack water if you want to stop at the small craft area. It is about 1 mile south of the main village. The state ferry docks are at Killisnoo Harbor, about 3 miles south of Angoon, facing Chatham Strait. For information phone (907) 788-3653.

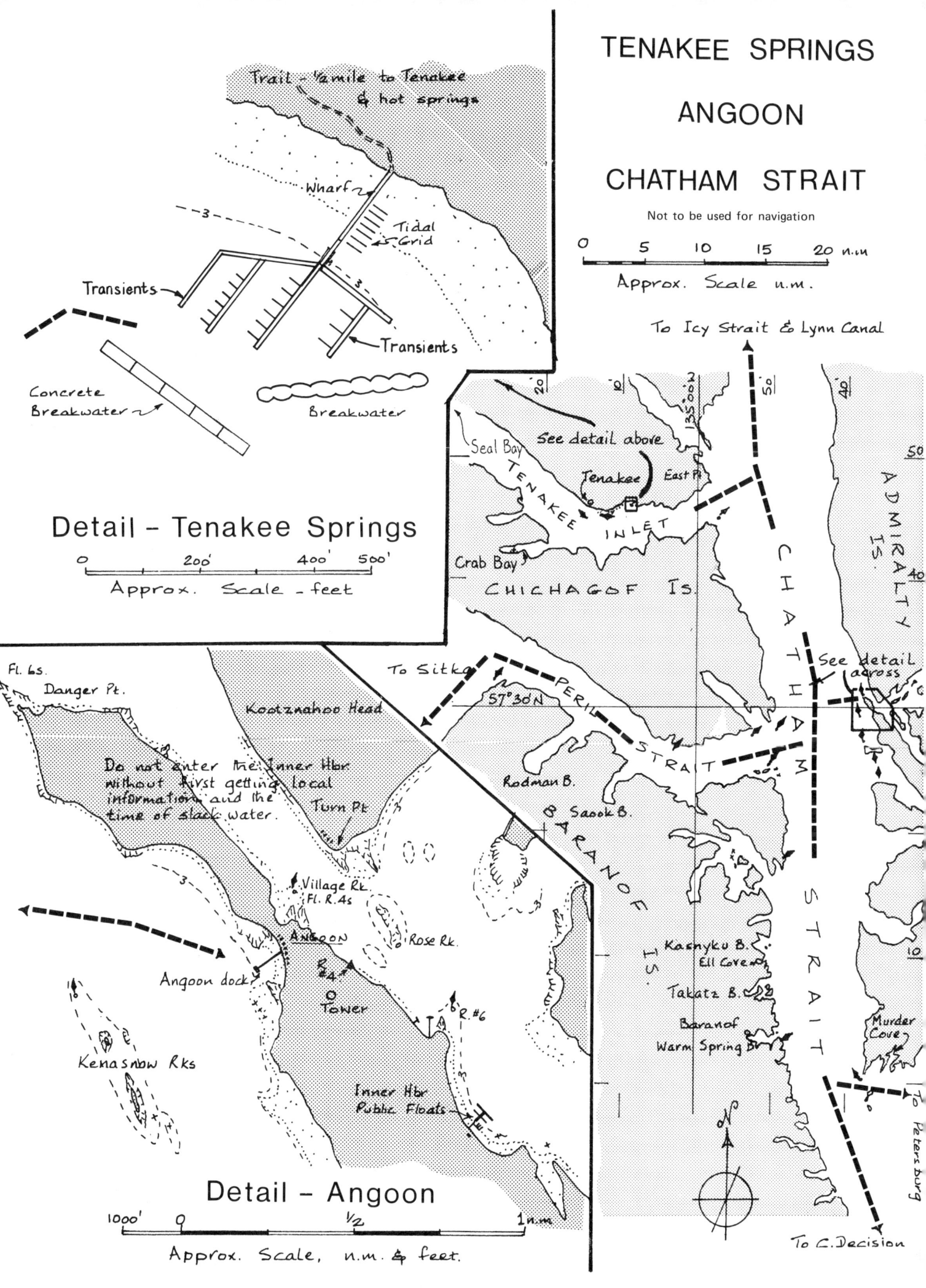

TENAKEE SPRINGS
ANGOON
CHATHAM STRAIT

Not to be used for navigation

0   5   10   15   20 n.m.
Approx. Scale n.m.

Trail - ½ mile to Tenakee & hot springs

Wharf

Tidal Grid

Transients

Transients

Concrete Breakwater

Breakwater

Detail - Tenakee Springs

0   200'   400'   500'
Approx. Scale - feet

To Icy Strait & Lynn Canal

See detail above

Seal Bay

TENAKEE INLET

Tenakee   East Pt

Crab Bay

CHICHAGOF IS.

ADMIRALTY IS.

CHATHAM STRAIT

See detail across

To Sitka

PERIL STRAIT

57°30'N

Rodman B.

Saook B.

BARANOF IS.

Fl. 6s.
Danger Pt.

Kootznahoo Head

Do not enter the Inner Hbr without first getting local information and the time of slack water.

Turn Pt.

Village Rk.
Fl. R.4s

Rose Rk.

ANGOON
R. #4

Angoon dock

Tower

R. #6

Kenasnow Rks

Inner Hbr
Public Floats

Kasnyku B.
Ell Cove
Takatz B.
Baranof
Warm Spring B.

Murder Cove

To Petersburg

Detail - Angoon

1000'   0   ½   1 n.m.
Approx. Scale, n.m. & feet.

To C. Decision

ANCHORAGES NORTH of WARM SPRINGS BAY

After passing out of Peril Strait into Chatham Strait there is a truly spectacular stretch of coast which can be followed southward along the west coast of Baranof Island. Several interesting anchorages can be found here.

The coast of Catherine Island must be passed for several miles before the first large bay opens. This is Kelp Bay, which divides into three long arms and a large basin behind Pond Island. As these arms are deep there are no recommended anchorages here, except in **Echo Cove** at the southeastern tip of Catherine Island which is open to the south and is useful only as a temporary anchorage. Kelp marks a submerged reef extending .6 mile south of Point Lull.

Cosmos Cove is about 2 miles south of Kelp Bay. One large and two small islands lie off the northern point of the cove, connected to it by shoals. Proceed well clear of their southern shores and enter the cove in mid-channel. The head and sides are shoal for some distance. Anchor about .5 mile in where there is good shelter, 4 to 6 fathoms, mud.

Kasnyku Bay is the next large opening. At the southern end is a magnificent waterfall that is visible from several miles away. This is Kasnyku Waterfall. Kasnyku Bay appears too open for shelter though there are several islands in it. At its western end are three islands and a Fish and Game Salmon Hatchery. A small anchorage can be explored above the northwest of the three islands. Here one can see another spectacular waterfall, Hidden Falls. The ruins of an old lumber operation are found here.

An especially intriguing anchorage can be found in the little reversed L-shaped cove south of Round Island, called **Ell Cove**. See US chart 17337. This little beauty spot is well protected, and as you approach it yet another waterfall will come into view when approximately due east of it. Ell Cove and Round Island can also be identified by the enormous semi-spherical bowl-like scoop in the rock face. The year-round snow-capped peaks and contorted rock faces with deeply water-cut gorges make travel along this coast most interesting.

Waterfall Cove, at Kasnyku Falls itself, appears too open and unprotected to be useful as an anchorage. Even if the southeast corner, the most protected part were used, the current from the waterfall would make it less than satisfactory.

About 4 miles further south is a large bay with several islands and arms—**Takatz Bay**. Entry is made around Point Turbot into the northern arm. Stay in mid-channel till past the outer rocks off the south point then favor the south side to pass the mid-channel rocks. Excellent anchorage in 6 - 8 fathoms, mud, is past the narrows then into the inner basin. Do not pass the largest islet .5 mile beyond the narrows, for shoals begin and reach to the head of the bay. It is only a few miles further to Baranof in Warm Springs Bay so Takatz Bay could be bypassed.

ARCTIC TERN

Kasnyku Falls   Round Is⁹   Kasnyku Bay   Cosmoc Cove

VIEW LOOKING SSE TOWARDS WARM SPRINGS BAY, FROM NEAR ST. CATHERINE Is.

Not to be used for navigation

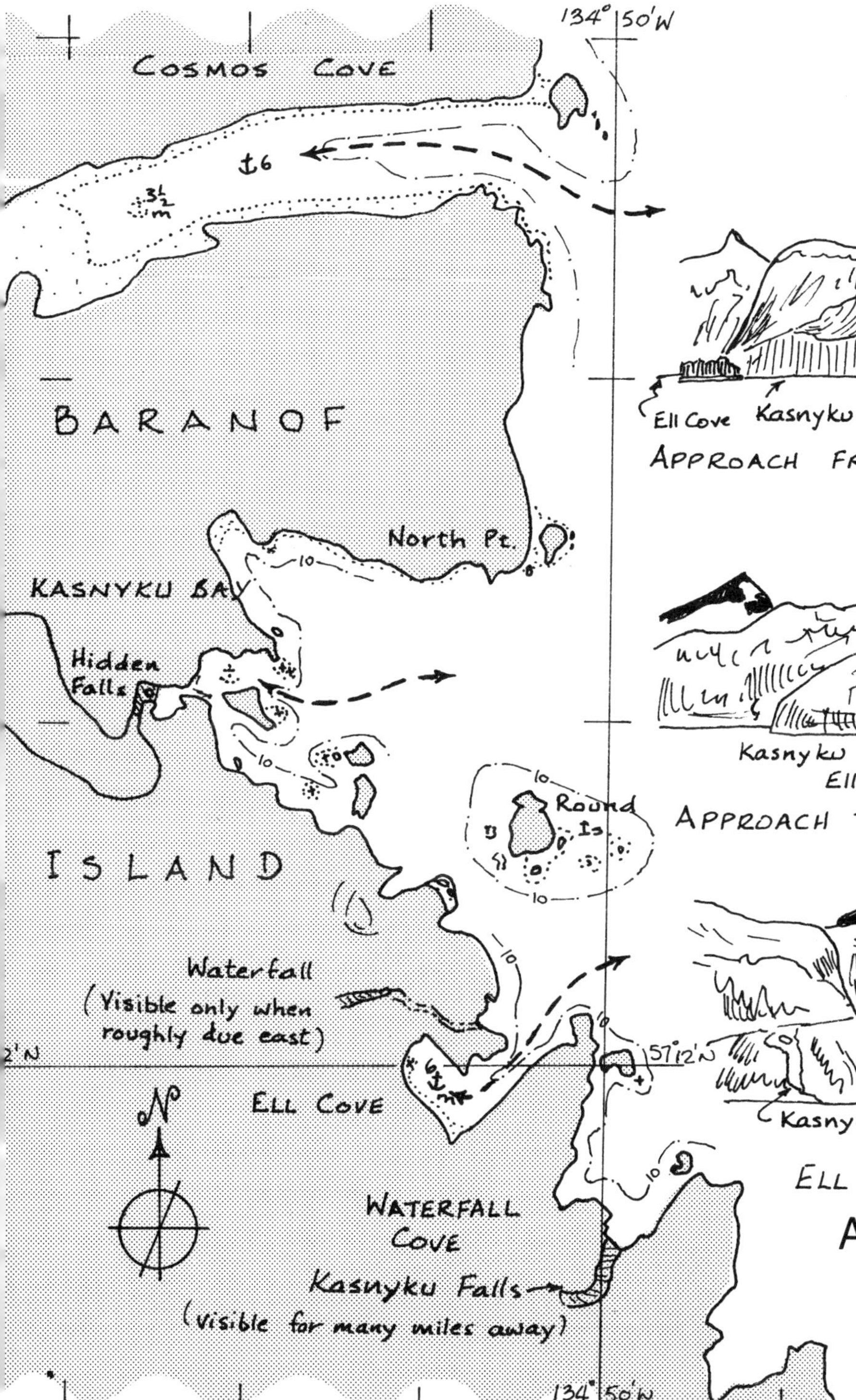

134° 50'W

COSMOS COVE

‡6

3½
1m

BARANOF

North Pt.

KASNYKU BAY

Hidden
Falls

ISLAND

Round
Is

Waterfall
(Visible only when
roughly due east)

2'N

ELL COVE

57°12'N

N

WATERFALL
COVE

Kasnyku Falls →
(visible for many miles away)

134° 50'W

Ell Cove   Kasnyku Bay   — To Cosmos Cove

APPROACH FROM NW TO COSMOS COVE, ETC. ANCH'S

Hidden
Falls

Kasnyku Falls   Kasnyku Bay
Ell Cove Entrance —   Round Is.

APPROACH TO ELL COVE FROM N.W.

Kasnyku Falls   Falls
To Ell Cove

ELL COVE FROM APPROX. DUE EAST.

ANCHS. N. OF WARM

SPRINGS BAY

CHATHAM STRAIT

Anchorage can also be found in the
inner basin of Takatz Bay, about
4 miles south of Ell Cove.

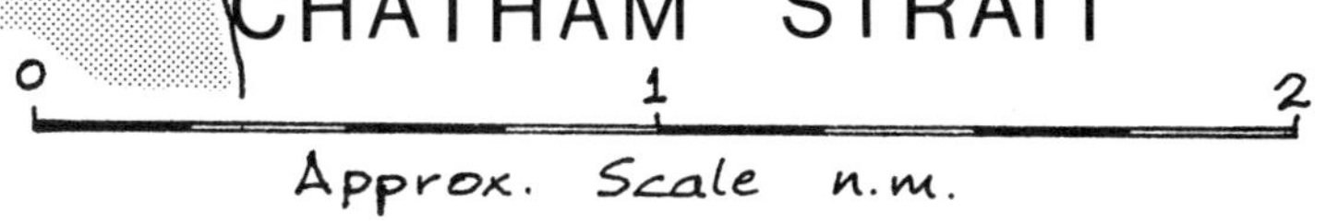

0   1   2

Approx. Scale n.m.

BARANOF, WARM SPRINGS BAY

A few miles south of Takatz Bay the steep slopes of the snow-capped mountains open to form the shores of Warm Springs Bay. A light is located on the southern point of the bay. Another identifying factor is the microwave reflector seen on the crest of the northern ridge.

A rock surrounded by kelp lies in the middle of the entrance. Pass on the southern side of this in deep water and proceed into the bay. The steep, green, forested slopes, the prominent white cascade at the head of the bay, the roofs of the few houses, and steam (sometimes trapped in the southern bights) give this place a special mood.

At the head of the bay the public floats lie east of a pier near the waterfall. Moorage can be taken on both sides of the 75 m (250-foot) float, but rafting may be necessary. The heavy current passing in front of the float should be taken into account when approaching it. The current affects the outer vessels of a raft more noticeably, so be certain that all vessels are well tied to the dock as well as to each other, preferably with extra lines to the dock. There is no fuel or electricity at the dock, only water. However, good fishing can be had right off the ends of the dock. Sometimes the cruise vessel, *Majestic Explorer*, comes in at night (all lit up) for a quick view of the falls—this is a cruise ship exploration trip!

If it hasn't become overgrown, a trail beyond the buildings leads to an interesting lookout over the falls and further on to Lake Baranof where the US Forest Service cabin is located at the south end of the lake.

If the wharf is full, anchorage may be taken in one of two coves on the south side of the bay, the westernmost being shallower at about 14 fathoms.

From Warm Springs Bay there are several routes that can be chosen. One route proceeds south along the west coast of Chatham Strait towards Port Armstrong and Port Alexander before crossing over to pass Cape Decision. A second route crosses Chatham Strait to anchorage at the Bay of Pillars or Tebenkof Bay before rounding Cape Decision. The third route turns at Point Gardner on Admiralty Island (7 miles southeast) to go up Frederick Sound. A light is situated on the westernmost of two rocks off Point Gardner. Pass between this light and a lighted buoy marking the rocky shoals around Yasha Island. Heavy tidal rips occur in this neighborhood, which is frequented by humpback whales.

On the eastern side of Point Gardner is **Surprise Harbor**; though not a good anchorage, it can be useful if strong winds are found in Chatham Strait. The next long indentation is **Murder Cove** (which got its name when a murder was witnessed here). It is best to enter at low water when the rocky hazards show clearly. Anchorage is fair off the ruins of an abandoned cannery about 1 mile into the cove.

BARANOF   FLOATS

BARANOF

WARM SPRINGS BAY

CHATHAM STRAIT

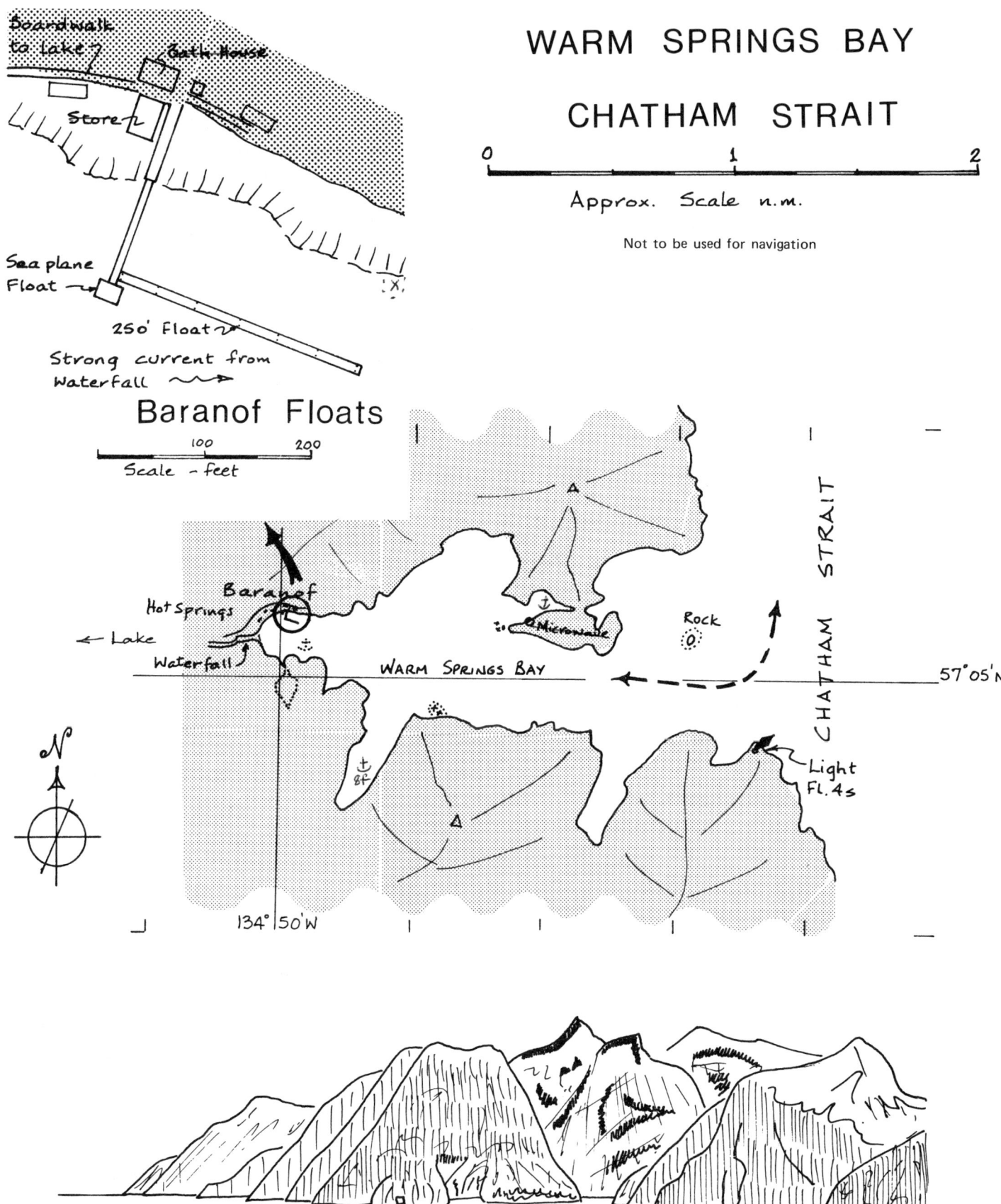

Boardwalk to Lake

Bath House

Store

Sea plane Float

250' Float

Strong current from Waterfall

Baranof Floats

100   200

Scale - feet

0   1   2

Approx. Scale n.m.

Not to be used for navigation

CHATHAM STRAIT

Rock

Hot Springs

Baranof

Micronesie

Light Fl.4s

← Lake

Waterfall

WARM SPRINGS BAY

57°05'N

N

134° 50'W

Rock

APPROACHING WARM SPRINGS BAY FROM NNW, distant about 1mile

TEBENKOF BAY

This large bay on the east side of Chatham Strait is the central feature of the Tebenkof Bay Wilderness Area of the Tongass National Forest. Located on the west side of Kuiu Island, it is 50 miles southwest of Petersburg. Extending 7 miles inland, the bay has a myriad of islands, islets, reefs, rocks and shoals within its boundaries and demands accurate navigation in order to reach safe anchorage. The low-lying islands are in stark contrast to the snow-covered peaks in the distance. The entrance to the bay is between Point Ellis on the north and Swaine Point on the South. An approach from the north is free of dangers. When entering from the south or leaving southbound care is needed to avoid Davis Rock and rocky patches and shoals to the southwest.

This is a cruiser's dream for there are numerous beautiful anchorages within the confines of the bay. In addition, Dungeness and Tanner crab, shrimp, herring and halibut are prolific in these waters. Wildlife often seen ashore includes black bears, wolves and foxes, plus many species of waterfowl including occasional sightings of trumpeter swans.

Happy Cove on the north shore of the bay is seven miles southeast of Point Ellis. Two islands (one bare, the other treed) identify the entrance to the bay. A narrow channel links the southern part of the bay to an inner cove, where anchorage may be taken with good protection. Several anchorages can be found in Elena Bay, the best one apparently having no name.

The southeast arm of the bay, **Petrof Bay**, is entered to port of the Tebenkof Bay Light, 2.1 m (14 ft.), located on a small island. A daybeacon is on a rock awash, 1.7 miles southeast of the light. There are several coves where secure, serene anchorage may be taken in 4 - 8 fathoms.

Thetis Bay, the southern arm of the bay, provides first-class anchorage well into the bay in 9 to 10 fathoms, good holding mud. Magnetic variations as much as 4° have been reported on the west shore of the bay.

Explorer Basin is part of a deep bay at the north end of Kuiu Island sheltered on the north by a phalanx of islands, rocks and shoals comprising Windfall and Troller Islands. Approach from the west where entry is between a rock (marked by breakers) off the southern Windfall Island and shoal water (identified by kelp) extendiing north of Swaine Point. Passable anchorage can be taken in coves to the south during southerly weather.

Gedney Harbor is about four miles south of the entrance to Explorer Basin. This harbor is popular with fishermen and cruisers since water, ice, fuel and limited provisions are available during the summer months at the scow anchored in the harbor. Care must be taken when entering. The entrance is on either side of a ledge .2 miles west of the island in the center of the bay. Rocky heads barely visible at high tide are on the NW and SE ends of the ledge. A mid-channel course on either side of the ledge leads into the bay. Anchorage can be taken anywhere in the harbor in 6 to 10 fathoms, good holding mud. Avoid shoal water indicated by kelp when moving in the area.

Tlingit Indians occupied this picturesque area in the past, and remains have been found of winter villages, seasonal fishing camps and gardens. In addition, vestiges of fur farms dating from the early part of the 20th century dot the shores of Kuiu Island as well as many other parts of the Southeast coast.

TEBENKOF BAY

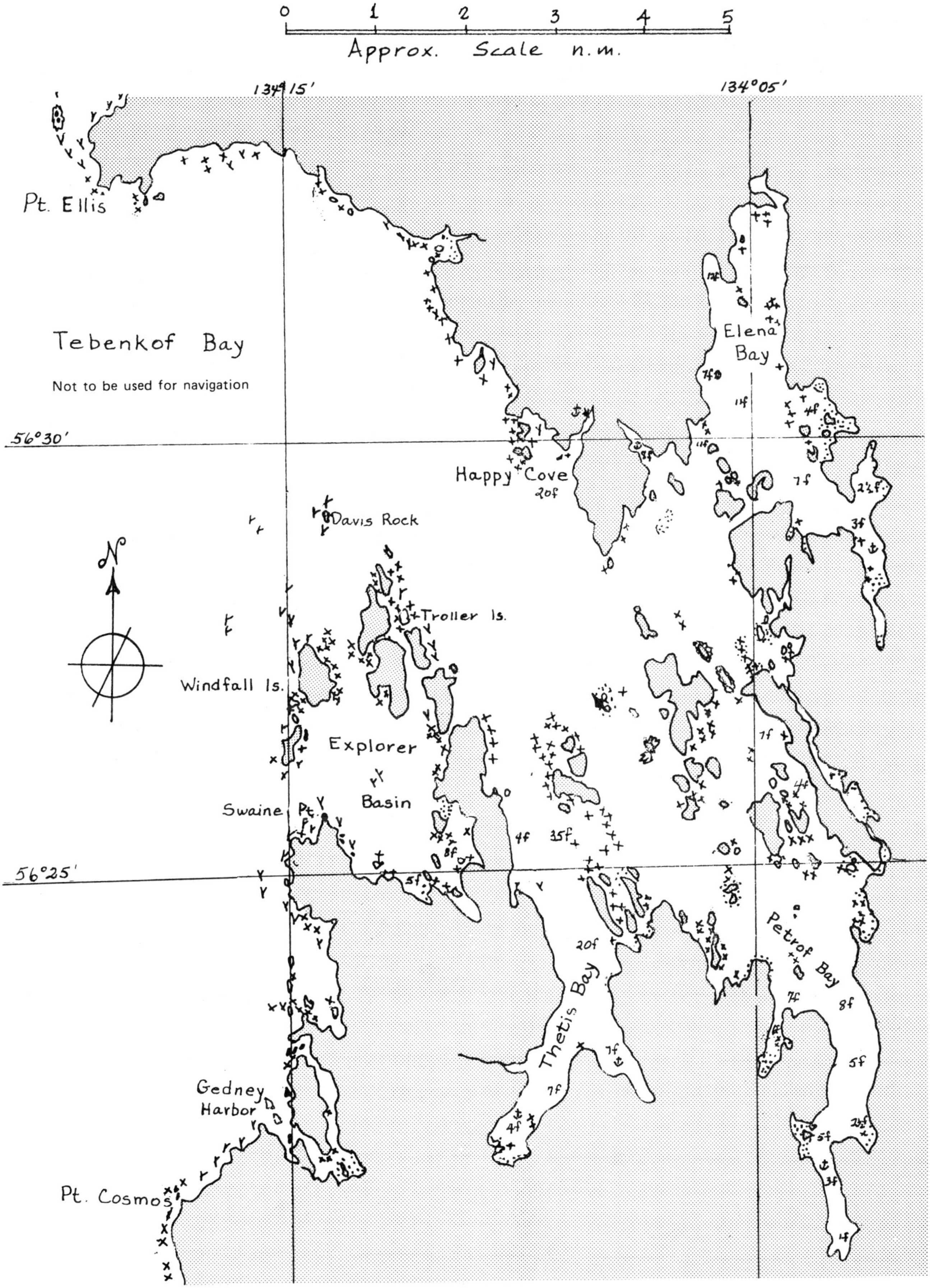

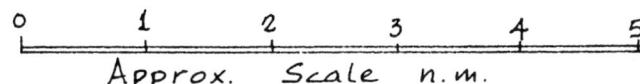

Approx. Scale n.m.

0   1   2   3   4   5

134°15'

134°05'

Pt. Ellis

Tebenkof Bay

Not to be used for navigation

56°30'

Happy Cove
20f

Elena Bay

7f
1f
11f

7f

2½f

3f

Davis Rock

N

Troller Is.

Windfall Is.

Explorer

Basin

Swaine Pt.

7f

4f

8f

4f
35f

1f

7f

56°25'

20f

Petrof Bay

7f

8f

Thetis Bay

20f

5f

7f

7f

Gedney
Harbor

7f

4f

2½f

5f

Pt. Cosmos

3½f

4f

PORT ALEXANDER

With the closing of Keku Strait a vessel proceeding from Chatham Strait to Sumner Strait has two choices. One is to go through Frederick Sound then down Wrangell Narrows, and on exiting turn westward into Sumner Strait. The other is to go down Chatham Strait and round Cape Decision into the entrance to Sumner Strait. If the latter route is chosen then Port Alexander is a suitable anchorage to await the best time to round Cape Decision This harbor lies about 5 miles north of Cape Ommaney at the southern tip of Baranof Island. The small community relies on fishing for its survival.

Two islands surrounded by shoals lie ENE of the entrance. Pass well south of them to approach from a little south of the lighthouse on the point. The entrance channel is 120 to 150 m (400 to 500 feet) wide. It lies between the lighthouse and a red buoy (N2) marking a shoal with rocks awash. A lighted range of 334° on two markers inside the harbor leads through the channel. A speed limit of 3 miles per hour is set for the harbor.

From well inside the entrance, turn northward up the harbor. Shoals occur well out from each side so stay roughly mid-channel. The main public floats are on the east side about .5 mile into the harbor, just north of a large wharf. This float is 140 m (450 feet) long and vessels can moor on either side, 3 fathoms, open mooring. Rafting may be necessary. Another public float is in the inner harbor about .25 miles further into the harbor, but the narrow channel is no longer maintained and it is advisable to get local advice if planning to use it.

Across Chatham Strait there are several good alternative anchorages in the **Bay of Pillars** and in **Tebenkof Bay** on Kuiu Island. In these more remote anchorages there is a good chance that brown bear can be seen; great care should be taken if shore excursions are planned.

Cape Decision lies about 13 miles southeast across Chatham Strait. It is a low, bare, rocky point with a square white lighthouse at the tip. Decision Passage, the route into Sumner Strait, is 1 mile wide and lies between the Cape and a string of islands, the Spanish Islands. When making the passage stay well off Cape Decision before turning.

Strong tidal rips and currents can be encountered in the area off Cape Decision and the stronger winds and weather of the open ocean can be felt here. Since fog often occurs in summer it is best to wait for good, settled weather before attempting to round Cape Decision.

More adventurous sailors can take the longer route around Coronation Island which is south of Cape Decision. This will take the vessel past Helm Point, a unique and spectacular sight. It is a flat tableland ending in sheer cliffs over 300 m (1,000 feet) high, where thousands of seabirds nest. If there is any possibility of stormy weather or fog this trip should not be lightly undertaken.

From Cape Decision it is about 10 miles northeasterly to Shakan Bay and the entry through Shakan Strait to wonderful El Capitan Passage.

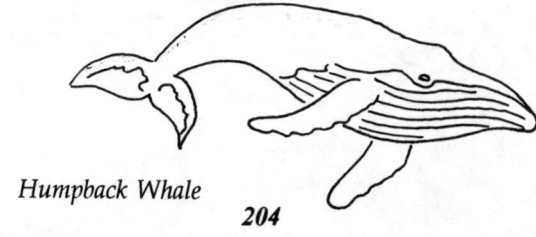

Humpback Whale

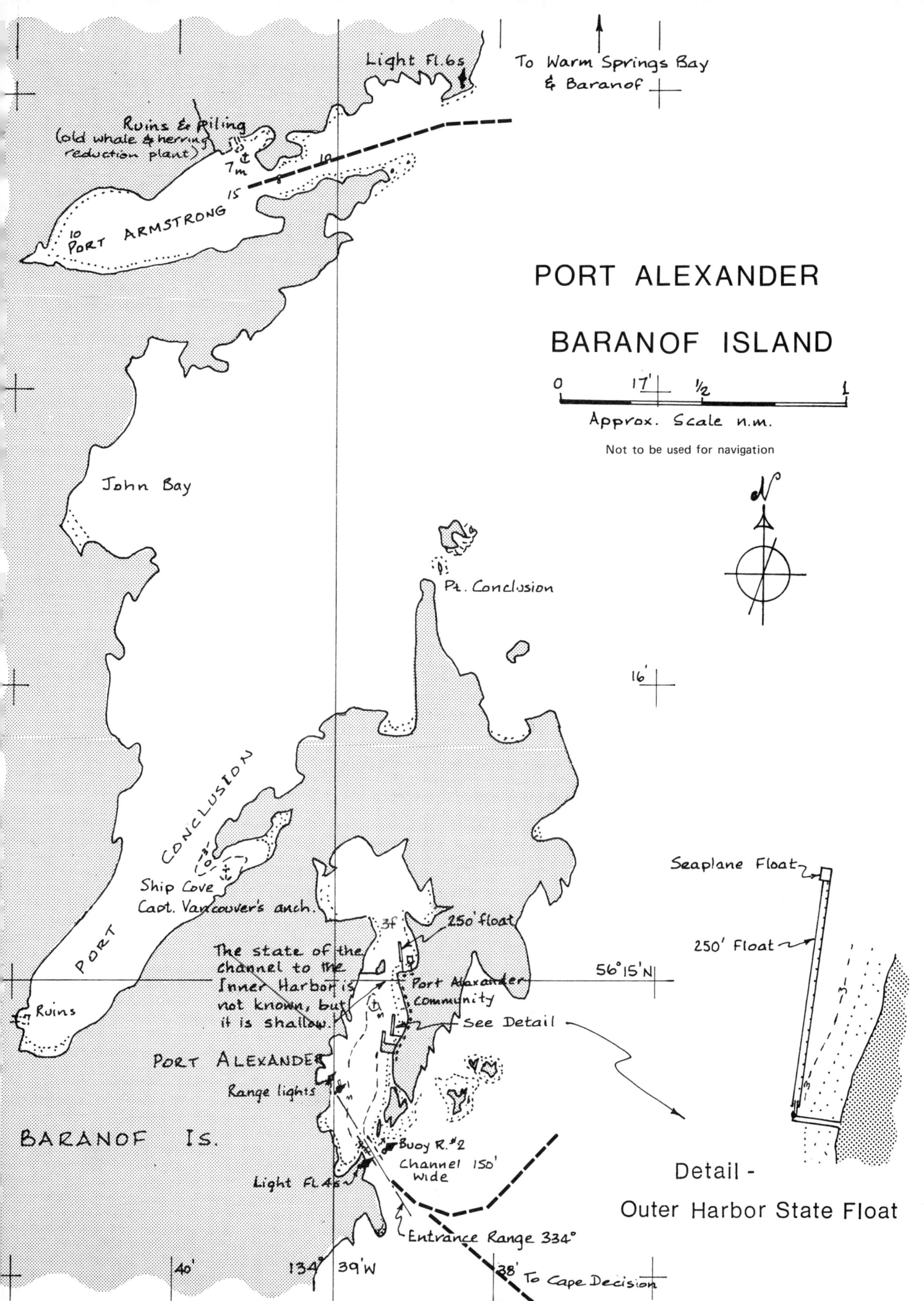

Light Fl.6s

To Warm Springs Bay & Baranof

Ruins & Piling
(old whale & herring
reduction plant)

7m

10

PORT ARMSTRONG

15

John Bay

Pt. Conclusion

PORT ALEXANDER

BARANOF ISLAND

0   17'   ½   1

Approx. Scale n.m.

Not to be used for navigation

N

16'

CONCLUSION

PORT

Ship Cove
Capt. Vancouver's anch.

3f   250' float

The state of the
channel to the
Inner Harbor is
not known, but
it is shallow.

Port Alexander
community

See Detail

56° 15' N

Ruins

PORT ALEXANDER

BARANOF Is.

Range lights

Buoy R.#2

Channel 150'
Wide

Light Fl.4s

Entrance Range 334°

40'   134° 39' W   38' To Cape Decision

Seaplane Float

250' Float

Detail -
Outer Harbor State Float

PORT PROTECTION

An alternative approach to Shakan Bay and E1 Capitan Passage is from the southern end of Wrangell Narrows, going west down Sumner Strait. Several isolated rocks marked by buoys act as mileposts along the way. The chart is the best guide. At Point Baker, the northwest tip of Prince of Wales Island, Sumner Strait changes to a north-south orientation. Across the strait to the north is the exit of Keku Strait which connects Sumner Strait to Frederick Sound, but all navigational aids have been removed to discourage any effort to transit this very challenging passage.

Point Baker, a small fishing community, has a state-operated small craft float in the harbor, which is in the gap between False Island and the northwest tip of Prince of Wales Island. Enter only from the north, between Point Baker light (with a red and white daybeacon to the west) and Point Baker anchorage daybeacon (on a smaller island to the east). Postal services, fuel, water, and provisions are available. Free moorage is found at the small dock on a first-come, first-served basis. A narrow, very shallow dinghy passage carries on behind False Island and Joe Mace Island to join Port Protection.

About .75 of a mile northwest of Point Baker is the bell buoy marking Helm Rock. The buoy is located about .25 mile north of the rock. At times there are heavy tidal rips and swirls around the rock. Small vessels would do well to avoid this rip by passing between the rock and Point Baker.

Port Protection is a large bay opening about 1.5 miles south of Point Baker. The same name is given to a small community in a well sheltered cove. The southern entrance point of the port is Protection Head which is a bold landmark visible from several miles. Port Protection light is on a red and white daymark on the point of an island on the north side of Wooden Wheel Cove. Note the detached reef with a daybeacon on it about .5 south of Joe Mace Island. Vessels can pass it on either side while giving the reef a wide berth.

Wooden Wheel Cove is boot-shaped, the toe of the boot facing southwest. Located behind Jackson Island, this small, well protected area has floats and some buildings. The 75 m (250-foot) public float is in the southern corner, unconnected to the shore. The southern end of the float is reserved for sea planes, but vessels can moor on either side of the remainder which has deep water alongside. Fuel, laundromat and showers are available.

There are several private floats around the rim of the cove. The large log cabin at the end of the largest float contains a small store. This a very pretty and peaceful setting, especially if you have come in to avoid the slop outside in Sumner Strait. Protected anchorage is found in the cove or further down the bay of Port Protection on the east side behind the islands where log booms are moored.

Many places (including Port Protection) were named by Captain George Vancouver who surveyed this area in the summer of 1793. The port itself received its name because the *Discovery* and *Chatham* sheltered here from a severe storm in Sumner Strait.

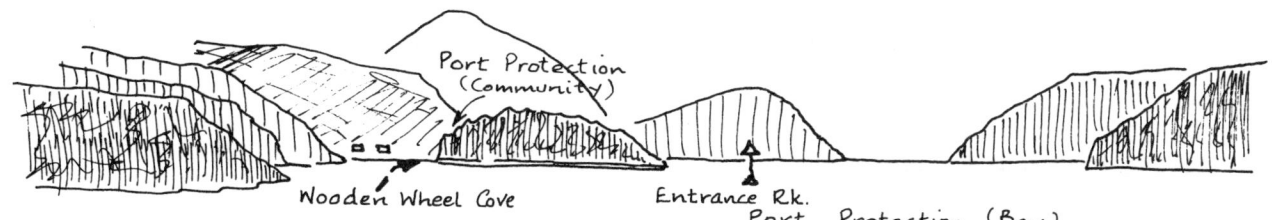

APPROACHING PORT PROTECTION (WOODEN WHEEL COVE) FROM WNW
distant about 1 mile.

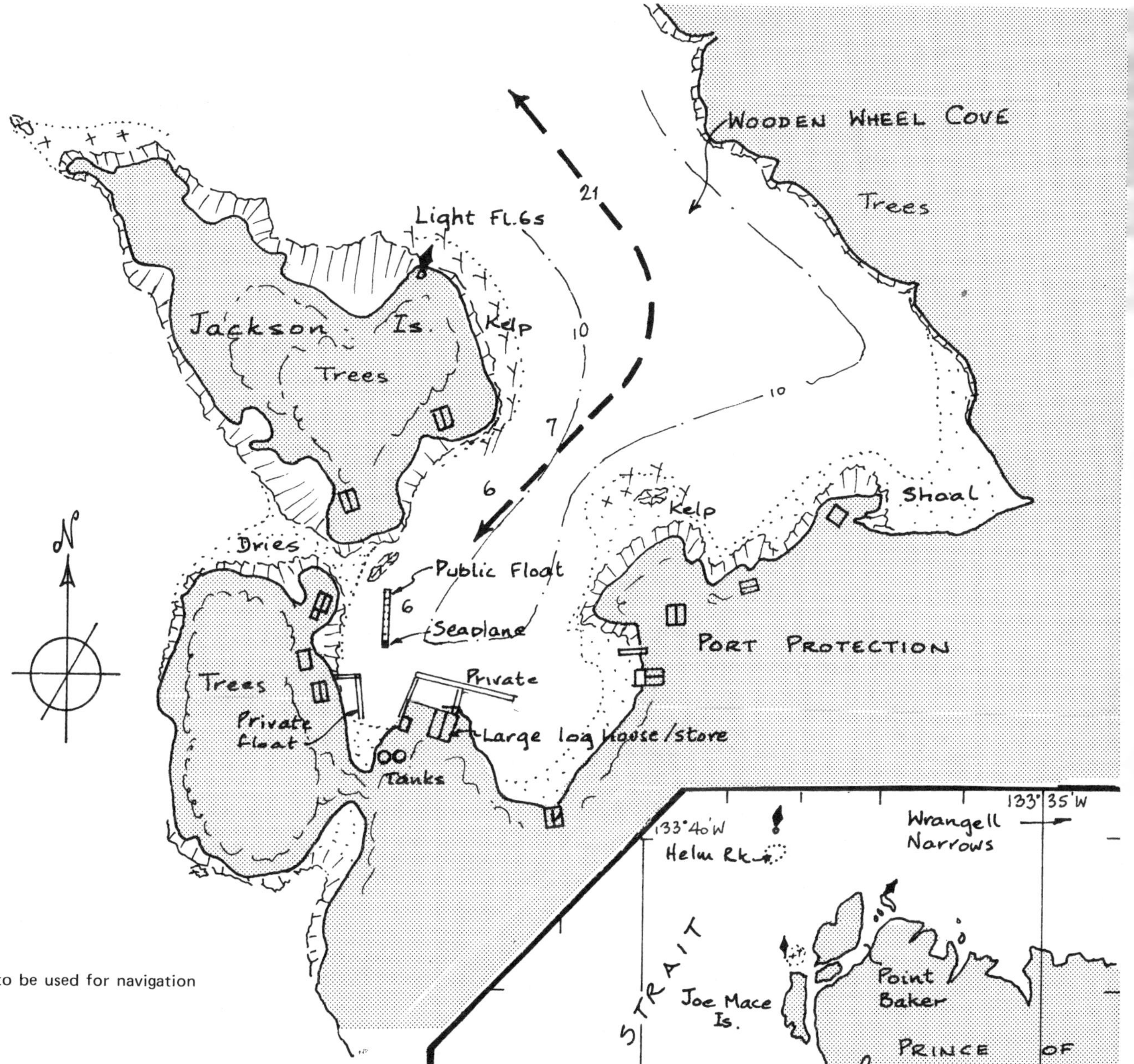

Port Protection
(Community)

Wooden Wheel Cove

Entrance Rk.
Port Protection (Bay)

WOODEN WHEEL COVE

Trees

21

Light Fl.6s

Kelp

10

Jackson Is.

Trees

10

7

Kelp

Shoal

6

N

Dries

Public Float

6

Seaplane

Trees

Private
Float

Private

PORT PROTECTION

Large log house/store

Tanks

Not to be used for navigation

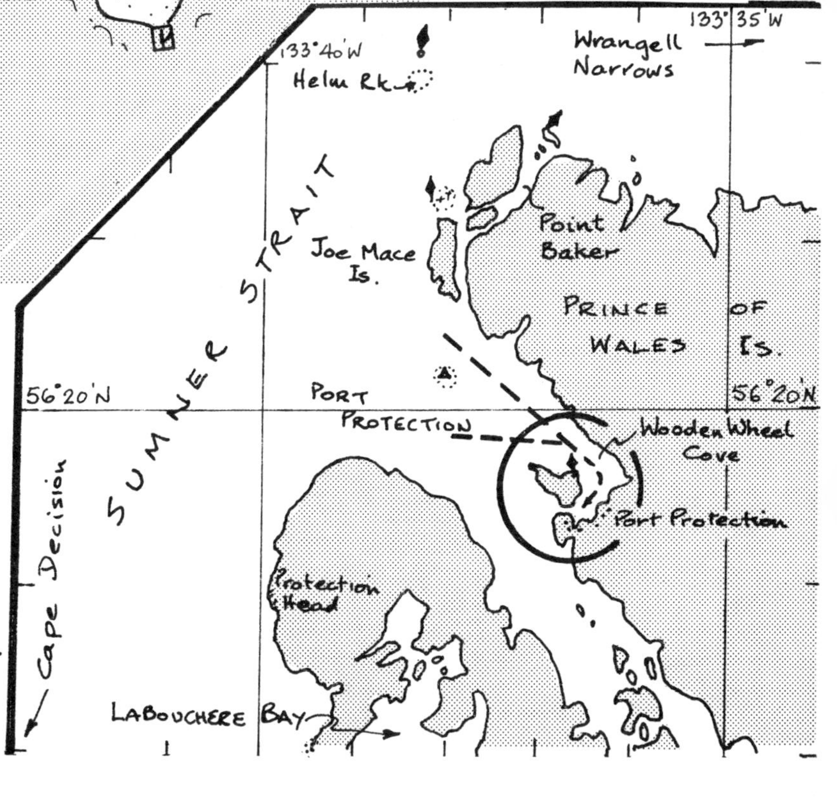

Helm Rk.

133°40'W

Wrangell
Narrows

133°35'W

Joe Mace
Is.

Point
Baker

PRINCE OF
WALES Is.

56°20'N

SUMNER STRAIT

Cape Decision

PORT
PROTECTION

Wooden Wheel
Cove

Port Protection

56°20'N

Protection Head

PORT PROTECTION

· SUMNER STRAIT

LABOUCHERE BAY

0   0   ⅛   ¼

Approx. Scale - n.m. (feet)

EL CAPITAN PASSAGE

The southern part of Sumner Strait is open to the Pacific and to southerly winds. However, with good weather one can reach over from Cape Decision, or run down from Port Protection to enter Shakan Strait on the east side of Sumner Strait. Enter in the center of the opening for there are many rocks and islands on each side, then steer for the south end of the largest island (Hamilton Island), where a daybeacon stands, and enter Shakan Strait.

At the end of Shakan Strait is an open bight to the east, where log booms are moored. El Capitan Passage leads off to the east with its entrance marked by a red beacon on a mid-channel rock. Anchorage can be taken a little further north in the bight in **Marble Creek**, or further on in **Calder Bay**.

El Capitan Passage is a little-known but fascinating part of Alaska. The passage follows a marked, narrow channel towards the east which is dredged to a controlling depth of 3 m (10 feet) and a minimum width of 21 m (70 feet). At Dry Pass the controlling depth is 2 m (7 feet) and it appears narrower than the width indicated on the chart. Chart #17387, with its enlargement of this part of El Capitan, should be used when negotiating the passage.

Before entering the narrows from either end call "Securite, Securite, Securite" on VHF Channel 16, to warn of your passage and to inquire of any vessel going the opposite direction. There are several wider spots where vessels can pass each other, but if a tug and boom are in the passage it is best to wait till they are through. There is no room to pass in the narrows. Currents of about 1 to 2 knots occur through the passage. Tidal change occurs at about the same time as at Sitka. Passage through is best near high water.

Beyond Dry Pass the passage widens, though it is still relatively shallow. Deadheads are hazards of shallow waters, resulting from use of the waterway by log booms, so it is wise to keep a sharp lookout at all times. After turning the bend, leave the small wooded island to the west. In the wider section that follows a logging camp is located on the small peninsula on the north side.

At Aneskett Point, the Passage turns southward and gradually begins to widen. About 3.5 miles south of this point the opening to Devilfish Bay is passed. A little further on, **Sarheen Cove** on the east, and an unnamed cove on the west (both about 2.5 miles further along) could be used as anchorages except during southerly weather. El Capitan Passage continues southward, widening, with beautiful vistas of low forested hills on either side and many islands. Five miles from Sarheen Cove is Burnt Island which has a light on it marking the main passage.

East of Burnt Island is **Sarkar Cove** where anchorage can be taken in about 6 fathoms, mud, near the head of the cove and off the ruins of Deweyville (once a gold-mining town). The main route continues directly south from Burnt Island, past the daybeacon at Hub Rock, then towards Tuxekan Narrows. Proceed around either end of El Capitan Island to visit the small community of Tokeen on the western side of the island where fuel and basic groceries may be available.

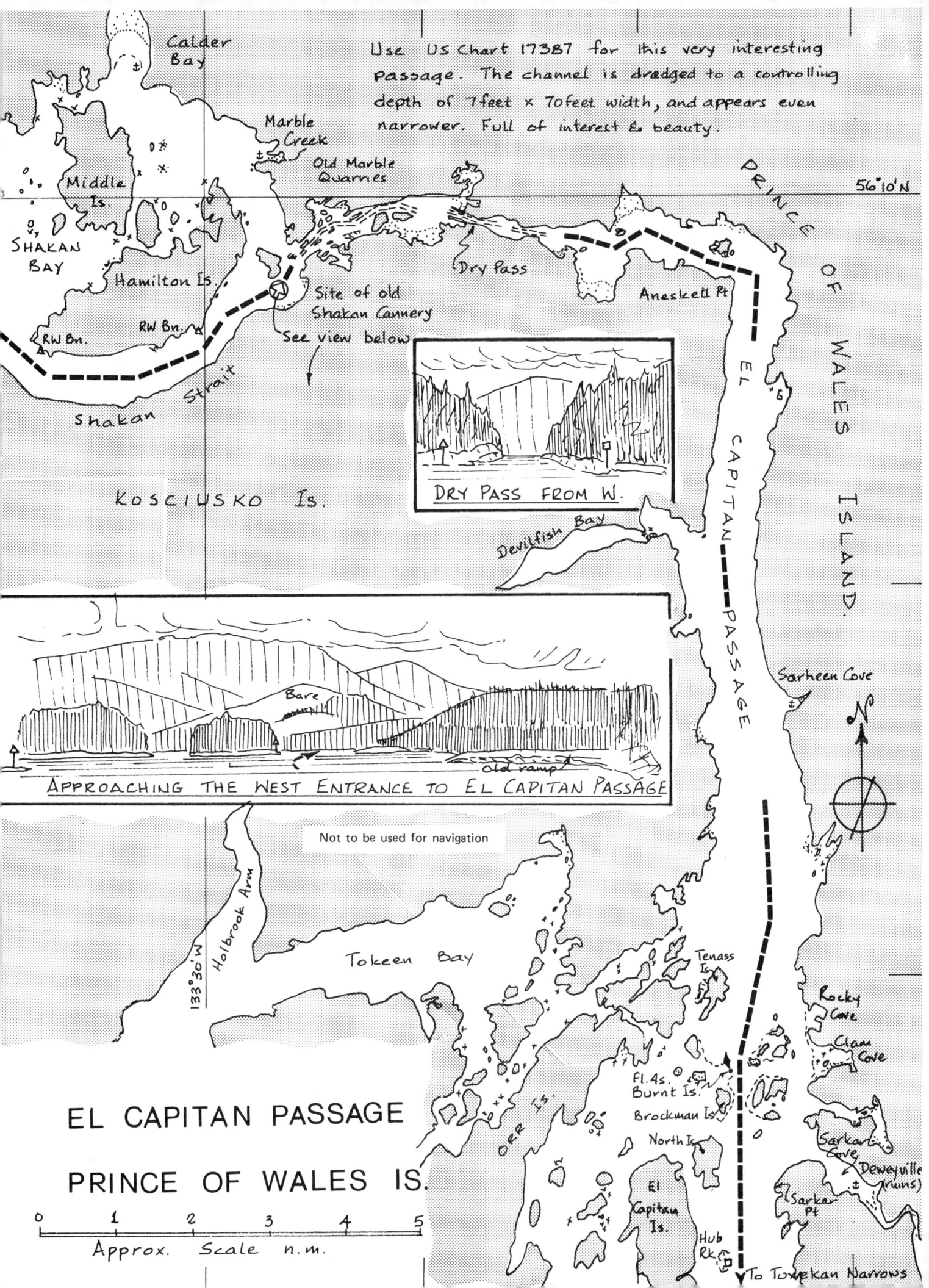

Calder Bay

Use US Chart 17387 for this very interesting passage. The channel is dredged to a controlling depth of 7 feet × 70 feet width, and appears even narrower. Full of interest & beauty.

Marble Creek

Old Marble Quarries

Dry Pass

56°10'N

PRINCE OF WALES ISLAND.

Middle Is.

SHAKAN BAY

Hamilton Is.

RW Bn.   RW Bn.

Aneskett Pt.

Site of old Shakan Cannery
See view below

Shakan Strait

KOSCIUSKO Is.

DRY PASS FROM W.

Devilfish Bay

EL CAPITAN PASSAGE

Sarheen Cove

Bare

Old ramp

APPROACHING THE WEST ENTRANCE TO EL CAPITAN PASSAGE

Not to be used for navigation

133°30'W

Holbrook Arm

Tokeen Bay

Tenass Is.

Rocky Cove

Clam Cove

Fl.4s.
Burnt Is.

Brockman Is.

North Is.

Sarkar Cove

Deweyville (ruins)

EL CAPITAN PASSAGE

PRINCE OF WALES IS.

El Capitan Is.

Sarkar Pt.

Hub Rk.

0   1   2   3   4   5

Approx. Scale n.m.

To Tuxekan Narrows

TUXEKAN NARROWS to SAN CHRISTOVAL BAY

This "inside passage" through the waters south of E1 Capitan Passage continues the very interesting and scenic route southwards. The series of large and small islands screen off this route from Sea Otter Sound and the open sea beyond. US Charts 17403 and 17404 should be used for navigation.

Tuxekan Narrows has daybeacons on the main rocky reefs. Aikens Rock is passed on the east side, but Village Rock can be passed on either side. The route passes about 90 m (300 ft.) east of the rock, keeping well away from Kinani Point on the Prince of Wales shore. A vessel is then aiming right into the 180 m (600 ft.) opening of Tuxekan Narrows. Though narrow, it is deep, and currents are not extreme. Thus, this passage is preferred by most vessels. (It is also possible to go around the west side of Tuxekan Island into Sea Otter Sound to join the route south through Karheen Passage.)

At the southern end of Tuxekan Narrows there is a village and logging camp at Little Naukati Bay, but anchorage is not recommended. A little further south on Tuxekan Island is **Nichin Cove** where good anchorage may be taken within the cove for small craft. Larger craft can find less protected anchorage off the entrance in 6 to 8 fathoms, mud bottom. A ramp and float are on the west side of the cove.

Tuxekan Passage is wide and about 10 miles long. The current is not strong, and the route is unmistakable. At Kauda Point (the southern tip of Tuxekan Island), Tuxekan Passage, Karheen Passage and Tonowek Narrows meet in a large, square bay which is littered with islands and reefs. Careful examination of the chart is needed. Enter Tonowek Narrows in mid-channel leaving the green daybeacon to the west and the red buoy NNE of Point Swift rocky shoal area to the east. Known locally as Little Skookumchuck, passage through the narrows is usually trouble-free since the current reaches a maximum of 3 knots.

When passing the first island on the west side within Tonowek Narrows look well above on the shoreline, where two mortuary poles and a burial box can be seen. The location on the island in the pass amid the tall guardian-like trees creates an atmosphere that engenders respect for the personage buried here. Pass by and do not disturb the quietness of this burial spot.

From Tonowek Bay there are two routes southward. One may proceed along the outer route into the Gulf of Esquibel, clear Curacao Reef and the rocks off St. Philip Island to enter San Christoval Channel. This route is exposed to the swell and these dangers must be identified. The preferred (inner) route stays in the channel behind Harmony Islands and the string of islands that follows, then behind Culebra and St. Philip Islands before exiting north of Blanquizal Island. Most rocks are visible, except for the mid-channel reef east of the north end of St. Philip Island.

At the southern end, St. Philips Island is joined by a sandy spit to a small island to the south where middens of white sea shells are seen. This is **Bob's Place**, the site of an old village. Good anchorage in about 5 fathoms can be taken in mid-channel, protected by the islands. San Christoval Channel, just a few miles further, leads through a well buoyed pass into San Alberto Bay.

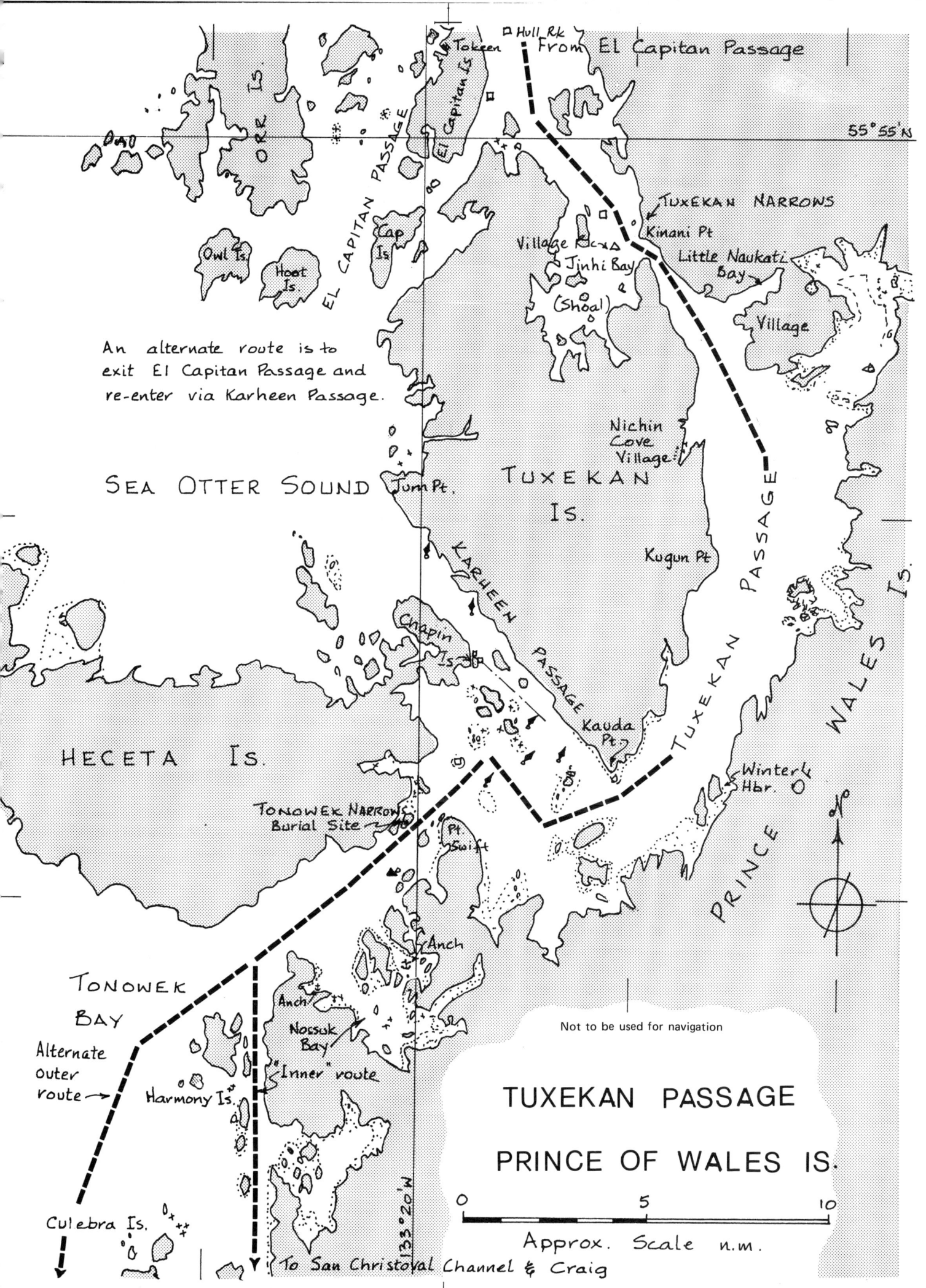

□ Hull Rk
● Tokeen   From El Capitan Passage

55° 55' N

El Capitan Is.

El Capitan Passage

ORR Is.

Cap Is.

Owl Is.

Hoot Is.

Tuxekan Narrows
Kinani Pt
Village Rocks
Jinhi Bay
(Shoal)
Little Naukati Bay

Village

An alternate route is to exit El Capitan Passage and re-enter via Karheen Passage.

SEA OTTER SOUND   Turn Pt.

Nichin Cove Village

TUXEKAN Is.

Kugun Pt

Karheen Passage

Tuxekan Passage

Chapin Is.

HECETA Is.

Kauda Pt

Winter Hbr. ○

WALES Is.

PRINCE OF

N

Tonowek Narrows Burial Site
Pt. Swift

Anch

TONOWEK BAY

Anch

Alternate Outer route →

Nossuk Bay
"Inner" route

Not to be used for navigation

Harmony Is.

TUXEKAN PASSAGE

PRINCE OF WALES IS.

133° 20' W

Culebra Is.

To San Christoval Channel & Craig

0   5   10

Approx. Scale n.m.

CRAIG

The northern approach to Craig is through the San Christoval Channel into San Alberto Bay, then southeast across the bay to the well buoyed channel between Klawock Reef and Fish Egg Island. This channel leads into Klawock Inlet. On turning south the town of Craig is visible on Craig Island which is joined to Prince of Wales Island by a causeway. The mountains on the large islands are steep, though not high, and make this a picturesque area. US Chart 17405 should be used when visiting this area. The most prominent landmarks are a brown water tank and a microwave tower on the southeast side of the island. Craig may also be entered from the south through Bucareli Bay and Ulloa Channel.

Craig is the largest community of Prince of Wales Island and is the economic center of the island. It is the service center and home port of a large commercial fishing fleet. In addition to marine services there are stores, a post office, banks and an ATM, laundromat, a library with internet service and a health care facility. Restrooms and showers are in the harbormaster's office at the head of the approaches to the cove. There are several wharves and structures connected with the canneries, a boat repair shop and garbage collection facilities. There is a magnificent collection of totem, memorial and mortuary poles in the park above the harbor.

There are two coves in town, one on each side of the causeway. Docks and floats for fishing vessels and other craft are along the north waterfront. The channel leading to North Cove is evident on the chart. A 90 m (300 ft.) main float has ~~two~~ four fingers at right angles. When approaching Craig call the Harbormaster on VHF Ch. 16 for moorage assignment. He controls moorage in both coves and will direct you to a temporarily vacant dock if necessry, but transient moorage is usually available at the public floats in both North and South (Shelter) Coves. The outermost finger, 50 m (175 feet) long, has transient moorage along its north (outer) side. Water and power are available at the floats and a fuel dock is north of North Cove Harbor.

Shelter Cove (the docks in South Cove) can be reached by going west around Craig Island, then passing through the buoyed channel between Craig and Fish Egg Reef. A controlling depth of 2.4 m (8 feet) is in the channel and float area.

The road across the causeway continues up the coast of Prince of Wales Island to **Klawock**, a Tlingit village towards the head of Klawock Inlet. Klawock can also be reached from Craig by boat by proceeding up the inlet, rounding Klawock Island, then through a narrow, marked channel. Public floats (max. 72 hours) are about .25 mile south of Klawock dock (the pier seen first). A small wooded peninsula resembling an island, projects out between the dock and the floats.

A number of caves have been discovered in the northwestern part of Prince of Wales Island and the Forest Service has daily tours to the most accessible cave, El Capitan.

Over 100 years ago this village was the site of the first cannery in Alaska.

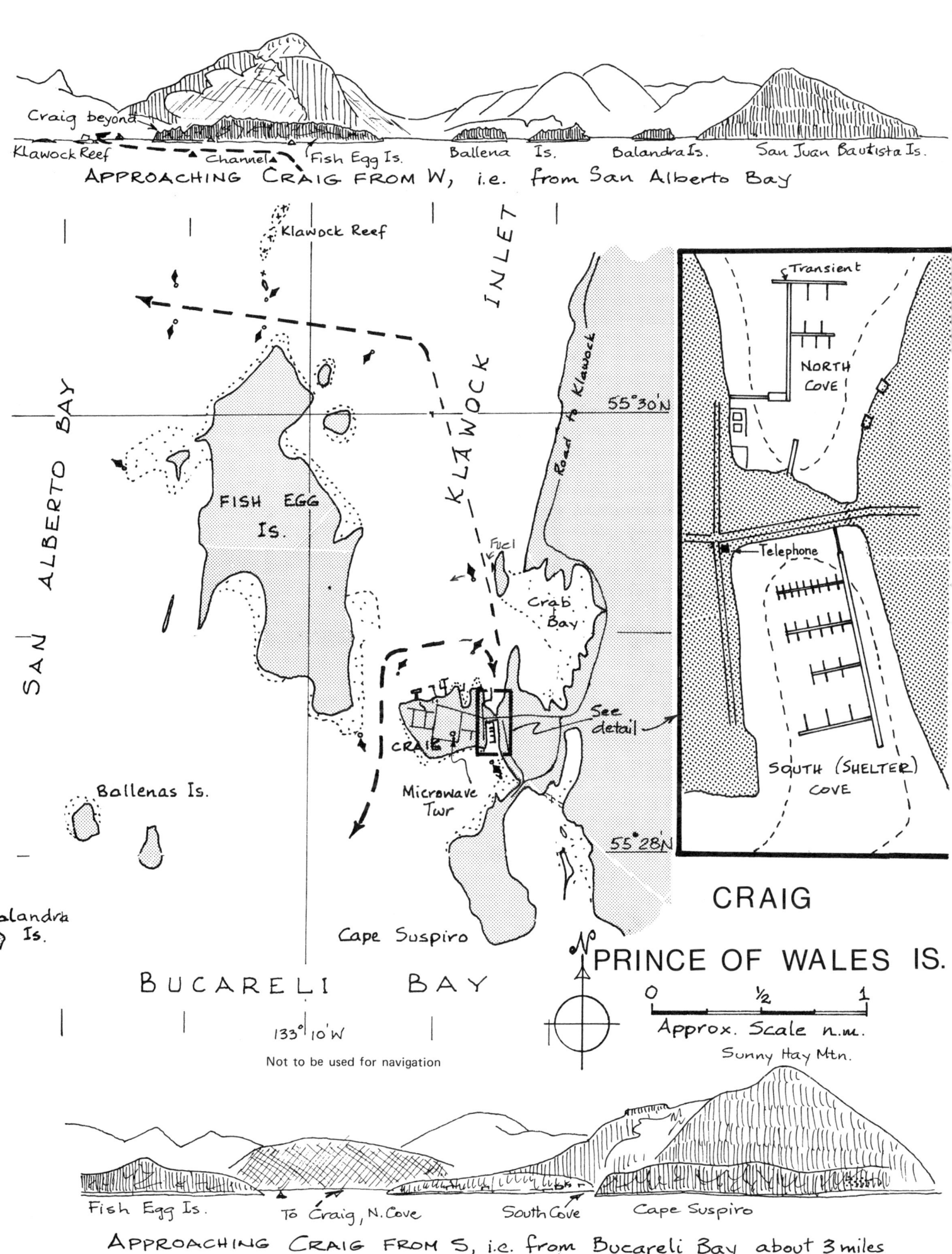

APPROACHING CRAIG FROM W, i.e. from San Alberto Bay

Craig beyond
Klawock Reef   Channel   Fish Egg Is.   Ballena Is.   Balandra Is.   San Juan Bautista Is.

Klawock Reef

KLAWOCK INLET

SAN ALBERTO BAY

Road to Klawock

55°30'N

FISH EGG Is.

Fuel

Crab Bay

NORTH COVE

Transient

See detail

Telephone

CRAIG

Microwave Twr

55°28'N

SOUTH (SHELTER) COVE

Ballenas Is.

Balandra Is.

Cape Suspiro

BUCARELI   BAY

CRAIG

PRINCE OF WALES IS.

133° 10'W

N

0   ½   1

Approx. Scale n.m.

Not to be used for navigation

Sunny Hay Mtn.

Fish Egg Is.   To Craig, N. Cove   South Cove   Cape Suspiro

APPROACHING CRAIG FROM S, i.e. from Bucareli Bay about 3 miles

BARRIER ISLANDS and CORDOVA BAY

It is a good day's run from Craig to the Barrier Islands in Cordova Bay, passing through Ulloa Channel, Tlevak Narrows and Strait and into and across Cordova Bay. There are several anchorages in this area.

The topography of Ulloa Channel—steep hillsides along a passage opening into a larger body of water—causes local fog to be trapped within, while the open water clears. White cottonwood fog banks at the entrances to the channels are a clear warning of these conditions. Navigation at these times needs care, even with the assistance of radar. Similar conditions can occur in other channels in this area.

Waterfall is an old cannery site on the Prince of Wales coast midway along Ulloa Channel. The cannery has been converted into a fishing resort, operating mainly during the summer with guests flown in from Ketchikan. Permission should be obtained for overnight tie-up at the dock. Some isolated pilings and an abandoned wharf create a hazard when it is foggy.

Tlevak Narrows is a short, narrow but deep passage opening into Tlevak Strait. Several islands and rocky groups occur on both sides of the narrows, but buoys and lights, and U.S. Chart 17407 are sufficient to navigate a vessel through. Currents are fairly strong inside the narrows where boils and swirls may be experienced, but the effect reduces rapidly with distance. Use this passage at or near slack water unless the strength of the current is low.

Once past the narrow section between Turn Point and Block Island Tlevak Strait is entered. Lively Islands are passed on their western side. If bound for **Hydaburg**, a principal village of the Haidas, stand to the ESE for Sukkwan Island and South Pass. There are public floats at Hydaburg.

If bound for Cordova Bay stand southeasterly down the Strait. Several deep coves indent the narrow length of Dall Island, though not all show evidence of being good anchorages. The mountainous backbone of the 40-mile-long island shows rugged, partially wooded peaks which appear to consist of marble. Ruins of canneries and/or logging camps are seen in some inlets.

There is a long reach across **Cordova Bay**. Wallace Rock, marked with a red buoy, lies to the north of the Barrier Islands and can be passed on either side. Once it is identified, the daymark at Guide Rocks to the ESE can be found. When nearing Guide Rocks the position of the Narrows leading to Eureka Channel becomes evident. A good anchorage can be found just past the Narrows in a small cove to the south. The sketch shows the anchorage. Another anchorage can be found behind the reefs west of the channel past the green daymark. Several similar anchorages could be discovered in the other passages of the Barrier Islands, though care should be taken because of the many rocks and reefs in the area.

Eureka Channel leads southward, past Mexico Point. There are many outlying rocks along the coast, and you should clear Nunez Rocks before attempting either to round Cape Chacon or to sail across Dixon Entrance to Prince Rupert.

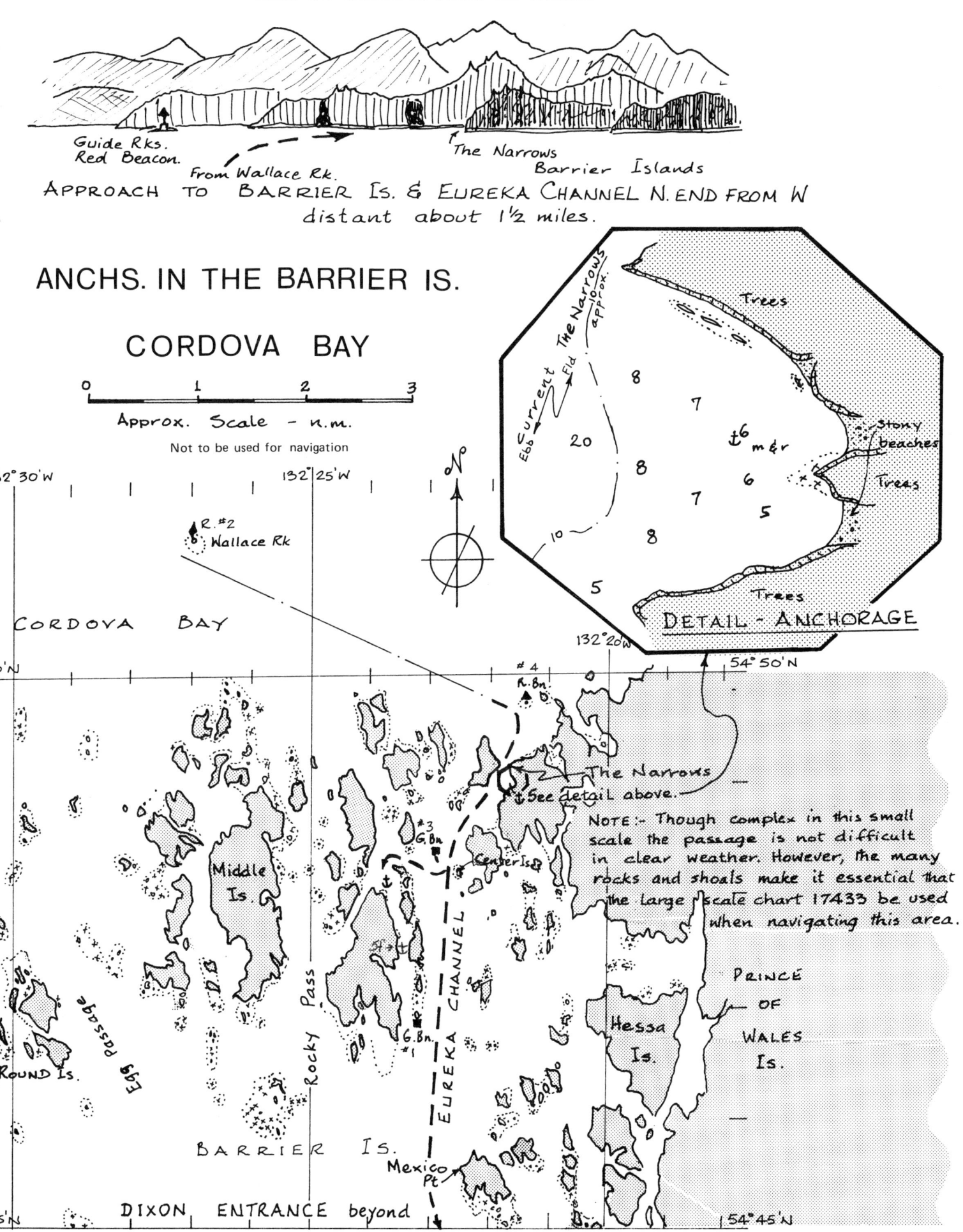

Hills on Prince of Wales Is. behind

Guide Rks.
Red Beacon.

From Wallace Rk.

The Narrows
Barrier Islands

APPROACH TO BARRIER IS. & EUREKA CHANNEL N. END FROM W
distant about 1½ miles.

ANCHS. IN THE BARRIER IS.

CORDOVA BAY

0   1   2   3

Approx. Scale – n.m.

Not to be used for navigation

132°30'W   132°25'W

R. #2
Wallace Rk

CORDOVA   BAY

N

DETAIL – ANCHORAGE

Ebb Current   The Narrows   Fld   10' approx.

8
7
20   t6 m & r
8   6
7   5
10
8
5

Trees

Stony beaches

Trees

Trees

132°20'W   54°50'N

#4
R. Bn.

The Narrows
t See detail above.

Center Is.

#3
G. Bn.

Middle
Is.

Rocky Pass

Egg Passage

Round Is.

G. Bn.
#1

EUREKA CHANNEL

BARRIER   IS.

Mexico
Pt.

DIXON   ENTRANCE beyond

NOTE:– Though complex in this small
scale the passage is not difficult
in clear weather. However, the many
rocks and shoals make it essential that
the large scale chart 17433 be used
when navigating this area.

PRINCE
OF
WALES
Is.

Hessa
Is.

54°45'N

ROUTES ACROSS DIXON ENTRANCE

It is necessary to stand out into Dixon Entrance when leaving Cordova Bay or the Barrier Islands for Prince Rupert. Several routes are available, the choice depending on wind, wave and weather conditions.

Going directly to Prince Rupert via Brown Passage is, harbor to harbor, about 90 nautical miles, of which 65 cross Dixon Entrance to Brown Passage. In good weather this can be a straightforward crossing, usually with quartering seas, and for sailors a good broad reach. Swells in Dixon Entrance are mostly from the west and southwest. Bad weather or fog should be waited out, and the crossing should be arranged to have daylight on the approach to Brown Passage. and Prince Rupert. An alternative destination for southbound travel is to turn SE from Georgia Rock, enter Porpoise Channel and proceed to moorage facilities in Porpoise Harbour. This choice will save some distance as well as time otherwise spent maneuvering in Prince Rupert Harbour. For details on Porpoise Harbour and Prince Rupert see pages 132 and 133a.

A shorter and slightly more protected route passes Cape Chacon crossing to Foggy Bay, about 65 miles, then on to Ketchikan or Prince Rupert. Shorter distances can be found to anchorages on Duke or Annette Islands. **Ryus Bay** is on the north side of Duke Islands, and it is an excellent, sheltered anchorage. **Tamgass Harbor** on Annette Island is also a good anchorage. If necessary, there are harbors and anchorages on the east side of Prince of Wales Island which are closer and in the lee of the land. If a cruise of the Queen Charlotte Islands is next on your itinerary it is just 50 miles across Dixon Entrance and a call to Canada Customs in Prince Rupert is all that is needed if you pre-registered and have a Canpass number. If you do not have a Canpass number you must first clear customs in Prince Rupert before approaching the Queen Charlotte Islands for Massett is not a Port of Entry.

Brundige Inlet on the north side of Dundas Island is another good anchorage which is also useful on the northward route.

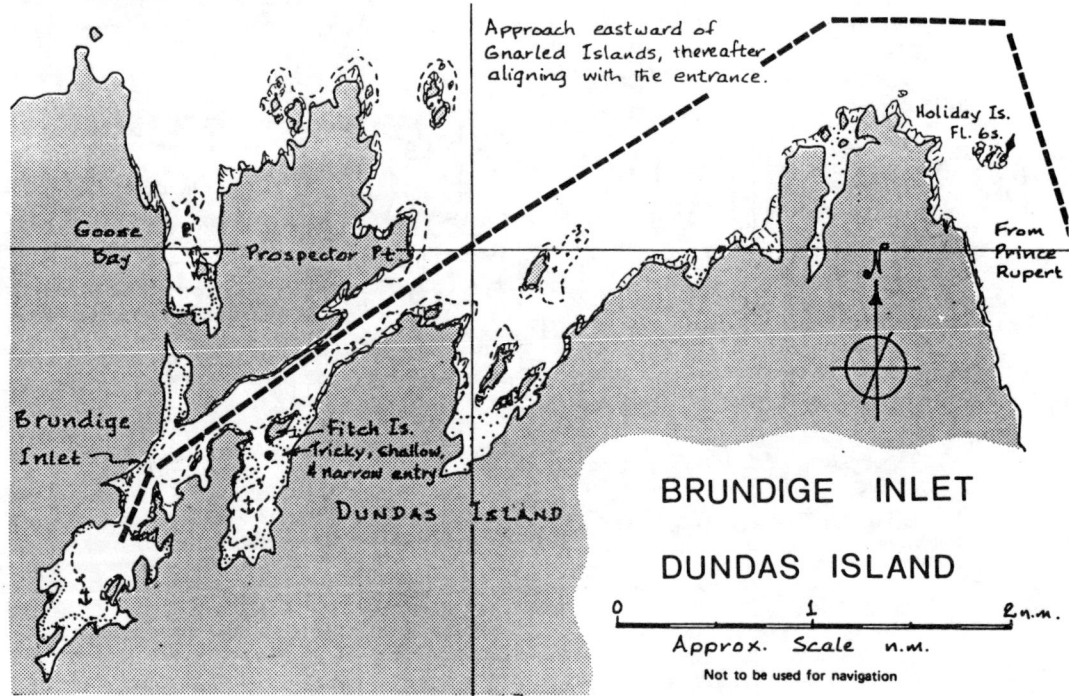

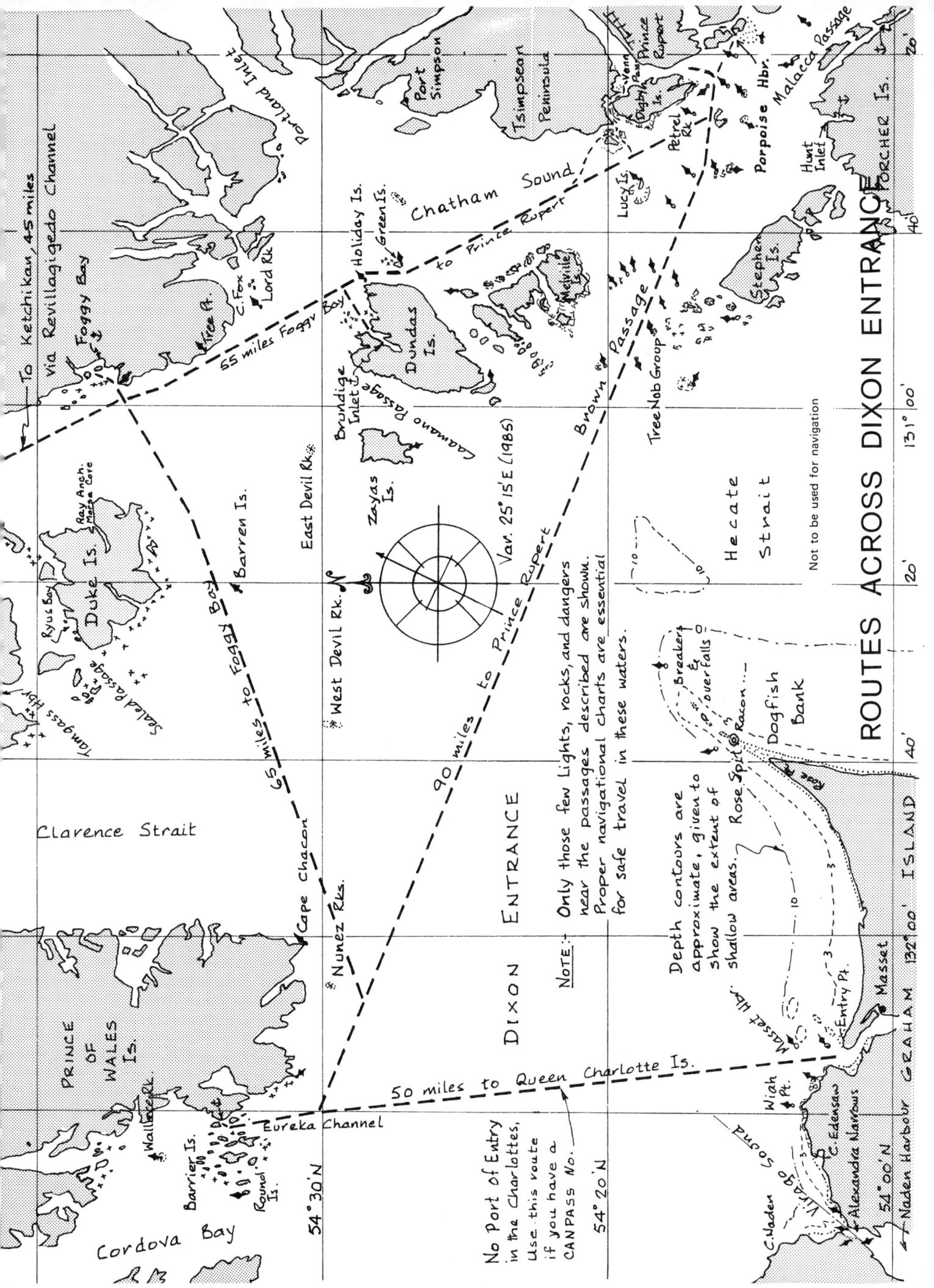

ROUTES ACROSS DIXON ENTRANCE

Not to be used for navigation

NOTE:- Only those few Lights, rocks, and dangers near the passages described are shown. Proper navigational charts are essential for safe travel in these waters.

Depth contours are approximate, given to show the extent of shallow areas.

No Port of Entry in the Charlottes, Use this route if you have a CANPASS No.

Var. 25° 15' E (1985)

DIXON ENTRANCE

Chatham Sound

Clarence Strait

Cordova Bay

Hecate Strait

to Prince Rupert

90 miles to Prince Rupert

65 miles to Foggy Bay

55 miles Foggy Bay

50 miles to Queen Charlotte Is.

To Ketchikan 45 miles via Revillagigedo Channel

Portland Inlet

Port Simpson

Tsimpsean Peninsula

Prince Rupert

Malacca Passage

Porpoise Hbr.

Venn Pass

Digby Is.

Petrel Rk.

Hunt Inlet

PORCHER IS.

Stephens Is.

Tree Nob Group

Brown Passage

Lucy Is.

Melville Is.

Green Is.

Holiday Is.

Dundas Is.

Brundige Inlet

Caamano Passage

Zayas Is.

East Devil Rk.

West Devil Rk.

Barren Is.

Nunez Rks.

Cape Chacon

Duke Is.

Ray Anch. Maize Cove

Ryus Bay

Scaled Passage

Tongass Hbr.

Tree Pt.

C. Fox

Lord Rk.

Foggy Bay

PRINCE OF WALES IS.

Wallace Rk.

Barrier Is.

Round Is.

Eureka Channel

DogFish Bank

Breakers & overfalls

Rose Spit

Racon

Masset

Entry Pt.

Masset Hbr.

Wiah Pt.

Jalun Sound

C. Naden

C. Edensaw

Alexandra Narrows

Naden Harbour

GRAHAM ISLAND

54° 30' N

54° 20' N

54° 00' N

132° 00'

131° 00'

40'

20'

40'

20'

APPENDIX I: CHARTS and PUBLICATIONS

Canadian Charts and Publications

3313	Strip charts of Gulf Islands
3311	Strip charts of Sunshine Coast
3312	Strip charts of Jervis Inlet and Desolation Sound
3462	Juan de Fuca Strait to Strait of Georgia
3463	Strait of Georgia - Southern Portion
3512	Strait of Georgia - Central Portion
3513	Strait of Georgia - Northern Portion
3538	Desolation Sound and Sutil Channel
3539	Discovery Passage and Seymour Narrows
3541	Approaches to Toba Inlet
3543	Cordero Channel (includes Green Point, Dent, and Yuculta Rapids)
3544	Johnstone Strait, Race Passage and Current Passage
3545	Johnstone Strait - Port Neville to Robson Bight
3546	Broughton Strait with plans for Port McNeill and Alert Bay
3547	Queen Charlotte Strait - Eastern Portion (including Stuart Narrows and Kenneth Passage
3548	Queen Charlotte Strait - Central Portion (including Blunden Harbour and Port Hardy
3549	Queen Charlotte Strait - Western Portion with detail of Bull Harbour
3550	Approaches to Seymour Inlet and Beliize Inlet
3605	Quatsino Sound to Queen Charlotte Strait, Scott Channel
3727	Cape Calvert to Goose Island including Fitz Hugh Sound
3779	Penrose Island
3921	Fifer Bay, Green Island Anchorages
3785	Namu Harbour to Dryad Point, Kliktsoatli Harbour, Namu Harbour
3720	Idol Point to Ocean Falls, Gunboat Passage, Troup Narrows
3728	Milbanke Sound and Approaches
3734	Jorkins Point to Sarah Island, Jackson Narrows
3738	Sarah Island to Swanson Bay, Hiekish Narrows
3739	Swanson Bay to Work Island, Butedale
3740	Work Island to Point Cumming
3742	Otter Passage to McKay Reach
3743	Douglas Channel to Kitimat
3745	Gardner Canal, The Kitlope
3772	Grenville Channel, Sainty Point to Baker Inlet
3773	Grenville Channel, Baker Inlet to Ogden Channel
3927	Bonilla Island to Edye Passage
3957	Approaches to Prince Rupert Harbour
3955	Prince Rupert Harbour, Detail of Venn Passage
3959	Hudson Bay Passage

Chart numbers are constantly changing as new charts are issued. The above list is intended merely to assist in choosing charts for the area covered.

APPENDIX I: CHARTS and PUBLICATIONS Cont'd.

B.C. Coast Pilot - Volume 1: South Portion (Juan de Fuca to Cape Caution)

B.C. Coast Pilot - Volume 2: North Portion (Cape Caution to Stewart)

Small Craft Guide - Volume 1: Port Alberni to Campbell River

Small Craft Guide - Volume 2: Boundary Bay to Cortes Island

List of Lights, Buoys, and Fog Signals - Pacific Coast

Canadian Tide and Current Tables - Volume 5: Juan de Fuca and Georgia Strait

Canadian Tide and Current Tables - Volume 6: Barkley Sound, DiscoveryPassage to Dixon Entrance

Radio Aids to Marine Navigation (Pacific)

A free brochure map, showing the extent and coverage of the charts can be obtained from the Canadian Hydrographic Service or any of its agents. It is useful for determining your own choice of charts.

United States Charts and Publications

17420   Hecate Strait to Etolin Island including Behm and Portland Canals

17360   Etolin Island to Midway Islands including Sumner Strait

17300   Stephens Passage to Cross Sound including Lynn Canal

17320   Coronation Island to Lisianski Strait

17434   Revillagigedo Channel

17430   Ketchikan Harbor

17385   Ernest Sound - Eastern Passage and Zimovia Strait

17382   Zarembo Island and Approaches

17367   Thomas, Farragut and Portage Bays

17363   Pybus Bay, Frederick Sound, Hobart and Windham Bays

17315   Gastineau Channel and Taku Inlet, Juneau Harbor

17316   Lynn Canal - Icy Strait to Point Sherman

17317   Lynn Canal - Point Sherman to Skagway

17302   Icy Strait and Cross Sound, Inian Cove and Elfin Cove

17318   Glacier Bay, Bartlett Cove

17303   Yakobi Island and Lisianski Inlet, Pelican Harbor

17321   Cape Edward to Lisianski Strait, Chichagof Island

17322   Khaz Bay, Chichagof Island, Elbow Pass

17323   Salisbury Sound, Peril Strait and Hoonah Sound

17324   Sitka Sound to Salisbury Sound

17338   Peril Strait - Hoonah Sound to Chatham Strait

17337   Harbors in Chatham Strait, Kelp Bay and Warm Springs Bay

17376   Tebenkof Bay

17375   Wrangell Narrows, Petersburg Harbor

17378   Port Protection, Prince of Wales Island

17386   Sumner Strait - Southern Part

17387   Shakan and Shipley Bays and part of El Capitan Passage

APPENDIX I: CHARTS and PUBLICATIONS Cont'd.

17403   Davidson Inlet and Sea Otter Sound

17404   San Christoval Channel to Cape Lynch

17405   Ulloa Channel to San Christoval Channel, Shelter Cove, Craig

17407   Northern part of Tlevak Strait and Ulloa Channel

17408   Central Dall Island and Vicinity

17431   North end of Cordova Bay and Hetta Inlet

17433   Kendrick Bay to Shipwreck Point, Prince of Wales Island

17435   Harbors in Clarence Strait: Port Chester, Metlakatla Harbor and Tamgass Harbor

U.S. Coast Pilot: Dixon Entrance to Cape Spencer (CURRENT EDITION)

Tide Tables, West Coast, North & South America

Tidal Current Tables, Pacific Coast of North America and Asia

Light List, Pacific Coast and Pacific Islands (CURRENT EDITION)

A free brochure map showing the extent and coverage of charts can be obtained from the National Ocean Service or through any of its agents. It is useful for determing your own choice of charts to your destinations.

APPENDIX II: MARINE WEATHER SERVICES from ENVIRONMENT CANADA

MARINE WEATHER ONE-on-ONE

Mariners can speak directly to an Environment Canada forecaster when on land. The $2.99 minute charge gets you detailed information on your specific area of interest. Both the accuracy and reliability of the forecast are greatly increased when the forecaster can take into account all of the variables which can affect the weather.

WEATHER CALL

When at sea, mariners can communicate with Environment Canada forecasters, by calling (604) 664-9033, or Fax: (604) 664-9081 to set up an account. Staying informed of potentially dangerous weather systems is vital for mariners. Weather Call allows mariners to stay abreast of any weather developments that could affect their safety.

WEATHER MENU

Extended marine forecasts can be obtained by calling 1-900-565-5000. An excellent tool in planning trips at sea. Weather Menu will let you know what to expect, helping you stay ahead of the unexpected.

MARINE WEATHER PHONE

This free service provides mariners with prerecorded marine forecasts around BC Call one of the following numbers to get an overview of the marine conditions you can expect:

Vancouver	604-664-9010	Commix	250 339-5044
Victoria	250-656-2714	Campbell River	250-286-3575
Victoria	250-656-2715	Port Hardy	250-949-7148
Nanaimo	250-245-8899	Prince Rupert	250-624-9009

MARINE FORECAST CONTENT

Marine forecasts are valid for 24 hour with an outlook for the following 24 hours.

SYNOPSIS

The Synopsis is given at the beginning of the forecast. It describes the location and intensity of weather systems which will affect the coastal waters and indicates what their movements will be during the forecast period. There is also a general description of present conditions.

WIND SPEED

The winds in the forecast are the average winds expected over open waters. Gusts or squalls are mentioned when they are expected to be higher than the average winds. With the rugged coastline of B.C. considerable local variation from the forecast winds are possible.

WIND DIRECTION

Wind direction refer to the direction from which the wind is blowing and these are based on true north, not magnetic north.

WEATHER and VISIBILITY

A brief description is given of sky and weather conditions. This is followed by a statement about visibility if it is expected to fall below 1 nautical mile.

OUTLOOK

This describes the winds expected during the 24-hour period following the main forecast.

MARINE FORECAST TIMES (Local Time)

0400
1030
1600
2130

APPENDIX III: UNITED STATES WEATHER STATIONS

Ketchikan	WXJ - 26	162.55 MHz
Wrangell	WXJ - 83	162.40 MHz
Petersburg	WXJ - 82	162.55 MHz
Juneau	WXJ - 25	162.55 MHz
Sitka	WXJ - 80	162.55 MHz

Continuous VHF - FM radio broadcasts are made on the above Weather 1 and Weather 2 stations. These are line-of-sight transmissions which are usually received 20 to 40 miles from the antenna site. Where the antennae are on hills or mountains, the range is extended. Broadcasts are taped and periodically updated. Weather information is also available from push-button boxes at major towns in Alaska.

APPENDIX IV
MARINE WEATHER REPORTING STATIONS, *WEATHER BUOYS* and <u>WEATHER REPORTS</u>

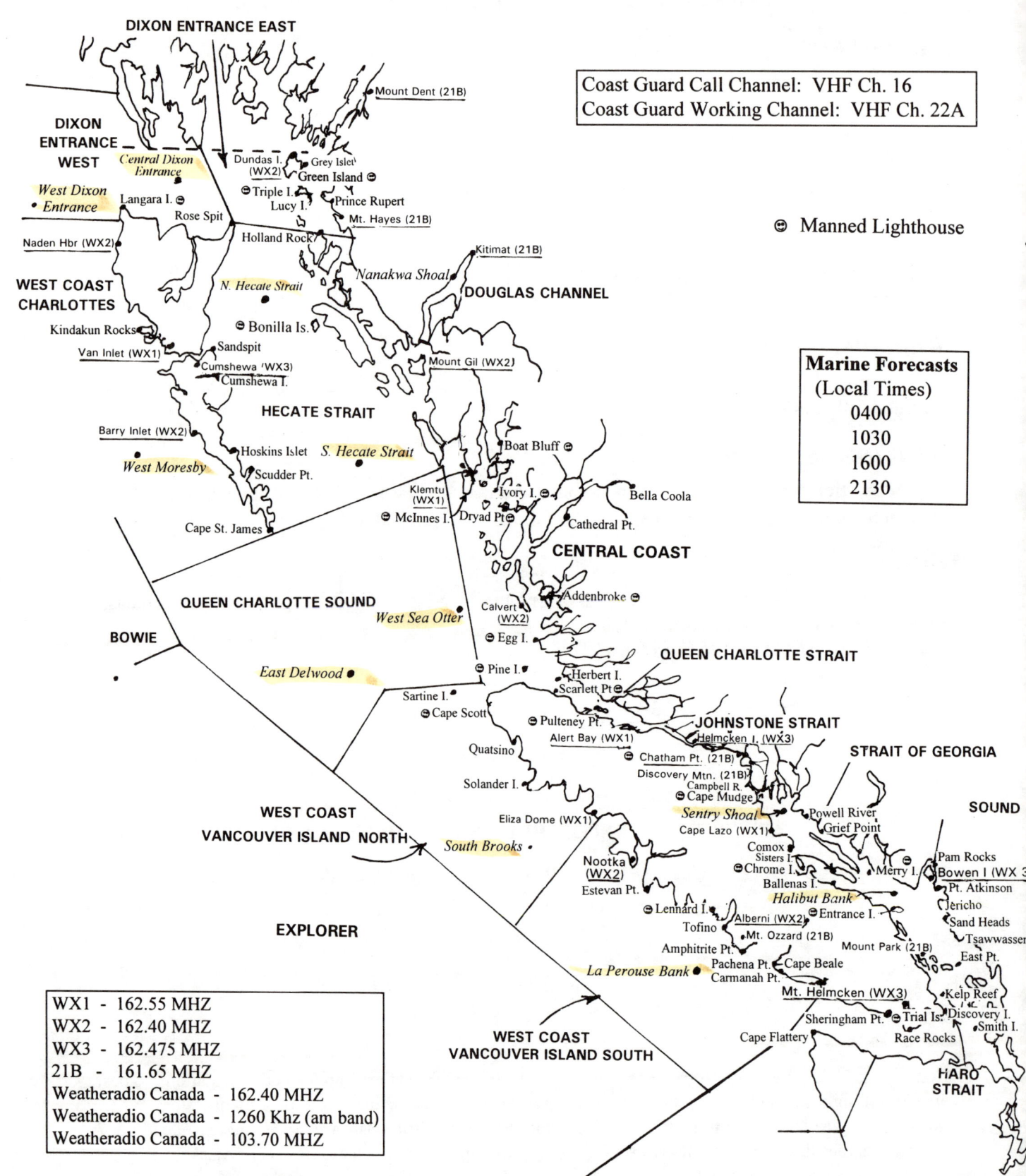

DIXON ENTRANCE EAST

Mount Dent (21B)

DIXON ENTRANCE WEST

Central Dixon Entrance

Dundas I. (WX2) Grey Islet Green Island ☺

West Dixon Entrance

Langara I. ☺ Triple I. Lucy I. Prince Rupert

Rose Spit Mt. Hayes (21B)

Naden Hbr (WX2) Holland Rock Kitimat (21B)

Nanakwa Shoal DOUGLAS CHANNEL

WEST COAST CHARLOTTES

N. Hecate Strait

Kindakun Rocks Bonilla Is. ☺

Van Inlet (WX1) Sandspit Mount Gil (WX2)

Cumshewa (WX3) Cumshewa I.

HECATE STRAIT

Barry Inlet (WX2) Boat Bluff ☺

West Moresby Hoskins Islet *S. Hecate Strait*

Scudder Pt. Klemtu (WX1) Ivory I. ☺ Bella Coola

Cape St. James McInnes I. ☺ Dryad Pt ☺ Cathedral Pt.

CENTRAL COAST

Addenbroke ☺

QUEEN CHARLOTTE SOUND

West Sea Otter

BOWIE Calvert (WX2)

East Delwood Egg I. ☺

QUEEN CHARLOTTE STRAIT

Pine I. ☺ Herbert I. Scarlett Pt ☺

Sartine I. Pulteney Pt. ☺ JOHNSTONE STRAIT

Cape Scott Alert Bay (WX1) Helmcken I. (WX3) STRAIT OF GEORGIA

Quatsino Chatham Pt. (21B) Discovery Mtn. (21B)

Solander I. Campbell R. Cape Mudge ☺ Powell River

Eliza Dome (WX1) *Sentry Shoal* Grief Point SOUND

WEST COAST VANCOUVER ISLAND NORTH Cape Lazo (WX1)

South Brooks Comox Pam Rocks

Nootka (WX2) Sisters I. Merry I. ☺ Bowen I (WX 3

Estevan Pt. Chrome I. ☺ Pt. Atkinson

EXPLORER Ballenas I. Jericho

Lennard I. ☺ *Halibut Bank* Sand Heads

Tofino Alberni (WX2) Entrance I. ☺ Tsawwassen

Amphitrite Pt. Mt. Ozzard (21B) Mount Park (21B) East Pt.

Pachena Pt. Cape Beale Kelp Reef

La Perouse Bank Carmanah Pt. Mt. Helmcken (WX3) Discovery I.

Sheringham Pt. Trial Is. ☺ Smith I

WEST COAST VANCOUVER ISLAND SOUTH Cape Flattery Race Rocks

HARO STRAIT

Coast Guard Call Channel: VHF Ch. 16
Coast Guard Working Channel: VHF Ch. 22A

☺ Manned Lighthouse

Marine Forecasts
(Local Times)
0400
1030
1600
2130

WX1 - 162.55 MHZ
WX2 - 162.40 MHZ
WX3 - 162.475 MHZ
21B - 161.65 MHZ
Weatheradio Canada - 162.40 MHZ
Weatheradio Canada - 1260 Khz (am band)
Weatheradio Canada - 103.70 MHZ

APPENDIX V

Table of Distances

The intersection of columns between two places is the approximate distance in nautical miles. Distances can be added between sections. Use only for planning. Measure the actual distances on your chart.

Example: Safety Cove is 222 miles from Prince Rupert, and 222 + 179 = 401 miles from Wrangell.

(Via Cape Decision & El Capitan) — Craig to Sitka = 144
(via Cordova Bay & Cape Chacon) — 156
(via Peril Strait) — 314

From	Sitka	Glacier Bay	Juneau	Petersburg	Wrangell	Ketchikan	Prince Rupert
Craig	144					156	
Sitka		148	162	159	170	224	314
Glacier Bay			94	188	220	290	380
Juneau				108	148	220	310
Petersburg					40	112	200
Wrangell						89	179
Ketchikan							90

From	Butedale	Klemtu	Bella Bella	Safety Cove	Port Hardy
Prince Rupert	100	138	180	222	277
Butedale		66	80	122	177
Klemtu			43	85	142
Bella Bella				42	97
Safety Cove					75

From	Alert Bay	Campbell River	Powell River	Pender Harbour	Nanaimo	Vancouver*
Port Hardy	26	108	140	161	183	207
Alert Bay		83	114	136	158	182
Campbell River			31	53	75	99
Powell River				26	52	70
Pender Harbour					30	48
Nanaimo						34

(Via Gulf Islands)

From	Silva Bay, Gabriola Pass	Montague Harbor, Active Pass	Sidney	Victoria
Vancouver*	27	40	50	73
Silva Bay, Gabriola Pass		23	35	58
Montague Harbor, Active Pass			17	39
Sidney				24

* At the entrance to Burrard Inlet

(Via Strait of Georgia) / **(Via San Juan Islands)**

From	Point Roberts	Blaine	Friday Harbor	Victoria
Vancouver*	32	45	50	80
Point Roberts		13	28	47
Blaine			31	53
Friday Harbor				27

SYMBOLS

- - - - -	Recommended route		Lights in line on bearing
⚓	Anchorage	⚓	Reported anchorage
×	Rock or reef underwater	⊛	Dangerous rock or reef
	Rocks exposed by tide		Shoal area exposed by tide
	Steep rocky edges		Sand or pebble beach
	Glacier		Land areas
☼ , ⚑	Lighthouse, navigation lights	△ , ▢	Beacons, not necessarily lit
_3_	Depth contour in fathoms	⟶	Flood current
4 , 4f	Depth in fathoms	⟵	Ebb current
S	Sand bottom	↻ , ↺	Eddies or whirlpools
m	Mud bottom	⌒⌒⌒	Rips and/or overfalls
r	Rock bottom	5 kn	Current velocity in knots

NOTE: All depths are given in fathoms, except where specifically mentioned in feet. Approximately 2 meters = 1 fathom and exactly 1.8 meters = 1 fathom.

INDEX

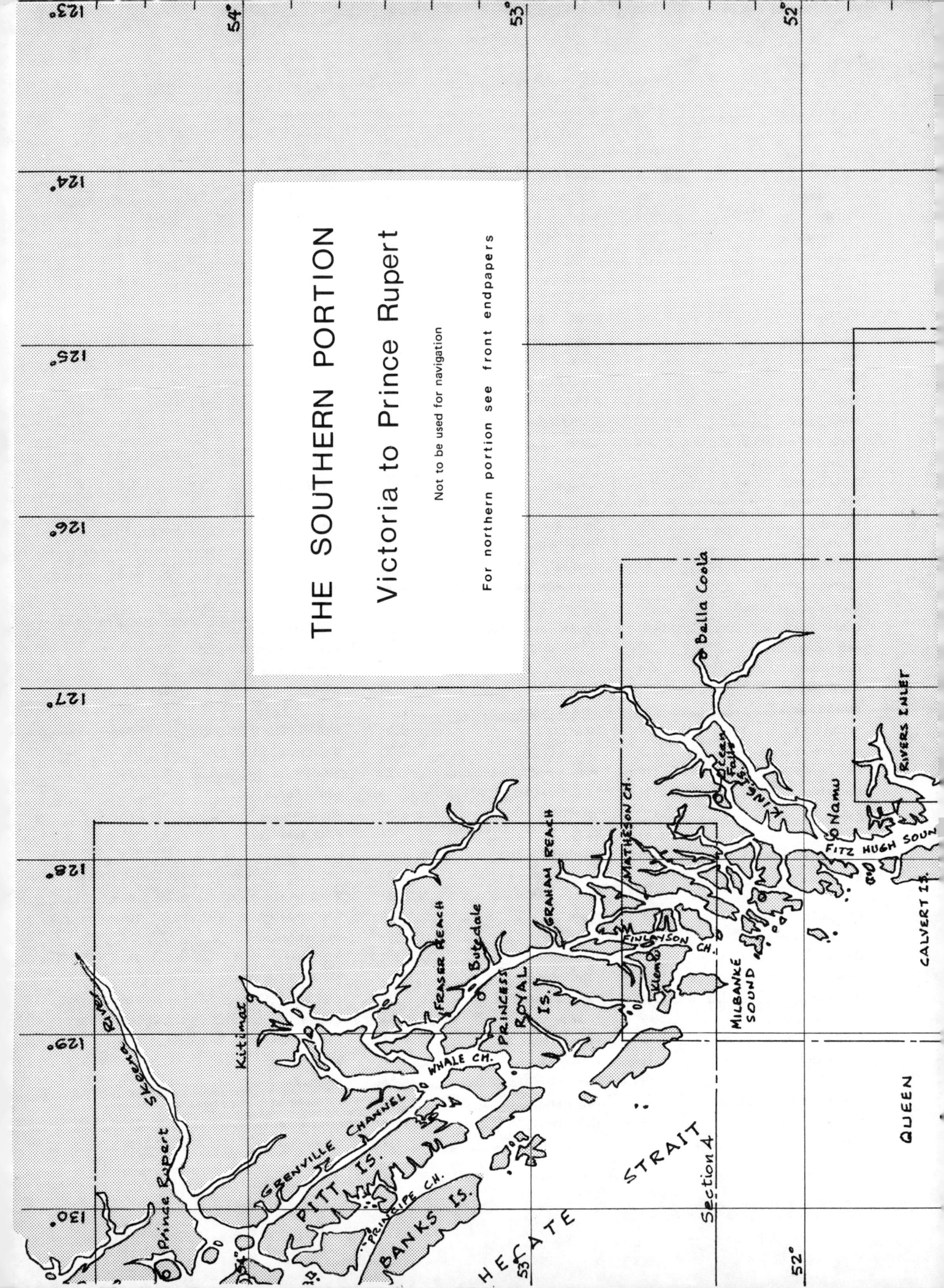

THE SOUTHERN PORTION

Victoria to Prince Rupert

Not to be used for navigation

For northern portion see front endpapers